To Mam

Matthew Williams

The Science of Hate

How prejudice
becomes hate
and what we can
do to stop it

faber

First published in 2021
by Faber & Faber Limited
Bloomsbury House,
74–77 Great Russell Street
London WC1B 3DA

This paperback edition published in 2022

Typeset by Faber & Faber Limited
Printed and bound by CPI Group (UK) Ltd, Croydon, CRO 4YY

A CIP record for this book
is available from the British Library

ISBN 978-0-571-35707-9

10 9 8 7 6 5 4 3 2 1

Contents

Prologue: Living with Hate

I've never talked about my attack. But now feels like the right time. It was a summer holiday weekend in the late nineties. One of those weekends you look forward to for months. I was in London visiting friends on a blisteringly hot day. It was my last chance to see them before I started my postgrad degree in journalism, so I made the most of it. The morning was spent basking in Regent's Park and we headed for lunch around midday. Many of us had just finished our final undergraduate exams so we went somewhere that served cool beer to celebrate. We ate like kings and imbibed enough to fuel a gush of reminiscing over good times at university. After one too many for a lunchtime, we convinced ourselves to carry on the party. The destination of choice was a bar on Tottenham Court Road well known for the diversity of its clientele.

A few hours into the sprawling celebration I stepped out of the bar to take five in the heavy London air. I was struck by the bright azure sky and took a moment for my eyes to adjust. A guy standing in the distance on the shimmering asphalt gradually came into focus. He sauntered over and asked for a light. Before I could flick the flint on my Zippo two other guys jumped me. All three had been waiting patiently for their target. This was something planned, considered, not something that came about through circumstance; not a crime of opportunity.

In an instant, without having to think, I knew what had happened. I was a victim of a hate crime. I remember the metallic tang of the blood pouring from my split lip. The din resonating in my head from the precision-placed punch. I got a glimpse of the three of them, laughing, enjoying their victory. I turned away, afraid of appearing resilient – giving them their prize in the hope they would move on. Some may call me a coward for not retaliating – I certainly felt like one. But all I could think of in those first few seconds was minimising the violence, and protecting those coming out behind me. Then one of them spat it out:

'Fucking batty-boy.'

That was all the confirmation I needed. I recognised the 'game' I was part of. They called it 'queer-bashing', a 'sport' played up and down the country, where the players on one team wait outside well-known gay bars for the players on the opposing team to emerge inebriated, less able to defend themselves when the game starts and the attack comes. The gamification of hate crime.

This felt different to one of those random acts of violence fuelled by alcohol on a Saturday night. This wasn't senseless violence. The attack was a message. What that was I couldn't fathom in that moment. But in the days and weeks following I would return to the attack again and again – it filled my thoughts until there was no space for anything else. An attack on your identity will do that. You don't ask 'Why me?' like most victims of violent crime. You *know* why me, and that is much more insidious. It gets right under your skin.

I couldn't stop the deluge of questions flooding my head. Did my attackers actually hate what I was? Is hate too strong a word for it? Did the attack affirm the heterosexuality of the guy who punched me? Or was it simply to do with protecting their turf? A signal to me and others that 'my sort' was not welcome in 'their' city. Whatever the motive (or mix of motives), the violence made me question who I was, my place in society, and my relationship.

I've not held my partner's hand in public since that day. I look back and feel like I was cheated of intimacy. The attack on my identity made me feel so unsafe that it reshaped me. The feeling of vulnerability was constant. It became tied up with my person. I lost something that day, and it still feels like I will never get it back.

The actions of those three men not only changed my personal life, but my professional life too. Soon after the attack I decided to abandon my desire to become a journalist and I signed up for a master's degree in criminology. The questions I had about my attack preoccupied me and the science was the place to find the answers.

My postgraduate studies were illuminating in ways I both did and did not expect. Most of the year was spent pacing up and down dimly lit library stacks, blowing dust off mildew-ridden books and losing myself in them. This I anticipated. In between the scholarly activity I took a part-time job in an internet cafe that provided a less formal and more unexpected learning experience. As the cafe rarely had customers I had a lot of time on my hands. To pass away the hours I took advantage of the high-speed internet access. It didn't take long before I witnessed my first incident of virtual hate. A small group of chatroom users went on a rampage, abusing others with racial epithets. Then they turned on me. Homophobic slurs flooded my screen.

In the same year I had experienced hate both on the streets and online. These experiences were formative and created in me a drive that wouldn't let up. To fuel it I signed over four years of my life to embark on a PhD. This was the start of my journey to make sense of the motivations of my attackers and others like them. That journey, on which I continue to travel, has involved looking into some of the darkest parts of the human mind to work out what makes a prejudiced thought turn into hateful and sometimes lethal action.

Introduction

Is hate hard-wired? I asked myself a similar question early in my journey: 'Is there something in the biology of my attackers that is somehow responsible for their act of hate against me?' The possibility was both comforting and disturbing. It would allow for a clear separation of myself from my attackers but it would mean hate is an even more intractable problem. The question serves as a good place to introduce this book. The nature versus nurture debate is as fundamental to understanding hate as it is to understanding every other part of what makes us who we are.

The majority of hate criminals are rather mundane and share similar characteristics to the general population. To me and you. They are not all pathological, not all monsters as portrayed in the mass media. The same foundations for prejudice and hate are present in everyone.

We all have a deep-rooted preference for people that we think are like us. This trait is common not just to humans, but to other species too. Far back in human history our ancestors developed this trait to ensure their groups flourished; forging tight bonds that fostered trust and cooperation was essential to survival. While less important to survival today, there is no getting away from the fact, however uncomfortable it might make us feel, that humans are predisposed to favour people from their own group over people from outside groups.

Scientists are now able to show how a possible consequence of this human trait can be observed in our brains. Long gone are the days when doctors had to crack skulls to take a look under the hood. Scanning technology such as functional Magnetic Resonance Imaging (fMRI), the type of scan a patient may have to identify the presence of a tumour, is now being used to produce three-dimensional images of the brain that show real-time reactions to external stimuli such as photographs. Under certain conditions, a predisposed preference for 'us' can turn into a learned aversion towards 'them', and the brain signals involved in this process have been found using this scanning technology.

People who say they don't hold prejudiced views of black people can be betrayed by their brain signals. Participants in neuroscience studies have been shown to exhibit differences in brain activity when they look at pictures of white and black faces. What is startling about this finding is that the area of the brain that shows the highest correlation with unconscious prejudice, the amygdala, is associated with fear and aggression (see first brain image in plate section). The amygdala is where 'prepared' fears (fears we learn more quickly) and learned fears are formed. Think of spiders and snakes versus exams and the dentist. The science shows the amygdala can generate a fear reaction when it processes images of people with darker skin tones (and this applies to both white and black study participants – more on this in Chapter 3). But it would be a mistake to assume we are born with parts of our brains pre-coded to react in this way.

To study brains in the wild, psychologists have looked at how young children interact. In our early years, when we have had little socialisation, adult ideas about other groups play a minimal, if not non-existent, role in our interactions with peers. Watching kids play shows evolution at work. From the age of about three, we begin to recognise the existence of groups, and develop a preference for being in one group over another.

Girls or boys, members of team Red or team Blue, fans of SpongeBob or Peppa Pig – what defines these groups doesn't matter (in fact, for our distant human ancestors, difference was unlikely to manifest in skin colour given the limits of migration). But kids become anxious about being excluded from the group they perceive they belong to. At this stage the consequences of a preference for the ingroup over the outgroup are minimal. Children at this phase of development don't actually turn this ingroup preference into harmful behaviours aimed at the outgroup. They don't steal toys or start tribal wars in the playground based on what group they belong to. But they may only share toys with members of their ingroup unless encouraged to share more widely.

Interactions between older children occur in a more complex social context than the preschool playground. From the age of about ten, the ability of children to reason means they begin to understand how society is organised into hierarchies. Opportunities for competition seem to emerge at every turn and begin to dominate play and more general behaviours. Kids still place importance on ingroup identity, such as who belongs, but more importantly, they start to keenly identify those who do not belong. Preference for the ingroup can begin to turn into seeds of prejudice against the outgroup, even when the groups are made up of very similar individuals.

Classic psychology studies show that when 'average' white middle-class adolescent boys are put into groups that have had no prior contact, they can rapidly form biases against each other based on group membership. This even occurs when the identities of those in both groups is similar (e.g. all-white middle class boys).[*]

---

[*] 'Average' white middle-class boys, or more generally people from Western, Educated, Industrialised, Rich and Democratic (WEIRD) societies, make up

When the groups come into contact for the first time, competition can result, especially when resources, like food, are scarce. While conflict is not inevitable, it can erupt if a share of resources becomes unequal. But group divisions are not ingrained, and they can be easily crossed. Give both groups a common problem to overcome and they can forget their differences and come together to get a job done for the benefit of all.

It is usually during adolescence when negative thoughts about other groups can turn into deeply harmful acts. Prejudice and hate targeting members of the outgroup can start to embed. This galvanising of prejudice, where acting on it in harmful ways can become normalised, is not inevitable. Within us we all have the internal precursors of prejudice, but it takes a specific set of external conditions to cultivate it. Contributing factors for this could include a failing economy or divisive politics; things that kids are largely protected from, which come to bear on most of us in early adulthood. When combined with other influences like negative norm and value transmission from peers, a lack of daily face-to-face contact with the outgroup, and gradual exposure to subversive subcultures and fringe online media, the seeds of prejudice can rapidly germinate into hate. But still, *not everyone* in this tinderbox will embark on a spree of hate crimes.

the bulk of subjects in scientific studies on human behaviour. This has led to the claim that most of what we know about human behaviour is not generalisable to the whole population of the world, but instead only represents people from WEIRD societies (J. Henrich et al., 'The Weirdest People in the World?', Behavioral and Brain Sciences 33 (2010), 61–83). What we currently know from the science about IQ, moral reasoning, fairness and cooperation, among other things, may only apply to a subset of the world's population. If you are from a WEIRD society, then the findings from these studies probably apply to you. If you are not, then we need more science in societies like yours to confirm if what we know applies more broadly.

The good news is the majority of us have learnt to suppress prejudice. Some researchers point to the 'civilising process' to explain why most of us now feel shame when we think in prejudiced ways.[1,2] Over hundreds of years of social change, and aided by the civil rights, women's liberation and gay rights movements, it has become unacceptable to think and behave in ways that disadvantage certain groups in society, and in particular, groups that are known to already be structurally disadvantaged.

But suppressing prejudice takes mental energy. Granted, there are those who would argue they don't have to suppress anything, because they are prejudice-free (a suppression in itself?), but many of us are careful to correct our thoughts when, in that split second, we associate a person from a group with a negative trait. A few might have to remind themselves that gay men are not sexual predators, disabled people are not welfare scroungers, Jews are not profiteers, and so on. But this suppression mechanism, if present, can fail under certain conditions, accelerating some towards hate.

The approach taken in this book

My journey has been to figure out what set of ingredients is necessary for someone to tip into hate offending and how this can rapidly spread to others – why at some points in time and in some places we can live together harmoniously, and why in others things get so divisive they reach genocidal proportions.

Understanding the gap between thinking something and doing something is the holy grail of the behavioural sciences. A vast amount is known about prejudice and how it is formed, and an equally vast amount is known about what happens when it becomes so extreme that it has violent consequences. It is agreed that while not everyone who has been exposed to prejudiced thoughts will become a hate criminal, all hate criminals will have been exposed to prejudiced thoughts at some point. But get a group of experts in a room and ask them to pinpoint that precise moment when prejudice tips into violent hate and you'll be met with multiple conflicting answers.

As a professor of criminology, I am fortunate to have studied a field that was formed long after many of the classic scientific disciplines, allowing it to borrow ideas unashamedly from all of them. Unlike some disciplines that often work in silo, criminology can come at the problem from many angles and from the extremes. This is absolutely crucial when tackling the question, 'Why do people commit hate crimes?' You cannot begin to understand hateful behaviour without looking at the whole picture, from how biology and early socialisation predispose humans to favour the ingroup, right through to how financial meltdowns, global pandemics and artificial intelligence (AI) can create the ideal conditions for hate to flourish.

Taking this wide-angle picture is key to understanding hate crime *now*. The current rate of the breakdown in social relations across the world is arresting. It is no coincidence that soaring hate crime figures are found in countries where the extreme right is rising. This trend is fuelled by the internet revolution and its corruption by masked individuals, the far right and state actors. Societal divisions are being prised wide open with the use of the internet in an attempt to garner support for populist leaders and ideologies.

Donald Trump's 2016 presidential campaign hired Cambridge Analytica and the Leave.EU Brexit campaign hired Aggregate IQ to use artificial intelligence to 'micro-target' those who would be most vulnerable to messages designed to stir up fears of the 'other'.[3] During the COVID-19 pandemic, social media was flooded with far-right conspiracy theories and hate targeting Jewish, Muslim, Chinese and LGBTQ+ people for supposedly creating and/

or spreading the disease (more on this in Chapter 10).[4] Beyond organised campaigns, the everyday internet user also took to social media to post hateful messages, triggered by disinformation and careless phrases, like 'Chinese virus' and 'kung flu', coming out of the White House (see Figure 1).[5] What is most worrying about this trend is that the research shows divisive messages from public figures are directly linked to tipping some people into hateful violence on the streets. In January 2021 the world witnessed an unparalleled example of this when the US Capitol Building was stormed by Trump supporters who had been whipped up by his polarising rhetoric. Many were photographed wearing T-shirts and holding flags emblazoned with far-right, neo-fascist and white supremacist symbols. The riot resulted in five deaths, including one police officer, and hundreds of injuries. Within minutes of the siege, Twitter, Facebook and YouTube removed Trump's content that praised his supporters, conceding that the posts incited violence. Later the three tech giants went a step further and suspended the president's accounts in an effort to prevent further unrest.

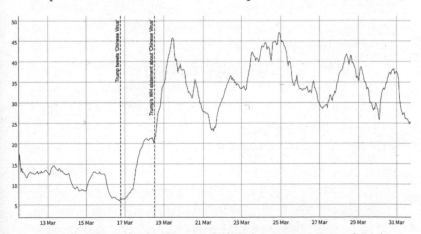

Fig. 1: Frequency of online hate speech on Twitter targeting East and South East Asians in the early stages of the COVID-19 pandemic

New technology has transformed hate, amplifying its power to inflict harm. Left unchallenged, the expression of hate in our modern connected society has the potential to become more widespread than at any other point in history. If we do not seek to fully understand this new context, using all the science at our disposal, we risk hate radiating beyond individual communities to whole nations.

This book is divided into two parts. Part One begins by examining individual hate crime cases to understand what it means to hate, before turning to the numbers to ask what qualifies as hate and how much of it is out there. It then delves into how our ability to hate is shaped by characteristics that are common to all humans – our evolved biological and psychological wiring and the influence of our rapid early learning.

Part Two explores how hate is shaped by ingredients that can layer on top of these human traits – *accelerants* that reduce our capacity to suppress our prejudices and edge us closer to hate. Hate comes about from a combination of the core traits we all share and these accelerating forces. While we all have the ability to hate, only some of us are exposed to enough accelerants to make it erupt. As this exposure (and safeguarding from it) is not equally distributed across society or time, hate appears more often in some groups and in some periods of human existence.

In unmasking the tipping point from prejudice to hate crime, I take you on my journey across the globe and from our ancestors in prehistory to artificial intelligence in the twenty-first century. I delve into hate crime cases to tell the stories of victims and offenders, speak to the experts and make use of the most cutting-edge scientific tools. By looking through multiple lenses, I present counter-intuitive and shocking explanations that defy commonly held perceptions about human behaviour, and at each stage, edge closer to explaining why some people act upon their prejudices, while others don't.

PART ONE

1

What It Means to Hate

Srinivas and Alok

In 2017, on an unusually warm February night in Olathe, Kansas, Srinivas Kuchibhotla and his friend Alok Madasani decided to cut short their day's toil at the GPS company Garmin and go for a cool beer. They had moved their families from India to the Sunflower State in the mid 2000s to start new lives. The 135,000-strong Olathe community had been warm and welcoming to both, and Austins Sports Bar and Grill on the strip mall, a typical American establishment serving good burgers and beer, had become their local.

At Austins, large TV screens blared out the University of Kansas versus Texas Christian University basketball game to a throng of patrons. Srinivas and Alok sat at a table on the outside patio, relishing the unseasonable 79 degrees. Over a pair of frosty Miller Lites they caught up on their day at work before segueing into conversation about Bollywood movies and Alok's impending fatherhood.

Mid-conversation, Alok noticed a white man wearing a T-shirt with military-style badges and a bandana stand up from his table and walk over. By the look on the guy's face, Alok immediately suspected something was wrong. With a pointed finger Adam Purinton asked, 'Which country are you from? Are you here illegally?'

Alok was silent, concerned the threatening tone of the aggressor's questions might be the preliminary to violence. Srinivas quietly responded, 'We are here legally. We are on H-1B. We are from India.'

Purinton fired back at him, 'We pay for your visas to be here. You need to get out of here! You don't belong here! . . . Sand niggers!' He then proceeded to poke Srinivas in the chest, shouting, 'Terrorist!'

Alok darted inside to fetch the manager, but upon his return found two patrons, one of whom was a local man named Ian Grillot, standing up for him and Srinivas and insisting that Purinton leave.

A short while later Purinton returned, this time in a different T-shirt and with his face covered with a scarf. Yelling, 'Get out of my country,' he pulled out a semi-automatic pistol and opened fire on his two targets. Srinivas took the brunt of the attack; four bullets to his chest. Alok was shot in the leg and fell to the ground. All he could think about was his unborn child, and how he had to live.[1]

Ian, the patron who had earlier defended them, counted the shots from beneath the table he was cowering under. At what he thought was the ninth he got up from the floor and gave chase as the terrorist fled the scene. But he had miscounted; one bullet remained in the magazine. Purinton turned and unloaded his remaining ammo, piercing Ian through his hand and chest.

As patrons at Austins frantically performed first aid on the two Indian men, Srinivas's wife, Sunayana, was trying to call him from home. She wanted to know what time he would be returning, hopeful that they could share a pot of tea in the garden and watch the sun go down. When he didn't pick up she started to scroll through Facebook and found a news post with the headline 'Shooting at Austins Bar and Grill'. She feared the worst.

Alok and Ian survived the attack. Srinivas died from his multiple gunshot wounds.

The police informed Sunayana that the shooting was premeditated – her husband was killed because of who he was, the colour of his skin. Sunayana had hoped the attack was random, like so many of the other shootings in the US which she had heard about on the news. Knowing her husband and his friend were targeted because of their nationality and race deepened the pain she felt. She struggled to comprehend Purinton's reason for killing her husband. What had hurt him so much to lead to this unthinkable action? What was he afraid of? Where did his anger come from? Did killing Srinivas take away his pain?

While Alok and Ian were still recovering from their injuries, both were approached by reporters from all over the world to give their take on what had happened. In one interview Alok said, 'I'm scared, for sure. One thing I really want people to know is that this is just hate.'

Eyes filled like pools, Ian said from his hospital bed, 'I was doing what anyone should have done for another human being. It's not about where he's from, or his ethnicity. We're all humans.'[2]

Days later Sunayana said in a press conference, 'I was always concerned. Were we doing the right thing by staying in the United States of America? . . . What will the government do to stop this hate crime? My husband would want justice to be done. We need an answer.' She had read about other hate crimes all over the country since the election of Donald Trump in 2016. She said to a reporter shortly after the attack, 'When the recent elections happened, we were watching it so closely. I was so worried; I just couldn't sleep.'[3] She recalled asking her husband, 'Srinivas, will we be safe in this country? I'm so worried.'[4]

After fleeing the scene Purinton drove 112 km to Clinton, Missouri, where he confessed to an employee at an Applebee's restaurant. Following apprehension by police he was charged with murder and manslaughter by the state, but specific hate crime charges could not be brought as they do not exist in Kansas law.*5 Only at the federal level would Purinton be charged with a hate crime. He admitted that his attack was motivated by the race of his victims. Two weeks before the shooting he had noticed Srinivas and Alok sitting at their usual table and said to the bartender, 'Did you see those terrorists on the patio?' Purinton pleaded guilty to all charges and was sentenced to three consecutive life sentences without the possibility of parole.[6]

Amid mounting pressure for a statement from both the American and Indian press, in front of Congress President Trump condemned 'hate and evil in all of its very ugly forms' six days after the murder.[7] Srinivas's funeral, in Hyderabad, was broadcast on Indian news and online. Mourners could be heard shouting, 'Trump, down, down! . . . Down with racism! Down with hatred!'[8]

A year after Srinivas's murder, Sunayana set up Forever Welcome, a not-for-profit organisation to support immigrants and to combat hate crime in the US.

What drove Purinton to murder that day? It is the job of a criminologist to provide answers to such questions. To take the stories

---

* At the time of writing, no dedicated hate crimes exist in Kansas law. However, provision does exist for a judge to impose a harsher sentence if a crime is known to be motivated entirely or in part by the race, colour, religion, ethnicity, national origin or sexual orientation of the victim. However, Purinton was charged with a hate crime at the federal level. The Matthew Shepard and James Byrd Jr Hate Crimes Prevention Act, signed in 2009 by President Barack Obama, makes it a federal crime to wilfully cause bodily injury, or attempt to do so using a dangerous weapon, because of the victim's actual or perceived race, colour, religion, national origin, gender, sexual orientation, gender identity or disability. It extended the 1969 US federal hate crime law beyond just race, colour, religion and national origin.

of victims and perpetrators of hate and to make sense of them using the best available science. Criminology emerged as a field of study in response to the problem of crime. It is therefore focused on informing government policy, and is driven by one big question: Why do they do it? Beneath this is a range of sub-questions that shape the research of criminologists who study hate: What is hate and is it useful in establishing motive? How much hate crime is actually out there? What are the consequences of crimes that target our identity? How do we stop the hate? Through the individual names and stories of victims and perpetrators, this chapter deals with the first of these sub-questions.

What does it mean to 'hate'?

As a younger man, Adam Purinton held a pilot's licence while in the navy, was an air traffic controller for some time and also worked in a skilled role in the IT industry. Then he suffered a series of losses that reshaped his life. His father died from cancer only eighteen months before he killed Srinivas. This contributed to excessive drinking and unemployment. He managed to get a few manual jobs, including as a dishwasher at a fast food restaurant. This toxic mix of personal loss, failure and frustration may have played a role in Purinton's decision to kill that day, but it can't fully explain it. It is possible that Trump's xenophobic rhetoric and his banning of Muslims from entering the US that same month played its part – did Purinton believe what he was being told, that his failings were not his own but could be blamed on immigrants? Maybe, but we don't know this. Even if he did, there are pieces of the puzzle still missing. Not everyone in the US who has suffered deep personal losses and believes divisive political messages turns to violence. So was it hate that made Purinton murder that day?

Much of our criminological understanding of hate stems from the study of prejudice. Prejudices feed off stereotypes, characteristics given to a person or whole group of people, based on crude generalisations and categories. Prejudices are formed when our attitude and feeling towards someone are shaped by our perceptions of a group we think they belong to. They therefore focus on what psychologists call the outgroup ('them') and the ingroup ('us').

When focused on the ingroup, prejudices are often associated with positive stereotypes, categories and feelings – a person who is one of 'us' is associated with competence and trustworthiness and generates warmth and compassion. On its own, our built-in, often unconscious preference for people like 'us' can result in discrimination against 'them' if we do not work to counteract it. Positive attitudes and feelings make it more likely that we will be nicer to 'us' than to 'them', and this is reflected in who we give our time, affection, money and resources to.

When prejudices are focused on the outgroup, they tend to be associated with negative stereotypes and feelings. Purinton thought Srinivas and Alok were a drain on America's resources ('Are you here illegally?') and a potential threat to life ('Did you see those terrorists on the patio?') – prejudiced attitudes and thoughts based on unsubstantiated stereotypes that generate negative emotions.

But it would be unfair to state that Purinton was *just* prejudiced against the outgroup of his victims. We all hold prejudices, but we don't all take to the streets to commit hate crimes. When a person harms or kills another because they belong to a particular group, they have moved beyond prejudice to something else. 'Hate' has become the normal word for this state of being, but what does it really mean, and is it a useful term in fully understanding motive?

Hate means different things to different people in different contexts, and is overly used, even misused, to political ends. If we begin with the simple use of the word in conversation, 'hate' is thrown around every day. A dinner-time tussle with my young nephew has often resulted in the exclamation 'I hate vegetables!' and a casual chat with my neighbour has ended with the utterance 'I just hate that president!' To both, there is something so inherently wrong with vegetables and that president that they can never see a day when they could accept them. Both are pushed away.

But hate is probably too strong a word to convey how they actually feel. My nephew dislikes the taste of vegetables, and maybe even experiences disgust when eating them. My neighbour holds the president in contempt, and may be greatly angered by his behaviour. All strong negative emotions, but short of actual hatred. The emotions will likely decrease in intensity over time, as my nephew gets older and his tastes change, and when my neighbour sees the president leave office.

Experiencing hatred is beyond the realm of the ordinary and commonplace, despite its use in everyday language. When we hear people say they truly hate an individual (called interpersonal hate), the situation leading to the state of mind likely involves a behaviour that impacted them directly. The abusive father is hated by his children, the unfaithful spouse is hated by her husband, the captor is hated by his prisoner. But even in such deeply personal circumstances, this state of mind can change over time, and may be better described as intense dislike, contempt or disgust.

In the scientific study of hate, the term is often reserved for the desire to remove a whole group because of an actual or perceived clash of worldview (called intergroup hate). An individual can still be the target of hate, but only because of their association with the outgroup. Srinivas and Alok were not targeted because of something they did to Purinton, but because of their association with a larger group that he believed was responsible for what was wrong with his country and possibly his own life.

Hate of this nature goes beyond the negative emotions of anger, contempt, disgust and so on (although these may be felt alongside it – see later in this chapter).[9] Emotions are felt when we are stimulated by information flowing in through the senses, memories, thought processes and chemicals coursing through our brain. For most of us they are ephemeral, sometimes so fleeting that we can wake up on the wrong side of the bed in a foul mood, but by lunchtime be full of enthusiasm for the day, fuelled by a few cups of coffee and a cinnamon swirl. Hate, on the other hand, especially its intergroup form, is more enduring, stable and consuming. It is this form of hate I focus on in this book.

The Pyramid of Hate

In the 1940s, a decade that saw the largest modern genocide in German-occupied Europe and the Moore's Ford mass lynching in Georgia, Harvard psychologist Gordon Allport could think of little else but prejudice and hate. These horrors and others like them that took place in the first half of the twentieth century spurred Allport on to reveal the underpinnings of human prejudice and the hateful conflict that could result.[10] His 1954 book *The Nature of Prejudice* went on to shape half a century of research on the topic.

Allport considered prejudice as antipathy towards a whole group of people. The examples he used in his work often related to negativity expressed towards religious and ethnic groups, namely Jews and black people. In his view, to be prejudiced you had to think of the whole group in a negative way, not just select individuals from that group. In adopting this view, he excluded other forms of prejudice, such as sexism (where generally positive attitudes can

18

be held towards women, though this still results in discrimination – now recognised in contemporary prejudice research and termed 'benevolent paternalism').

Based on his early definition of prejudice – negativity towards a whole group – Allport proposed a scale to demonstrate that not all prejudices are equal (see Figure 2). In the first stage, termed *Antilocution*, hate speech is used increasingly by sections of the ingroup, ranging from jokes to outright slurs targeting the outgroup. In this stage, hate speech ebbs and flows depending on the state of social relations and the occurrence of divisive events, as is so clearly visible on social media platforms today.

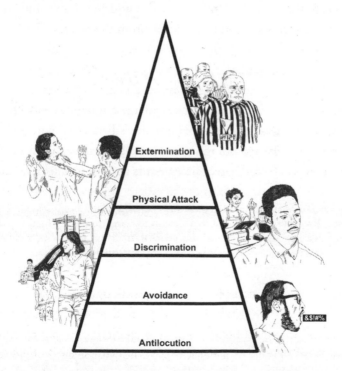

Fig. 2: The Pyramid of Hate (adapted from G. W. Allport, *The Nature of Prejudice*, 1954).

In the second stage, *Avoidance*, we see the separation of the ingroup and the outgroup. This ranges from the ingroup 'organically' avoiding certain establishments or parts of a city or town because they are known to be frequented by the outgroup, to the state forcing segregation in its institutions, such as schools, public transport and housing.

In stage three, *Discrimination,* we see the outgroup denied access to opportunities, goods and services, stifling their ability to advance in society. The outgroup is prevented from gaining a certain level of education, achieving employment in certain areas, receiving the best healthcare, and being afforded equal protection under the law.[11]

The Jim Crow era in the American South, from the late nineteenth century through to the 1960s, is a good example of this third stage. Many of those in power, including influential religious figures, politicians, business leaders and scholars, ensured the belief that African Americans were inferior in every way to white people was ingrained within the fabric of society, creating a racial caste system that saw the subjugation and abuse of black people.* Today many governments continue to discriminate

* The notion that race is biological and hierarchical has been debunked by science. Race and ethnicity are social constructs used to classify humans into groups. Race generally refers to physical characteristics, such as skin colour, while ethnicity generally refers to cultural characteristics, such as language and religion. The terms are sometimes used interchangeably, but their meanings and uses are often confused and contested. For example, most scholars argue that talking of race in terms of genetic differences is inappropriate given that the ancestry of every person on the planet is made up of a core group of common ancestors. This has ensured the average genetic differences between socially constructed racial types are typically very small. Human variation is real, but it does not map neatly onto the conventional and everyday descriptions of race. Most of the academic research and policy literature uses the term 'race' to refer to groups within populations that exhibit physical differences in skin colour. While this is a widely accepted practice it is not scientific and is a remnant of European

against parts of their populations, including at least sixty-eight countries (at the time of writing) that make it criminal to engage in same-sex relations, with the death penalty still in place in some for those caught doing so.[12]

The discrimination stage is also accompanied by subtle forms of aggression. In using their privilege to exercise power over the outgroup, the dominant group frequently commit verbal and behavioural *micro-aggressions*.[†] These include *micro-assaults* that are explicit and target the identity of the outgroup.

The fourth stage, *Physical Attack*, is the conscious extension of the behaviours found in the previous stages to full-blown aggression. The physical violence may not be tolerated under the law of the country or state in question, but authority figures are likely to turn a blind eye. In some situations, authority figures such as the police may actually perpetrate the violence illegally.

Physical attacks against black and LGBTQ+ citizens perpetrated by members of the public and the police were prevalent in the US in

---

colonial expansion and empire building. However, this does not mean race as a social category is unimportant, as it has become imbued with meaning through the interaction of humans classified into races. In this book I borrow the use of the term race from the research and policy work that I include, but I do not support its use in a scientific way that attempts to ascribe inherent differences between populations.

† The term micro-aggression describes words and/or behaviours that result in unintentional discrimination against an outgroup. In addition to micro-assaults, micro-aggressions can include micro-insults: words, conversations or actions (often unconscious) that are rude and insensitive, but are not explicit (e.g. asking a disabled person how they got a job over an able-bodied person); and micro-invalidation: words, conversations or actions that exclude based on identity (e.g. a white person asking a UK-born Asian person where they are 'really' from, or a white person saying to a black person 'I don't see colour', negating the importance of their identity and heritage). These are more common to stage 1: Antilocution. D. W. Sue, 'Racial Microaggressions in Everyday Life: Implications for Clinical Practice', *American Psychologist* 62 (2007), 271–86.

the middle of the last century and still continue to this day (Purinton's attack would fall into this stage, and see also the case of Frank Jude Jr later in this chapter). Similar behaviours continue around the world today, including horrific physical attacks on gay men and women in Russia by members of the public and law enforcement.[13]

The fifth and final stage, *Extermination*, sees deadly violence towards the outgroup become desirable and in some cases legal.[14] The Holocaust is the prime example of this stage, but genocides are not consigned to the past. Since 2016, an estimated 24,800 Rohingya Muslims have been wiped out by the Buddhist majority in Myanmar, and as many as 700,000 have been forced out of the country.[15] This, and the recent genocides in Bosnia and Herzegovina (1992–5), Rwanda (1994) and Darfur (2003–) serve as continuing reminders of what is possible when a society allows hate to flourish.

The push/pull factor

Any scale of hate is imperfect. Distilling this darker side of human nature to account for all circumstances is a tough task. What Allport's attempt does show us is that weak to moderate prejudice (up to stage 2) can see the ingroup *avoid* the outgroup, while more extreme forms of prejudice that might tip into hatred (stage 4 and up) can see the ingroup *pursue* the outgroup, in order to attack and exterminate. A key difference between prejudice and hate may therefore be this push/pull factor. The push factor can result from negative thoughts experienced when in the presence of the outgroup: unease, uncertainty and anxiety generated by a lack of knowledge about 'them', or the fear of causing offence or looking prejudiced.[16] The pull factor can result from a desire or a need to act against the outgroup, to take out frustrations, to eliminate a perceived threat or to 'correct' behaviour.

Purinton falls into the physical attack stage, and hence the pull category. He had seen both Indian men at Austins on previous occasions and had labelled them as a threat, calling them 'terrorists'. While his encounter with them was likely happenstance, their presence was not a surprise to him. Instead of ignoring them or moving tables to get out of earshot of their talk of Bollywood movies, he pursued them. He invaded their space and questioned their right to be in the US. After being thrown out of the bar, he went home, armed himself and returned to kill.

At the extreme end of the spectrum, extermination requires the allocation of a great deal of resources to hunt down and eradicate the outgroup. People go out of their way to locate the outgroup, instead of avoiding them. In Nazi Germany during the Second World War, the cost of exterminating the Jews and others could have instead been used on the war effort. This kind of illogical behaviour has more in common with extreme passions or obsessions than with a dislike of a group and negative emotions. In line with passions and obsessions, people who hate often believe they are embarking on a moral cause of some kind. There is a belief that their hate and the actions that stem from it are virtuous. The hated outgroup is perceived as doing something that undermines the very morals the haters are trying to uphold. The ends can then justify the means, even if the means involve the extermination of whole ethnic or religious groups.[17]

Feeling hate together

Alexei

In 2014, twenty-year-old Alexei was working as a drag queen in Moscow, Russia. Ahead of each show he would transform in front of the mirror in his local gay club, freeing himself from the heterosexual persona that he had to wear every day when in public. Since the passing of the anti-gay 'propaganda' law in Russia in 2013 that claims to protect minors from knowledge of 'non-traditional relationships', attacks on LGBTQ+ people have increased at a staggering rate.

Human liberties groups say the law is an attack on LGBTQ+ rights and a way of banning all forms of public expression that deviate from a heterosexual way of life. The reported widespread support for the law amongst the public means hiding in plain sight has become the only way to survive for people like Alexei in modern Russia. Simply holding hands while walking down a busy street in central Moscow invites homophobic taunts and even physical violence from passers-by.[18]

The club where Alexei worked provided a surrogate family; his real one was lost when he came out as gay. Away from the hostile streets it offered a sanctuary that helped him maintain hope that things might change one day. For a few hours a night, Alexei's true identity sparkled in the limelight, captivating crowds of other outcasts who accepted him for who he really was. But following the passing of the anti-gay propaganda law this safe haven had turned into a war zone.

Within months the once discreet club was targeted. A large neon sign was erected above the entrance, beaming the letters 'Gay Club Here ↓ ↓' to all who happened to pass by. The building's owners, reported to be a Kremlin-controlled railway company, were behind it.[19] The dangerous stunt placed a target on the back of every patron who dared visit. A 'Morality Patrol' van took up its position outside, surveilling all those who entered the club.

Soon after the violence came. First, two men harassed patrons as they queued outside the club, and when refused entry they fired off gunshots into the crowd, leaving bullet holes in the entrance door.

Then came the gassing. Hydrogen sulphide, a potentially lethal chemical known to cause brain damage, was pumped through the ventilation system. Some of the five hundred club-goers suffered headaches and vomiting, but luckily no one was permanently harmed. Finally, the club was besieged by a fifty-strong mob of men who eventually stormed the building, ransacked it and set the roof ablaze.

Organised hate groups were behind the attacks. Dmitry 'Enteo' Tsorionov, the leader of 'God's Will', an extremist Christian group, continues to spearhead campaigns against homosexuality in Russia. 'Homosexuality is no different than paedophilia . . . It's a real plague, a real virus that needs to be destroyed. We need to stop this tumor so it doesn't metastasize,' he said in an interview.[20] The group campaigned to get the anti-gay propaganda law passed, with the hope it would pave the way to outlaw homosexuality in Russia with a maximum penalty of death. God's Will have reported connections with the neo-Nazi group Occupy Paedophilia, who entrap gay men and film them being abused and beaten, then upload the footage to YouTube. Both groups have significant followings on VKontakte, Russia's version of Facebook.[21]

The gunfire, toxic gas attack and harassment eventually proved too much and the club Alexei called home shut its doors in March 2014. With his surrogate family gone, like so many other LGBTQ+ people in Russia, Alexei made plans to leave his country to escape persecution by the likes of God's Will and Occupy Paedophilia.[22]

Such groups provide the lifeblood of hate. They accelerate the negative attitudes towards the outgroup by using like-minded others to validate them. God's Will provided a space where prejudice against homosexuals could turn into hateful violence, fuelled by a group of people who share the same attitude, sentiment and moral code.

The act of coming together to express shared hatred has the effect of minimising the individual within the group. Psychologists call this *deindividuation*. Hate groups react as one where the sense of individual responsibility necessary to put the brakes on bad behaviour gets lost in the mob mentality.[23] The individual and the group become 'fused' (more on this in Chapter 8). Instead of the outgroup being seen as threatening or challenging the morals of the individual, now they are perceived as challenging the entire group.

While hate of this kind is not considered by most scientists as an emotion in itself, it is accompanied by a range of negative feelings that are amplified in group settings. These group-based emotions, which Allport referred to as 'hot emotions', play a fundamental role in how conscious prejudice is nursed into full-blown hate.

Anger is a common feature of hate and it can be felt towards whole groups, as well as individuals. When anger is felt with hatred the source is often unresolved or displaced frustration. Frustration stems from various situations including unemployment, insecurity, poverty, ill-health, loneliness and lack of fulfilment. Individuals who are angry about one of these things often take it out on an outgroup that are misperceived to be the cause – 'I am unemployed because THEY take all the jobs'; 'I am less safe because THEY are all terrorists'; 'I am poor because THEY are clogging up the welfare system.' The hate group is a place where these frustrations can be shared. You are told your failings in life are not your own, but the fault of others who also act as a group in direct opposition to your own – 'WE are sick because THEY are overburdening the health service'; 'WE are isolated because THEY have taken over our neighbourhood'; 'WE have fewer opportunities because THEY are the priority.'

A bedfellow of hateful anger is fear. Often the targets of hate elicit fear in the hater, and this is frequently threat-based, resulting in a sense of powerlessness.[24] We are all familiar with the usual negative stereotypes: immigrants will take our jobs, school places and hospital beds. Gays will want to have sexual relations with our children, and will undermine our masculinity, family values and the institution of marriage. Jews only want to control the media and industry to shape society in a way that favours them, and hence discriminate against us. Muslims will gang-rape our children, plot terror attacks and replace our values with sharia law. All misperceived threats that the hater feels they have little power to overcome. Fearful, angry and powerless is how most of us imagine a hateful person to be, and it is certainly how I imagine Adam Purinton.

The intense emotions of humiliation and shame can also inspire hateful actions. These deeply affecting emotions can arise from one-on-one negative interactions, but in the case of intergroup hate they often arise from the projection of individual humiliation onto an outgroup. When felt in isolation, humiliation and shame often result in avoidance of the outgroup. This may have been how Purinton felt following his cascade of life losses that turned a productive lifestyle into a dysfunctional one. In isolation he possibly used alcohol to numb these intense feelings.

Shared in a group, humiliation and shame can inspire reactions that see the outgroup pursued for revenge. The knowledge that your pain is not just your own, but shared with others around you, generates feelings of collective injustice and unfairness that beg for closure. Collective humiliation and shame, accompanied by hate for the outgroup, can thus lead to extremist behaviour, including terrorism (more on this in Chapter 8).[25] Might Purinton's individual humiliation have turned into the collective form when he was told the misfortunes of many unemployed Americans were not of their own making but instead the fault of illegal immigrants taking their jobs? If so, was this collective humiliation then projected onto his eventual victims?

Failure to empathise is also an ingredient of hate that can thrive in groups. A lack of emotional empathy – resistance to sharing the feelings of another – stems from unwillingness to engage in cognitive empathy – refusal to see the situation from the perspective of 'them'. Psychologists have technical terms for similar phenomena. The process of *mentalising* involves imagining what it is like to be 'them', emotionally. Having *theory of mind* means being able to comprehend another's beliefs, intentions and persuasions.

Both of these types of empathy are less likely to emerge when the ingroup rarely has contact with the outgroup. Conversely, positive contact can inspire empathy, and in turn reduce hate.[26] But in the absence of one or both of these forms of empathy, compassion is unlikely to arise, allowing negative stereotypes to intensify to a point where entire groups are depersonalised. If you cannot bring yourself to imagine what it is like to be a member of the outgroup, you can only conceptualise 'them' as a collective, meaning the individual is lost. With no sight of individuals in the throng, it only takes a few additional steps to dehumanise all of 'them'.

'Gut-deep' hate

Kazuya

In the dead of night on 26 July 2016, Kazuya Ono slept silently in his care home in a leafy suburb of the city of Sagamihara in Japan. The care home housed hundreds of people with disabilities aged between eighteen and seventy, including forty-three-year-old Kazuya, who is autistic and has the mental capacity of a toddler.

Around 2 a.m., ex-employee Satoshi Uematsu smashed a window and entered the care home. He knew that most of the two hundred staff would be off duty, leaving around a dozen to patrol the wards. He walked through the home confidently, knowing the layout well and where the night staff would likely congregate. Turning a corner he encountered a member of staff, who challenged him. Uematsu quickly grabbed one of five knives he was carrying in his rucksack. Waving it at the now quivering member of staff he instructed them to put on handcuffs. With the coast clear, Uematsu pressed on towards the wards.

On the first ward he found Kazuya sleeping in his room. Knife still drawn, he slashed at Kazuya's throat. In sheer terror, Kazuya threw up his arms to protect himself, deflecting the knife downwards where it sliced his torso. Thinking he was done, Uematsu moved on. Ward by ward, room by room he calmly slit the throats of his sleeping victims. The attack became the largest mass murder in Japan since the Second World War, with Uematsu claiming nineteen lives.*

Along with twenty-six other residents who were badly injured, Kazuya survived. But the emotional scars run deep. His family described in a later interview how when agitated he claws at his face and arms shouting, 'Blood, blood, blood!'[27]

Following a guilty verdict Uematsu was sentenced to death. However, as Japan does not recognise that crimes against people with disabilities can be motivated by hostility towards their identity, he could not be found guilty of a hate crime.[28] Uematsu was not

---

* The names of the other victims were kept off the public record by police, who claimed they were sparing the families any shame from being associated with a disabled relative. I feel that not publicly acknowledging the victims only serves to support the murderer's hateful aim and further entrenches the 'otherness' of disabled people in Japan.

diagnosed with a mental illness and was deemed fit to stand trial. He was trained as a teacher, had a good work record at the care home before he left, and was regarded as personable and good with children. He did not act on a whim or explode in a moment of rage. He meticulously planned his attack, articulated his motive, carried out his murders with cold precision and accepted his punishment.

Months before the atrocity he wrote a letter intended for Japan's Parliament, stating he had 'the ability to kill 470 disabled people' and was 'aware that this is an outrageous thing to say'. The letter never got to its destination, but instead fell into the hands of the police, who had Uematsu undergo a psychiatric evaluation. He passed and was deemed not to be a threat. After the attack he told reporters he imagined 'a world where disabled people . . . are allowed to be peacefully euthanised' as they had 'no point in living' and that he had acted 'for the sake of Japan and the world'. Before his hate crime he posted on Twitter, 'Are people who from birth to death make those around them miserable really human beings?' He later admitted his actions were inspired by Hitler's directive to eradicate disabled people in Nazi Germany.[29]

I recall thinking when I read about this case that Uematsu's actions could not be explained by anything other than hate and the deeply negative emotions that often accompany it. He was fuelled by a visceral or 'gut-deep' form of hate. The feeling of disgust it generated led Uematsu to perceive disabled people as less than human, allowing for their cold and calculated extermination.

When visceral emotions like disgust enter the mix, dehumanisation is the likely outcome. Members of the outgroup are no longer people, but instead vermin, cockroaches, parasites. Not only are they from an alien moral universe, they are imagined as a different species. To these subhumans, no obligations are owed, no rules apply, and their victimisation is tolerated.[30] Dehumanisation therefore allows for the outgroup to be treated with indifference and contempt. As objects at the disposal of the ingroup, their lives and deaths become inconsequential.

'Gut-deep' hate is not reserved for particular outgroups. It can fuel violence towards any target who is thought of as physically or morally less than human. The words of Dmitry Tsorionov, the leader of God's Will, make it clear members of his group find homosexuality disgusting and consider those who practise it to be from a different moral universe. When commenting on the Russian anti-gay propaganda law he invoked the terms 'plague' and 'virus', accompanied with the need to 'destroy'. Like Uematsu, these individuals and groups make it their mission in life to eradicate their target.

Profiling the hater

Hateful killers like Satoshi Uematsu are thankfully rare. Through the myriad factors explored in this book, this small group of offenders have been accelerated towards a position of all-consuming hatred that can only be serviced by embarking on a mission to subjugate and exterminate the outgroup of choice. To distinguish between these and the more common hate offenders, criminologists have created a typology.[31] Based on the examination of around 170 Boston Police Department hate crime cases, Professors Jack McDevitt and Jack Levin of Northeastern University came up with four types of hate criminal. These profiles provided the first hint at psychological motivation – what drives the hater – and environmental factors – what triggers the hater.

The *mission hater* occupies the top spot for seriousness and dangerousness. These are the recidivists who make a career out of hunting down the outgroup. They tend to specialise in hateful activity and avoid other forms of petty crime, such as theft. Their drive is a moral one, and they see themselves as tasked with a 'mission' to 'send a message' to the wider community and to teach a lesson to the outgroup, to subjugate them and, if that fails, to eradicate them. They fall firmly into the 'pull' category described earlier. The modus operandi is extreme physical violence and murder. These are the serial killers of the hate criminal fraternity and include David Copeland who committed the 1999 nail bombing in London, Satoshi Uematsu in Japan, Anders Breivik in Norway, Brenton Tarrant in New Zealand, and Dylann Roof, Robert Gregory Bowers, Patrick Crusius and the 1970s white supremacist Joseph Paul Franklin in the US (I delve deep into the pasts of Copeland and Franklin in Chapter 6).

Retaliatory haters take second place, and also form part of the 'pull' category, but only for short periods of time. The retaliatory profile describes those who engage in vengeful violence. More often than not, the revenge is exacted on innocent members of a group associated with a wrongdoer. This kind of hate crime has become common recently in reaction to extremist Islamic terror attacks. In the US in the year following 9/11, the Federal Bureau of Investigation recorded 481 hate crimes with a specific anti-Islamic motive, with a staggering 58 per cent of these occurring within two weeks of the attack.[32] Similarly, in the month of the 7/7 attack in London hate crimes against Muslims rose by 22 per cent in the UK.[33] Retaliation comes in many forms, but the most likely is street-based harassment and violence. The majority of perpetrators are part-time haters who are emboldened and/or threatened by actual or perceived wrongdoing, and seek to take out their frustration for a limited period on those who share similar characteristics to the wrongdoer, before returning to their usual law-abiding behaviour or petty crime.

Defensive haters take third position. Unlike the mission and retaliatory haters, this profile forms part of the 'push' category. Their attitude towards the outgroup falls somewhere between high prejudice and hate, and it is only acted upon when they feel that their territory is being invaded or their resources threatened. Defensive hate crimes tend to occur when the outgroup moves into a majority ingroup area, and the 'invasion' is perceived to devalue property, corrupt children and attract crime. This is the one type of hate crime where women are more likely to play a role, either in perpetration or by encouraging men to act.

Thrill-seeking offenders take the final spot. Unlike the other categories, these offenders may not hold hateful attitudes towards their targets, and instead may be motivated by their peer group and a desire to be one of the gang. A degree of prejudice likely plays a role in who they decide to target, but this only plays a limited role in the activity. Gang socialisation and proving one's masculinity are also key components.[34] These perpetrators are most likely to be young men who regularly take part in petty criminal activity, and hence do not specialise in hate crime.

Profiles are never 100 per cent accurate, and there are some haters who fall outside of this typology or move between categories. A hater can go from a defensive hate crime pattern to a retaliatory one, depending on the circumstances. Hater profiles can also be counter-intuitive. Although hate crimes against Muslims and LGBTQ+ people are more likely to involve groups of young strangers, hate crimes against disabled people are more likely to involve older individuals known to the victim. Hate crimes against mixed-race victims are sometimes perpetrated by members of their own racial groups, while bisexual and transgender people can find themselves being victimised by gay perpetrators. Those from ethnic minority backgrounds who are also LGBTQ+ can suffer hate crimes perpetrated by their close family and friends.

There is no one hater profile, meaning it is difficult to accurately assess how many of the different types are on the streets and online. Next I delve into the attempts across the world to quantify the rising tide of hate and I reveal why not everyone who suffers at the hands of violent bigots gets counted.

2

Hate Counts

Eudy

On 27 April 2008, thirty-one-year-old Eudy Simelane was celebrating with friends in the Noge Tavern in KwaThema township, South Africa. Her new job as a merchandiser for a prestigious pharmaceutical company in Pretoria was big news. None of her friends had ever imagined an out lesbian being considered for such a position, and the regular monthly salary meant she could support both of her retired parents.

Eudy was used to success, despite the disadvantage black lesbians face in South Africa. At the age of four she started to play football with her brother, and by the time she reached her teenage years it was clear she had talent. Starting out as a midfielder for the local Spring Home Sweepers, she went all the way to play for the national women's team, Banyana Banyana, and eventually qualified as an international referee. Eudy was all set to serve as a line official in the 2010 men's World Cup. This success, and her brave move of coming out at a young age, meant she had attained local celebrity status. She used it not to serve herself, but to support HIV and LGBTQ+ charities in the area.

On the same night Eudy was celebrating, Thato Mphiti was sitting across the tavern drinking bottles of Carling Black Label. Around his fourth bottle at 10 p.m. he was joined by his friend Themba Mvubu and two other men. Upon leaving the tavern at around 1 a.m. the four men noticed Eudy walking home ahead of them. Collectively they decided to rob her.

Mphiti held Eudy at knifepoint as the three other men searched her for cash. Frustrated with finding nothing of value, he instructed her to remove and hand over her trainers. At this point Mvubu recognised Eudy as the famous lesbian midfielder, and the men decided to take her to a nearby field, a site notorious among locals as a dumping ground for bodies. As her arms were held down against the coarse grass, one of the men proceeded to rape her. Mphiti then stabbed Eudy repeatedly, before her limp corpse was discarded in a stream at the end of the field, just two hundred metres from her home.

The next day her body was discovered by locals. Eudy's brother was called to identify her. His sister had been stabbed twenty-five times, in her chest, legs, face and the soles of her feet.

The attack on Eudy became one of the first high-profile cases of 'corrective rape' in South Africa, a growing trend that involves young men raping lesbians because they believe these women need to be 'cured'. At the time of writing there is no law in place to recognise the homophobic element of these hate-fuelled rapes.

In the first sentencing of the men found guilty of Eudy's rape and murder, the judge said her sexual orientation had 'no significance' in her killing. A second hearing brought about by months of campaigning by gay rights groups found the practice of 'corrective rape' likely played a role, and the first ruling was overturned. Mphiti and Mvubu received lengthy prison sentences, but the other men were acquitted on a lack of evidence. This was the first time a hate element had been considered in such a case in a South African court.[1]

The murder of Eudy and the subsequent trials demonstrate how some countries still have trouble putting a number on hate crime. The context in which Eudy's rape and murder took place gives us confidence that her sexual orientation was central to the perpetrators' motivations. There are a reported five hundred cases of 'corrective rape' a year in South Africa, and even after the second hearing which saw it recognised for the first time, there are still cases where it goes unacknowledged. Almost three years to the day after Eudy's murder, and in the same township, twenty-four-year-old Noxolo Nogwaza, a prominent lesbian activist and mother of two, was raped, stabbed with shards of glass and bludgeoned to death with blocks of concrete. The case was not recorded as a hate crime by the police or courts. In a statement a spokesperson for the South African Police Ministry said that 'Murder is murder' and that they did not look at sexual orientation when carrying out their investigations.[2]

This chapter deals with the second sub-question that preoccupies scientists who study hate: how much hate crime is actually out there? The official statistics on hate crimes in any country are more a reflection of the process of reporting, recording and prosecution rather than the actual number of hate crimes being committed. Much of hate crime goes under the official radar in all countries. The US and UK feature heavily in this book. This is an artefact of the volume of scientific research conducted in these countries, which in turn has shaped the way governments have attempted to deal with the problem. Governments who have a good record on dealing with hate crimes have developed mechanisms for counting instances of hate, including laws guiding the actions of enforcement agencies, and statistics departments analysing large national victim surveys. For these mechanisms to come into being, there needs to be a general recognition that a problem actually exists in the country.

Once accepted, hate crime statistics have been used by governments and others to monitor trends upwards and downwards. These trends are shaped by three factors.

How and when they count

First, laws are inherently place-specific, and therefore they vary by state and country. In some cases, police forces and lawyers have to work out which jurisdiction a crime may have been committed in, for example if a perpetrator has crossed state lines, and therefore which law should apply. What is certain is that there are no universal laws against hate crime, and this means not every member of the public (nor law enforcement for that matter) can be expected to know what a hate crime is.

Increasing knowledge of the law amongst the general public can ingrain the acceptance that certain behaviours count as hate crimes. Thought of the other way around, introducing new laws that criminalise the behaviours of minorities, such as gay men, can motivate perpetrators to increase their activity and tip otherwise law-abiding citizens to become hate crime offenders. We have seen this happen in Russia with the introduction of the anti-gay propaganda law. Law acts as a mode of communication from the state conveying to citizens the standards to which they should aspire. When I was attacked in the late nineties, there was no law protecting LGBTQ+ people specifically from hate crime. If there had been, and my attackers had known such a crime would carry a harsher punishment, maybe they would have thought twice before jumping me.

Second, the willingness of victims and witnesses to make a police report can also impact hate crime trends. LGBTQ+ communities all over the globe have at some point been over-regulated and persecuted by the police, and only recently has the relationship improved in some larger cities in the western world. Relations between black communities and the police the world over are also hampered by the over-policing of ethnic minority neighbourhoods, unwarranted stop-and-search and the killing of unarmed black men, women and children. Where trust has been eroded between minority groups and law enforcement it is unlikely that members of these communities would expect a police officer to take their report of a hate crime seriously, and in the extreme they might fear being victimised a second time by the police. In one case a gay man in the UK in the mid-1990s reported having been raped by another man only to be arrested himself for the act of 'buggery'. He was left in a cell overnight without medical or psychological care.[3]

Third, hate crime trends are also affected by levels of acceptance among police officers that such crimes have taken place. This is the end of the statistics-generating process that is often neglected in research.* From my interviews with police officers, it is clear that recording an incident as a hate crime begins a process that is more time-consuming for the officer and the force compared to a non-hate crime. In the UK the definition of hate crime is perspective-based – if a victim or a witness thinks an identity has been targeted with hostility, then they have a legal right to have it recorded as a hate crime, regardless of the evidence. But when it comes to prosecuting the alleged perpetrator, evidence on their motivation is needed, and a victim statement is not enough to secure a conviction. Supporting evidence is required: perhaps a prior prosecution for hate crime, membership of a far-right group, or the use of hateful slurs during the attack that were heard by others. The police know this (and often the victims don't), and therefore they can often enter a negotiation of sorts with the victim

---

* There may also be later stages, such as decisions on which crimes get sent to government agencies that release statistical summaries to the public. Minor hate crimes, such as public order offences, may not get sent by police to government agencies.

to discover 'what really happened'. At times this can result in the 'hate' element of a crime being dismissed due to a lack of evidence that would prove essential in securing a conviction.[*]

A warped world of hate

All three factors, criminalisation, victim and witness willingness to report and police training, combine to produce a pattern of hate crime statistics across the world. Map 1 (a choropleth) in the plate section shows the number of hate crimes in total in 2019 across countries that report into the Office for Democratic Institutions and Human Rights (ODIHR).[†] This map colours countries by the frequency of hate crimes recorded by the police in each nation, with colder shades of green and blue indicating low levels, and hotter shades of orange and red indicating high levels.

The UK, one of the smaller countries on the map, is shaded a deep red, indicating the highest count of hate crimes (some 105,000 in England and Wales).[‡] This is much higher than the number recorded in the US and Russia, which both have much larger populations. In the US, there were a recorded 7,314 hate

---

[*] This process also avoids instilling false hope in the victim that the perpetrator will be convicted of a hate offence. A failure of conviction for the hate element of a crime is the most frequently cited reason for dissatisfaction amongst victims with the court process in hate crime cases in England and Wales (see M. L. Williams and J. Tregidga, 'All Wales Hate Crime Research Project: Final Report', Cardiff: Race Equality First, 2013).

[†] In the UK this includes hate crimes targeting race, religion, sexual orientation, disability and transgender identity. Not all countries recognise hate crimes in all these categories (see hatecrime.osce.org). Some countries that do collect hate crime statistics are not included on this map.

[‡] Total for England and Wales excludes Greater Manchester due to technical issues with police systems.

incidents (8,559 offences – there can be more than one hate crime offence in an incident, such as vandalism and assault) in 2019, significantly lower than the UK's tally. Based on such comparisons, the UK seems to be an incredibly intolerant and hateful nation. This assumption is made even more stark when we look at Map 2 (a cartogram) in the plate section. In a cartogram, the size of each country represents the volume of what is being measured, in our case hate crimes reported to police. Through the lens of hate crime statistics the world looks like an unfamiliar place, with the UK dominating the planet, and most of Europe, Asia and Russia squeezed into a fraction of their actual size. But this is a warped lens that says more about how hate crimes are reported, recorded and prosecuted in different countries than about the actual prevalence of victimisation. Put differently, the UK is likely to be the best country at reporting, recording and prosecuting hate crimes in the world, while most others are quite poor.

Maybe most surprising is the low number of hate crimes reported to the FBI by law enforcement agencies. Map 3 in the plate section shows the 'dark figure' of police-recorded hate crime in the US. Each dot represents a police department serving over ten thousand people that reported zero hate crimes in its jurisdiction in 2019.[§] The map shows some surprising dark spots where you might expect to see some volume of hate crime reported. Texas and Florida, each home to over sixty organised hate groups, including the KKK, are peppered with dark spots that call out for a deeper analysis.

A useful alternative to these official police numbers is found in the statistics produced by national crime victimisation surveys.

§ Map adapted from a similar visualisation of police records showing zero/low hate crimes produced by ProPublica's Documenting Hate Project.

If you are one of the lucky ones to have been sampled, you will have opened your door to a government-appointed interviewer who was desperately hoping you wouldn't slam it on them when they asked you to respond to a series of questions. If you were polite, like me, you would have sat patiently while the stranger took about an hour to ask you all about your life in the last year, including your experience of crime. Because these interviewers are not police officers, and tend to be mild-mannered, interested people who have all the time in the world to learn about your life, they get good information out of you. This includes experiences of hate crimes you may have suffered that you did not bother reporting to the police for one reason or another. In criminology we use these victim surveys to provide a more accurate reflection of reality.

Taking the UK and US for a comparison, data from the Crime Survey for England and Wales shows 190,000 hate crimes a year on average (2017–20),* while the US National Crime Victimisation Survey shows around 305,390 hate crimes a year on average (2018–19).† Both surveys define and measure hate crime in

---

* Victims are asked about their perception of the offender's motivation for the incident, which is an indirect measure of hate. Fifty-five per cent of these crimes were perceived as racially motivated, 26 per cent as disability motivated, 22 per cent as religiously motivated, 12 per cent as homophobically motivated and 4 percent as transgender identity motivated. The total does not sum to 100 per cent due to rounding and because more than one type of bias can be attributed to each incident. Importantly, these figures exclude crimes where no individual victim can be identified or interviewed, such as some public order offences (e.g. racial slurs that do not target an individual but a group) and homicide. The former constitutes a significant amount of police-recorded hate crime in the UK.

† Fifty-seven per cent of hate crimes were racially motivated, 27 per cent transgender identity motivated, 26 per cent homophobically motivated, 16 per cent disability motivated and 8 per cent religiously motivated (2013–17 averages). The total does not sum to 100 per cent due to rounding and because more than one type of bias can be attributed to each incident. Like the CSEW, the NCVS does not measure all types of hate crime.

roughly the same way, though the UK survey includes gender motivation while the US survey does not.

This does narrow the gap between the countries considerably, but there is still something unconvincing about the US data given their population is near five times the size of the UK's. The US is also more ethnically diverse (around 60 per cent white compared to the UK's 87 per cent), meaning there are more ethnic minorities to victimise (race hate crimes are often the most prevalent).[‡] So what specifically could be going on to discourage individuals from reporting hate crime to the police or government interviewers in the country with both the largest immigrant population and the largest number of organised hate groups on the planet?[§]

Criminalising hate

To find out we must return to the various factors that shape hate crime statistics. While at the federal level hate crimes are clearly defined in the US, at the state level there is significant variation. Some states have comprehensive hate crime laws, while others have none, not even enhanced sentencing for crimes motivated by hate (three at the time of writing: Arkansas, South Carolina and Wyoming, covering a total of around 9 million Americans).[¶] Georgia was on this list until it introduced hate crime laws in July 2020.

‡ The counterfactual is that more ethnic minorities makes the US more multi-cultural and more tolerant. This is unlikely to be the case as ethnic minorities are not evenly spread across locations and they tend to cluster.

§ The Southern Poverty Law Center identified 838 hate groups operating in the US in 2020: https://www.splcenter.org/hatewatch.

¶ S.B. 622 (2021) in Arkansas has been described as a hate crime law, but it has been criticised for not being specific in identifying protected characteristics, likely rendering it ineffective. Indiana's S.B. 198 (2019) has been criticised on similar grounds.

Arkansas is the reported headquarters of the Ku Klux Klan and home to its leader, Thomas Robb. South Carolina is where Dylann Roof callously murdered nine members of the Emanuel African Methodist Church in Charleston in 2015. His crimes could not be regarded as hate-motivated by the state, and he had to be charged with hate crimes at the federal level. Wyoming was the home and is now the resting place of Matthew Shepard, the student who was tortured and murdered for being gay by Aaron McKinney and Russell Henderson in 1998. The murder provoked national outrage and eventually resulted in the federal hate crime legislation of 2009 that extended the groups protected to include LGBTQ+ individuals.[*] Georgia is where unarmed Ahmaud Arbery was hunted down and shot dead while jogging on 23 February 2020. The two white assailants, Travis McMichael and his father Gregory, were charged with the murder over ten weeks later, but with no official recognition of its racial motivation.

The ability to rely on federal hate crime law is sometimes used to justify a lack of state legislation in the US, but this is a false argument. If the hate crime in question is deemed as less serious (e.g. racial or homophobic harassment) then the federal law is less likely to be used. In these states, being anything but a white heterosexual Christian makes you less safe.

The absence of comprehensive hate crime laws at the state level also communicates to citizens that the local government and the police care less about the victimisation of minorities than they do about conflicting principles, such as freedom of speech. In such contexts, the notion of a 'hate crime' is less likely to exist at the forefront of the consciousness of a victim, and much less so a witness of a crime that includes an element of bias against an aspect

* Matthew Shepard and James Byrd Jr Hate Crimes Prevention Act 2009.

of identity. Can we therefore expect minority groups in US states with limited or no hate crime laws to even recognise themselves as hate crime victims, let alone report to the police?

Sophie

In the early hours of Saturday 11 August 2007, twenty-year-old Sophie Lancaster and her boyfriend, twenty-one-year-old Robert Maltby, were heading home from an evening at a friend's house in the small town of Bacup, Lancashire. On the way they stopped off at the Total petrol station on Market Street to buy cigarettes.

They had been dating for about two years, and both planned to start university that October. They were a solitary couple, mostly keeping themselves to themselves, but they occasionally joined in with the local 'goth' scene. Their look was distinctive – brightly coloured braided hair, and nose and lip piercings – and it had attracted the wrong kind of attention in the past. Defiant and free-spirited, Sophie and Robert never changed their appearance and they looked perfect together. Just a month before they had talked about marriage.

At the petrol station they encountered a group of teenage boys on the forecourt. They got into a friendly conversation and shared the cigarettes they had bought. Instead of continuing home, Sophie and Robert decided to continue hanging out with the boys at the local skate park.

Upon arriving they were introduced to other members of the gang, including sixteen-year-old Ryan Herbert and fifteen-year-old Brendan Harris. Both boys were nonplussed by the arrival of two goths, or 'moshers' as they disparagingly referred to them. Herbert and Harris showed their disapproval by moving to the other side of the skate park.

Sophie and Robert continued to exchange friendly banter with their new friends, their piercings attracting much of the attention. Meanwhile Herbert and Harris were joined by several other boys. All of them eavesdropped on the conversation and leered over. One of the boys called out to his friend who was talking to Robert, 'Why the fuck did you bring them here? Weirdos. Let's bang him!'

The mood quickly turned. Harris launched himself at Robert, landing a punch to his head. 'Get off him!' Sophie screamed. A mob descended on Robert and kicked him to the ground. They booted him from every angle until he lost consciousness.

Sophie begged them to stop and put herself between Robert and his attackers. She cradled his head and cried. The mob told her to move, but she wouldn't leave her boyfriend's side.

Herbert kicked Sophie so hard that she flew backwards and hit the ground. Harris then joined the attack. Sophie was simultaneously kicked in the head by the two boys from opposing sides. Herbert delivered one final stomp to her skull. The force of the impact was so great that Sophie's face was left with an imprint of his trainer.

Sophie and Robert's facial injuries were so dreadful that the paramedics could not identify either's sex when they arrived at the scene. As both were rushed to hospital, the boys boasted about their attack to other locals: 'There's two moshers nearly dead up Bacup park . . . You want to see them, they are a right mess,' said Herbert.

Robert eventually regained consciousness in the hospital but lost all memory of the night. Sophie was in a coma for thirteen days and died in her mother's arms after her family agreed to turn off life support.

Five boys were arrested following the attack. During questioning, police said, Harris was 'laughing and joking' about the attack with his mother. Harris and Herbert were found guilty of murder and the remaining boys were found guilty of grievous bodily harm with intent.

At the sentencing the judge stated, 'I am satisfied that the only reason for this wholly unprovoked attack was that Robert Maltby and Sophie Lancaster were singled out for their appearance alone because they looked and dressed differently from you and your friends . . . This was a terrible case which has shocked and outraged all who have heard about it. At least wild animals, when they hunt in packs, have a legitimate reason for so doing, to obtain food. You have none and your behaviour on that night degrades humanity itself.'

Life sentences were handed down to Harris and Herbert, and the other boys received between four and six years.[4] An account of the brutal attack and murder is well captured in the 2017 BBC film *Murdered for Being Different*.

The attack on Sophie and Robert was not included in 2007's official police hate crime statistics in the UK. Despite the country having some of the most inclusive laws in the world, they are still limited to certain individual characteristics: race, religion, disability, sexual orientation and transgender identity. Of these characteristics, only race and religion have specific hate crime offences attached to them in law. Hate directed against the remaining characteristics is only dealt with at the sentencing stage of a case, where a judge can increase a sentence if there is evidence that the crime was aggravated by hostility towards the victim's identity.

Differences in law have consequences. The judge in Sophie's case decided that the perpetrators had attacked her and Robert for who they were. The attackers' crimes were aggravated by hostility towards their 'goth' identity, and their sentences reflected this aggravating factor. But as there is no specific law for hate crimes against alternative subcultures, they were not counted. Treating groups of people differently in law sends out a message that one group is less worthy of protection than another.

Because there was no anti-gay hate crime offence in law at the time of my attack, the police would have recorded my experience as a crime against my body but not my identity, had I reported it. This made me feel as if I mattered just a little bit less than others in the eyes of the establishment.

Lack of recognition, even persecution, continues around the globe. Who a country or state sees as a 'legitimate' victim therefore greatly influences the official number of hate crimes. Even with some of the most advanced and inclusive laws, gaps still remain that make it difficult to get a true picture of all crimes motivated by hate.

Beyond the countries that recognise hate crime in law, the complete absence of statistics from some countries, such as Japan, can be explained by their governments' repeated refusals to acknowledge that hateful motive in crimes should be criminalised or carry a harsher penalty. The mass murder in the care home in Sagamihara was not recognised by the police or other officials as a hate crime against disabled people, despite the clear admission by the killer in writing and in a spoken confession that he felt 'It is better that the disabled disappear.' While some discrimination laws exist that protect certain minority groups against unfair treatment by government agencies and in workplaces, there are no laws in Japan that criminalise offences motivated by hate. The closest the government has come to passing such a law was in 2016 when it introduced an anti-hate speech act, following international condemnation for allowing widespread demonstrations and online abuse directed against Japan's ethnic Korean (Zainichi) minority by ultra-right-wing organisations. However, the Japanese Constitution protects freedom of speech, which is taken to include hate speech. Therefore the new act contains provisions to prevent such demonstrations, but not to take action against protesters if they do go ahead.

For many this does not go far enough to recognise the discrimination and hate many ethnic groups suffer in Japan.[*] Part of the issue is that ethnicity is not recorded in the census, a tool the government claims is used to inform good policy making (which would include criminal justice policy, no doubt). This has led some to claim that the official stance is that race is of little importance in Japanese culture. The Japanese government has claimed the country is monocultural, monoethnic and homogeneous. This is an odd position to take when we know hundreds of thousands of Chinese, South Korean, Filipino and Brazilian nationals live there, along with minority Japanese ethnic groups such as the Ainu and Ryukyuan peoples who have suffered discrimination over hundreds of years.[5]

Japan is not alone. Of the countries that send official hate crime statistics to the ODIHR, only a small minority always publish comprehensive data, covering a range of motivations and types of crime (at the time of writing these include the UK, Finland, Sweden and the Netherlands). Countries including Russia, Bosnia and Herzegovina, Croatia and Serbia, which are known to exist in a climate of ethnic and religious tension, report tiny numbers of hate crimes. Within these countries and others that share similar characteristics, it is likely that the concept of 'hate crime' is lost

---

[*] In December 2019 the Tokyo district of Kawasaki passed an ordinance that bans discriminatory speech against foreign people in public spaces, with a maximum punishment of 500,000 Yen. The district houses one of the largest Korean communities in the city.

in the much wider debates common in post-conflict nations. In these contexts, suitable laws do not exist, local police are not well trained and government programmes are not developed to protect minority groups from persecution.

'Signal' hate acts and criminalisation

Sadly, it often takes a 'signal' act of hate, an act so atrocious that it attracts international attention, to bring about legal change. In the case of Sophie and Robert, while the law in the UK was not changed to include 'goths' or alternative subcultures as a protected group, many police forces now recognise them as such. It took Sophie's death to effect change, although limited. The 1993 racist murder of Stephen Lawrence in London, and the subsequent mishandling of the case by police, brought about the UK's hate crime legislation in 1998 (though it took five more years for anything but race to be protected in law, and an imbalance still exists between characteristics). The racist murder of James Byrd Jr in Texas in 1998, and the homophobic murder of Matthew Shepard the same year, resulted in the introduction of federal hate crime legislation in the US in 2009.

Some countries that still have inadequate laws are now going through similar transitions following their own 'signal' acts of hate. The racist murder of Shehzad Luqman in Athens in 2013 put hate legislation on the agenda in Greece. The 2007 attack on Budapest Pride march led to changes in the law in Hungary to protect LGBTQ+ people. The violent tension over disputed territory between Georgians and South Ossetians, lasting from 1989 to the present day, and the 2012 attacks against an LGBTQ+ demonstration, including discrimination by police in Tbilisi, inspired change in Georgia. It will be decades before hate crime counts which reflect a fraction of the true magnitude of victim-isation emerge in these countries and many others, but change is afoot due to the hard work of human rights organisations and some inspirational people.

Perceiving versus proving hate

Beyond a general recognition in law that hate crime exists and should be punished are the all-important details.[6] There are too many to outline here, but one which greatly shapes hate crime counts is the definition of hate crime at the police recording stage. The broadest definition of hate crime is 'perception-based', mean-ing the police record a hate crime when a victim perceives they have been targeted because of their identity, or when a witness perceives that this is so. The alternative definition is strictly 'evi-dence-based', meaning the police record a hate crime only when the evidence supports this conclusion, regardless of what the vic-tim or witness perceives. Evidence might include the use of rac-ist or homophobic slurs during the commission of the crime, the presence of extremist iconography, a known link between the per-petrator and an extremist group (either online, offline or both), and/or a history of hate crime perpetration.

The evidence-based definition may seem reasonable, but it fails to acknowledge that not all acts of hate are accompanied by an utterance or by hate symbols carved on skin or walls that declare motive. Nor are they only committed by repeat-offender hardened bigots. Things also get complicated when the victim states there were slurs used during the attack, but there are no witnesses. The narrowness of the strict evidence-based definition inevitably means fewer hate crimes get counted. The UK follows a perception-based approach, while many other countries adopt the alternative. This partly explains the UK's high police-recorded hate crime count in comparison to other countries.

While the perception-based approach has a greater chance of counting more hate crimes, a downside is its mismatch with the requirements of a court proceeding. In 2018 there were 111,076 hate crimes counted by the UK police, but only 18,055 got to the courts. Some of this discrepancy comes down to less serious hate crimes being dealt with by police (called out-of-court disposal) where the perpetrator admits guilt and the victim gets to decide on a community punishment. Difficulty in locating a perpetrator of a hate crime, especially in random acts of violence by strangers, can also mean that a record is generated but there is no progression to court. But the most likely sources of this 'justice gap' are victim withdrawal and a lack of solid evidence that a crime was motivated by hate.

It is incredibly difficult to prove beyond reasonable doubt that a criminal act (what lawyers call actus reus) is a result of a hateful attitude in the perpetrator's mind (called mens rea). A lawyer can easily show a criminal act was committed, but it is much more difficult to prove the act was motivated by hate towards the identity of the victim. Even if the victim testifies that a hateful slur was used during the attack, there may be no witnesses to back this up. The defence could also argue the slur was motivated by fear or anger, and not hate. These complexities mean only the most clear-cut hate crimes reach the courts – those where witnesses heard the use of slurs or saw hate symbols (demonstrating hostility), the perpetrator had prior convictions for hate offences, and/or they had links to extremist ideology (demonstrating motivation).*

* Section 145 of the Criminal Justice Act 2003 (England and Wales) imposes

Where countries have well-developed laws and operate with broad definitions, any significant difference in counts of hate crime then comes down to the relationship between citizens and the police.

The police and hate

Frank

In the early morning of 24 October 2004, friends Frank Jude Jr and Lovell Harris, both black men, attended a housewarming party in the middle-class white neighbourhood of Bay View in Milwaukee, Wisconsin. The party was hosted by a Milwaukee police officer, Andrew Spengler, and by the time they arrived many of his guests were soused on hard liquor.

Frank and Lovell had been invited by two white women, Katie Brown and Kirsten Antonissen, and their arrival together as a foursome raised eyebrows and caused chatter amongst the other guests. When Katie and Kirsten went to the bathroom together, Spengler, flanked by four of his officer friends, peppered Frank and Lovell with questions: 'Who have you arrived with?' 'Who do you know at the party?' 'Have you brought anything to drink?'

---

a duty upon courts to increase the sentence for any offence that involves either: a) the offender demonstrating towards the victim hostility based on the victim's membership (or presumed membership) of a racial or religious group; or b) the offence being motivated (wholly or partly) by hostility towards members of a racial or religious group based on their membership of that group. These are alternatives. This means that in a case where a demonstration of hostility can be proved, there is no need also to prove motivation, and vice versa. (CPS 2020, Racist and Religious Hate Crime – Prosecution Guidance). The Crime and Disorder Act 1998 creates specific offences for crimes that demonstrate hostility towards race or religion or show hateful motivation.

At around 2.45 a.m. the foursome left the party because they felt unwelcome. As they were about to drive off in their truck, Spengler and about nine other off-duty officers confronted them. Spengler's police badge was missing, and Frank and Lovell were his prime suspects. When both men denied taking the badge and refused to get out of the truck, one of the officers shouted, 'Nigger, we can kill you!'

The officers then rocked the truck and smashed the headlights as Lovell cried out for help from the sleeping neighbours.

'Nigger, shut up, it's our world!' one of the officers exclaimed.

When both women got out of the truck to offer up their handbags for inspection, four officers grabbed Frank by his legs. He held onto the headrest in fear of his life as the four men tugged at him before pulling him free. After dragging him across the floor they turned to Lovell and forcibly extracted him from the truck. An unsuccessful search of both men served to intensify the violence.

One of the officers walked Lovell at knifepoint a few metres up the street, jutting the blade into the back of his head. As Lovell was instructed to sit on the kerb the officer asked menacingly, 'Nigger, who you think you is?'

Lovell remained silent. The officer then slowly drew the knife across his face, carving a deep gash into his cheek. Lovell recalls the officer relishing the moment.

'Now let me stick this knife in your ass, nigger,' said the officer.

As he instructed his victim to stand, Lovell took his chance. He pelted down the dark street, cradling his bloody face.

Meanwhile two officers were holding Frank's arms behind his back while the others took turns to beat him. After taking multiple hits to his body, Frank fell to the floor, where he was kicked several times in the head. His face was drenched in blood.

More questions were darted at Frank. While he was held in a tight headlock an officer asked him for the badge. Frank repeated he didn't know anything about any badge and pleaded with them to stop. With a final decisive strike to his head, Frank lost consciousness for a moment and dropped back to the floor with a thud.

As the violence was unfolding, Kirsten managed to call the police. 'They're beating the shit out of him!' she screamed into the cell phone.

Spengler noticed her on the phone and ordered her to hang up. When she didn't comply, he twisted her arm behind her back, ripped the phone from her hand and threw it against the truck, smashing it into pieces. Katie then frantically called the police only to have her phone seized too. The other house guests watched on from the porch. Their phones remained firmly in their pockets and handbags.

Around 3 a.m., two on-duty police officers arrived at the scene. To the horror of Katie and Kirsten, the beatings continued with one of these officers joining in. After Frank was handcuffed on the ground the violence took a sickening twist. An officer took a pen out of his pocket and whispered to Frank, 'You're gonna tell me where the badge is or I'm gonna put this pen in your ear.'

The officer made good on his threat. With a stabbing motion he pushed the pen deep inside Frank's ear, drawing copious amounts of blood. Frank's screams were not enough to stop the officer from doing the same to his other ear. The torture continued as two other officers bent several of Frank's fingers so far back that they snapped. At this point Frank recalls 'crying like a baby'. 'Please, stop, please,' he begged.

From all sides the officers hammered Frank, their fists falling fast and heavy. An officer then spread Frank's legs apart and kicked him in the groin with such force that his body left the ground. As Frank cradled himself in excruciating pain, the on-duty officer took the opportunity to stamp on his head until bones could be heard cracking.

The host of the party then held a gun to Frank's head and said, 'I'm the fucking police. I can do whatever I want to do. I could kill you.'

In a final effort to find the missing badge, the officers ripped apart the truck in a rage and cut Frank's clothes off him with the knife. They turned up nothing. It wasn't until a third on-duty officer arrived at the scene that the violence stopped. It stopped because Frank was arrested, despite him not fighting back at any stage of his brutal torture. The officer found Frank bleeding, naked on the street, unable to stand.

He immediately drove Frank to hospital, where the emergency room doctor felt compelled to take photographs as evidence because his injuries were so unusual and extensive. He had injuries to his scalp, face, ears, neck, chest, abdomen, back, arms, legs, buttocks and perineum. In twenty years of emergency medicine the doctor had never seen injuries like these. Following his initial examination, Frank grabbed the doctor by the hand and asked her not to leave him alone because he was afraid his attackers would 'finish the job'.[7]

In the days following the vicious attack and torture of Frank Jude Jr and Lovell Harris, none of the officers was arrested, and the police department was uncooperative. Only when a local paper published the doctor's photos of Frank's shocking injuries and detailed the likely lifelong disabilities he would suffer, did anything happen. Public demonstrations in the days after the story broke pressured Milwaukee Police Department to fire those involved. But at a state trial, Spengler and two other officers were acquitted by an all-white jury, who had heard false testimony from officers and party guests. Some of them claimed to have 'suffered memory loss'.

Protests following the verdict prompted a federal investigation. Eventually seven of the officers involved were convicted. Some of the off-duty officers who formed part of the baying mob that night were reinstated and allowed to continue patrolling the streets of Milwaukee.

I was totally taken aback and horrified when I read about this case. I respect the work that police officers do. This respect came about through my research work with police forces, but also because my sister and her husband joined their local force shortly after I started my PhD. I know how hard the job has been for my close family, and how they, like so many other officers, have put their lives on the line to protect us. I came to believe the police are the public, and the public are the police.

The police can only do their jobs effectively if the people they serve approve of their role, powers, actions and behaviour. We trust the police to protect us *all* and not to discriminate by protecting some but not others. When this trust is abused public respect wanes, and at the extreme police legitimacy is undermined. We stop recognising the police as a service that works for the good of the people, and instead see a corrupt, self-serving organisation. At worst, this results in the breakdown of social order as citizens question and wilfully break the laws officers are employed to enforce. At best, citizens disengage from the police – they refuse to cooperate with inquiries, to come forward as witnesses and to report crimes. Both of these responses were seen across the US in the aftermath of the murder of George Floyd by Minneapolis police officer Derek Chauvin in May 2020.

Trust in police and the corresponding willingness to engage can shape the hate crime count. Even when someone knows they have been a victim of a hate crime, reporting it to the police is dependent on trust. In Russia, Alexei never reported the attacks he had suffered because he feared further persecution, and even if he had it is doubtful the police would have taken the report seriously.

I did not report the hate attack on me over twenty years ago. Why? I didn't want to tell a police officer I was gay. Growing up and going to school in the late 1980s in a small village in Wales shaped what I thought of the authorities. Section 28 of the Local Government Act was introduced in 1988 under Margaret Thatcher, forbidding teachers to discuss or promote 'the acceptability of homosexuality as a pretended family relationship', and at that time the police were known to target and entrap gay men for bogus 'sex crimes'. Section 28 was not repealed until 2003.

In the US the relationship between black communities and law enforcement has been marred by a string of police brutality and murder cases over the past few decades. Many cases have attracted widespread news attention, including those of Frank Jude Jr and Lovell Harris in Milwaukee, Wisconsin in 2004, Sean Bell in New York City, New York in 2006, Oscar Grant in Oakland, California in 2009, Trayvon Martin in Sanford, Florida in 2012, Michael Brown in Ferguson, Missouri in 2014, Breonna Taylor in Louisville, Kentucky in March 2020, George Floyd in Minneapolis, Minnesota in May 2020, Tony McDade in Tallahassee, Florida in May 2020, and Rayshard Brooks in Atlanta, Georgia in June 2020.

Research by Professor Matthew Desmond and colleagues at Harvard, Yale and Oxford Universities noted that in the US there are clear racial disparities in police use of force. Black teenagers and adults are more likely to be beaten and killed by police even when other contributing factors are considered (such as resisting arrest and officer training).[8] Desmond and colleagues sought to test the effect highly publicised police brutality cases have on the black community's willingness to report crime to law enforcement agencies. The hypothesis was that well-publicised cases of police brutality against unarmed black men would reduce crime reporting in black neighbourhoods – the theory being that such cases reduce confidence and trust in the police and this can result in lack of engagement.

The researchers focused on the effect of the beating of Frank Jude Jr and Lovell Harris. They measured the number of 911 calls before and after the story broke in the news. In the year following the story an estimated 22,200 fewer 911 calls were made in Milwaukee, representing a 20 per cent reduction on the previous year. The reduction was much more marked in black neighbourhoods, where calls dropped by 13,200, while in white neighbourhoods they fell by 8,800. But what was more concerning to the researchers was how long the reduction seemed to last in black neighbourhoods. Based on their calculations the reduction in these neighbourhoods lasted well over a year after the story broke. It lasted only seven months in white neighbourhoods.

The researchers also found that the killing of Sean Bell by police in Queens, New York, the day before his wedding in 2006, had an effect on the reduction of 911 calls made in black neighbourhoods in Milwaukee. This analysis provided evidence that non-local cases of police killings also impact local crime reporting. The study concluded that cases of police brutality can have a nationwide effect on reducing 911 calls, and that this is more likely to impact black neighbourhoods than white ones in terms of volume and duration.

Lack of reporting creates a vicious cycle where an absence of police and apprehension of offenders means crimes are allowed to flourish, making black neighbourhoods less safe. In the Milwaukee study, murder rates increased by 32 per cent in the six months after the Frank Jude Jr case, when 22,000 fewer calls were made to the police. That summer was the deadliest in seven years in the city.

The murder of unarmed seventeen-year-old Trayvon Martin in Florida in 2012 by a white neighbourhood watch officer resulted in rallies and marches across the US, and after the acquittal of the shooter, President Obama said in a speech, 'Trayvon Martin could have been me thirty-five years ago.'[9] The killing of eighteen-year-old Michael Brown in Ferguson, Missouri in 2014 by a white officer, which involved six shots to the chest, sparked three rounds of protests – following the shooting itself, the trial, which was unusual and some say biased, and the eventual acquittal of the officer in question. A year later a Department of Justice investigation found the Ferguson Police Department had engaged in misconduct by discriminating against African Americans. As a result of the shooting, Obama committed to spend $75 million on police body-worn cameras to provide more evidence in future trials of this nature. The police killing of George Floyd by strangulation in Minneapolis in 2020 resulted in the officer concerned being charged with unintentional second-degree murder, and in violence-inciting tweets from President Trump, demonstrations globally, and the worst widespread civil unrest in the US since the assassination of Martin Luther King Jr in 1968.

The local, national and global news coverage of these and similar incidents inevitably erodes trust in regional government officials and law enforcement agencies amongst large swathes of the population. The lack of reporting of criminal victimisation within black communities as a result means thousands of hate crime cases go unrecorded in the official statistics.

Is the hate count rising?

There remain questions over the apparent rise in police-recorded hate crime. Many on the right of the political spectrum would rather explain away the association between events such as the Brexit vote or the election of Donald Trump and the highest rise in hate crime in recent history. To do so they argue that changes in recording and reporting offer likely explanations for the upward trend.

These arguments are not without merit. Over the past ten years, police services throughout the UK, US and many other countries have put in additional resources to fund campaigns aimed at increasing the reporting of hate crime by victims and witnesses. These campaigns have focused on challenging the reasons why as many as 50 per cent of hate crimes have gone unreported in the past: distrust in the police and the fear of secondary victimisation among minority communities, and worry over making the situation worse (for example, where the perpetrator is a neighbour). The evidence suggests they are working. Thankfully, police culture in many countries has changed dramatically in the last few decades, and officers have taken part in record levels of training in recognising hate crime and increasing detection and recording. There is little doubt that part of the rise in police-recorded hate crime over the past decade can be attributed to these factors.

But the astonishing rises in hate crimes around the Brexit vote and Trump's election, and after high-profile terror attacks, cannot be explained by these factors alone. At the time of the Brexit vote, according to an editorial in the *Spectator*, 'Perhaps the referendum did lead to a rise in hate crime. Then again, perhaps it didn't. But despite the angry reports blaming Brexit, the only thing that is clear is that there is little proof either way.'

To get a definitive answer, the UK Cabinet Office Behavioural Insights Team and my HateLab at Cardiff University set out to generate the most complete picture of hate crime in the UK by pulling together every source of information, from police records to data on Facebook posts. In the face of right-leaning newspaper headlines such as the *Daily Mail*'s 'Great Brexit Hate Crime Myth', we set out to explore whether the divisive polarising narratives promoted by the Leave.EU and Vote Leave campaigns directly led to a genuine rise in hate crimes that continued for many years.

Our first hypothesis was that the Leave campaigns legitimised, for a temporary period, hate crimes towards members of the outgroup in an attempt to protect the resources of the ingroup, whether economic (e.g. threats to jobs, housing, NHS waiting times) or symbolic (e.g. threats to 'our way of life'). Such resources were increasingly portrayed as under threat from EU migrants by the Leave campaigns in the weeks running up to the vote. The two most frequently covered issues in the press in the weeks leading up to the vote were immigration and the economy, with particular groups (Turks, Albanians, Romanians and Poles) receiving negative coverage.

Our second hypothesis was that places with the largest spike in Brexit-related hate crime also had demographic characteristics that meant certain members of the ingroup were more susceptible to the divisive propaganda emanating from the Leave campaigns. We expected to find that the areas with the highest spike in Brexit-related hate crimes also had high levels of migration, unemployment and Leave vote share. Many of the areas that voted overwhelmingly to leave the EU had seen migration rise in the decade prior to the vote. In some Leave voting areas, immigrants, who previously made up one in fifty of the local population, numbered as many as one in four at the time of the referendum. These places had also suffered the biggest cuts in jobs and services.

Migration to these areas, concentrated in the North and on the south coast of England, is largely comprised of younger, non-English-speaking, low-skilled workers. The combination of unemployed locals and an abundance of employed migrants, competing for scarce resources in a time of recession and cutbacks, creates a greater feeling of 'us' versus 'them'. A lack of inter-cultural interactions and understanding between the local and migrant populations results in rising tensions. Combined with the galvanising effect of the referendum result, these factors create the perfect conditions for hate crime to flourish.

In our analysis we used statistical models that take account of a number of factors known to have an effect on hate crimes. In each of the populations of the forty-three police force areas of England and Wales we measured the unemployment rate, average income, educational attainment, health deprivation, general crime rate, barriers to housing and services, quality of living, rate of migrant inflow, and Leave vote share. To account for the argument put forward by right-wing thinktanks that the increase in hate crime was down to more reporting, we controlled for the frequency with which each police force raised awareness of the problem of hate via their social media channels, where they encouraged the public to report hate crimes as victims or witnesses. We also cancelled out the effect of a large number of other events that may have caused the hate crime rate to rise, including terror attacks at home and abroad, such as the murder of Jo Cox days before the referendum.

Even when controlling for these influential factors the referendum still emerged as a powerful explanatory factor in its own right. The month after the vote saw 1,100 more hate crimes (29 per cent greater) than would have been expected in the same period in the absence of the vote. Of the other factors that may have had an impact (migration inflow, unemployment, educational attainment etc.), only the Leave vote share emerged as a significant predictor of hate crimes. The higher the Leave vote in an area, the greater the increase in hate crimes after the vote. This gives us confidence that the vote result acted as a signal to would-be hate crime offenders to take to the streets. The counter-argument that the spike in hate crimes could be explained by more victims coming forward to report did not hold up. We found police forces that most frequently encouraged reporting on social media did not record more hate crime than those forces that encouraged reporting least frequently.

Similar analysis has found the 2016 election of Donald Trump was associated with one of the greatest increases in hate crimes in recent American history, second only to the dramatic uptick in crimes targeting Muslims following 9/11[10] (the end of his presidency and the COVID-19 pandemic was associated with the second greatest increase – see Figure 2). Even when controlling for alternative explanations, counties that voted for Trump by the widest margins experienced the largest increases in hate crimes.

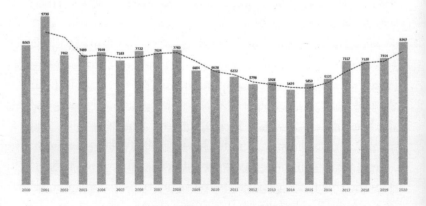

Fig. 3: Total number of hate crime incidents recorded by the FBI (2000–2020)

In countries where hate crime recording standards are moderate to good, meaning they capture a partial picture of victimisation that is relatively stable over time, the data point to an upward trend. There is no doubt this trend is influenced by a range of factors, but the one that stands out from all others as particular to our time, and which exerts the greatest influence, is the divisive nature of political rhetoric.[11] It is the case that in some parts of the world hate is being allowed to flourish on the streets and online, and for a significant number of people, at no other point in their lives have they been so encompassed by it, so affected by it, and so ill-equipped to challenge it.

In the sciences, it is rarely possible to make a definitive conclusion based on the data available at the time, and therefore unwise to make an ultimate statement on a phenomenon. We know hate crimes are happening today across the globe, but governments, police, witnesses and even victims in some countries and states are so incapable of recognising hate for what it is that we cannot be certain that there is more hate now than at any other point in history.

As it is not possible to directly measure hate crime with accuracy, an alternative is to measure the ingredients that we know feed hate – the social, economic and political *accelerants*, and our foundational human biological and psychological traits. Increases in inequality, political polarisation, divisive events and abuses of the internet, among other things, can give rise to hateful sentiment, and if we can measure and better understand these, then we can figure out when, where and in whom hate might erupt. Before we delve into understanding the accelerants, we must first take a closer look at how our evolved internal wiring can lay the foundation for hate in us all if we don't fight against it.

3

The Brain and Hate

On a cold February day in 2016, music journalist John Doran took a break from editing his online magazine, *The Quietus*, and went for a stroll down his local high street in Hackney, London. John had grown up in Liverpool in the 1970s and worked on the factory floor for years before moving to the capital to become a writer, his work published by *Vice* magazine and the *Guardian* among others.

Nothing in particular caught John's attention as he strolled down Stamford Hill Broadway that day. The street was not overly busy, and he saw some familiar faces. But then something strange happened. As he passed one of the many independent coffee shops, John heard a voice shout out, 'I'll cut you open, you big-belly cunt!'

He looked around and saw a portly man walking by. He asked himself, 'Was it him that said that? If it was, why is no one else on the street reacting?' Then a man in joggers passed by. The voice erupted a second time: 'Why don't you get a fucking job, you lazy fucking prick!?'

John still couldn't pinpoint where it came from, and again there was no reaction from bystanders. It dawned on him. No one was screaming out these words. It was his own voice he was hearing, loud and clear, but in his head.

More inner-voice tongue-lashings followed as others passed him by, this time pure racist, homophobic, misogynist bile. Profane and violent rants. John had no control over these words being spouted by his mind, all of them hateful. Disgusted, confused and terrified, he darted home, head down, hoping the voice would stop if he averted his eyes from anyone who might trigger it.

About four months before this strange incident, John had been cycling to work after dropping off his child at school. Just two minutes into his journey he came across traffic chaos – it was the school run, so nothing unusual. Two cars blocked John's path as they locked horns. Neither driver would reverse to let the other pass. 'Best not get in between them,' John thought. He went around the back of the car closest to him. It was the wrong decision. The driver angrily shifted into reverse and slammed down the accelerator before John could manoeuvre to safety.

It was a psychedelic blur from then on for what seemed like days, but was only sixty seconds of unconsciousness. Bystanders reported seeing John being launched off his bike with incredible force by the reversing car. He landed head first on the asphalt, splitting his helmet clean in two. When he came around, he saw the car bumper above him. Within the half-hour an ambulance arrived, and the paramedics performed a series of tests to assess the damage. They asked him his name, and he could only remember 'John'. His age, he said, was twenty-one. Oddly, he felt elated, as if on a ketamine high at a rave – in his psychedelic unconsciousness he relived his early twenties in under a minute. Apart from these two lapses in memory and difficulty using his smartphone, which appeared to him as a puzzle, John seemed fine, better than fine – he was actually happier than he had been in a while. That was, until some of his memory returned and he realised he was actually forty-five.

In the hours after he only suffered aches and pains. A slight concussion that required two weeks of 'cognitive rest' (i.e. no work, TV or reading) was the worst of it, or so it seemed. Things started

to get a bit weird later on the day of the accident. As a music journalist, John has sharply defined tastes and loud opinions about
bands he doesn't like. That afternoon, while waiting for his dinner in his favourite fish and chip shop, his girlfriend noticed he
was enjoying the background music from an indie rock playlist,
air-drumming and smiling to the Libertines, Muse and Reef. More
of the same came on, track after track, and he couldn't believe his
ears. This stuff was incredible. Bemused, his girlfriend asked if he
knew who the tracks were by. After all, he'd made some pretty
scathing comments about them in the past. He knew exactly who
they were, but his taste in music had changed since the accident
that morning. From there things went further downhill. He struggled with memory and vocabulary. If his daily itinerary was not
written down, he would get confused and flounder.

John decided to take two months off work, but some weeks
later he began to get the deeply disturbing hate-filled thoughts.
Encountering strangers in the street would bring them flooding
out, especially when he was tired. Black, Asian, female, gay, over-
weight, slightly scruffy-looking – all triggers for the epithets that
part of his mind spouted out uninvited. Even when he had struggled with alcoholism earlier in his life, finding himself in a dark
suicidal hole, he had never come close to thinking such things.

While talking about his experience with me, he said, 'I'm not
going to say any of the things I was thinking, but just think of the
worst, most vile and aggressive things you can. It was horrible, and
I couldn't stop it.'

John battled this inner voice during most encounters. He would
try to block out the thoughts, but to no avail. Avoiding encounters
was the only way to silence it. 'I had enough presence of mind to
realise something was wrong . . . I felt like I'd aged thirty years in
a day,' he told me.

Feeling feeble-minded and ashamed, John became a recluse. The content published in his music magazine publicly defined him as anti-racist, anti-misogynist and anti-homophobic. Where did these inner outbursts come from? Was their genesis to be found in his childhood? 1970s Liverpool was progressive compared to many parts of the UK, but the National Front were active, and race relations were at a low point. This was reflected in the conversations overheard in the factories where he'd worked. Maybe this stuff was somehow stored deep inside his brain, and it was now rising up with force – but why?

John was later diagnosed with a moderate to severe traumatic injury to his brain (the prefrontal cortex, to be exact). The connections (axons) between neurons in the front of John's brain had been stretched to the point of snapping by the force with which his head hit the ground that November. His symptoms were put down to the accident. He was relieved at the news. He lived his life in a certain way, held non-prejudiced attitudes, and then one day was hit by a car and started to perceive an inner voice that spewed bigoted bile. The damage only changed his inner voice in this way for a short time, and he never verbalised or acted on it. The voice eventually stopped after two months, and John returned to his former self. The axons had been repaired, restoring his brain back to its normal function.

Neuroscience research suggests that in cases like John's, parts of the brain responsible for emotion regulation and moral decision-making are damaged by injury or disease, such as head trauma or a tumour. One of the very first studies of behavioural change due to brain injury was the 'American Crowbar Case' involving railroad worker Phineas Gage. In an industrial accident in 1848, an iron rod was blasted through Gage's left cheekbone, travelling behind his eye, through his brain, exploding through the top of his skull and ending up twenty-five metres away, covered in blood and some of his left frontal lobe.

Gage remarkably survived and is rumoured to have walked away from the accident with little help from his co-workers. In under six months, with a good portion of his brain missing, he was working on his parents' farm. Although there was no impairment in his movement, speech or intelligence, his personality was reported to have changed – before, he was well liked, responsible and convivial, but afterwards, rude, profane and erratic. The area of Gage's brain that was responsible for the emotional element of rational decision-making was damaged, resulting in a new Gage, at least for a while.[1] The immediate changes in his personality reportedly faded over time. Years later his antisocial behaviour was minimal, indicating that other parts of his brain may have compensated for the damage caused in the accident.

There are now dozens of documented cases where brain damage has been associated with extreme changes in behaviour. In the early 1980s, a British man who had been in a traffic accident at the age of twenty-six developed uncharacteristic sexually deviant behaviours and went on to commit three sexual assaults, for which he was sent to prison. A brain scan revealed accident-related damage to his prefrontal cortex.[2] In 2007, a woman in her sixties living in Chile killed her mother by drowning her in a bath, and she attempted to do the same to another relative in 2009. Examination of her brain found a lesion in her prefrontal cortex from a botched nasal polyp removal.[3] In 1994, a thirty-two-year-old man was convicted of murder and rape in the UK. Before trial he was assessed by psychiatrists and diagnosed as schizophrenic and delusional. His mother recalled that he had been a shy child, but prone to unprovoked aggression. After his incarceration a brain scan revealed a tumour in his left amygdala, the part of the brain responsible for fear and aggression.[4] A tumour pressing on the amygdala was also found in the famous case of Charles Whitman, who stabbed his wife and mother in the heart and then shot and killed fourteen other people at the University of Texas in 1966. Before the attack he complained of headaches and extremely violent urges.[5]

On the surface, such evidence seems to point to a key role for the brain in criminal behaviour. But we must ask ourselves, with hundreds of brain tumours diagnosed every day in the UK and US combined, and many more cases of brain injury, why do we not see more murders and massacres? The brain damage in the cases of John Doran and Phineas Gage, the former mild and the latter extreme, did not result in any form of criminal behaviour. And what do we say about the non-tumorous and lesion-free brains of others who commit grotesque acts, such as the 2017 Las Vegas shooter, Stephen Paddock?[6]

It is tempting to think of people guilty of the most heinous crimes as having something physically wrong with their brains, as that would easily demarcate them from us and the rest of society. We could put them in a box and more easily rationalise their behaviour as the result of some terrible biological anomaly. But the brain in isolation is rarely, if ever, solely responsible for human wickedness. I cannot say for sure, but I would be very surprised if brain tumours or lesions were to blame for the hateful rhetoric spouted by alt-right and far-right figures such as Milo Yiannopoulos, Richard Spencer and Stephen Yaxley-Lennon.*

Aside from brain anomalies, over the last few decades in which new medical scanning technology has been developed, scientists

---

* The term 'alt-right' is used to describe the far-right subculture that emerged around 2010, and is primarily associated with US white nationalist Richard B. Spencer.

have begun to study how the 'normal' brain processes hate. The scientific consensus is clear: no one enters this world with their brain preloaded with prejudice or hate. What we do start life with is a brain that appears to be predisposed to distinguish 'us' from 'them', but who 'us' and 'them' are is learned, not fixed. This ingrained neurological mechanism means we all have the most basic foundations from which prejudice and hate can form. We are all capable of hate when a certain combination of events and environment is layered on top of this human trait.

Under soft grey armour

The brain evolved to support human survival under a dizzying array of situations that changed over time. It's done a great job getting us here, but despite the astounding things our brains can handle, some may think evolution has done us a disservice, as nature has not bestowed upon us the protections afforded to other species. We have no natural armour to protect our vital organs, no natural weapons such as horns or fangs, and no natural camouflage to disguise ourselves when threats are present. Armadillos, snakes, octopuses and many others that we share our planet with are equipped with specific biological features to defend against, attack or dodge a threat. We have to rely on the soft grey armour inside our skulls to defend ourselves.[†]

This may at first seem unfair considering the sometimes remarkable defence mechanisms available to other species (what human wouldn't want to fly away to avoid a predator?) – but our brains are remarkable, even more so than the power of flight. Remarkable enough that we have been able to create artificial defence

† The brain is actually made of up grey and white matter.

mechanisms that surpass those found in nature. Our brains are responsible for self-repairing armour, 3D-printed organs, life-prolonging drugs, earthquake warning systems – the list is long.[*] Only the human brain can develop such advanced technology to mitigate threats and contribute to the survival of our species.

We have not always been able to rely on incredible feats of engineering and medicine. If we consider the whole period of the existence of our species, we've only had these enhanced forms of protection for a tiny amount of time. But our brains weren't just being lazy for all those years. They were busy evolving to recognise threats from predators – animals that wanted to eat us, members of neighbouring tribes who wanted our food, water and shelter, and freak weather and natural disasters. Through the experience of seeing our family mauled by animal predators, our homes pillaged by neighbouring tribes and whole villages wiped out by flash floods, our prehistoric brains learned to recognise threats to personal and group safety. This learned process over millions of years shaped the brain in a way that allowed modern humans to cope with and eventually dominate our environment.

Ancient brains in a modern world

Despite the adaptability of our brains, this coping mechanism is only so flexible. There are still some parts of our brain that are

* One I was particularly impressed by was created at Cardiff University by Dr Rhys Pullin and colleagues, in partnership with Microsemi, a Californian defence company. They ingeniously created a system that uses ultrasound in real time to detect when a soldier's body armour has received micro-damage that is not visible to the naked eye, but which is enough to seriously weaken its protective capability. This innovation has the potential not only to cut back significantly on the $c.5$ million armour units routinely sent around the world for x-ray inspection to find micro-damage, but more importantly, to save lives in war zones.

stuck in the past. Optical illusions provide a good example of this. One of the best known is the hollow mask illusion (see Figure 4). When the mask is turned around, although we know it is hollow, our brains process the image of the face as if the nose, lips, brow, cheekbones and chin were all protruding, not inverted. On an intellectual level we know what we are seeing is not real, but our brain refuses to interpret it correctly. This is because millions of years of evolution tell us noses are projected, not inverted.

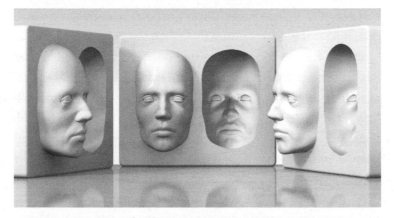

Fig. 4: The hollow mask illusion.
Animated Healthcare Ltd / Science Photo Library

The cognitive processes underpinning the mask illusion are hard-wired and operate on an unconscious level. Our perceptions of self, and of the groups to which we think we belong and don't belong, also rely on out-of-date wiring. Because the brain is incapable of processing all the information out there in the world, it creates shortcuts. We have evolved processes that predispose us to think with the aid of categories, and in doing so they work by making a series of approximations. We have done this for as long as there has been a human mind. These categories are formed by identifying differences between individuals and then generalising to groups of people – 'this type of person is lazy, so everyone in their group is also lazy'.

Predisposed to prefer 'us', but not to hate 'them'

As well as crude categorical thinking, there are core psychological processes that predispose us to prefer people like ourselves. A famous experiment conceived in the 1970s by Henri Tajfel showed that even the slightest of differences between groups can result in greater reward for the ingroup ('us') than the outgroup ('them').[7]

Tajfel allocated his students into two groups, but they were not divided by gender, race, age, hair colour, attractiveness, shoe size or any other discernible personal characteristic. Instead one group were labelled as 'underestimators' and the other 'overestimators', based on their estimations of the number of dots in a picture. Unbeknownst to the students, they were actually allocated to the groups randomly, and it had nothing to do with their estimations at all. To make the difference between groups even more insignificant, no group members met each other – they were all kept separate and told only that they belonged to this group or that group.

So Tajfel had two groups who believed they were separated by the tiniest of meaningless differences – what he called 'minimal groups'. He then asked each subject to distribute money between the groups, telling them they couldn't benefit personally from the allocation. The arbitrary difference between groups resulted in subjects allocating more money to their own group, despite no personal gain. Almost every time this experiment is performed under the original conditions, the same result occurs. The experiment acts like a mirror on the real world – based on the most minimal conditions, people consistently favour their ingroup over the out-group – you give the person like you the larger tip, the slightly more expensive birthday present, the job.

These automatic processes of categorisation and preference for the ingroup help us navigate the world – who to avoid and who to engage with. But people are complicated; they are multifaceted and while some aspects of their identity may relate to the group to which they belong, other parts may diverge, and even contradict these traits – an outgroup member may even share traits with the ingroup. This is when the brain's automatic processes fail to provide the necessary information to make the right decision. These psycho-logical mechanisms common to us all – categorising and automatic-ally preferring people like us over those who are not like us – can be the precursors to prejudice and hate if we do not work against them.

'I don't see difference'

Our brains are tuned to recognise differences between ingroup and outgroup characteristics. 'Change blindness' experiments show this phenomenon in action (see Figure 5).

The initial greeting

**Original desk attendant
ducks behind desk**

**Replacement
desk attendant pops up**

**The subject fails to
recognise the swap**

Fig. 5: Change blindness.

Cleverly switching white desk attendants halfway through a transaction results in no recognition from the subject. This is achieved by having the original white attendant duck under the desk to fetch a folder, where the other white attendant is ready to pop up to finish the transaction.

Following the experiment, when the subject is told about the switch they commonly report no recollection of it, and often express shock upon viewing a video of the transaction and swap. Even when the second attendant's clothes and hairstyle are different, the same change blindness remains. But switch the race or gender of the desk attendant, and most subjects notice. Our brains are highly sensitive to these differences – so when a person says they are blind to race, gender and physical impairment, their brain is not.

Much of what our brain gets up to is automatic – we have no conscious idea it is processing information in a certain way, or when this information is being used to inform our decisions or behaviours. This is necessary, as the alternative – being aware of every process – would be so distracting it would render us paralysed with information overload.

Brains and unconscious bias against 'them'

When this automatic processing favours people from our own group, and in doing so disadvantages people from another group, we call it unconscious bias against the outgroup. Another term for it is *implicit prejudice*. When implicit prejudice relates to characteristics like race, religion, sexual orientation, disability or gender identity, the brain is not acting alone. We have to learn these differences after birth for the brain to use them in this unconscious way.

Take race as an example. The skin colour of people a newborn encounters in the first year of life, the types of relationships a toddler sees depicted in children's books, the characters and their relations a preschooler watches on children's TV, and the stereotypes conveyed to a primary-schooler by teachers, parents and friends all shape how the automatic part of their brains processes 'us' and 'them'. If a child is primarily exposed to only one skin colour and one culture early in life, to a narrow representation of relationships and to negative stereotypes of racial others, then their brain will automatically distinguish 'us' from 'them' in those terms. The brain must be fed this information for it to be layered on top of the wiring. Much of this cultural 'feeding' early in life goes unchecked and unnoticed, meaning we remain unaware of its effect on us in later life unless we make an effort to recognise it.

Measuring unconscious bias

If not faced with a situation that brings the brain's automatic biased processing into clear view, we may say that we are not prejudiced, and we may genuinely believe it. The culturally bestowed privilege of whites, cis males, heterosexuals, Christians and those without physical or mental impairment can blind many to how their thoughts and behaviours (or the lack of these) contribute to the plight of 'them'. When faced with a situation where we are asked to make a decision that will benefit one person over another, we may believe we always make the fair choice. But during the decision-making process bias will often creep in without us being aware of it.

Knowing the degree of implicit prejudice we hold, and towards what groups, is a difficult challenge. As prejudice is generally frowned on, scientists cannot trust subjects' own declarations as to their attitudes. Therefore, indirect measures have been developed to get around the *social desirability bias* that is found in responses to interviews and surveys which try to measure prejudice. The most widely used technique is Harvard's Implicit Association Test (IAT).[8]

The IAT is based on a sorting task that taps into the decades' worth of cultural 'feeding' and personal experience – the stuff that informs the automatic processing we are largely unaware of. It can be used to assess attitudes to many characteristics, including gender, sexual orientation and weight. In the version which looks at race, the subject is presented with white and black faces and with pleasant and unpleasant words (e.g. 'disaster' and 'peace', 'sweet' and 'agony'). In the first task, the subject is asked to press a key with the left hand when they see either a white face or a pleasant word, and a different key with the right hand for either a black face or an unpleasant word. In the second task the process is partially reversed: the subject is asked to press the left-hand key for white faces and unpleasant words, and the right-hand key for black faces and pleasant words.[*] If the subject has an automatic preference for white faces over black faces, this second task takes them longer to complete because it is mentally easier for them to associate white faces with pleasant words than with unpleasant words. In the subject there is a kind of cognitive bond, based on years of experience and exposure to the cultural 'feed', that creates a mental 'stickiness' between white faces and good words but not black faces and good words.[†]

About 75 per cent of the millions of white test subjects who have taken the race IAT show an automatic preference for White

[*] The IAT has poor test-retest reliability so the inventors suggest it is taken around ten times over a few weeks to create an average score. Scientific reviews also question the relationship between test scores and behaviours.

[†] In the original experiment half of subjects did the two tasks in the other order, to rule out any effects of learning one keystroke pattern before the other.

Americans over African Americans. Interestingly, almost 50 per cent of black test subjects showed some degree of preference for White Americans over African Americans.[9] This suggests the unconscious preference being measured by the IAT is shaped by the culture 'feed' we are exposed to during socialisation.

Few of these white and black test subjects would actually classify themselves as racially biased if asked. In the years since the test was developed, many research studies have shown those with a preference for White Americans over African Americans are more likely to engage in behaviours that may be linked to prejudice. These include laughing at racist jokes and rating them as funny; doctors providing unsatisfactory care to black patients; and voting for McCain instead of Obama in the 2008 US presidential election.[10]

Another indirect measure of prejudice that attempts to tap into the brain's inner workings is the Linguistic Intergroup Bias (LIB) test.[11] Subjects are asked to look at images or videos in which a person from their ingroup performs an activity and then a person from the outgroup performs the same activity. For example, white and black people are shown helping an old person cross the road, and starting a fight in a bar. Subjects are then asked to describe what they saw.

The words used in their descriptions of members of the ingroup and outgroup performing the same activities are analysed and compared. The scientists look for words describing a person's failings either as situation-specific and fleeting (e.g. verbs that describe behaviour with a clear beginning and end) or as innate and constant (e.g. adjectives that are detached from specific behaviours and instead describe general personal dispositions).

The research shows that in cases of aggression, a member of the ingroup is more likely to be described as 'hurting someone' (indicating a temporary behaviour – i.e. 'our group is rarely like that'), whereas one of the outgroup is more likely to be described as 'aggressive' (indicating a more general disposition – i.e. 'their group is like that all the time'). In the case of helpful behaviour, the opposite is observed. An ingroup member is more likely to be described as 'helpful' (indicating a more general disposition), whereas an outgroup member is more likely to be described as 'helping' (indicating a temporary behaviour). The assumption made in the LIB test is that subjects are not policing their choice of words as they are not explicitly told the experiment is about prejudice and stereotypes. But through close linguistic comparison, differences in word choice can indicate stereotyped thinking.

Both the IAT and the LIB test were developed before brain scanning technologies were widely available. Although the former has been widely used in research for decades, the increasing sophistication of imaging technology now means psychologists and neuroscientists can look directly into the brain, bypassing conscious human input, to see the parts involved in the processing of prejudice and hate.

Locating hate in the brain

Medical science has figured out how most of the human body works. The hepatologist has mastered the liver, the nephrologist has figured out the kidneys, and the cardiologist knows the heart like the back of their hand. We have written most of the manual on how humans work. But one part still challenges science: the brain. Although neuroscientists have a grip on many disorders and diseases of the brain, such as epilepsy and brain cancer, the manual is missing a few pages on the location and processing of emotions, attitudes and social behaviour.

Imagine assembling IKEA's most complicated flat-pack with an instruction manual that is missing three quarters of its pages. You know the final picture, that every part is meant to be there and that they all have a function, but you just don't know what all those functions are or how everything fits together. This is a fraction of the challenge facing neuroscientists who study hate. They have seen the outcomes of hate (they may have personally felt it) and they know many parts of the brain are needed to feel and act, but in the beginning they did not know which parts functioned to process hate and its behavioural outcomes, or how they related to each other.

Working from a partial instruction manual, neuroscientists have mapped elements of hate onto the brain. The tricky part was taking human-constructed concepts like prejudice, threat, disgust and empathy, and locating them in the brain to understand how they all come together to create the human concept of hate. The advent of new brain imaging in the 1990s made this task a little less daunting. Over the last three decades neuroscientists have spent much of their time recruiting test subjects, people like us, to take part in their brain imaging studies. Extremely expensive scanners can now take internal pictures of our brains in action as we are exposed to stimuli such as photos of faces or emotive symbols, and record what our brains show about our innermost thoughts. But 'thoughts' is probably the wrong way to put it.

These scanners can't read minds, at least not like Deanna Troi from Star Trek. Instead they record the flow of blood around the various regions of the brain and the electrical signals fired off by neurons, as test subjects are exposed to images on a screen. This activity provides an insight into which parts of the brain may be involved in processing phenomena like prejudice and hate. The majority of this research has been conducted on racial prejudice. However, much of what has been found is likely to be applicable to any type of prejudice.

The parts that process prejudice

The latest neuroscience research suggests that a 'network of prejudice' exists in the brain, and that the cognitive processing of hate is spread across this complex web of neurons.* Some of the first brain imaging studies from the turn of the century indicated the amygdala may play a part in prejudice.[12] It is an almond-shaped region of the brain and comes as a pair. These nutty structures sit at the bottom of each hemisphere (see Figure 6).[13]

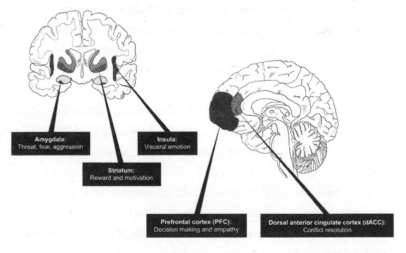

Fig. 6: The prejudice network.

In these early studies white test subjects' brains were scanned using fMRI while they were asked to look at pictures of black and white faces. Beforehand they took tests to measure their implicit and explicit prejudices as a comparison. For some test subjects, the amygdala seemed to activate when black faces, but not white

* I am grateful for the conversations on the brain and hate with professors David Amodio and Jay Van Bavel. Any errors in the reproduction of the conversations here are my own.

faces, were shown in the scanner – blood flowed to this part of the brain, and this oxygenation was picked up by the fMRI, indicating increased activity (e.g. see brain images in the plate section). In the same way our leg muscles need more blood and oxygen when we go for a run, parts of the brain need more blood and oxygen when they are processing the information streaming in through our sensory organs.

The amygdala is responsible for triggering fear and aggression in response to threats in the environment – anything from spiders to potential human attackers.* When a threat is detected it communicates with other parts of the brain to initiate 'red alert' – the 'fight or flight' response. The heart races, blood pumps to the muscles and action is taken.[14]

This extreme response only comes with high levels of amygdala activation. In the first of these pioneering studies in the US, activation was too weak to initiate red alert, but a faint signal in the 'noise' was picked up by the scanner in some white subjects. The signal was also linked to subjects' IAT scores. Those who had an implicit preference for White Americans over African Americans showed greater amygdala activation when viewing black faces than when viewing white ones. Interestingly, all subjects said they held pro-black views before the experiment.[15]

These early studies were far from conclusive, and big questions remained over the role of the amygdala in prejudice and hate. Because the amygdala is known to process threat detection, did its activation by the sight of black but not white faces provide the first evidence of racism in the brain? As not all of the white

---

* I use 'fear' and 'aggression' interchangeably to describe the amygdala's responses in this section. Fear and aggression are the possible outcomes of detecting threat and relate to the 'fight or flight' response.

subjects' brains reacted in the same way, were some of them less threatened when viewing black faces, or were they controlling their inner reaction, motivated by not wanting to look prejudiced? Is there a conscious part of the brain that engages 'manual control' to cancel out a signal automatically generated by the threat-detecting amygdala?

Disengaging the amygdala autopilot

The amygdala is an ancient part of the brain. Like one of our ancestors in prehistory it isn't particularly smart, but it is super-fast at detecting threats. It evolved as an early warning system that picked up information from the environment before any other part of the brain. When our distant ancestors faced extreme threat[†] (think of an encounter with a sabre-toothed cat) information entered through their eyes, bypassed all other brain regions and darted direct to their amygdala.[16] As if on autopilot, in a split second our ancestor either ran away from or threw their spear at the perceived threat.

After the amygdala, our prefrontal cortex evolved. The prefrontal cortex sits at the very front of the brain and acts as the executive control area where detailed processing is performed (see Figure 6).[‡]

---

† Before the agricultural revolution around twelve thousand years ago, humans almost exclusively relied on hunting and gathering to survive. It is commonly thought that the main threats to the survival of hunter-gatherers in this period were animal predators, environmental hazards and other humans (and likely in that order).

‡ The prefrontal cortex is divided into regions, each with their own specific function. The two most important for understanding hate are firstly the dorsolateral (on the top outside of the) prefrontal cortex (dlPFC): the smart part where the rational decisions are made – i.e. 'What are the consequences of making this decision?' And secondly the ventromedial (on the bottom inside of the) prefrontal cortex

It's where information is evaluated, emotions are considered and decisions are made. Do I want McDonald's or KFC? Do I walk towards and smile at the stranger or do I keep my distance and avoid eye contact? How would my friend feel if I told them what I really think about immigrants?

Importantly, the smart prefrontal cortex puts the brakes on the fast-but-dumb amygdala when it figures out a perceived threat is actually benign. It switches the brain from 'autopilot' to 'manual control' mode. As our ancestor had a smaller and less sophisticated prefrontal cortex, their amygdala was free to detect threats everywhere with incredible speed, even where there weren't any. This wasn't so much of a problem as it was often better to be safe than sorry. In modern humans the amygdala still acts as an early warning system. But in the absence of carnivorous four-legged predators and marauding tribes,* does it still react in its super-speedy way?

Other neuroscience studies have been able to see how the brain works in its amygdala-driven 'autopilot' mode. Rather depressingly, showing black faces to white test subjects in brain scanners for milliseconds, instead of seconds as in the early studies, resulted in a threat-detection signal from the amygdala. Rapidly

(vmPFC): the emotional part that throws our feelings into the decision-making process – i.e. 'How would my decision impact the emotions of others and myself?'

* The extent of the threat posed by marauding tribes in pre-agricultural times remains unclear. From this period archaeologists have found human remains (some in mass graves) with broken bones, smashed skulls and fragments of spearheads embedded in bone, indicating violent deaths at the hands of other humans. But these finds are rare. Before the cultivation of land, humans had few belongings to protect and remained mobile. Instead of fighting, different tribes encountering each other probably cooperated to hunt, gather and share food. Things got much more violent between humans when agriculture introduced sedentariness, dependency on a limited number of food sources and resource inequality.[17]

flashing the images didn't give the prefrontal cortex enough time to register them as faces, let alone black or white. The amygdala, on the other hand, lit up like a Christmas tree. It misrecognised the black faces as potential threats almost immediately.[18] The prefrontal cortex could not register the faces fast enough to do its job, meaning the amygdala was free to carry out its prejudiced threat detection.

The purpose of the amygdala shortcut is to ensure survival. The amygdala doesn't care much about the detail of what we are facing; just registering it as a *potential* threat is enough to take some sort of action. But the cost of this expediency is accuracy. The detail can be important, and when it's not a sabre-toothed cat we are facing, it's worth the brain spending a bit more time on working out whether the potential threat is friend or foe.

Most of the time we don't see rapidly flashing images of black faces outside of the lab, so our prefrontal cortex can process the face for what it really is and order the amygdala to stand down. The majority of us do this because we are motivated not to act on our automatic prejudiced threat detection: we either personally reject prejudice, feel socially pressured not to come across as prejudiced, or feel guilt when we think in a prejudiced way.[19]

In those who experience a prejudiced threat response during an encounter with a black person, and who are not motivated to override it, the neuroscience suggests that their prefrontal cortices will either underreact or react in a non-regulating way, allowing the amygdala to shape behaviour. In social encounters the most likely outcome is anxiety-induced social awkwardness – the person with a prejudiced threat response may pay less attention to the black person, frown more, laugh less, make slips of the tongue, hesitate and engage in verbal microaggressions. Outside of social encounters, this brain response can lead to discrimination (in employment, housing, finance, education, healthcare, criminal justice . . .). Unfortunately, the unruly amygdala is not confined to those prone to a prejudiced threat response. In a range of real-life situations, usually well-meaning people can see their brain's 'autopilot' threat-detection win over 'manual control'.

Simply being overly stressed, tired or under the influence of drugs or alcohol can inhibit the speed at which the prefrontal cortex can keep a check on the amygdala.[20] When some busy and exhausted commuters only offer their seats on the rammed subway to people of the same race, and some drunken friends in a bar pause and give a prolonged look to someone of a different race who's just entered, there is a good chance their amygdalae have been cut loose to initiate anxiety by suboptimal performances from their prefrontal cortices.

A devastating consequence of autopilot failing to disengage

In August 2011, a twenty-nine-year-old black man was suspected by London's Metropolitan Police to be in the process of procuring a firearm from a criminal contact. An unmarked police vehicle tailed Mark Duggan as he left the contact's address in a taxi. On his way back from East London three police cars boxed in the taxi, forcing it to stop. Mark was ordered to get out. Within seconds he was shot dead by an armed police officer.

The police claimed that Mark was holding the firearm when he was shot. During a search for evidence after the shooting a gun was found some fourteen feet away from the vehicle over a fence. At the court hearing none of the eleven officers at the scene reported seeing Mark throw the gun. How it got there remains a mystery. Two witnesses alleged that it was taken from the vehicle after the killing and placed over the fence by one of the officers.

While the Metropolitan Police did not accept liability for wrongful killing, they did pay out an undisclosed sum to Mark's family following a civil case. At the inquest into his death, a witness stated that Mark was holding a mobile phone when he was shot. Mark's killing triggered the worst riots in modern British history.[21]

In this case the science says police were more likely to shoot because of the colour of Mark's skin, regardless of whether he was holding a mobile phone or a gun. The same applies to hundreds of killings of black men by law enforcement worldwide in situations that required ultra-fast reaction times.

In many police shootings of black men, a claim is often made by the officer(s) involved that the same outcome would have resulted if the assailant was white – that skin colour had nothing to do with the decision to shoot. The science says otherwise. Research into the decision to pull the trigger shows that white shooters' brains exhibit a weaker prefrontal cortex signal when faced with black versus white suspects.[*] [22] To grossly oversimply the brain process, when faced with a black suspect holding a phone, the fast-but-dumb 'autopilot' response to shoot is left uncontrolled by the weak prefrontal cortex signal, and it is allowed to rapidly engage the motor cortex – the officer's finger squeezes the trigger. When faced with a white suspect holding a phone, the stronger prefrontal cortex signal forces 'autopilot' to stand down, resulting in the motor cortex being released from its command – the officer's finger eases off the trigger.

---

[*] The shooters in this study were students not formally trained in the use of firearms. The meta-analysis mentioned in the next paragraph includes shooters from a wide range of backgrounds, including those trained in the use of firearms.

A meta-analysis of forty-two studies on decisions to shoot, involving just under 3,500 shooters, found all the evidence pointed in the same direction. Shooters were more likely and faster to pull the trigger on armed and unarmed black targets relative to white targets. Depressingly, shooters required less certainty that a black target was holding a gun to shoot them, compared to white targets. Those shooters who endorsed negative cultural stereotypes of black people showed the greatest bias.[23] The foundational study in the field found black and white shooters showed the same level of bias, indicating this is a learned reaction.[24]

The inability of the brain's executive control area to disengage autopilot fast enough in these high-stakes life-threatening encounters with black suspects can be disastrous. As this process is learned there is hope that a form of unlearning or deprogramming can undo it.

Prepared versus learned amygdala responses

We have established the amygdala activates and can initiate red alert when images of black faces are encountered in the lab, and it can take over our reactions when split-second decisions are needed, often resulting in devastating consequences. So why don't we see even more violence towards black people?

The research shows the amygdala doesn't come preloaded with this prejudiced threat detection. What and who it sees as a threat is learned through fear conditioning. The amygdala feeds off prepared fears and learned fears. Prepared fears we learn very easily – we learn to fear spiders much more quickly than taking exams. Fear of exams comes from experience and exposure to information from within our culture over time. The amygdala's response to the black faces in the lab is learned, not prepared. The learning required to fear black faces is dependent on experience from within cultures.

An innovative brain imaging study backs this argument up. The study showed that playing 'Straight Outta Compton' by NWA while white subjects viewed black faces in a brain scanner resulted in a stronger amygdala activation. In comparison, playing 'Only One' by Slipknot – heavy metal, more commonly associated with white audiences – resulted in no greater activation.[25] * One explanation for this is that for these white test subjects, rap music was a racial stereotypical cue and so a stimulant for prejudiced threat detection – a cultural creation, not an innate biological one.

The amygdala also speaks to the hippocampus, the brain region responsible for memory.[26] Under conditions of extreme threat, it can instruct the hippocampus, which usually stores unemotional facts (think cramming for exams), to store extreme fears in long-term memory (think a knife pulled by a black person on the street). Seeing a similar knife held by a black person in another context, such as a carvery restaurant, can trigger the memory of the street incident in the hippocampus, which sends a signal to the amygdala to engage red alert. It's functional, in that the brain is trying to protect us from attack, but the rate of false positives (fear initiated in the wrong context) is high in modern society where the number of threats is much fewer than that faced by our distant ancestors. The storing of extreme fears in long-term memory is a feature of post-traumatic stress disorder (PTSD). Treatments such as cognitive behavioural therapy have been successful in reprogramming the brain to disassociate the fear of past traumas from current events.[27]

---

* To confirm this finding a replication with black participants is needed.

Unlearning prejudiced threat detection

While at first it may not sound like it, this process of learning prejudiced threat detection is good news, as we can more readily address the fears that don't come prepared (like the fear of spiders and snakes) in our brains. Studies that ask subjects to imagine an outgroup in a positive light (e.g. black doctors or sports stars) before taking prejudice tests show a reduction in implicit bias.[28] Amygdala studies also show that viewing images of black celebrities results in no activation, indicating that prejudiced threat detection can be reduced if subjects learn to view black people in general in a more positive light.[29]

Research shows the amygdala doesn't begin to react to black faces until adolescence, around the age of fourteen, meaning it learns prejudiced threat detection through childhood development and increased exposure to culture.[30] Those children with a more diverse peer group showed less amygdala activation when viewing black faces, indicating that interracial mixing before the age of twelve limits the effect of learning prejudiced threat detection.*[31] A surprising set of results showed that both white and black children aged fourteen and over exhibited amygdala responses to black faces, indicating that black children learn this prejudiced threat detection in the same way as their white counterparts. This finding was replicated in a study of black adults.[32]

Despite these encouraging findings regarding the power of positive association in countering learned racial bias, prejudiced threat detection is easier to acquire than to remove. Even when a person manages to unlearn a fear of an outgroup, they can often fail to

---

* The reverse may also be true: those with less implicit prejudice, as measured by amygdala activation, may be more inclined to mix with a diverse peer group.

do so permanently. Their amygdala will continue to learn from what it is exposed to, and choosing what goes into their brain and what does not is difficult when the cultural tap cannot be turned off. If the information from the media, family and friends that led to the original prejudiced processing doesn't change, then their amygdala will continue to feed off it, gradually recalling the unlearned fear. When the person encounters black people in the future, if their prefrontal cortex remains dormant (because of a lack of motivation to reject prejudice, inhibition from extreme stress or intoxicants, or the jeopardy and speed of the encounter), their autopilot reaction can result in anything from anxiety to killing in self-defence. Based on this insight, the answer lies beyond the brain, in society itself – we must reform society and its institutions if we are to change what the amygdala is exposed to and in turn what it detects as potential threats.

The parts that can edge us towards hate

More recent research on the role of the amygdala in the prejudice network casts some doubt on the universality of its role. In 2008, a brain scanning study by Professor Jay Van Bavel and colleagues at NYU found that mixing images of black and white faces with team badges shifted the response of the amygdala away from the black faces to the team subjects associated with.[33] The team's badge proved a stronger stimulus than the black face. This suggests the amygdala adapts to what seems most important to the subject in the context of the moment.

All prejudices are not equal, and the amygdala can only account for prejudiced processing of threat (threats are seen where there are none because of the decades' worth of biased information it learns from) in some situations. In the brain's processing of hate, the mounting evidence suggests that the amygdala doesn't act alone. It has partners in crime that can amplify prejudice.

Most of what has been discussed in this chapter so far relates to 'push' behaviours as a result of implicit prejudice – avoidance, microaggressions, discrimination, and violence in self-defence. Neuroscience has indicated the insula, an inverted pyramid-shaped structure deep in the brain (we have two, like the amygdalae), as a candidate for the processing of more extreme prejudices and hate resulting in 'pull' behaviours – where the target is actively pursued (see Figure 6, p. 85).

In addition to an array of other functions, the insula plays a key role in the *salience network* that processes what is important to us in our environment – think of how you pick up on emotional expressions on a partner's or friend's face quicker than on a stranger's face. It has a part in processing learning from painful events – think of an incident where you were hurt by someone from another group and how that made you feel towards that group. It processes perception of pain in others – think of a time when you saw someone get hit in a sensitive area of their body and how it made you wince. And it also processes deep visceral emotion, including extreme fear, dread, aversion and disgust – think of a time when you encountered a grotesque sight or pungent smell that made you feel something in the pit of your stomach.[34] Each of these has something to do with the brain's processing of hate.

Recognising facial expressions on other-race faces

The salience network is a series of brain regions that communicate with one another to determine what is important to us in various contexts, and to influence our subsequent reaction.* To grossly oversimplify, the network shines the spotlight of attention and then tells us how to behave.[35] The role of the insula in this process is to call up emotions related to what is important to us in the environment. What is deemed important and the shape of the resulting behaviour varies dramatically by the individual.

The salience networks of heroin addicts and medical doctors will activate differently at the sight of a hypodermic needle. In the case of the heroin addict, the network jumps into action, shining a bright spotlight on the needle. 'Gut-deep' emotions and memories of the last hit are awoken, creating a sense of craving (processed by the insula). Signals are then quickly sent to the striatum, the part of the brain that processes reward, motivation and action (see Figure 6, p. 85). As the craving for another hit intensifies, the addict engages the prefrontal cortex, which frantically begins to figure out how they are going to find the money to buy some heroin. For the medical doctor, the 'spotlight' of the salience network passes over the needle, barely registering it as important, given an unemotional attachment to it and its everyday appearance.

Interestingly, for a recovering heroin addict, the network acts slightly differently than for a current addict. The spotlight is still shone on the needle, but instead of the reward and motivation centre (striatum) taking over, another part of the network kicks in: the dorsal anterior cingulate cortex (dACC), responsible for conflict resolution (see Figure 6, p. 85). The dACC forms part of the executive control area, which includes the prefrontal cortex, and so it allows the recovering addict to select the correct response – move on and ignore the emotional memory and the urge for a hit.

---

* The salience network consists of the anterior insula, (the largest part of the insula), the amygdala, the striatum and the dorsal anterior cingulate cortex.

The salience network also activates when we see facial expressions. As social beings, we are acutely aware of the emotional states of others. A perplexed expression on a colleague, a sad expression on a family member, a disappointed expression on a partner and an angry expression on a stranger will all evoke a reaction from the salience network. We recognise the expression, feel an emotion in reaction, remember the last time we saw such an expression on the person and then decide what to do. We explain our business plan to the colleague, we console the family member, we make up for forgetting the wedding anniversary, and we move away at pace from the stranger. The ability of the salience network to recognise emotional states from facial expressions is at its most effective during adolescence. This is an emotionally turbulent and challenging time for most teenagers, and it's good to know they are better equipped to spot a friend in distress than most adults.[36]

The salience network overlaps with the prejudice network. Researchers in China wanted to find out if facial expressions made a difference to the way subjects' brains processed images of the faces of people of other races.[37] They found that subjects who showed implicit prejudice on the IAT more readily recognised negative emotion in other-race faces compared to same-race faces, and were more likely to label emotions as negative in other-race faces when the expression was ambiguous. In the brains of these Chinese test subjects, when black faces with expressions of disgust were shown, the insula and amygdala both activated; a toxic combination of the spotlight of attention, a reaction to the disgust in the image, and a threat response. In the test subjects who showed less implicit prejudice on the IAT, the salience network operated differently. The insula activated but the amygdala remained dormant. Instead the dACC activated, indicating a conflict resolution process. Whatever emotion was felt in relation to the disgusted black face was quickly dampened by the regulating influence of the brain's executive control area.

Hate and feeling pain

From a very young age (around three years), we anticipate that the harm inflicted by someone from a threatening outgroup will be more frequent and more painful.[38] But it's not that this harm actually *is* more frequent or painful, more that we are extra sensitive to pain intentionally inflicted by a group we already feel threatened by.

When the harm has a moral dimension, such as a hate crime that communicates the perpetrator's objection to a way of life, the insula, in partnership with other brain regions of the victim,* automatically registers disapproval at lightning speed. This happens way before the smart part of the prefrontal cortex weighs in and rationally pieces together what happened. Literally without thinking, the victim's brain registers the attack for what it is and negatively evaluates the perpetrator and others associated with them. Violent attacks that do not have this moral dimension (e.g. an attack from a member of one's ingroup†) are unlikely to generate the same brain activity, meaning the victim is likely to feel less emotional harm.[39]

When the attack is serious, for example where physical injury is inflicted, the insula can work in tandem with the amygdala and hippocampus to embed the event into long-term memory both as a painful incident and as one with a morally challenging

---

* The left orbitofrontal cortex and amygdala.

† An exception would be violent betrayal by a member of the ingroup as it has a moral dimension.

dimension. This human trait ensures that in the future, incidents with similar potential predators are avoided. In extreme cases, acts of aggression from members of the outgroup that both inflict pain and challenge a moral position can generate bias in the victim towards the offending group.[40]

As well as biased processing of direct pain, the insula has been shown to activate along racial lines when viewing the pain of others. A study by Professor Xu from Peking University, Beijing showed the insula in white and Chinese college students lit up when they watched cheeks get pricked with a needle, but only if the face was from the same race as their own.[41] This finding was replicated in more recent studies with other Chinese and white subjects, and with white and black test subjects.[42]

However, this racial bias in the brain registering others' pain is undone when the other-race person belongs to a *superordinate ingroup* (an ingroup that trumps another in terms of its perceived importance). If they attend the same university as us (hence they are in our superordinate ingroup that trumps race) then the insula will activate when we see them in pain, but not if they attend a rival university (which would put them in the superordinate out-group).[43] It seems there is a hierarchy at play, as with the amygdala, and both will switch to what is most important to us in that context: being from the same university, company or even city can trump racial difference when it comes to empathising with pain.

In the absence of a superordinate ingroup, the consequence of the brain not registering the pain of other races can be severe. With less empathy comes less willingness to help ease others' suffering – a lower likelihood of sharing resources or providing physical aid and emotional support. This is why charities in predominantly white countries appeal to superordinate ingroups when seeking donations for causes in predominately non-white countries.

Showing the suffering of other-race children alongside their distressed parents activates the insulae of potential white donors who are also parents. Being a parent (superordinate ingroup) trumps the difference of race. This effect can also extend to grandparents, uncles, aunts and so on.

The brain's processing of 'gut-deep' hate

Much of the research on the insula has focused on its role in processing disgust. The insula evolved to protect us from another type of threat – things we should avoid ingesting. Before drinking and eating, our ancestors tested water or food for safety by tasting and smelling. A slight funky odour or taste would immediately engage the insula, which would in turn send a message to the stomach creating a sense of nausea, and the food or water would be spat out to avoid potential poisoning. This function persists today, but the role of the insula has expanded.[44]

Professors Lasana Harris and Susan Fiske at Princeton University's Centre for the Study of Brain, Mind and Behaviour conducted a brain scanning study to identify if the insula could be activated by people regarded as the lowest of the low in society.[45] To demarcate the lowest of the low, they used the Stereotype Content Model that classifies people into four groups.[46] The model suggests we stereotype people along two axes: warmth and competence. Those we consider to have high warmth and high competence, such as superhuman Olympic athletes, we have pride in. Those we consider to have high warmth and low competence, such as elderly people or those with disabilities, we pity. Those we consider to have low warmth and high competence, such as filthy-rich people, we envy. And those we consider to have low warmth and low competence, such as homeless drug addicts, we consider disgusting.

This model is not perfect, and plenty of us would balk at the idea that we all make such simplistic generalisations, but for the purposes of Harris and Fiske's brain imaging study, these examples were used. The results were fascinating. The first three categories, superhuman Olympic athletes, elderly and disabled people and the filthy rich, only activated the prefrontal cortex. As well as its previously discussed roles, this area kicks into action when we think about a person. Imagining what it is like to be them, emotionally and in terms of their beliefs, intentions and persuasions (known in psychology as mentalising and theory of mind, respectively), informs our decisions about them. To grossly oversimply again: when the prefrontal cortex activates, subjects are empathising and hence humanising. The final category, the homeless drug addicts, activated the insula and amygdala but not the prefrontal cortex. For the so-called lowest of the low, there was no empathising or humanising; quite the opposite – disgust, dehumanising and a sense of threat.

Other neuroimaging studies have found the brain's disgust response can be triggered when white subjects view other-race faces.[47] This may be linked to white subjects associating other-race faces with particular notions about culture and all they imagine it entails: for example, eating habits, hygiene practices and rituals. The insula was not designed to activate in response to people from other cultures, but when we ascribe qualities to them which disgust us, it will light up. When it is activated without the corresponding activation of the brain's executive control area (e.g. prefrontal cortex and dACC), the result is more disgust and less empathy for the outgroup. Add in a fundamental difference in morals and/or beliefs and a process of dehumanisation can occur, a prerequisite for 'gut-deep' hate. Thinking of the outgroup as less than human paves the way for unspeakable treatment – and we take one step closer to genocide.

Hacking the brain to hate

Generally, humans have a hard time hurting other humans. Research into the willingness of soldiers and police to kill others shows that the behaviour does not come naturally to us. Studies of soldiers in the Second World War showed that many did not aim at their targets, and a significant number (purported to be around 70 per cent) never fired a single shot. Although the exact numbers have been disputed, the analysis resulted in the military establishing psychological training that increased the propensity of soldiers to feel 'gut-deep' hatred towards the enemy, making it easier to kill them on the field of battle.

Twenty years after the Second World War, over 90 per cent of soldiers in the Vietnam War fired their weapons.[48] The psychological techniques used drew heavily on *deindividuation*, *displacement* and *dehumanisation*. Deindividuation is a psychological process whereby the individual feels divested of responsibility because they perceive themselves to be part of a larger group. In war, the notion is that failing to kill the enemy will not only endanger yourself, but your unit. Displacement of responsibility onto an authority figure, the psychological process of conformity identified by Stanley Milgram, allows soldiers to divest themselves of guilt when the decision to kill is made by a superior officer.

Finally, and arguably most disturbingly, dehumanisation involves seeing the enemy as subhuman. The enemy are envisaged as cockroaches, vermin and parasites, and their behaviours and beliefs are placed in direct opposition to those of the soldiers. The enemy, they are told, eats foul food and animals that we keep as beloved pets; they don't wash for weeks at a time; they smell of sweat and faeces; and they deny the weakest in their society basic human rights. They are an infestation and a contagion that must be removed. They are the opposite of super-human Olympic athletes – they are subhuman, on a par with those homeless drug addicts.

If this psychological brainwashing works, when faced with one of the enemy the soldiers' prefrontal cortices remain dormant while their insulae and amygdalae light up like it's the Fourth of July. Now it's just that little bit easier to take away the enemy's freedom, separate them from society, pull the trigger.*

Like the amygdala, the insula evolved to keep us alive, but the modern conditions in which we now live have made many of its functions less essential to survival. Of course, it is still useful for quickly recognising our partner's expression of disgust when we are caught picking our nose, empathising with a friend's pain when they stub their toe, and helping us out when we sniff the carton of milk that's gone beyond its use-by date, but it wouldn't kill us if we couldn't do these things.

The science shows the insula adapted its skills to our ever more complex social environment. In doing so, it applied its survival tricks to dealing with other humans. Because it learns from information fed to it, like the amygdala, its processing can be prejudiced. It can more readily pick up negative expressions on the faces of people of other races, register pain differently depending on who dealt it, limit capacity to feel the pain of those not like us, and initiate a disgust response when we encounter a member of the outgroup.

Simply put, when a prejudiced insula and amygdala work together, in the absence of a regulating signal from the brain's

---

* This process is captured brilliantly in the 'Men against Fire' episode of Netflix's *Black Mirror* series, written by Charlie Brooker. In the episode soldiers are brain-washed via a chip implanted in their brains that makes the 'enemy', referred to as 'roaches', appear as something other than human, making it easier for them to be exterminated.

executive control area, a member of the outgroup can be seen as threatening, angry-looking, capable of inflicting long-lasting pain, disgusting, undeserving of empathy, and subhuman. A response that bears the hallmarks of hatred.

What is the rest of the brain doing while we hate?

Research has identified other parts of the brain that also play a role in processing hate. The striatum activates more when subjects view same-race faces, and this is important because it affects how we make decisions relating to risks and rewards. So viewing a same-race face makes us feel we may get a better outcome from an interaction with that person, meaning there is an increased chance we might actively prefer them over people of other races.[49] The parts of the brain that process vision, and hence faces, have also been found to react differently to same-race and other-race faces.[50] The part of the brain called the fusiform face area is responsible for telling us if we are seeing a face or not – think the face of your grandmother versus a toaster. If this area is damaged, a person will find it difficult to tell other people apart (but luckily, they can still tell their grandmother is not the toaster and vice versa). In several brain imaging studies this area has been shown to activate quicker to same-race faces than to other-race faces. This is known as the cross-race or same-race effect.[51] Slower fusiform face area activation may mean a person is slower to recognise other-race faces as individuals. They process other racial groups at a more abstract, category level, meaning they see them less as individuals and more as part of a separate other whole. The implications for remembering and distinguishing between other-race faces and hence stereotyping are significant.

*

As hate is a human concept, trying to find a single region or set of regions in the brain that are *fully* responsible for it is a fool's errand. We cannot point a finger at part of the brain, remove it, and then claim we've excised hate. What neuroscientists have attempted to do is to locate parts of the brain that react when presented with stimuli which may elicit a response that relates to a component of hate. The results tell us the human concept of hate has something to do with the brain's *learned* processing of threat detection and fear (by the amygdala) and disgust, pain, emotion recognition (by the insula), and how empathy and internal conflicts shape decisions (involving the prefrontal cortex and dACC). These latter two areas of the brain control prejudice and hate and they are by far the most sophisticated.

From the perspective of the brain, we don't really have an excuse for acting on hate if we are motivated to reject prejudice. Saying 'my brain made me do it' just doesn't ring true when we can slam on the brakes courtesy of the most advanced executive control system of all species.[52] Even after brain damage to the executive control area, hateful thoughts can still be stopped from becoming hateful actions. John, introduced at the beginning of this chapter, managed never to vocalise or act on his temporary, unbidden hateful inner voice.

All my reading about neuroscientists peering into brains looking for hate created a mental itch. As I moved from one brain region to another during my research, I had this strange sensation of their presence in my own grey matter. In the same way I could feel my heart pump and my bones click, I began to imagine my amygdala tingling when I saw a spider and my insula juddering when I smelled sour milk. Of course, there was no actual tingling or juddering, but the increased awareness of my brain's constituent parts made their role in shaping my thoughts and behaviours more apparent than ever before. I had to know what my brain was doing when it processed black and white faces, and there was only one way of doing that – allow a neuroscientist to peer into it.

4

My Brain and Hate

From the age of about twelve I knew I wasn't like the majority of other boys. My friends' bedroom walls were strewn with overlapping posters of Manchester United, *Rambo* movies, and Cindy Crawford in that bathing suit. My walls were adorned with neatly placed posters of the periodic table, *Star Trek* movies, and David Hasselhoff sprawled over that car.*

Despite knowing I probably wasn't heterosexual, I remember still holding biased views about same-sex relationships. For a short time I felt shame when I eventually realised what I was. Shame emanating from decades' worth of cultural 'feeding' that flooded my young impressionable brain with the notion that homosexual relationships were wrong. This was only bolstered by the negative portrayal of the LGBTQ+ community in the media that reached its height during the HIV/AIDS epidemic in the late 1980s.

On top of this, in 1988 Thatcher's government banned all school teachers from talking to students about gay relationships. The genesis for the Section 28 rule was a children's book about gay parents, *Jenny Lives with Eric and Martin*, found in a library in a Labour-held inner London Education Authority (it was actually only available for teachers). I recall seeing this headline in a copy of the *Daily Mail* my father had bought: 'Save the children from sad, sordid sex lessons'. When debating the Bill in the House of

* For those born well after the 1980s, I'm referring to KITT from *Knight Rider*.

Commons, Thatcher said, 'Children who need to be taught to respect traditional moral values are being taught that they have an inalienable right to be gay. All of those children are being cheated of a sound start in life.'

My brain absorbed this information like a sponge and I had no way of stopping it. The result was confusion. I recall seeing two men kiss for the first time on a TV show, and my brain automatically processed them as 'other'. At first, it didn't feel as if I was seeing someone like me. My conscious mind knew I was the same as them, but I couldn't stop that automatic split-second judgement.

Not long after this a friend told me he was gay. My response was laconic. Instead of supporting him and making him feel he wasn't alone, I pushed him away. The torrent of anti-gay propaganda my brain had been exposed to, like almost everyone else's brain during the 1980s and 90s, warped my views, held me back from supporting my friend and ensured I remained closeted for longer.

After several years, my brain eventually stopped the culturally programmed separating of 'them' from 'me'. Once I realised what my brain was doing, came to terms with being gay and started my new life, the cultural feeding of my childhood brain was undone. I was motivated to deprogramme my brain. Instead of shame I felt pride. I got in touch with my old gay friend, came out to him and apologised. Thankfully he understood, as he had also gone through the same process of deprogramming.

Coming out in my early twenties forced me to confront the prejudices I held towards gay people. By challenging my internalised homophobia head on, I came to recognise my brain's automatic processing in a range of other categories. When prompted by a conversation or encounter with someone from an outgroup I would take time to reflect and question any prejudices and the stereotypes I held.

*

The way the brain feeds off culture and experience means that negative encounters with members of the outgroup can shape how we judge others later in life. A heterosexual man who encounters a gay man for the first time in a social setting may see a negative stereotype further ingrained if that interaction is sexually predatory. A Christian who encounters a Jewish person for the first time in a financial exchange may see their negative stereotype ingrained if they feel short-changed. A white man encountering three young black men for the first time outside a London gay bar may see his negative stereotype ingrained if the interaction turns violent.

First encounters with members of the outgroup are foundational. In my case, I probably held stereotypical views of young black men in my early twenties because of my limited opportunities to interact with black people while growing up. My home town, like many towns outside of the cities in Wales, is incredibly white, and there were no black pupils at my schools when I attended. While studying at Cardiff University in the mid 1990s there were no black students on my undergraduate degree course. For the most part all I had to go on was the media, and I was being told mostly negative things. Of course, I had the intellectual wherewithal to question what I was being told. But it will probably come as no surprise that I didn't spend that much time questioning if young black men were any different from me. That may have changed after I encountered the three men outside that London bar. After the attack I can't actually recall if my attitude towards young black men changed. All I do remember was the anxiety the attack caused and how long it lasted. To this day I still look over my shoulder when exiting a gay bar. It wasn't until I began researching the neuroscience of hate that I began to wonder if the identity of my attackers might have shaped my brain's automatic processing of young black men since the hate crime.

Finding a neuroscientist with a brain scanner

'But what if the scan shows you are prejudiced?'

This was the warning from my husband, parents and siblings, who were all ill at ease with my idea of getting my brain scanned for prejudice and hate. Nevertheless, I wanted to know what it felt like to be part of one of these neuroscience studies. What did it feel like to have my brain scanned, prodded, computed, rendered and pored over by a group of neuroscientists in white coats looking for hate? (Fortunately there was no actual prodding of my brain, I'm happy to report.*) I was prepared for the likelihood my brain would send out different signals when presented with black versus white faces. We all harbour implicit prejudices, including those of us who study hate for a living. But I was unsure what these signals would mean in the context of *me*.

If present, might the signals indicate my exposure to old-fashioned media in the 1980s and 90s that flooded my amygdala and insula with racist stereotypes? Might they indicate a sense of threat left over from my attack decades ago? If the attack was a source of information that fed my brain, then surely it would shape my unconscious reactions. Or was I worrying over nothing? My brain might come back neutral, so to speak. No signs of prejudice or hate.

I emailed staff at the Cardiff University Brain Research Imaging Centre (CUBRIC) to find someone interested in helping me on my journey. CUBRIC is a well-funded facility with state-of-the-art neuroimaging equipment. At the time of opening in 2016 it was regarded as the most advanced brain imaging facility

---

* Although actual prodding with electrodes has been performed in studies using invasive electroencephalography!

in Europe. A post-doc, Dr Zargol Moradi, replied to my email. Dr Moradi, who had done her PhD at the University of Oxford, explained that the scanning process would be completed in two stages.

The first stage was to generate an overall map of my brain, using their Diffusion Magnetic Resonance Imaging scanner. The scanner uses high-powered magnets and radio waves to detect the flow of blood in the brain. By tracking the movement of blood, it produces a picture of the brain's white matter. This is considered an indirect measure of brain activity, as the scanner can't see the firing of neurons – the actual process of brain activity.

The second stage would involve my undertaking a task in a MEG (magnetoencephalography) scanner, which picks up signals in the brain more quickly than Diffusion MRI. Instead of tracking the flow of blood to parts of the brain, the MEG scanner looks at the electrical signals produced by neurons, a direct measure of what my brain is doing.

The Diffusion MRI: Mapping my brain

In the first scan I had no tests to perform while in the machine, and I got to lie down for half an hour after my lunch – easy, I thought initially. However, the atmosphere of the CUBRIC facility took me back to a traumatic operation I had as a child. The feeling deepened when Dr Moradi asked me to change into a hospital gown and to remove all items of metal on my person. She warned me that the scanner was sixty thousand times more powerful than the earth's magnetic field, meaning any piercings, rings or implants would rip from their moorings and zip through the air (and possibly through me) if they were not removed. I reported I had no piercings, and my worry subsided a little.

All the talk of strong magnetic fields got me thinking about how MRI technology actually works. Our bodies are 60 per cent water, much of it contained in blood. Water contains hydrogen protons that are like tiny versions of the earth, having a north and a south pole and constantly spinning on their axes.* Like the earth, the spinning hydrogen proton creates a magnetic field. Naturally, these protons spin about randomly in the body, but when exposed to a strong external magnetic force, they can all be made to spin in the same direction. When the magnetic field of an MRI scanner is turned on, the hydrogen protons in the water inside our blood line up like the strings on a guitar. Radio waves are then fired in pulses at the protons knocking them out of alignment. After each pulse, the magnets bring the protons back into line, and the speed with which they jerk back depends on how much oxygen there is in the blood. The effect is like strumming guitar strings with a plectrum. This 'tune' is then picked up by radio frequency coils which act like ears, placed around the head. These readings are then sent to a computer for analysis.[1]

Before the first scan Dr Moradi spoke with evident pride about the Diffusion MRI technology, dubbed the 'Connectome' (referring to the complex network of neural wiring in the brain connecting some 86 billion neurons). She told me that by tracing water molecules around the brain it is capable of generating images ten times the quality of MRI scanners in most hospitals. It is the Hubble Telescope of neuroscience, and CUBRIC has one of only three in the world.

'We'll be building a complete picture of your white matter, but also focusing very closely on parts of your brain hypothesised to

---

* If you remember your school chemistry lessons, you may know water consists of two hydrogen atoms and one oxygen atom, and atoms consist of protons, neutrons and electrons.

be related to prejudice,' said Dr Moradi, as she jotted down my details on a clipboard.

She weighed me to make sure I wasn't too heavy for the machine – it has an upper limit of 100 kg. To Dr Moradi's surprise I came in at 101 kg (I hide it well), but I was told it was within acceptable tolerances. A series of health questions were then asked, including my medical doctor's address. 'I need it just in case we find anything anomalous, like a tumour,' she said.

My mind darted back to the childhood operation and my heart raced. 'Deep breaths,' I whispered to myself.

Everything was bathed in clinical white apart from the array of computer screens in the control room that displayed the data coming in from the scan. I was taken to the scanner and asked to lie down on the bench. After popping in some earplugs, my head was guided into the radio wave coil and jammed in tight with foam pieces.

'Try not to move, otherwise we'll have to start over,' Dr Moradi warned. A heart monitor was attached to my finger, and a small balloon lodged in my hand. 'Squeeze on this hard if you have a panic attack.' Her muffled voice just registered.

Dr Moradi and her assistant moved into the control room, away from the impending gargantuan magnetic field. 'Are you okay to go?' she said over the intercom.

I gave the thumbs up and was slowly entombed in seven tonnes of magnet. From this point on I experienced a cacophony of hellish whirs, beeps, clicks and bangs as the giant magnets engaged and radio waves were fired into my head. Dr Moradi intermittently checked on me with her reassuring tone: 'Only twenty minutes left now, Matt.'

And it was over. I came out a little dizzy, but happy with my performance – I didn't panic, move (despite having an itch on my forehead) or sneeze. The perfect test subject, I thought. As I hoped, Dr Moradi was impressed with my behaviour. But the whole experience was tarnished with her final comment.

'Given your weight, I expected a larger brain.'*

The MEG: Finding a signal in the noise

I waited two weeks for the second brain scan. Dr Moradi met me in the MEG lab at the very end of the sprawling CUBRIC research facility. The MEG was tucked away to minimise magnetic interference from the MRI machines. As the magnetic field of a brain is very weak (over a billion times weaker than a fridge magnet), to detect any activity in its billions of neurons the MEG uses some of the most sensitive detectors available.

These detectors, called superconducting quantum interference devices, or SQUIDs, must be kept at -270°C and shielded from other magnetic fields to function properly. SQUIDs are so remarkably sensitive that they have been compared to hearing a pin drop at an AC-DC concert.[2] They are used to detect gravitational waves, undulations in space-time emanating from cataclysmic events in the universe like a star going supernova or the collision of two black holes 1.8 billion light years away.† They have also been used in attempts to detect axions, the ghostlike particles with virtually no weight that were candidates for the dark matter that makes up 85 per cent of the universe. More locally, they have been used to study brain activity in sufferers of epilepsy and Alzheimer's disease.

* Months later she told me this was a joke! I'm happy to report my brain size is slightly above average.

† This first direct observation of gravitational waves was made in 2016, with help from my colleagues at Cardiff University.

It may come as no surprise to learn that the theory underpinning SQUIDs, the Josephson junction, won its namesake the Nobel Prize in Physics in 1973. Looking into my brain to find signals of prejudice sounds easy compared to these giant scientific undertakings and achievements, I thought.

As Dr Moradi attached three wire sensors to my head, she casually asked, 'Are you wearing any face cream or eyeshadow?'

'No,' I replied. Curious, I asked why she was concerned.

'The MEG sensors will pick up the tiny traces of metal present in some products and will interfere with the scan, so it's best to remove them before we start,' she explained.

I was guided into a metal-lined room, wires dangling from my head. Inside was the MEG. A large leather white chair was attached to a massive cylinder about one metre wide and two tall. There was a hole at the bottom where my head would fit, making it look like a ridiculously large hood hairdryer from the local salon. This hood contained the SQUIDs and a serious amount of liquid helium to keep them deep-frozen.

I was placed in the seat and told to squeeze my head as far into the cylinder as possible. In front of me a screen lit up, peppered with indecipherable computer code. Dr Moradi explained that once the experiment started, black cross hairs would appear in the middle of the screen. My only task was to press a button with my right index finger when the black cross hairs turned red. She repeated the same warning from the first scan: 'One thing you must not do is move your head. If you do, the readings will be off.'

The whole experiment was to last around twenty minutes – no problem, I thought. Dr Moradi closed the five-inch-thick metal door and bolted me into the magnetically shielded room. I was left with only a small speaker and microphone to communicate with the outside world.

'Matthew, are you okay to go?' her voiced crackled through the speaker.

'Ready when you are,' I replied tentatively.

The screen in front of me flickered for a moment and then the computer code was replaced by the message 'Get ready'. I cleared my throat to steady myself. The black cross hairs flashed up and behind them was a white man's face, neutral in expression. The cross hairs turned red and I hit the button, turning them black again. Then the white face was quickly replaced with that of a black woman, angry in expression. The cross hairs turned red again, so I clicked.

I began to ponder the set-up of the experiment. Was Dr Moradi measuring the speed at which I pressed the button after the cross hairs turned red? Was my speed affected by the race and emotion of the face being flashed up? Did seeing a black male angry face before the red cross hairs speed up my reaction, and what could this possibly say about any implicit prejudice I might hold?

White male angry face
Black cross hairs
White female neutral face
Red cross hairs – click . . .

After five minutes my head was spinning. All I could do was focus on the cross hairs:

Black cross hairs
Black female happy face
Red cross hairs – click . . .

To my tired eyes the faces looked like they were all merging into one. I was barely conscious of their gender, race or expression.

Black male neutral face
Black cross hairs
Black male angry face
Red cross hairs – click . . .

Twenty minutes in, the screen went dead, and the noise of the heavy door opening brought me back into the cold metal room. I rubbed my eyes.

'Did I remain still enough?' I asked Dr Moradi.

'Still enough. I think you had a spasm in your back which came through on the scan, but we can compensate for that,' she said as the probes were detached from my head.

After the experiment I asked how it worked. Dr Moradi revealed that my speed of response to the red cross hairs appearing had nothing to do with measuring implicit prejudice. It was a process to focus my attention; to put my executive control area under pressure. This allowed the SQUIDs to detect any brain signals thought to be linked to unconscious bias processing.

Following the scan Dr Moradi entered the data into CUBRIC's supercomputer, which took forty hours to process all the information captured from the task. This information was then combined with my detailed Diffusion MRI scan to produce three-dimensional images of my brain activity.

Did my brain show signs of prejudice?

Before I received my brain scan results I took the Implicit Association Test. I was keen to know if both sets of results married up. I took the online version of the race IAT twice. The first results indicated that I had a slight automatic preference for black faces over white ones, and the second results, a few days later, indicated a slight automatic preference for white faces over black ones. Not a huge variation, given the scale goes from slight to moderate to strong automatic preference. I therefore assumed the test was telling me I was somewhere in between having a tiny preference for black faces and a tiny preference for white faces.* This made sense to me, as I don't consciously feel I have a preference for either. But this test looks for unconscious or implicit bias, so I took the results for what they were.

I travelled into Cardiff city centre by bus to get my results from the brain scans. During the journey I pondered what my results would mean for me and for this book. A result that showed areas of my brain reacting to black faces but not white ones might indicate implicit prejudice. The IAT result suggested this was a possibility. I reminded myself that we all harbour prejudices and it's what we do about them that counts. Also, a 'positive' result would make for a more interesting read!

I met Dr Moradi in a coffee shop where she showed me the images of my brain. Three orientations were presented – front, side and top – and parts of my brain were coloured in a heatmap of vermilion red through to sun-bright yellow (see second set of brain images in the plate section).

'These are areas of activation,' Dr Moradi said. 'We saw activation when you were exposed to black male angry faces.'

'So my brain didn't react in the same way to black male neutral or happy faces, or black female faces?'

'No,' she said.

'What about white angry faces?' I probed.

'Just black angry faces,' she clarified.

This startled me a little. I asked Dr Moradi which areas lit up. Pointing to the sides of my brain on the images, she said, 'That's the insula.' She moved her finger to the centre of my brain. 'And that's the dorsal anterior cingulate cortex.'

---

* As stated in an earlier footnote, the test is not meant to give a definitive result in one try. The inventors suggest you take it about ten times over a few weeks and average your score.

I asked why my amygdala wasn't showing up.

'The MEG is great at detecting neurons as they fire, but it can't go deep enough into the brain to scan the amygdala,' she explained.

I recalled some of the research I had done while waiting for the brain scan results. If my insula activated when presented with black male angry faces, it may have had something to do with my salience network processing deep emotion in relation to where my 'spotlight of attention' was while in the scanner. The activation of my dACC, part of my brain's executive control region, might have related to a need to resolve an inner conflict. The co-activation of the insula and dACC in other studies was associated with less implicit prejudice on the IAT, mirroring my earlier results.

To me it seemed plausible that black male angry faces elicited a deep emotion in me and my brain's executive control area then regulated this emotion. I had previously told Dr. Moradi about my attack and posed this hypothesis to her.

'Could this be related to the hate crime?'

'It is possible that this co-activation relates to your attack all those years ago,' she said.

I dug around my bag, pulled out a research paper from *Nature: Neuroscience* and paraphrased from a highlighted section: 'We know the insula speaks to the amygdala . . . and that both are involved in emotional memory. Is it possible that seeing black male angry faces forced my brain to recall the emotion felt around the time of the attack?'

She agreed, and added further insight: 'But because the attack happened so long ago, your dorsal anterior cingulate cortex may have put the brakes on the insula . . .'

I finished her thought: 'Allowing me to rationalise that there is no need to feel now whatever emotion was recalled from the past.'

'Possibly. But you must remember, neuroimaging research is done on multiple subjects, and we'd never draw conclusions from one scan.'

Despite Dr. Moradi's caution, research backs up the train of thought we shared when poring over pictures of my brain. A team of psychologists from Harvard, Columbia and Michigan State universities devised a study to test whether learned fears were more difficult to unlearn if the source of that fear was a black male. The first stage of their experiment involved administering electric shocks to test subjects as they viewed images of black and white female and male faces, while monitoring galvanic skin responses – a physiological measure of fear. Naturally, every time a subject was shocked they registered fear.

The second stage showed the same faces but without the electric shock. The galvanic skin responses in this stage showed that fear continued to be felt in response to seeing black male faces only, in the absence of the electric shock. The study concluded a bad experience with a black male is harder to forget than the same bad experience with anyone else.[3]

As this study suggests, it is possible the memory of my attack was made more powerful because of the race of the perpetrators. The insula* processes pain differently according to whether it is inflicted by a member of the ingroup or the outgroup, especially if it carries a moral message.[4] In an instant, without thinking, I knew I was a victim of a hate crime. I immediately negatively evaluated the perpetrators – they were a threat to me and my worldview. When they uttered their homophobic slur my pre-frontal cortex rationally pieced together their motive. The physical nature of the attack may have spurred my insula, amygdala

---

* In conjunction with the left orbitofrontal cortex and amygdala.

and hippocampus to work together to embed the painful and morally challenging incident into my long-term memory, to be abruptly recalled then regulated every time I saw a black male angry face afterwards. When I try hard to think back to that time, the attack is one of only a few vivid memories I hold. There is no question the violence stuck with me, but it surprised me that the race and sex of my attackers might have something to do with the persistence of the memory.

In the end, the scan raised more questions than it answered. If I had not been a victim of that hate crime twenty years ago, would my results have looked different? Did their prejudice directed towards people like me create prejudice in me directed towards people like them – young black men with angry faces? What if my attackers had instead been white? With these questions came doubts over whether the scan could tell me anything about the implicit prejudices I held. Dr Moradi understandably didn't have answers to these questions. It seems the neuroscience of prejudice and hate still has a long way to go before we can draw firm conclusions.

Where the neuroscience of hate falls down

The salmon of doubt

A brain imaging study like no other was presented at the 2009 Organization for Human Brain Mapping conference in San Francisco. But there was something fishy about it. The scientists presented results of an fMRI scan of a dead salmon's brain. That's no typo. They actually put a dead salmon bought from the local supermarket into a multimillion-pound brain scanner. Like proper neuroscientists, they scanned its brain as they would a human subject's, and wrote up the results in the usual way:

The salmon was approximately 18 inches long, weighed 3.8 lbs, and was not alive at the time of scanning . . . The task administered to the salmon involved completing an open-ended mentalising task. The salmon was shown a series of photographs depicting individuals in social situations with a specified emotional valence. The salmon was asked to determine what emotion the individual in the photo must have been experiencing.[5]

Despite the salmon having been dead for some time, the fMRI scan picked up brain activity during the task. The results got everyone talking and were taken in good spirit, as was intended by the authors. Their paper was a (not so fresh) reminder to the neuroimaging community that brain images can produce erroneous results when statistical corrections are not applied.

Only a year earlier a group of scientists from MIT had questioned the number of studies being published in respected journals that found strong evidence for locating psychological phenomena, such as hate, in the brain.[6] In no other field of social or behavioural enquiry were there so many astonishing breakthroughs in such a short space of time. Instead of sticking a dead salmon into an fMRI scanner, the MIT researchers opted to conduct a forensic statistical review of fifty-five neuroimaging studies. They concluded twenty-eight of them had got their statistics wrong (due to the non-independence error[*]), leading to incorrect results. Many

---

[*] The non-independence error arises from a two-step procedure in brain imaging. In step 1, multiple areas of the brain are correlated with a psychological measure, say prejudice. In step 2, the data from areas where high correlations are found (e.g. the amygdala and insula) are averaged to produce the published results. This approach distorts the picture by only selecting highly correlated results from the 'noise', thus presenting the pattern that is being searched for. This is akin to the selection bias problem (see E. Vul et al., 'Puzzlingly High Correlations

of these studies focused on brain regions like the ones covered in this and the preceding chapter, including the amygdala and insula, and claimed to have shown evidence that they were strongly linked to psychological states and behaviours.

The authors of the criticised studies quickly defended their work. By 2009, a type of statistical correction required to discount these false results (correction for multiple comparisons[†]) became widely used by neuroscientists. But this controversy in the field encouraged scientists to question what signals in the brain actually mean. It is widely assumed that when more blood is called to a region of the brain, this is because it requires oxygen to perform, like our leg muscles when we go for a run. It is a reasonable assumption to make, given what we know about how our bodies work, but beyond this assumption, what else can be concluded beyond reasonable doubt? For example, in many of the studies previously mentioned, the amygdala is consistently identified as a site for processing fear that is assumed to be related to threat and prejudice. But these are big leaps to make based on the finding that as one thing increases (e.g. IAT score for implicit prejudice) so does another (e.g. amygdala activity). Statistical issues aside, how can scientists conclude that amygdala activation is directly related to a test score or the presentation of a face, when it is also known to activate in relation to intense smells, sexually explicit images, badges of rival sports teams and, perhaps

in fMRI Studies of Emotion, Personality, and Social Cognition', *Perspectives on Psychological Science* 4 (2009), 274–90).

† This correction is used when multiple tests for statistical significance are performed, as they are in brain imaging studies. The more tests for significance, the more likely a significant result will be found that is erroneous (a false positive, where brain activity appears to have been observed in the statistics when there actually is none).

most importantly, to the experiences of being tightly wedged into an fMRI scanner and being tested for prejudice – both of which are anxiety-inducing. Does a fear of being entombed in the bore of a seven-tonne magnet that can rip metal objects on your person from their moorings mean you are prejudiced against fMRI scanners? Probably not.

Once a collection of brain imaging studies spot the same areas of the brain lighting up in response to prejudice-eliciting stimuli, there is a temptation to stop looking elsewhere for answers. We stop asking questions because the scans confirm what we already knew – prejudice and hate exist, and we can locate them in the brain.

Looking at the pattern of activity in my brain scan, I began to think about my quest to find meaning in the noise. Humans repeatedly see order in patterns, even when there is none. It seems to be an inescapable trait. Imagine being a neuroscientist in the first brain imaging study of implicit bias. The results show part of the brain is active when subjects look at black and white faces, but more so for black ones. This area, the amygdala, has been associated with fear and aggression in previous studies, so we try to create a rationale for the activity: in some subjects, but not all, seeing black faces results in activity in the amygdala, which indicates fear, or maybe a perception of threat, which we link to prejudice. We stop asking questions. We don't consider in too much detail why some subjects' amygdalae lit up in response to white faces, or why other parts of the brain didn't show activity. We publish and move on to the next study. But then in this second study another part of the brain lights up that we didn't expect. It's the insula, known from previous research to be related to pain and deep emotion – we can work with that, and weave it into our narrative that prejudice is also related to these things. Then the next study shows another area activate, the dACC, which is involved in resolving conflicts and so must be about regulating prejudice – so now we have a 'prejudice network' in the brain. We make sense of the patterns presented to us, and will sometimes minimise information when it contradicts our story.

This process of neuroscientific discovery has led to some rather unusual claims. In 2005 a team of researchers from UCLA and Caltech claimed to have found the Halle Berry neuron.[7] Epilepsy patients who had electrodes placed in their brains to locate the origin of their seizures were asked to look at a series of pictures including landmarks, objects and famous faces. In one patient the scientists found a single neuron that only fired on pictures of Halle Berry, Halle Berry dressed as Catwoman, and the letter string H-A-L-L-E B-E-R-R-Y. It refused to fire on other pictures, including other celebrities and other women dressed as Catwoman.

This was the first time a study had isolated a single neuron that related to a specific stimulus, and it flew in the face of conventional neuroscience wisdom – that there simply aren't enough neurons in the part of the brain in question for it to work in this way. But a neuron was found that only fired when Halle Berry popped up. There the questions should not stop. Although other faces were shown, along with landmarks and objects, the scientists could not show an exhaustive list. Maybe that neuron would fire on another image which shared a trait with Halle Berry. But the scientists had to craft their story to get published, and now we have the Halle Berry neuron.[*]

---

[*] This neuron was only found in one subject, and the authors do not suggest we all have a Halle Berry neuron.

Can neuroscience answer the big questions about hate?

The Halle Berry neuron study and others like it rely on visual proof of brain activity. There is no doubt that showing fancy pictures of the inside of our heads overlaid with coloured pixels is a powerful way to get an argument across. Peering into my own brain and seeing parts lit up was such a heady experience that my knee-jerk reaction was to assume Dr Moradi had found what I was looking for. In that moment I was suffering from what Professor Joe Dumit from the University of California, Davis calls 'brain overclaim'.[8]

In his book *Picturing Personhood*, Professor Dumit questions the claims of brain imaging. I called him to get his take on scanning brains for hate. He said a key test for the neuroscientists is to answer the question 'Could I go backwards from this result?' Take this example: specific patterns of activity in a brain area can indicate epilepsy. Neurosurgeons can even pinpoint problematic areas for extraction to reduce the number of seizures suffered by a patient. This is a good example of 'going backwards' from a brain scan to a diagnosis. The same cannot be done for scans that look for the existence of social and psychological phenomena in the brain. A neurosurgeon would not look at activity in the amygdala and/or insula on a scan and conclude that a person was prejudiced or hateful. These parts of the brain give off signals for a huge variety of reasons, and because of this there is just too much noise to be sure beyond reasonable doubt that they are activating because the person is feeling hate.

Much of the problem comes down to the fundamental question these scientists pose – can we locate a human social construct, such as hate, within the brain? Although we can all agree hate exists, we cannot agree upon its definition. Multiple definitions have existed throughout time and space. First, racial prejudice was recognised and legislated against, then came gender, sexual orientation, physical and mental impairment, religion and so on. But where and by which institutions these prejudices were recognised varied enormously, as it still does. Compared to some countries, citizens in the UK enjoy an array of protections from hate, but this has come hard won, and only recently have some groups been afforded equal protection. And there are still some groups fighting for recognition. The concept of hate shifts depending on place and time. How can we expect such a slippery social construct to be located within the brain? Does the brain update its wiring every time there is a change in the law to recognise a new type of hate? What if scientists were able to find a new type of hate in the brain? Should the law then take notice?

The reason I used the phrase 'beyond reasonable doubt' earlier was to draw attention to the burden of proof required in courts of law. Neuroscientists now claim to have found evidence linking features of the brain to diminished responsibility – adolescence, diminished mental capacity, psychopathy, addiction-related risk-blindness to name a few.[9] 'My brain made me do it' becomes a more compelling argument when juries can see differences in images of the 'normal' versus the 'diminished responsibility' brain. Brain images are often not allowed as evidence in a case because a judge may consider that they will be prejudicial – that the impressive-looking scans with their perceived scientific certainty will likely confuse or mislead a jury.

It doesn't take much imagination to conjure up a situation where the brains of 'at-risk' people are scanned for prejudices, and those found hateful – perhaps due to high levels of activity in the amygdala and the insula in response to viewing black faces, and a lack of activity in the executive control area – are placed in rehabilitation programmes. Orwell's notion of 'thoughtcrime' from *Nineteen Eighty-Four* realised. Proceeding with caution is the sensible thing for the law, and the rest of us, to do in this space.

Beyond the brain

Impressive brain scanning technologies can locate sites of activity when certain stimuli are presented. But questions over what activation actually means, and how one stimulus can be disentangled from others, cast doubt over the ability of neuroscientists to tell us everything we need to know about hate. Even if we could locate hate in the brain with certainty, how would this help us tackle the problem? How would we deal with people whose brain activity tells us they hold hatred towards a group, but who insist they do not? Do we believe the brain scan or the person? What if the person admits they feel hatred towards a group but that they are able to control its expression, so it never manifests as a behaviour? Do we trust that under all conditions they can stop hateful thoughts from turning into hateful acts? If not, should we cut out the parts of the brain we think are responsible for processing hate, just as we cut out the problematic areas of the brain responsible for seizures in epileptics? How might this reduce their ability to identify other threats in their environment?

There is strong evidence showing we are predisposed to prefer people like us. This is the most basic ingredient of hate. But graduation to hate is not inevitable, and prejudiced thinking during encounters with other humans is something that our brains learn, not something innate. Most neuroscientists agree that the brain is only part of the equation. While there may well be a neural component to hate, brain images tell us little about contexts outside of the scanner – which personal, social, economic and environmental factors may turn a relatively benign preference for 'us' into prejudice and hate. To answer this question we must look beyond the brain, beginning with *group*-based threat.

5

Group Threat and Hate

Bijan Ebrahimi was born in Iran in 1969 and moved to the UK to join his two sisters at the turn of the millennium. He had stayed behind in his native country to care for his dying parents. When given indefinite leave to remain as a refugee in 2001 he moved to Bristol. Keen to contribute to society, he studied plumbing and carpentry at a nearby college, but a physical impairment prevented him from working. He also suffered from mental health issues and a speech impediment. To be close to his sisters he settled in Capgrave Crescent in Brislington. He was one of only a few residents that were black or minority ethnic. During his time on the crescent, Bijan was victimised by some white residents.

He loved gardening, but the neighbours' children would destroy his flowers and plants. His cat was tormented by a neighbour's out-of-control dog. When he reported this to the council, the dog was set on him. His life was routinely threatened. He reported around fifty incidents to the police, including five cases of criminal damage, seventeen assaults, seven threats to kill, five cases of harassment, twelve public order offences and one of cruelty to an animal. He felt all were racially motivated and often provided video evidence from his phone to back up the claims. One of Bijan's sisters witnessed some of these attacks, and recalled him being called 'foreigner', 'cockroach' and 'Paki', and being told to go back to his own country, by both young and old residents on the crescent.[1] The police noted racial aggravation in sixteen of the reported incidents. The result of all this was the caution of one neighbour for criminal damage.

As if this torment was not enough, some of his neighbours started the vicious rumour that Bijan was a paedophile, despite him never being charged with a sexual offence in his life. These distressing claims were rife within the small community of Capgrave Crescent, and when twenty-four-year-old Lee James moved onto the street to be with his girlfriend and young children, fellow residents were at pains to warn him of the 'local child predator'. Although James knew of Bijan, he only encountered him on a few occasions. One of those occasions was on a warm summer's night, Thursday 11 July 2013. James was drinking cans of Budweiser while watching his children play on the green in the shadow of the homes on the crescent. From his flat, Bijan saw that James was drinking alcohol and decided to take video evidence. Given Bijan's heritage he frowned upon drinking, especially in front of children. James noticed the phone in Bijan's hand and angrily marched over to his flat to confront him. 'Don't you dare take pictures of me, alright . . . Stop taking pictures of my fucking kids,' yelled James.

During the altercation the police were called. Upon arrival at the flat the police arrested Bijan for breach of the peace, but not James. Outside a group of about fifteen white neighbours had gathered to eavesdrop on the ruckus. As Bijan was marched to the police car the mob cheered and shouted slurs. The next day Bijan was released without charge. The police found the pictures he had taken were not of the children, but of James drinking. Aware of the tension on the crescent, the police told Bijan to call the station if he felt unsafe at any point. He arrived back to his home to taunts from neighbours: 'Paedophile!' 'Where are your handcuffs?' 'Why have you come back?' He called the police several times to no avail. On the Saturday, Bijan was so afraid for his safety that he stayed locked in his flat.

As the sun fell and the night came, James and his friends started drinking again on the green. In an inebriated state they bawled slurs and threats at Bijan as he remained indoors, scared for his life. Hoping his tormentors were asleep, Bijan waited until 1 a.m. on Sunday to water his beloved plants. But James was only just heading back to his flat and spotted him. A confrontation ensued and a fight broke out. One neighbour recalled hearing James shout, 'Have some of that,' as he stomped on Bijan's head. James said that as he beat Bijan to death he kicked him 'like a football . . . I had so much anger in me.' Then with the help of a neighbour, James dragged Bijan's lifeless body onto the green where his children had been playing a few days before. With no remorse, and still furious, James poured white spirit over the corpse and set it alight for all the crescent to witness.

James was sentenced to a minimum of eighteen years for murder, but not a hate crime.* Because James pleaded guilty to the murder charge, no witnesses from the crescent were called to a trial to give evidence on whether the murder was motivated by or demonstrated hostility toward Bijan's impairment or race. There was just not enough solid evidence to charge James with a hate-related murder.

But the absence of concrete evidence does not mean hate did not play a role (see the section on proving hate in Chapter 2). At the sentencing the judge said the accusations that Bijan was

* Lee James was charged with the basic offence of murder without a weapon under the Homicide Act 1957 (amended by the Criminal Justice Act 2003, schedule 21), the penalty for which is a minimum of fifteen years in prison. There was not enough evidence to charge James with murder that demonstrated or was motivated by hostility towards Bijan's race or impairment. If he had been charged with and found guilty of such an offence, the penalty would have been a minimum of thirty years in prison.

a paedophile were baseless. A review of the case concluded that from 2005 until his murder, Bijan had been subject to a pattern of repeated harassment, assault and criminal damage, some of it serious and much of it racially aggravated. It also stated that there had been a number of cases documented in which disabled men had been similarly erroneously labelled as paedophiles, then targeted and murdered because of such labels.[2]

At the trial Bijan's sister, Manizhah Moores, gave an account of the impact of the crime:

> He lived in Bristol throughout his time in the UK and met many good people. Unfortunately he was also subjected to horrendous bullying by bad people on a daily basis. Call it racism, call it prejudice, it doesn't really matter what you call it, the things our brother was subjected to were barbaric . . . In our view this prejudice amongst some members of the local community helps explain why events escalated to Bijan being kicked to death and burned . . . When Bijan was brutally murdered on 14th July 2013 our lives changed forever. There are no words on this earth that can describe the emptiness we feel. Part of us died with him. Three or four times a week my sister drives to Brislington, sits in her car and cries . . . On Sundays Bijan's chair is empty. Burning Bijan's body took away the opportunity for us to pay our respects to our brother as we could not view his body before he was laid to rest. To us this felt like Bijan being murdered twice. The loss of Bijan has left a hole in our lives that we can never fill. Our life will never be the same again.[3]

A review of the police handling of Bijan's case found evidence of institutional racism.[4] They had branded Bijan a serial complainer, having put their belief in the mass of white neighbours on Cap-grave Crescent who made counter claims against him and spread the vicious rumours that he was a threat to children. The review noted that in Bijan's dealings with the police he always remained respectful, cooperative and calm, despite the extreme distress he suffered at the hands of his neighbours and the services that were meant to protect him. The Chief Constable of Avon and Somer-set confessed the police failed to protect Bijan. His death could have been prevented if they had simply done their job correctly, without prejudice. After the investigation, two police officers were jailed and four were fired. In total, eighteen officers were investi-gated, including sergeants and inspectors.

Some of the earliest scientific work identifies group-based threat as a primary motivation for prejudice and hate.[5] Throughout human history group threats represent the main source of conflict – com-peting tribes, armies and nations battling it out for the top spot. Today, apart from high-level territorial and ideological conflicts, actual group threat at the lower level is rare. For most of us, group threat is imagined – from the outgroup causing indiscriminate deadly infection and crime waves, to the theft of precious jobs and the eradication of local and national ways of life. But even imagined threat can have consequences for intergroup relations.

It is hard to escape the rabble-rousing headlines: 'Britain threatened by gay virus plague', 'Britain's towns shamed by Asian grooming gangs', '3 million UK workers are now foreign' and 'Sharia courts getting prominent in Britain'. Often, the percep-tion of group threat is all that is needed to activate a defensive response from the ingroup. Bijan was the subject of a 'local belief' that was never challenged by the police; their silence was likely taken as confirmation that he was a threat to children. Was this perception all it took for Lee James to stamp on Bijan's head until he was dead? That is too simple an explanation given the history of hateful abuse he suffered.

Bijan's victimisers had something in common – they believed their community was somehow jeopardised by his presence and what he represented. Why else would his abusers have yelled at him to 'go back to your own country' and called him a 'foreigner' and a 'cockroach'? Was the murder of Bijan an act of defensive aggression to oust him and to provide a warning to anyone else from his 'group' thinking of taking up residence on the crescent?

Stories similar to Bijan's are repeated throughout time and place, and the science is definitive: in over a hundred psychological studies covering over a hundred thousand people across twenty-eight countries since the 1960s, one finding endures – members of dominant groups are more likely to express prejudice and hate when they perceive a threat from a subordinate group.[6] Bijan's death is a tragic reminder that this phenomenon persists beyond the university labs where it was first identified.

The evolution of group threat detection

The previous chapter showed how our brains evolved to ensure the survival of our species. The brain did this by inclining us to form a tight bond with our own group, which generated trust and cooperation. This bond ensured successful hunting and gathering and defence against outside threats from animal predators, the environment and possibly competing species of human. Defence against aggressive competition was key to survival. Aggression can erupt when the ingroup wants to increase its status and resources, and when it must protect itself against real or imagined threat from an outgroup.

The ability of *Homo sapiens* to adapt to multiple threats in the environment is unrivalled, mainly due to superior brains which allowed for sophisticated language, cooperation and problem-solving. Other species of human, while potentially physically more powerful, likely failed to adapt to the wide range of threats in the same way. Like the predisposition to bond with the ingroup, the threat response is likely to have evolved over time. *Homo sapiens'* ability to recognise threats, including those posed by outgroups, helped ensure genes were passed down the evolutionary chain. The alternative is that our ancestors would have been killed off by freak weather, animal predators and possibly our other human competitors.

We plan an escape when faced with a superior aggressor in a dark alley, recalling our path up to the point of the threat, and tracing back an escape route. We adapt our strategy when faced with an unfair exchange of goods in a market, using laws or subterfuge to redress the imbalance, so that we can still feed our family. We reduce contact with a poorly work colleague so we can avoid infection and continue earning money. Each of these adaptations to threat is associated with an emotional response. The aggressor generates fear, the cheat anger, and the infected person disgust. When faced with repeated threats of a similar nature these emotions can intensify, increasing sensitivity and the speed and magnitude of our response.[7]

The feeling that our group is constantly under attack, whether real or imagined, not only makes us acutely aware of the threat, but also makes us see threats where there are none. Like the overly sensitive belt alarm in your car that goes off every time you put your bag of shopping on the passenger seat, our ability to detect threat can become so sensitive that it raises false alarms. That person in the alley was not an aggressor but an out-of-towner asking for directions; that salesman in the market was not a crook, he simply gave the wrong change; that colleague was not infected with the feared virus, they just had the hangover from hell.

But what leads some of us to jump to such extreme conclusions so quickly about each of these potential threats? Perhaps the out-of-towner was black and wearing a hoodie; the salesman was Jewish and was wearing an expensive watch; the work colleague was Chinese and had just returned from a trip to China. Each one possibly a member of an outgroup (depending on your own identity), each with discernible characteristics that allow us to (mis) classify them quickly.

In milliseconds our threat detection mechanisms can be triggered by visual cues that draw on the negative stereotypes in our heads. Black and hoodie equals violence, equals fear, equals threat; Jewish and greed equals dishonesty, equals anger, equals threat; Chinese and poor food hygiene equals health risk, equals disgust, equals threat. With each misclassification of threat based on stereotypes and misread signs there is a chance of prejudice. The out-of-towner gets lost and feels unwelcome, the salesman gets wrongly accused, tarnishing his reputation, and the Chinese colleague is avoided and excluded.

Our threat meter, which was essential to human survival, is now out of date and not fit for purpose. We are burdened with a biological system akin to a smoke detector – designed to overreact because it is better to be safe than sorry. But the likelihood of experiencing false alarms is not evenly distributed across the population. Those who fail to acknowledge the power of their biology to influence behaviour, to resist mass media brainwashing and to swap competition for cooperation are far more likely to detect threats where there are none, and often with a hint of prejudice.

Our biology and threat

In 2010 students at the University of Amsterdam received an email inviting them to take part in a strange psychology experiment. The text of the email mentioned test subjects had to be male and that they would participate in a study on the effects of medication on decision-making. The reward for taking part was ten euros. The email was signed off by Professor Carsten De Dreu. Around 280 Dutch men replied offering themselves up. All were asked a series of questions that would determine their suitability for the experiment. Regular smokers, heavy alcohol and drug users and those on medication for mental illness were excluded. The applicant group was whittled down to seventy.

The first test subjects arrived at Professor De Dreu's lab at midday. The men were instructed to sit at computers in individual cubicles to ensure they could not see each other during the experiment. They were asked to read a page of information and provide a signature giving their consent. Those who were happy to proceed were then handed nasal sprays with the instruction to self-administer their contents. After a vigorous round of snorting, the computer screens flickered into action, and the men began a series of calibration tests.

Around forty minutes in the real experiment began. A Moral Choice Dilemma task popped up on the computer screens. The men were presented with five hypothetical high-stakes choices where there was no correct answer, but where their decisions would determine the fate of other people, such as the following:

1. A trolley is running toward six people who will be killed if nothing is done. Hitting a switch will divert the trolley, where it will kill only one person.

2. Six explorers are stuck in a cave. One caver is lodged in the exit, which is too tight for an adult to fit through. Hitting a button will blow a larger hole, allowing the rest of the cavers to escape, but it will kill the one who is stuck.

3. A ship sinks stranding six sailors at sea. They all swim to a lifeboat, but it can only accommodate five safely. Denying one access to the lifeboat will save five lives, but a sailor will drown.*

For each of the scenarios the scientists specified the characteristics of the person who dies to see whether the subjects were more likely to sacrifice a member of the ingroup or the outgroup. For the ingroup condition, the person who would die if the choice was made to save the other five had a typical Dutch name, such as Dirk or Peter. For the outgroup condition, the person who would die was given a typical Arab or German name, such as Mohammed or Helmut. The five people who would be saved by making the choice were nameless in both conditions. The seventy Dutch male test subjects were randomly allocated to take either the ingroup or the outgroup version of the task, meaning any variation in prejudice held by group members would not shape the overall results.

When it came to the results, the group of test subjects were split right down the middle. Half were less likely to sacrifice Dirk or Peter and more likely to kill Mohammed and Helmut, while the other half showed no bias towards either type of name. But why were the one half more likely to protect the ingroup over

* These are common scenarios used in the Moral Choice Dilemma task and are presented here as illustrations of the tasks given to the Dutch male test subjects.

the outgroup? Because of the random allocation it could not be because they held prejudices against Arabs or Germans.

Recall the nasal sprays self-administered before the experiment. Half of the group snorted the hormone oxytocin, the chemical released when we fall in love and by pregnant women, while the other half inhaled a placebo. Those that snorted the 'love drug' were significantly more likely to save a member of their own group and sacrifice the outsider. Professor De Dreu had found the first evidence that our naturally produced hormones can foster human ethnocentrism.[8]

The previous chapter showed how threat detection relies heavily on certain regions of the brain. There are also chemical processes that influence how these regions work, sometimes turning us into that oversensitive smoke detector. Oxytocin is widely assumed to increase trust and empathy and reduce aggression in groups.[9] But Professor De Dreu's experiment showed it is the 'love drug' only up to a point.

The darker side to the 'cuddle chemical' was exposed, and De Dreu thinks its Jekyll and Hyde nature came about through evolution.[10] In order to survive, humans need well-functioning groups whose members can be trusted to generate resources, and not to overuse these resources for personal gain. For groups to work in this way, humans have evolved an ability to judge who to trust and who not to trust. More trust within a group meant better cooperation, with the result that its members were more likely to survive, while those who were less well integrated died out.

The hormone oxytocin can play an active role in this preference for 'us', whatever the dividing lines may be between 'us' and 'them'. Snort oxytocin and within the hour we become more trusting and cooperative with our ingroup. But the love has a limit, and De Dreu showed we only share the cuddles with people like us, and not discernible outgroups. This is known as *ingroup favouritism*.[11]

Having shown evidence that oxytocin motivates humans to sacrifice 'them' if necessary to protect 'us', De Dreu and colleagues went one step further with the next experiment. They wanted to see if, in addition to oxytocin's ingroup favouritism effect, it also made the subjects more likely to actively harm 'them', known as *outgroup derogation*. This is an important distinction, because outgroup derogation can occur not only when a choice has to be made between 'us' and 'them', as in a Moral Choice Dilemma, but also when no such choice is needed, meaning it edges us closer to hate.

The experiment split a group of Dutch men into two, gave one group oxytocin and the other a placebo, and had them all take the Implicit Association Test (IAT). The advantage of the IAT over the Moral Choice Dilemma tasks is that it measures unconscious bias instead of relying on subjects telling the truth. For some of the subjects, the Dutch or Arab names in the Moral Choice Dilemma tasks may have alerted them to the true nature of the experiment – this is testing levels of prejudice – and since most of us are affected by social desirability bias, they may have consciously altered their choices to look less prejudiced. The IAT gets around this (see the section on measuring unconscious bias in Chapter 3). The results indicated the scientists were on the right track. The Dutch men given oxytocin were significantly more likely than those given the placebo to associate negative terms with Arabs, but not Germans or Dutch. This was a sign of outgroup derogation. But was this finding enough to say oxytocin increases prejudice and aggression towards an outgroup? Not quite.

In another experiment De Dreu and colleagues used an economic game based on the Prisoner's Dilemma, in which a subject must decide whether or not to cooperate with another 'prisoner', with no communication allowed between them. A higher reward is on offer if both cooperate, but if one betrays the other, that one receives a lesser reward and the other gets nothing at all – meaning fear of betrayal may override desire for the higher reward. De Dreu's version assigned participants to groups and set different levels of reward to manipulate subjects' fear that their ingroup would lose out. Those participants given oxytocin were far less likely to cooperate with the outgroup than those given a placebo, but the result was only significant when fear of the outgroup was manipulated to be high; desire for the reward alone did not have the same effect. The experiment therefore showed oxytocin stimulates humans to be defensive against the outgroup, but only when that group was perceived as a threat.[12] As De Dreu put it, oxytocin promotes 'tend and defend' actions.

In their most recent experiment, groups were pitted against each other in another economic game, with some group members being given oxytocin and some not. Those given the 'love drug' proved far more successful in coordinating their attacks on other teams. Their cooperation with the ingroup increased and their attacks were more precise, targeting other groups when they were at their weakest and posed least threat.[13] This is the first evidence that oxytocin plays a role in improving the efficiency of offensive aggression – attacking when threat from the outgroup is low.

The body of evidence on the role of oxytocin in intergroup relations is growing, but the early results show this hormone can promote aggression in humans in response to an outgroup. But in the absence of oxytocin nasal sprays, which you can't just buy from the local 7-Eleven or Co-Op, when is this hormone produced in humans? We know it is produced when we first meet a potential love interest. It is also why new mothers, and to a lesser extent new fathers, go 'gaga' over their own and other babies. There is evidence that it is produced during cultural rituals too, such as when New Zealand's All Blacks perform the Haka before a rugby match.[14] In all examples, when faced with a member of an outgroup who appears to threaten something we care about – a challenging suitor on the dancefloor, a man wearing a trench coat hanging around a playground, or a large Welshman dressed in red singing the Welsh national anthem 'Hen Wlad Fy Nhadau' – this oxytocin release can inspire aggression.

Oxytocin may have a role to play in hate, especially when the perpetrator is likely to have produced it (e.g. if they are a parent caring for a young child), and when they feel under threat from a discernible outgroup (e.g. a racial other).

Bijan as the threatening racial other

The claim that Bijan Ebrahimi was a paedophile is known to have been manufactured purely to demonise and further 'other' him, but it was this rumour that Lee James clung to as his motivation, and not his victim's race or physical impairment. In the face of James's statement and the court's decision to take him at his word, several charities supporting victims of hate crimes wrote to the attorney general to formally complain that the judge had turned a blind eye to the torrent of prejudice experienced by Bijan at the hands of some white residents on Capgrave Crescent.

These charities have a strong and serious point. Bijan was routinely subjected to racially motivated crimes over many years by his neighbours – the neighbours who started the unfounded rumour he was a paedophile, binding them and their hateful motivations to his killing. The court could only infer James's motivation from the available evidence on the nature of their encounters in the weeks and days before the murder of Bijan. None of the white witnesses from Capgrave Crescent were required to come forward to confirm whether James had used racist language while committing the act itself, or during his interactions with his victim in the days before. From a scientific standpoint, this lack of admissible evidence does not rule out the role of hate towards Bijan's race or physical impairment in the motivation.

If professors Michael Gilead and Nira Liberman from Tel Aviv University were asked to take a look at this case, they would consider whether James's caregiving role with his children interacted with Bijan's race to produce the fatal outcome. Their research has looked at the effect of the *caregiving motivational system* on bias against the outgroup. Compared to other species, humans spend an inordinate amount of time rearing and protecting their children. Human children remain vulnerable for many years and we have evolved a suitable caregiving system that helps to assist the survival of our group in the face of outgroup threats.

Professors Gilead and Liberman set out to test whether being a parent makes us more likely to express prejudice towards people not like 'us'. Nearly a thousand adults from Israel and the US were recruited for the study. Half of the participants were 'primed' with a caregiving stimulus by being tasked with either recalling in detail the first few days after giving birth to their child or looking at pictures of infants. The other half were tasked with either recalling what they had seen on TV in the last few days or looking at pictures of the countryside. Those that had their parental caregiving motivational system activated by the priming tasks were significantly more likely to express racist attitudes towards Arab Israelis and Arab Americans.[15]

To reduce any doubt that the process of caring for children makes us more prejudiced when faced with group threat, in another study the same scientists actually had subjects turn up to the lab with their babies. Sixty-six women accompanied by their children under the age of five, many of whom sat on their parents' laps while the experiment was conducted, were asked to read a news article on the influx of African immigrants and associated criminality (rape, murder, burglary – pretty threatening stuff). Another sixty-four women read the same article, but their children had been left at home. After studying the article for a few minutes, both groups of women were then asked to opine on government refugee policies, such as: 'The government should deport all African refugees,' and 'The government should allow in more African refugees each year.' Those with children on their laps were significantly more likely to agree with deporting refugees compared to those whose children were absent.

Parents, especially those with young children in their presence, can be made hypervigilant to threats from a member of the outgroup by the mechanisms of this evolved caregiving motivational system. It is therefore reasonable to at least hypothesise that James was influenced by such a mechanism when faced with Bijan recording him as his children played on the green that day. Bijan's mislabelling as a child predator may have been the first trigger for this mechanism, but the science above shows race may have been a second.

We must also ask ourselves what motivated the creation of the child predator rumour before James moved to the crescent. If Bijan had been white and not disabled, would the residents guilty of its creation have demonised him in the same way? If not, then its creation is intertwined with Bijan's identity as a disabled Iranian refugee. His race (and possibly his physical impairment) were perceived as threats by some, who manufactured the child predator rumour to make him appear a threat to everyone. But it remains to be explained why these aspects of Bijan's identity seemed so threatening to a minority of his neighbours.

Society, competition and threat

In 1954 psychologist Muzafer Sherif, masquerading as a camp supervisor, took a group of white American middle-class eleven-year-old boys to a summer camp in Oklahoma's Robbers Cave State Park. None of the boys knew each other before the trip, so the scientists had them take part in bonding exercises. The boys gathered wood, collected water and built rafts. During one of the tasks a few of the boys saw a rattlesnake and the group dubbed themselves the Rattlers. They made a flag for their newly named tribe and flew it over their camp. Within a short space of time the boys felt as if they owned the park at the foothills of the Sans Bois Mountains.

This feeling of security was about to be challenged. Unknown to the boys, a second group, the Eagles, had been placed there by Sherif as their direct competitors. This was to become famously known as the 'Robbers Cave Experiment'.[16] The experiment was designed to prove that prejudice and conflict arise between groups because of competition for limited resources, and not because of individual differences, like race, sexual orientation, or physical or mental impairment. Sherif's drive to prove his theory came from the violence he had witnessed during the Greek genocide of 1913–22, which saw the mass murder of almost three quarters of a million Greek civilians by the Turks under the Ottoman Empire. Unlike his contemporaries, he turned his back on the psychology labs and instead ran his experiment in the wild, literally.

In the first part of the study, the Rattlers and the Eagles, groups of equal size, were kept separate. Over a few days each group developed an identity, and the boys were showing signs of belonging to an ingroup. The second phase of the study set the stage for the germination of animosity between the groups.

First, they were made aware of each other's presence. They heard unfamiliar voices in the woods, but could not catch sight of the others. The boys initially assumed the other group might be of a different race – a sign of the times. The immediate reaction was to challenge them and scare them off. Shouts of racial slurs echoed through the forest. Once the two groups had seen each other and realised they were all white American boys, the imagined racial threat was replaced with whatever other minimal difference they could grasp – 'cheating' Eagles, 'sissy' Rattlers, the nature of the divide was irrelevant.

The scientists, in the personas of camp counsellors and care-takers, then pitted the Rattlers and the Eagles against each other in tasks where only one team could win the prize: candy, pen-knives, the kind of things eleven-year-old American boys val-ued in the 1950s. They competed in almost every game you can imagine playing at camp: tent pitching, beanbag tossing, baseball, tug-of-war. The scientists also assessed cabin tidiness, singing and improvisation, which they manipulated to increase the tension by unfairly awarding points to one group over the other. An early Rattlers' winning streak shook the Eagles, and on one night the chiefs declared war.

The Eagles lowered the Rattlers' flag, burnt it and re-hoisted the scorched rag. At this point the scientists stepped back from their manipulations and just watched as the two tribes fought it out. The Rattlers' revenge was to raid the opposing camp, which motivated Eagle talk of engaging in physical violence. Chaos descended and fighting broke out. The scientists intervened and closed down the camp for a period to ensure no one was hurt. Sherif had proved his point – two groups of decent all-American white boys can come to hate each other and engage in violence if forced to compete for what are perceived as scarce resources.

Although in Sherif's experiment competition between the Rattlers and the Eagles formed the primary threat, the groups naturally developed distinct cultural traits that also divided them. It was the Eagle way to swim naked and to avoid cursing, while the Rattlers were more modest but foul-mouthed. These traits were precious to each group, and any threat from either tribe to these customs invited retaliation. A Rattler skinny-dipping or an Eagle cursing became symbols of treachery and possible infiltration.

Different values and belief systems held by the ingroup and the outgroup have been the source of many conflicts throughout history. The moral dimension of hatred was covered in Chapter 2 – those embarking on such behaviour often see themselves as on a crusade to correct the beliefs of their targets, or to eradicate the source of those beliefs. A threat to our culture or ways of life can exist independently from threats to our resources, although they are often intertwined.

New Mexico State University's Walter and Cookie Stephan combined both types of threat, dubbed *realistic* and *symbolic* threats, into one concept they called Integrated Threat Theory (ITT).[17] In ITT both types of threat can work at the group and individual level: members of the ingroup can perceive that they as individuals, their group, or both are being threatened by some outgroup. When a threat is perceived as emanating from a member of the outgroup, say immigrants taking local jobs or buying up closed pubs and turning them into mosques, members of the ingroup can feel fear and anger as a result. But threats do not have to be real to have this effect. Simply the *perception* of threat, including the manufacturing of a sense of threat by nefarious politicians, can result in tensions between groups. All over the globe, ITT has been shown to predict negative attitudes towards other races, genders, nationalities, sexual orientations and even those with cancer and HIV.

Context and threat

Sherif's concept of competitive threat and the Stephans' concepts of realistic and symbolic threats all operate within context. With each of our misunderstood outsiders introduced at the beginning of this chapter – the out-of-towner, the market salesman and the hungover colleague – the wider context can worsen their fate. The feeling of being constantly under threat can be caused or worsened by political, economic, social and health conditions that increase our feeling of vulnerability. In times when political figures spread divisive rhetoric about 'dangerous' immigrants, our threat meter goes off the scale when met by the out-of-towner in a hoodie; in times of recession and scarce resources, our threat meter will misfire when we feel cheated by the privileged salesman; in a time of intolerance and misinformation about health risks, our threat meter will misregister the hungover work colleague as the harbinger of death.

People like Bijan are frequently labelled as economic threats in the context of a global recession. In the eyes of some of his white neighbours he was an Iranian refugee taking up scarce housing on an estate where many were dependent on state benefits. He was also disabled, meaning he may have been in receipt of additional benefits, and locals may have felt resentful about this. Perceived preferential treatment of refugees in times of austerity entrenches the notion that people like Bijan threaten the way of life for 'local people' (i.e. British-born white people). This was exacerbated by Bijan's preference to live close to his sisters, meaning he was placed in an estate with very few people from ethnic minority backgrounds.

Research shows hate crimes are as likely to happen in majority white areas, compared to more mixed areas, because the sense of economic threat becomes stark when the 'other' stranger moves in (see later in this chapter). Context therefore first made Bijan a 'double threat' to some on the crescent – an immigrant with a physical impairment taking up scarce resources. His malicious labelling as a child predator created the 'triple threat' which led to his murder.

My attackers perceived me as a threat in the context of a time of intolerance towards LGBTQ+ people. At the turn of the millennium Section 28 was still in force, meaning they had no formal exposure in school to positive perceptions of people like me. The ongoing HIV epidemic, claiming millions of lives globally in the 1990s, would have likely shaped their views. The absence of legislation criminalising LGBTQ+ hate crime would have also sent the signal that the state did not care enough to afford me additional protection.

Our perception of threat always operates within context, and the science shows that the harsher the context, the more threats we see and the more extreme they seem. A study of twelve European countries found that those which were suffering from economic downturns and which had large minority immigrant populations had a much higher level of racial prejudice than those with strong economies.[18] Economic downturns, hostile political environments, terror attacks and pandemics are just a few contexts that can hyperactivate the human threat detection mechanism (more on this in Chapter 7). When this hyperactivation occurs in the presence of an apparently threatening outgroup, prejudiced hostility can result.

To create the right context and set of divisions for the generation of threat, Sherif constructed his experiment carefully. He created two groups with strong identities. He made sure there was no contact between the groups beforehand. He limited resources, so there was only one prize to be won during competitions. In society there are no scientists to manipulate these conditions. There don't have to be, as the conditions arise naturally.

The Great Recession of 2007–9 and the decline of the UK's coal, steel and car manufacturing sectors over the past few decades impacted some towns and cities more than others. This economic downturn has been combined with a rise in inward migration, generating the conditions for local populations to perceive immigrants as posing realistic and symbolic threats. These perceived threats are exacerbated in areas where there is low employment amongst locals but high, although precarious and temporary, employment amongst migrants.

In the UK almost all of the places affected by a combination of deindustrialisation and immigration are north of London. Many have been selected by Conservative governments as asylum seeker dispersal areas and receive a disproportionate share of the load. Almost 60 per cent of asylum seekers are placed in the poorest towns, adding further strain on local resources in times of recession.[19] All the places in the UK that saw the largest proportional increase in foreign-born settlement between 2005 and 2015 also saw steady rises in racially and religiously motivated hate crime. The most staggering increase was in West Yorkshire, where hate crime rates per thousand of the population have reached the same level as in London, and significantly above the national average.

In West Yorkshire the rate of foreign-born settlement nearly doubled between 2005 and 2015. In 2016, 2,369 asylum seekers were living in the five Labour-run county councils that make up the area. This is compared to zero asylum seekers in the eight Conservative-run county council areas bordering North Yorkshire. Eastern Europeans also migrated to these areas, most of whom were young, low-skilled and unable to speak good English. An estimated two in five Polish migrants living in London have higher education qualifications, but among those migrating to the poorer parts of the UK only about one in four has the same qualification standard.[20] The language barrier results in a lack of interaction between the local and migrant populations which puts up other barriers. These barriers foster the perception of threat, as without shared language there can be little common understanding. Where local and migrant workers do interact on a daily basis and are enabled by a shared language, for example in London, we see a reduction in the perception of threat and greater levels of acceptance and tolerance.

In 2016, in response to the question, 'To what extent do you agree or disagree that your local area is a place where people from different ethnic backgrounds get on well together?' only 53 per cent of residents agreed in Kirklees, West Yorkshire's second most ethnically diverse local council, where 21 per cent identify as non-white and 10 per cent foreign-born.* In one ward, Dewsbury East, agreement dropped to 41 per cent. This compares to the national average of 85 per cent agreement, and 89 per cent agreement in Camden, London, where 34 per cent identify as non-white and 40 per cent foreign-born. These results are symptomatic of poor integration that is due to failings on both sides – minority and white populations keep themselves to themselves and resist attempts at integration imposed upon them by local councils and national governments.

---

* Kirklees CLiK 2016 survey: Strongly agree: 14 per cent; Tend to agree: 39 per cent; Neither agree or disagree: 34 per cent; Tend to disagree: 9 per cent; Strongly disagree: 3 per cent. 2011 UK Census: Non-white includes Mixed/multiple ethnic groups, Asian/Asian British, Black, African/Caribbean/Black British and Other ethnic group. Foreign-born excludes Republic of Ireland.

The town of Dewsbury in Kirklees has been labelled by the national media as one of Britain's 'failed spaces' of multiculturalism, assisted by a string of racially charged events and related local news coverage. On one side, far-right organisations have capitalised on poor race relations in the town. The British National Party (BNP) were implicated in a race riot in 1989 over a dispute concerning white children being sent to a majority Asian primary school, and an English Defence League (EDL) rally in 2013 motivated a failed extreme Islamist bombing of the event. In 2016 the MP Jo Cox was murdered by a right-wing extremist in the neighbouring village of Birstall. On the other side, Dewsbury has become known for being the home town of one of the perpetrators of the London bombings on 7 July 2005, and of the youngest suicide bomber from the UK, who travelled to Syria in 2015.

These are signals not only of failed integration, but also of mutual distrust and group isolation that has gone so far as to create a toxic feeling of 'us' versus 'them'. Taking Dewsbury as an example, the greater the sense of 'them' as a threat, the more extreme the public discourse becomes. At the most extreme, local whites may say local Muslims are to blame for terrorism and paedophile gangs, while local Muslims might say local whites are to blame for rising hate crime and the demise of traditional values. When the discourse is so polarised and widely adopted, political groups like the EDL, the BNP, the United Kingdom Independence Party (UKIP) and the Brexit Party can capitalise on the ill-feeling and propose extreme policies, such as banning the burka and deporting foreign-born residents, with little resistance from locals – things that would not be accepted where discourse is less antagonistic. The aim of the far right has been to create the conditions, or capitalise on those that already exist, to allow them to shift public opinion further to the right. On the other side, knowledge of the local broad acceptance of extreme policies that threaten Muslims' way of life creates opportunities for proponents of radical ideology to step in and convert normally peaceful members of the community into potential terrorists (more on this in Chapter 8).

Threat in their own words

While writing this book I had the opportunity to work on a documentary on the rise of hate crime for the BBC. I was tasked by the production team to analyse the statistics. The other members of the team travelled up and down the country speaking to victims, perpetrators and recruits to nationalist movements. In a town in West Yorkshire, not far from Dewsbury, a young man was willing to talk to the team about his understanding of the 'problem' facing the country. Much of what he said chimes with the types of threat conceptualised by Sherif and other psychologists. When asked why he thought a lot of the race hate victims in West Yorkshire were Eastern Europeans, James (not his real name) said:

Because people are losing their jobs . . . there's huge competition for jobs, there is rising poverty, there is rising unemployment. You've got whole estates now where people have lost their industries, they've lost the things that they, that made their areas great, they've lost their ways of life . . . And then they see the last few jobs disappearing and going and being given away and unfortunately some of those people direct their anger in a very misguided way.

In response to being asked to reflect on the argument that immigration creates economic growth, James said:

These people [politicians] will continue to flood Britain with immigrants as much as they can because it is part of their plan and they will claim it grows the economy, they will claim it brings wealth here, but it doesn't. It might grow the economy in size, but it makes the average person on the street worse off, worse off in terms of hospital waiting lists, worse off in terms of GP waiting lists, worse in terms of class sizes for their children, worse in terms of space, in terms of congestion, it takes them longer to get to work in the morning.

For James, hate crimes against Eastern Europeans can be explained by perceived realistic threat: threats to jobs, the health service and education. As Integrated Threat Theory suggests, these realistic threats are also related to symbolic threats, the loss of the identity of places where industry was a cornerstone of their character. The 'greatness' of these places is somehow felt to be threatened and diminished by immigrants. James went on at length, fleshing out his ideas:

You walk through areas of Bradford and you see people in burkas, you see all the different shops that these people have brought in, you see these giant mosques with thousands of people flooding into them on a Friday. That isn't Britain, that isn't Europe. Now I'm not saying these people shouldn't exist, there is a place for these people in the world, but that place is not here in Britain . . . Everyone else who has come here, these immigrants, are all allowed to celebrate their culture, their way of life, they're allowed to embrace their heritage, whereas if you're white English you can be accused of being racist simply for wanting to fly the St George's Cross or celebrate St George's Day.

'Burkas', 'different shops' and 'giant mosques' with brown people flooding into them are symbols that threaten James's vision of how Britain and Europe should be. Much of his interview was repetitive and it reads like he was careful not to go off script. He admitted to preparing, which is not surprising as he expected to be on national television (his interview was never aired), and may explain why he was at pains to deny he was a racist.

> When you use terms like racist . . . those terms aren't really going to have an effect on me, I don't really acknowledge that word . . . because it's an ideological word used to silence people who have a legitimate point of view, it has no intellectual weight to it, it's a silencing tactic . . . I want to make this very, very clear, I don't hate anyone because of their culture, their colour or their ethnicity, I just don't believe that every culture, colour and ethnicity has the right to live in Britain or in Europe.

His denial gave those in the room the sense that James was more of a *white* nationalist than the nationalist he portrayed himself to be.

Regardless of James's politics, he is not alone in expressing concerns about the economic downturn, the loss of 'Britishness' and the rate of immigration of foreign-born nationals. The difference is the majority do not combine them in the way that James does. The economic downturn and perceived change in culture are only exclusively related to immigration for those who are hypersensitive to threats of this nature.

Not all areas of the UK with large increases in foreign-born migration and a significant number of hate crimes share the same industrial past as West Yorkshire. The economic pains of deindustrialisation and the challenges to working-class British identity therefore play less of a part in explaining crimes targeting minority groups in these areas. Compared to West Yorkshire, Essex has a near polar opposite demographic character. It is a Conservative heartland with the UK's second most prosperous economy (after London). It has strong agricultural, electronics, pharmaceutical and finance sectors, high employment and wages above the regional and national average. It is 91 per cent white (the UK average is 87 per cent) and the whole county has received only sixty asylum seekers at the time of writing. The population of the city of Chelmsford, county town of Essex, is only 6 per cent black and minority ethnic and 7 per cent foreign-born. It housed only one asylum seeker up to 2016. The town of Maldon is even whiter – the population is 2 per cent black and minority ethnic, 3 per cent foreign-born and there are zero asylum seekers. However, it has seen its immigration rate more than double between 2005 and 2015, despite the overall number of migrants remaining small. Maldon voted 63:37 to leave the EU, in line with the whole county (not one of the fourteen councils that make up Essex voted to remain). Castle Point and Thurrock voted 73:27 and 72:28 respectively, the third and fourth highest leave-voting areas in the whole of the UK. These councils are located at the very south point of Essex, which houses the majority of the small number of asylum seekers in the county. In the wake of the Brexit vote Essex saw a 58 per cent rise in race and religious hate crime, one of the highest in the country.

Dr Alita Nandi and colleagues at the University of Essex have shown that minorities living in very high majority white areas are significantly more likely to report experiencing racial harassment. This risk decreases in more multicultural areas where there is low support for far-right groups, such as in some areas of London, but increases in multicultural areas that have high support for these groups, such as West Yorkshire.[21] Taken together, the evidence from more multicultural poorer places and more monocultural richer places suggests something similar is happening in both to trigger hate crimes. In both contexts, the majority group feel a need to defend their communities from outsider threat.

The producers of the BBC documentary I was involved with also interviewed three self-confessed hate criminals from a coastal town in the south-east. Like James, two of these men, Doug and Phil (not their real names), reference both realistic and symbolic threats as their motivation for committing hate crimes against immigrants.

Doug: You feel sort of segregated in your own, in your own town, in your own place, you know? . . . It's a feeling of being pushed out of somewhere which was a nice area where you used to feel safe growing up and now it, you, you, you don't feel safe.

Interviewer: So you feel that actually you didn't have a problem until you felt there was a threat?

Doug: No, didn't, didn't have a problem with them at all, you know, when they first started coming over here it was like the odd one here and there, weren't a problem, and then all of a sudden we ended up being, like now as English people we are a minority where we live, you know, and that ain't right.

Interviewer: And have you ever taken the law into your own hands?

Phil: Yeah, I have, yeah, of course we have.

Interviewer: How have you done?

Phil: Smashing the shit out of them.

Interviewer: Smashing the shit out of them?

Phil: Yeah, fucking right, what else can you do, you know what I mean, that's only, that's the only defence we've got, do you know what I mean.

Doug: I mean from like my point of view is at the end of the day they're only coming here for one thing and that's just to take our benefits, take our housing . . . It's a free ride, you know, we used to be Great Britain, now we're just Britain, ain't nothing great about us, you know . . .

Interviewer: But you're not racist?

Phil: No, no, no, no, no, listen, hear me out, I've got, I've got Muslim friends, I've got coloured friends and all this, yeah. I am racist towards the immigrants, yeah, the immigrants, yeah. For the simple fact is what they're doing to our country, yeah, they're coming over and they're just taking us for a free ride, they're taking the absolute piss [out] of it. How can you not be racist when something like that, do you know what I mean, like, and that's, and that's, like I'm not being funny.

Doug: They've made us, they've made us racist in that way, like I say not racist towards like, say, um like black people or people that wanna like sort of follow some, like whatever religion they wanna follow, that's down to them. But when it comes to people who's like basically getting on a boat, jumping off, coming over here, taking the piss, yeah, that makes you racist in that way because you're like, you think they're scumbags.

Phil: Well, do you know what I mean, a lot of people ain't having it, people have had enough of it, do you know what I mean. It is gonna get to the point where everybody's just gonna come together, it's gonna cause, it's gonna basically cause well like not racial war, but. And do you know what, yeah, do you know what, I know it might sound stupid, yeah, but I can't wait for that day, do you know that?

Doug: So yeah, yeah, that's, that is how we sort of used to deal with things and it, it is violence, that's, that's the action is violence basically, you know, to get them to understand that they're not welcome, we don't want them here, we've had enough.

The rationalisation used by young offenders, of defending their turf from 'alien' outsiders, is repeatedly referenced by other perpetrators across the globe. The notion of defended communities, first developed in 1972 in the US, helps explain this kind of racialised territorial behaviour.[22] Fears that invasion by outsiders will threaten community identity motivate defensive actions, which can manifest in hate crimes against the minority group. The theory has attracted empirical support in New York and Chicago.[23] But unlike the run-down estates in West Yorkshire, the parts of New York and Chicago studied to test the theory were affluent and majority white, much like many parts of south-east England.

The results from the statistical analysis lent further support to the idea that hate crimes are more likely to be perpetrated when an outgroup is seen as posing a threat, even under conditions of relative affluence. Unlike general crime, which flourishes in areas that are socially disorganised and run-down, the evidence from the US shows that hate crimes, especially those against ethnic minorities and immigrants, also seem to erupt in locations that are socially organised and affluent. The perpetrators in these areas fear that contamination by outsiders will change their way of life for the worse – those people will devalue their expensive homes, pass on subversive ideas to their kids at school, date their daughters.

There are some strong commonalities between white lower-class and white middle-class perceptions of threats posed by the racial or national 'other'. Surveys show that irrespective of social class or location of household, white people generally hold misconceptions about Islam.[24] There is also evidence to suggest that in respect to immigration, those on higher wages, with better qualifications and in professional and managerial occupations are as negative towards immigration as those on low wages, with few qualifications and in service and manual labour occupations. For this more affluent group it is more about symbolic threats (to values) than realistic threats (to economic self-interest).[25]

Perception of threat from the outgroup and the hate crime that can stem from that perception are not confined to areas with large minority populations, struggling economies and extreme politics. The very opposite demographic and economic political contexts – small minority populations, strong economies and moderate politics – can generate the same sense of threat from the presence of a small outgroup. In the former industrial towns of the North of England, minorities are a scapegoat that can be easily punished for all that is wrong and bad with the place. In the richer South, they are told stories of what has happened elsewhere and become fearful that the same fate may befall their place if they don't defend what is 'rightly their own'. It is this telling of stories that can infect others with negative stereotypes of the outgroup and create a sense of threat where there really is none.

The culture machine, group threat and stereotypes

In prehistoric times, the information that our threat detection mechanism learned from was unmediated – we saw first-hand who killed our kin and stole our food. Since the birth of oral story-telling this information has been adulterated, to the point where in modern times it has been weaponised to manufacture threats and fear in the masses. This mis/disinformation is what feeds our stereotypes of outgroups.

Stereotypes are the pictures we hold in our heads of people from other groups. These pictures tell us something about these groups – their culture, temperament, level of threat – before we even interact with them. They are efficient because they draw on categories instead of all possible information out there about other cultures or groups. They are also comforting, as they set out the world and the groups of people in it as predictable. But more often than not, these stereotypes are an exaggerated and distorted view of reality.

The residents of Capgrave Crescent held stereotypical views of Bijan, the disabled Iranian refugee, that placed him in direct opposition to their version of 'white English' heritage. They didn't take the time to find out who he really was personally, or if they shared any similar values, hopes or tribulations. If they had, they would have found much in common, and the negative stereotyping that divided them would have come crashing down. Instead they fed the stereotype of the alien invader, the benefit scrounger, the child predator.

What was responsible for the stereotyping of Bijan that turned him into a threat in the eyes of his white neighbours? In part, it was their own version of their 'white English' culture. Broadly, culture refers to our ideas, values, history, religion, language, traditions and social behaviour. It is transmitted to us at an early age through our parents and other relatives, our friends, the education system, religion and the media, including print, online and broadcast mediums. A country can be host to multiple cultures, but reference will be made to a dominant culture that encapsulates the way of life of a majority. The UK is made up of the indigenous population (including second+ generation immigrants) and people migrating there from all over the world, each subscribing to their own cultural heritage, but also to the broader values of the place they call home. There are also subcultures bound to place and identity that adapt the dominant culture to the values of that community. People can subscribe to some parts of the dominant culture, while deviating from others where they have a more community-specific understanding. This can lead to situations where the dominant culture may reject prejudice, but some of these subcultures may endorse it. When these subcultures limit contact outside of their group, prejudice can persist and flourish.[26]

Stereotypes of others and their culture or group are always compared to our own, and where deviations occur we make snap judgements, either positive or negative – I envy the work–life balance of their culture; I respect the focus on family in their culture; I am disgusted by the food hygiene and the treatment of animals in their culture; I am appalled at the treatment of women in their culture. The information we draw on to make these judgements rarely comes from the other culture or group, via their people or institutions. It usually comes from our own culture machine, which is made up of the dominant group and its institutions, and so presents a warped and often ill-informed view of others.

Sometimes this is purposeful, especially in the midst of a culture war. During the Cold War, US and Soviet cultural institutions pumped out propaganda about the opposing side. After the Second World War, the CIA invested heavily in European international television infrastructure (called Eurovision, not to be confused with the song contest) and encouraged the sale of US shows to western Europe, to spread the ideals of American culture, and hence diminish communist influence. The goal of this culture war was for one group and way of life to dominate over the other. For the US, achieving this goal required getting non-Americans (i.e. Europeans) on side. The US could not rely on patriotism, so communism was communicated as a threat to all cultures.

More recently, politicians have spread disinformation about other groups to foster negative stereotypes in an effort to create a sense of threat and garner support for their campaigns. During the 2016 US presidential election campaign, Donald Trump promoted stereotypes and created threats out of Muslims and Mexicans; during the 2016 EU referendum campaign, Nigel Farage and others promoted stereotypes and created threats out of immigrants; and during the 2018 Brazilian general election, Jair Bolsonaro promoted stereotypes and created threats out of the indigenous population and LGBTQ+ people.

Most often the misrepresentation of other cultures is a result of a lack of information, misunderstanding and/or an unwillingness to get the detail and a balanced view. Parents, friends and teachers, either wittingly or not, can implant negative stereotypes in children as young as five. Children who are not much older can begin to associate a sense of threat and negative feelings with these stereotypes, including fear, aversion, contempt and disgust. It is no surprise that in divided societies such as Northern Ireland, children as young as three were able to indicate their allegiance to one religion over another, and at age six expressed fear, aversion and a sense of threat towards either Protestants or Catholics. Most of this stereotyping was done at a distance, with less than 4 per cent attending mixed schools, and very few ever socialising after school with those of a different religion.[27]

The most influential cultural feed that shapes stereotypes and the threats they conjure up is the media. Depictions of minority cultures in TV, radio, popular music and the news can get inside our heads just as much as the views of our parents, friends and teachers. This is partly because these mediums are designed to be entertaining, and they use every trick in the book to grab our attention and keep it for as long as possible. Most of us would prefer to watch TV or listen to our favourite band than chat to our parents or a teacher. But like our parents and teachers, the media can also misinform.

Thinking back, many of you will remember shows like *The Dick Tracy Show*, *Tom and Jerry*, *Hong Kong Phooey*, *The Lone Ranger*, *Jonny Quest* and *Looney Tunes*. All had their part to play in misrepresenting other cultures. Many are now off air, but if made available via streaming services they tend to come with warnings about their content. Yes, they were of their time, but they demonstrate how our understanding of those different from ourselves was shaped by these rather innocent shows.

Perhaps more shocking were the British comedies of the 1960s and 1970s that marshalled racial threat as a device for laughs. Many British readers will recall Alf Garnett from BBC1's *Till Death Us Do Part* (1965–75), who became the bigot's hero through his routinely spouted racist slurs and whining about his fears of 'contamination' from black people. The show ran for a decade and spawned many spinoffs featuring Alf until 1998. They may also remember Spike Milligan's BBC comedy series *Q . . .* (1969–82) that saw him frequently use blackface and depict Pakistanis as Daleks exterminating household pets to put into curry. He went on to make ITV's *Curry and Chips*, blacking up as a Pakistani-Irish immigrant that won him the nickname 'Paki-Paddy'. ITV's appetite for racist comedies culminated in *Love Thy Neighbour* (1972–6), which depicted the threat of a West Indian family encroaching on a white English couple's turf. The creators of the show found it humorous to have the white protagonist label their invaders as unintelligent, cannibalistic and sexually deviant.

The writers of these shows claim their creative efforts were satire that poked fun at white male middle England, but it appears that was lost on the majority of viewers. In a BBC-sponsored poll of 563 children and 317 parents in 1974, the majority agreed with the sentiments expressed by the racist characters that they were supposed to disagree with and pity.[28] The white racist men who were supposed to be the butt of the joke were in the end relatable. Their anxieties, attitudes and behaviours towards the other-race characters connected with audiences, both adults and children. Their views were being reflected back at them on mainstream TV, and in turn reinforced them. The BBC buried the report, fearful it undermined the claim that their comedies satirised racism and proved instead that they actually bolstered illiberal attitudes.

Much of this misrepresentation stems from the continuing systemic bias in the production of media outputs and the lack of minority groups in non-stereotypical roles. The US is the world's biggest media producer. Around 40 per cent of the US population is made up of minority racial groups. In 2018–19 people of colour made up around 28 per cent of lead roles in top theatrically released films, compared to 11 per cent around a decade earlier. Around 30 per cent of Hollywood films released in 2018–19 included a cast that was close to or over-representative of the minority US population at the time. Just under a decade earlier this figure was an astonishing 10 per cent. In 2019 white actors still got the lion's share of film roles in Hollywood (67 per cent), with black (16 per cent), Latinx (5 per cent) and Asian (5 per cent) actors significantly under-represented. Broadcast TV in 2018–19 looked better, with just over 50 per cent of shows (up from around 10 per cent around a decade earlier) including a cast that was close to or over-representative, and black, Latinx and Asian actors making up around 40 per cent of actors.[29]

Not all the media's output is guilty of perpetuating negative stereotypes of the other as a threat. Some shows actively work against it by presenting minority characters in a positive light. The embrace between *Star Trek's* Captain Kirk and Lieutenant Uhura in 1968, fabled for being the first interracial kiss broadcast on TV (although earlier interracial TV kisses have since been found), caused a stir at the time. Soon more TV shows also boldly went where few had gone before: *Julia, What's Happening, 227, The Cosby Show, The Oprah Winfrey Show, The Fresh Prince of Bel-Air, Noah's Arc, Black-ish, Tales of the City, The Ellen DeGeneres Show, Queer Eye, Will & Grace, Queer as Folk, The L Word, Looking, Glee, Pose, Transparent, I Am Cait, Speechless, Atypical, Special.* These and many other TV shows, pioneering films and news programmes have made great strides to show a more balanced and less threatening view (although never perfect) of society's minority groups.

Anecdotally we know that what is watched, read and listened to day in, day out, can shape how audiences think. Many of us have had that conversation over the holiday period with the grumpy older relative. They spout some ill-informed prejudiced comment and when challenged on it the source is revealed as something they read or saw on TV. We roll our eyes and lament the all-powerful culture machine within our liberal bubble of friends and acquaintances. Advertising and marketing companies rely on it to sell products, politicians spend millions on it to garner votes, and governments depend on it to spread messages of safety in times of crisis. But can the science explain the media's power to influence?

Psychologists have shown that watching comedy which utilises prejudice as a device to get laughs can change behaviour for the worse. In one study, researchers found male test subjects were more reluctant to give a charitable donation and more willing to cut funding to a women's organisation after reading and hearing sexist jokes, but not neutral jokes.[30] In other studies, listening to sexist, anti-Muslim and anti-gay jokes increased acceptance of discrimination against women, Muslims and gay people.[31] The conclusion the psychologists came to was not that the comedy made the test subjects prejudiced, rather that the humour temporarily released them from having to regulate the prejudiced attitudes they already held, which they routinely suppressed due to wider societal pressure to appear non-prejudiced. Sexist, racist and homophobic jokes are a 'releaser' of prejudice that shapes behaviour.

In the same way that the culture machine can divide, it can also bring people from different backgrounds closer, even if they never meet. Popular shows that break down negative stereotypes have increased acceptance and reduced prejudice amongst audiences.[32] The research shows the average viewer can connect with fictional 'minority' characters, especially where they experience prejudice, fostering perspective taking and empathy.[33] This process goes on to shape attitudes and behaviour in the wider world, sometimes to the point where we see real change. Experimental work in Germany lends support to the idea that watching western TV shows depicting the successful integration of different cultures, as opposed to Soviet-influenced TV which tended to feature little content on other cultures, generated tolerance and reduced hate crimes against immigrants.[34] On the progress of popular support for gay marriage in the US, Vice President Joe Biden said in 2012, 'I think *Will & Grace* probably did more to educate the American public than almost anything anybody's ever done so far. And I think people fear that which is different. Now they're beginning to understand.'[35]

Despite the apparent power of the culture machine to make and unmake negative stereotypes and their associated threats, there are few scientists who would agree that we are all the dupes of those who control the message. Most young children excluded, we can resist what we are told in the newspapers and on TV. As active consumers of the media, we pick and choose. Those who invite knowledge and have an egalitarian view of the world can question the negative stereotypes beamed into their homes and embrace the positive in the hope they will help lead to a more fair and just society. Equally, those who reject knowledge, and who view the world as a ruthlessly competitive jungle in which the strong win and the weak lose, can reject the portrayal of positive stereotypes and use the negative to bolster their preference for unequal relationships. Of course, there is always a middle group of the undecided and swayable, those who tick 'don't know' on the survey, who are happy to be told what to think, maybe because they are time-poor, disengaged or ill-equipped to enlighten themselves.

Neutralising the *perception* of threat

There was a third phase of Sherif's Robbers Cave experiment. After successfully dialling up competition and sense of threat between the two groups of boys to the point where violence would have been inevitable, the scientists introduced one final manipulation. Sherif's main objective of the study was to see if a common challenge could inspire a kind of inter-group cooperation that would undo all of the threat and hatred generated over the previous weeks. The first *superordinate goal* – a term used by psychologists to describe tasks that can only be achieved by the cooperation of two or more people – was to restore the water supply to the camps, which had been shut off by the scientists. At first the Rattlers and the Eagles went about solving the problem separately. They traced the water supply up the mountain to a tank, near which the scientists had hidden the missing valve under a rock slide. Each group took it in turn to move the rocks, still reluctant to interact. As the heat of the day took its toll the walls built up over the previous two weeks began to fall. The boys worked out that they could clear the rocks quicker if they formed a single team and passed them down a chain.

That evening over dinner signs of an end to the antagonism were evident. The resounding success of the first communal task was a surprise to the scientists, and they quietly planned a second. The boys were told it would be possible to rent the movie *Treasure Island* for a viewing that night, but there was a lack of funds in the central kitty. Each group was asked to contribute a small amount. At first there was resistance: 'Make them pay,' said some boys. Then an Eagle suggested each individual should give an equal share, and all of them voted as one group in favour of the proposal. The researchers saw this as a further step towards peace.

A storm presented itself as an opportunity for a third superordinate goal. Members of both groups were camping by the lake and only had time to erect one tent before the rain hit. Rattlers and Eagles bedded down for the night together, under the thunder and lightning – great cover to save face. Finally, the scientists planned a trip to the next state, with the boys being told each group would travel in its own bus. All the boys were excited at the news, but then the challenge presented itself. One of the vehicles was out of commission – the trip was off. 'We can all go in the one truck,' cried one of the boys. There was little dissent from the others and off they went. The final scenes of the experiment have the boys drinking soda together, having their picture taken at the state line and singing Rodgers and Hammerstein's 'Oklahoma' on the trip home.

In an earlier study, a kind of pilot for the famed Robbers Cave experiment, two groups of boys, the Pythons and the Panthers, had actually refused to go to war, despite Sherif's team going to extreme lengths to manipulate the situation: they stole, ripped down flags, pulled down tents and damaged property, placing the blame on either the Pythons or the Panthers. But none of the boys would bite, finding non-contentious reasons to explain some of the happenings, and then blaming the scientists for the more extreme wrongs – they had been rumbled.

The key difference between the two experiments was that in the first the Pythons and the Panthers had got to know each other before they were put into direct competition. This was carefully avoided by Sherif in the second study, and the Rattlers and the Eagles were complete strangers to each other at the point of first contact in the camp. Although Sherif saw the first experiment as a failure, and did not report its findings at the time, the harmony between the Pythons and the Panthers tells us something. Positive contact between groups actually diminishes the feeling of 'us' versus 'them'. Even in the face of strong competitive threat, tension and hate is much less likely to result if both groups personally know each other. Under these conditions negative stereotypes will be less likely to stick, regardless of the efforts of others to manufacture them (more about this in the final chapter).

Beyond threat

Humans have one of the most highly developed threat detection mechanisms of all species. What ensured our domination over our once hostile planet is now being deployed to detect threats in an environment that is the safest in our history. Most of us sitting in our secure and air-conditioned or heated homes never have to contend with freezing or overheating to death, or being eaten alive by animal predators. These were the arduous challenges faced by our ancestors, who relied heavily on their overly sensitive smoke detector-like threat mechanisms. This system has not caught up with the modern environment. Our out-of-date biology and psychology register threats where often there are none.

The perception of threat is a foundational part of prejudice and hate. Yet not everyone who perceives a threat from an outgroup – even if they are full of oxytocin, in the middle of a recession, and obsessed with watching reruns of 1970s British racist comedies – takes to the streets to commit a hate crime. Sherif is famed for showing us that hate and the aggression that can stem from it is inherently a group phenomenon. Threats to groups motivate a reaction, more than threats to individuals (unless the attack on the individual is perceived as an attack on the group). What Sherif did not stress in his study was that some members of the Rattlers and the Eagles had shorter fuses than others.

Some of these rose to become gang chiefs. They led their tribes into battle and quashed any dissent from within. Some boys left the camp, uneasy with the way things were unfolding – maybe not convinced that the threats from the opposing tribe were worth getting all worked up over. There were also residents on Capgrave Crescent who did not play a part in demonising or victimising Bijan, despite being part of the ingroup. And not every heterosexual man that passed me outside that gay bar in the late 1990s felt the need to physically harm me. Not everyone feels threatened by an outgroup, and not everyone who does commits a hate crime. But those who do commit hate crimes routinely identify the perceived threat posed by their target's group as their motivation.

The first part of this book has outlined the foundations upon which we all build to navigate the social world – the biological and psychological parts that we all have in common, and the widespread exposure to culture that we all learn from as part of our early socialisation. In isolation, these core ingredients are unlikely to result in behaviours that we would associate with hate, but they are necessary for it to germinate. In Part Two we take a forensic look at the science on the *accelerants* that edge us closer to the worst of human behaviour. It begins with an exploration of the individual histories of those guilty of hateful actions by examining how their traumas and deeply personal losses experienced in childhood are linked to their hateful violent ways later in life.

PART TWO

6

Trauma, Containment and Hate

In mid-August of 1980, Joseph Paul Franklin set off from the small town of Johnstown, Pennsylvania and drove two thousand miles along interstate 80 in his maroon Camaro, stopping at a motel in Salt Lake City, Utah. To the surprise of the motel receptionist, Franklin demanded a room that had not previously been slept in by a black person. Spotting Franklin's racist tattoos, the receptionist thought better of questioning why and handed over the keys. Some time after his check-in Franklin drove around the city to get his bearings. On his way back to the motel he pulled up to the kerb to procure the services of a sex worker. On the drive back, Franklin engaged her in casual chitchat before segueing into an intense conversation on racial integration, calling black people 'dumb apes'. He then asked if she knew where 'black pimps' hung out, and if there were establishments known to be frequented by interracial couples in Salt Lake City. They got to the motel and spent their time together. Before she left he told her he was a 'hit man for the KKK' and that he would kill her pimp if she wanted. She didn't accept his offer.

Over a few days hopping from motel to motel using various fake identities, Franklin gathered information about the city and learned that the residential area around Liberty Park was racially mixed. On 20 August, he scouted the park and talked to another sex worker about her views on African Americans before returning to the motel. Around 9 p.m. the same day he set off in his

Camaro back to Liberty Park. He drove fast and made mistakes on his journey, having to make a U-turn and running a red light before leaving his car in a vacant lot at an intersection. From there he made his way into the park with a rifle. He settled on a spot among some reeds and made his sniper's nest.

The same evening, Ted Fields and his friend David Martin had decided to go for a jog. They headed out and on the way picked up Karma Ingersoll and Terry Elrod. The four, two young black men and two white girls, decided on a route in Liberty Park that Ted and Karma had navigated the day before. Around 10 p.m. Ted was leading the run, with Karma, Terry and David trailing behind. Under the cover of tall reeds, Franklin spotted the inter-racial group. In his kneeling position he carefully positioned his rifle and took aim.

David was hit first, taking a bullet to his right arm. Less than a second later Terry's arm was struck by shrapnel. Ted stopped and turned to see his friends cradling their wounds, blood pouring onto the grass. Then a second bullet hit David, this time ripping through his chest and exiting his back. As he turned away from the direction of the shots a third bullet hit him from behind. His body went limp and he crashed to the ground. Ted darted over and cradled David's blood-soaked body.

'Oh, my God, Ted, they've got me,' whimpered David.

In panic the girls tried to drag David's body onto the side-walk before being told to run by Ted. After getting to a safe distance, Karma looked back and saw Ted struggling to move David's body out of the sniper's sight. Then Ted hit the ground. Franklin had fired off two more shots, one hitting Ted's heart and the other his lung.

Satisfied his victims were dead, Franklin ran back to his car, threw the rifle in the trunk and drove out of the city. After it was clear the shooting had stopped, two witnesses rushed over to David and Ted to give first aid. By the time the ambulance arrived Ted was dead. David died hours later in hospital.

The women Franklin had met in the days before heard the shots ring out over the city, and when they learned the victims were black, they immediately suspected him as the culprit. They never reported their suspicions to the police, fearful they would be arrested for prostitution. It took a month for the police to locate and arrest Franklin.

The racist sniper murders in Liberty Park, Salt Lake City, were not Franklin's first. In the late 1970s he had embarked on his mission to kill the 'enemies of the white race', and he often selected interracial couples as targets. His aim was to maintain the 'purity' of the white race, and this meant sending a message to both black and white people. He also targeted Jews and admitted to the attempted murder of the pornography magnate Larry Flynt (leaving him partially paralysed) for his inclusion of interracial couples in *Hustler* magazine.

Franklin eventually admitted to claiming over twenty lives in his mission to start a race war. His murderous rampage took him from Tennessee to Wisconsin, Missouri to Georgia, Oklahoma to Indiana, Ohio to Pennsylvania and Virginia. While on death row, Franklin tried to explain his acts to those who would listen. He renounced his racist views and blamed his traumatic upbringing, and in particular his authoritarian mother, for warping his opinion of black people. Franklin was executed for his crimes on 20 November 2013.

Evolution shaped how our brains work to influence our behaviour. Human behaviour is also shaped by events much closer to home, so close in fact that we can remember them – our own individual pasts. Our personal histories of conflict, anxiety, loss and trauma shape how we interact with others.

Past experiences that stay with us, like rings in a tree trunk, can act as the primary drivers of our behaviour, overriding basic impulse. We do not all respond to that stranger in the dark alley in the same way, despite many factors remaining equal, such as how our brains work. Humans bring with them 'baggage' from their upbringing and later life, meaning each response to an event is painted in a unique individual colour palette. We cannot begin to fully understand behaviour until we acknowledge these deeply personal, and sometimes traumatic, pasts.

This psychosocial criminological approach to behaviour can be especially useful in understanding crimes caused in part by the senses of grievance and frustration, such as terrorism and hate crime.[1] 'Instrumental' crimes, such as burglary and theft, can often be understood as a product of wider social and economic forces. Economic downturns, cuts to state benefits, widespread unemployment, increases in school expulsions, income inequality and poor rental housing stock can all combine to explain much of the variance (the total amount that can be explained in a statistical model) in the propensity of someone to burgle a home or shoplift.*[2] Their commission is often rational – 'I have no money, it's easier to get it illegitimately than legitimately, and the chances of getting caught are low.' But these 'big issue' drivers do not explain so much of the variance in hate crimes. Most hate crimes seem irrational to us because they are often driven by the unresolved frustrations of offenders that are rarely revealed. To unearth them involves looking into their pasts.

* Association with deviant peers, a lack of self-control, and a sense of strain, among other factors, also contribute to explaining the remaining variance in instrumental crime.

By digging deep into the histories of offenders we can locate the losses and traumas that played their part in fostering hatred. If we take the perspective that those guilty of the worst of human behaviours can be understood by seeing them as a product of their own personal experience within the world, this humanises them. It takes away the convenient ability to demonise them, and instead offers a way to rationalise these kinds of behaviours as something we could all be capable of.

The 'average' hate criminal

There are few scientific studies that involve the direct participation of hate crime offenders. Those convicted of hate crimes rarely admit to the 'hate' element of their offences, so when asked to participate in research, they decline, sometimes politely. Most say that racism, homophobia or any other prejudice had nothing to do with the reason they targeted their victims. Those who do agree to be studied are often male and part of an organised hate gang – they are hyper-violent and have something to say about their 'mission'. This bias in sample selection can mean the science only reflects a minority of hate offenders.[†]

Manchester University's Professor David Gadd is one of the few criminologists to get in the room with ordinary people who have committed acts of racial violence. In 2008 he interviewed fifteen violent white men from Stoke-on-Trent in the West Midlands region of England. Stoke has experienced the kind of rapid

---

† This chapter focuses primarily on race hate due to the lack of data on the personal histories of other types of hate offenders. It also focuses exclusively on white men due to the small number of white female hate crime offenders. Despite this, the concepts and arguments presented are applicable to other types of hate offenders and women.

economic and demographic change that creates toxic environments where locals turn on minority groups in hard times.

Two of these men, Greg and Stan (not their real names), represent the 'average' perpetrator of hate.*[3] Greg is a good example of the many young people who become involved in defensive hate crime, part of the 'push' category described in Chapter 1, where the outgroup is avoided and punished when territory is felt to be invaded. Stan represents those hate offenders who occupy the more troubling 'pull' category, those who have developed ideological leanings towards the far right, leading to hate crimes that are more retaliatory and mission-orientated.

Greg

Greg, who was sixteen at the time of interview, had never been convicted of a hate crime but was known for racist violence, despite claiming that he did not hold racist views. Bouts of domestic violence ended his biological parents' relationship before he was old enough to know his father, but he occasionally saw him driving around in an expensive car. Greg was brought up by his mother and stepfather and he admitted to being so scared of his stepfather that they rarely spoke. Greg had a rocky relationship with his half-brother, whom he beat up with a metal bar after he found him pushing his mother in an argument. He was closer to his stepbrother, Lenny, who was five years older. When Greg turned nine, Lenny introduced him to smoking cannabis, and later, at age fourteen, to drug dealing. Greg was not as close to his other younger siblings, whom he considered 'mouthy'.

---

* I am grateful to Professor Gadd for the discussion we had about his study and the subjects he interviewed. The interview extracts presented in this chapter are taken with permission from his original transcripts and from a series of publications detailing his analysis.

Greg's relationship with his mother was complicated. He tried to act as her protector and attacked those who threatened her. A physical attack on his half-brother's girlfriend for arguing with his mother resulted in a charge of assault and placement with a foster family away from his housing estate. Initially this greatly unsettled Greg, as he had never been away from home. But after some time with the foster family he came to consider it as a respite from the chaos – he had routine, understanding carers, no annoying younger siblings and his own space. This arrangement didn't last long, however, and he was back with his mother and stepbrother in a matter of months. Despite his protective stance towards her, Greg complained that his mother failed to provide for him and that she refused to buy him nice clothes and trainers when he was younger.

Greg was also trouble at school. He would start fights with other pupils, attack the headmaster and throw chairs at teachers – delinquency that got him expelled and moved to a boarding school. This took him away from his family again, a punishment that had an unexpected effect. He began to behave – on the promise that he would be moved back to his old school and his family. Following transfer, the good behaviour was short-lived, and he began to bully other pupils, in particular a Czech boy. He was eventually attacked by four lads who set out to teach him a lesson. Greg was excluded again for threats of retaliation. Embracing exclusion, he went on a spree of drug dealing, shoplifting, joyriding and burglary. At the age of fifteen, he developed a £200-a-day cocaine habit.

Greg's drug use was out of control – he was snorting seven grams of cocaine a day – and everything fell to pieces. His friends abandoned him, his mother refused to speak to him and his girlfriend gave him an ultimatum. Greg fell into depression, drink and violence. He became embroiled in a drawn-out confrontation with local Asian kids, and while most of the time it was just banter, on one occasion Greg's close friend physically attacked one of the Asian boys, resulting in his arrest and prosecution for racially aggravated assault. Despite the impression that this turf war was racialised, Greg did not admit to holding racist views, and would describe other out-of-town Asians and black people as 'dead sound lads', especially those he sold drugs to.

In spite of his insistence that he was not racist, Greg openly admitted to not liking asylum seekers, who he felt were taking over his town. In response to this 'invasion' he confessed to vandalising a Turkish man's car before throwing a bottle through the window of his house. One of the deciding factors for throwing the bottle was Greg's realisation that the Turkish man was dating a white woman from his estate: 'I just thought, the cheeky twat. Taking my white woman and that . . . not my woman, but my race,' he said after the incident. He recalled feeling exhilarated after throwing the bottle: 'I was buzzing at the time.'

On being asked if seeing a white girl with a man of a different race had made him feel like that before, Greg said that it had, 'every time I see a white woman with an Asian bloke or a Turk. I don't mind about black men, they can have as many white women as they want. It's just Asians, Turks, Albanians, whatever you want to call them. It's just I don't like seeing them with white women.'

After the incident immediate revenge was enacted and the Turkish man tried to hit Greg with a metal bar. In the tangle, Greg's mother, who had arrived at the scene moments after the attack, took a crack to her head, resulting in admission to hospital. Greg recalled having murderous thoughts after the attack. 'It got in me head, just messed with me . . . I was going to kill him if I got hold of him . . . if it were up to me he'd be lying in his coffin now.'

Greg eventually got himself back on track. The threat of losing his girlfriend was too much to contemplate. They had been through a lot together, including an abortion forced upon them by her mother. Greg thought the world of his girlfriend: 'She's closest thing [*sic*] to me . . . she's helped me through a lot . . . just looks out for my best interests . . . she don't want nothing off me . . . I would do time in jail . . . I'd either hurt someone . . . or go back into dealing and I'd end up doing somebody over that way,' he opened up. Losing her would have been the end of Greg. He managed to avoid custody by becoming a volunteer drug support worker.

Stan

Stan, a race-hate offender who was nineteen at the time of interview, had a history of involvement with the far right and violence against ethnic minorities. As in Greg's case, Stan's father abandoned the family just after he was born. The story went that his father had moved in with another family to raise 'a good son' (i.e. not Stan). Stan's mother went on to date men who were violent. One strangled her in front of the children, and she only survived due to an intervention by Stan, aged five, who ran from behind the sofa where he had been cowering and smashed a fish bowl over the attacker's head. After the police broke down the door to gain entry, Stan remembers all the neighbours staring in.

Stan was introduced to sex at around age eight by his babysitter, who used to make him engage in sexual acts with her after watching pornographic films. This had a destabilising effect on his behaviour, manifesting in sexually explicit outbursts at school. He would ask other pupils to 'suck [his] dick' and suggested to a teacher that she should have children with him. He was also violent, and would overreact to the smallest of things. He locked teachers in cupboards and threatened the headmaster. Stan's perception of sex was further warped when he witnessed his mother being raped when she was asleep. He tried to repress these images but to little avail. The domestic violence continued with successive partners, and his mother began to drink heavily. On one occasion she became violent towards Stan, and in the process her dressing gown came off, revealing her naked body to him and his friends who were present.

Declaring himself a 'proper little racist', at fifteen he joined the National Front, a far-right organisation, over the internet. The National Front had Stan's back. They looked after him and provided a feeling of security that his home did not. In secondary school Stan was involved in fights with gangs of Asian students, which he referred to as 'Whites versus Pakis'. In the interview he said, 'These Pakis, they walk around [saying] "You can't do nothing to us, we fucking own this planet," and that . . . Nothing but fucking scroungers . . . I hate them when they are in their gangs.' Stan also admitted that he and his friends in the National Front coordinated mass fights in the local fields, saying: 'There was blood everywhere. It was heaving man. No holds barred shit. Serious, it was fucking evil. People stabbed in the neck, stamped on. It was just mad. [Laughs] A right little rampage. [Laughs] I hit all of them . . . All of them got hit.'

Some time later, Stan narrowly avoided prison for attacking a man of Kosovan descent who he believed had made sexual advances towards his girlfriend. His victim was beaten so badly that he had to eat through a straw. Stan felt no remorse: 'I don't feel bad . . . about it. Just think it's a laugh, a buzz. I break someone's jaw. I break someone's nose, I think it's a laugh. I love fighting I do. I don't know why.'

Stan's final act of violence before prison was committed against an Asian man. A young white female friend, whom Stan had sexual relations with, was attacked by a kebab shop owner after she refused his sexual advances. This put Stan into an uncontrollable rage: 'I thought, Fuck it. That's it. Paki bastard . . . I've got the pool cue at the side of me, like the fat end . . . I've said to him . . . "Can I order some food?" . . . As he's looking down. Pulled it [out]. "Want this", bam, bam, bam, about three or four times over the head with it. Then I've just legged it.' Stan was charged with racially aggravated threatening behaviour, affray, actual bodily harm and criminal damage. At the time of his interview he was serving a two-year prison sentence.

Like Greg and Stan, the other thirteen hate crime offenders interviewed by Professor Gadd were male, young, poor, emotionally damaged and socially marginalised. For the most part, these characteristics did not differentiate them from the average non-hate crime offender. What did differentiate the hate offenders was the way in which they dealt with their emotional problems. Emotional childhood scars can thwart psychological development to a point where normal coping mechanisms are either malfunctioning or absent. Without the safety net of these coping mechanisms, and in the face of what seem like extreme external pressures, most non-hate offenders find blame in themselves, their family or friends. But for Greg and Stan, blaming the usual suspects was more difficult, more inconvenient, than blaming the racial 'other'.

Greg and Stan's pasts share several similarities that help explain their trajectories towards racist violence. Both expressed a sense of rejection and loss in relation to their parents, particularly their fathers. Greg said of his father, whom he had never met but had seen driving around in a Mercedes: '. . . he didn't even know who I was. So I wasn't really bothered . . . If he wanted me he would have got in touch with me.' Stan came to believe his father had left to raise 'a good son' who later become a successful sales representative.

189

They maintained contact on and off, but his father stopped visiting with no explanation when Stan was around nine. Years later his father wrote to him, and sent him packages in prison. But his father's absence around Stan's release date inspired deep anger and rejection: 'Yer you knob head. You fucking . . . Go and kill yourself you cunt,' he said in the interview.

These are both examples of 'rejecting the rejector' – attempts to stem the pain of being rejected again.[4] But burying these deep feelings of childhood rejection is a temporary solution, and certain forms of instability or stress later in life will tear that Band-Aid off and open up old wounds. When the source of this pain – such as the absent father – cannot be directly challenged in a way that rebandages the wounds, alternative targets are sought; in Greg and Stan's cases, immigrants, Turks, Asians.

Both mothers were victims of repeated domestic abuse, scarring violence witnessed by their sons, and sometimes involving them. Greg's biological parents split because of his father's violence, and Stan's mother entered several relationships with abusive men. Repeated episodes of domestic violence witnessed at such a young age can erode the innocence, personal security and love that every child needs to ensure healthy psychological development.[5] These battered mothers appeared painfully vulnerable and powerless to their sons, and hence difficult to identify with as the boys grew up in a violent and masculine world.

Their mothers routinely failed in their roles as protectors, emotionally and physically, after their fathers abandoned them. Greg blamed his mother for his involvement in crime, saying she refused to provide for him despite having the money to do so: '. . . me mum never really got me anything so I went out and thieved it . . . I see her open her purse, she got loads of money.' He also felt she failed to protect him from his stepbrother's bullying, from school expulsion and from his early introduction to drugs within the family. Regardless, Greg always defended his mother, and felt like he could have murdered the Turkish man that accidentally hit her with a metal bar. Stan's perception of relationships and love was blighted by his exposure to abuse and sexual violence at an early age. His neighbours and friends witnessing this abuse humiliated him, eliciting murderous thoughts towards the perpetrators – thoughts later projected onto his Asian victims, whom he perceived as sexually predatory towards white girls and women.

Failures of containment

Unresolved feelings of dependency are key to understanding the racist actions of people like Greg and Stan. The painful loss that rejection from loved ones engenders, and the inability of protectors to give much-needed security, can lead to the exploration of alternative avenues for support.[6] Greg resorted to drug dealing and petty crime to provide for himself where his mother could not, eventually turning to his girlfriend who acted as a mother figure. Stan took a different course, his relationships with the opposite sex troubled by his childhood experiences. He was adopted by the National Front, an alternative family: 'I'd know I'd have that big, big thing around me. Like I know I've got my protection then. It's like a big rod for my back, if you know what I mean. You know they've got my back and that . . . They'll look after me,' Stan said in the interview.

This seeking out of alternative forms of support is a possible response to *failures of containment* during childhood psychological development.[7] In psychoanalysis, containment is the process a parent provides for a child who is too young to deal rationally with events that cause physical or emotional pain. Consider a toddler who falls and grazes their knee for the first time. The child does not know how much pain to anticipate, if the pain will ever stop, or if the graze is a serious or minor injury. The responsible and caring parent who is present quickly consoles the toddler and explains that the pain will not worsen, that it will stop soon, and that it is only a minor graze. The parent acknowledges and 'contains' the toddler's pain, allowing them to rationalise and get through it. For the toddler, the very fact of having a parent available to act as a 'container' makes the pain more tolerable. Over time, the need for this containment in the event of another graze is reduced as the child internalises the parent's coping strategy. Psychoanalysts believe that the process of containment, which continues throughout life with parents, lovers and close friends, is central to the development of psychological stability.[8]

What we see in violent racists like Stan and Greg are multiple failures of containment throughout their lives, starting in early childhood and persisting throughout adolescence and early adulthood. Bad experiences and feelings are 'uncontained' in the absence of anyone who cares or can care, leaving them in their disturbingly raw and unmanageable forms. Consider who was available to contain the horrors of domestic violence for Stan when he was growing up. Who could tell him that the violence would stop, that it wouldn't get worse, or that its consequences could be managed? Not his mother, who time after time ended up with boyfriends who abused her, undoing any attempt at containing the effects of the violence. Nor Stan's father figure, whom he saw rape his mother while she was unconscious. Imagine Greg's childhood world, the effect on his psychological development of learning that his father left after abusing his mother, and that his mother could not protect him from his stepbrother, from expulsion or from falling into crime. Being taken away from his family twice, first to live with a foster family and then sent to a boarding school, further removed opportunities for the containment of his feelings of powerlessness and vulnerability.

The other perpetrators of hate in Professor Gadd's study had similar histories – child abuse, destitution, homelessness, exclusion, abandonment, bereavement, mental illness, drug and alcohol abuse – each factor alone damaging. When multiple factors were combined, as was commonly reported, this undoubtedly hindered their ability to cope in later life. During times of stress, the failure to contain their pain opened up the possibility of racist violence.

Hate as a container of unresolved trauma

Most of us are able to keep our prejudices in our minds and rationalise them away before they get a chance to affect our behaviour. This ability requires a good deal of mental stability, especially when an interaction with a member of the outgroup is potentially contentious. We learn how to do this by picking up non-contentious psychological coping mechanisms during childhood, often from our parents. These can then be called upon and deployed in later adult life during a stressful encounter. Because of failures of containment during upbringing, people like Stan and Greg are less able to develop the mental machinery to contain their prejudice within the mind at certain times of extreme environmental and personal stress.

Households that are neglectful, rejective, overly critical or inconsistent can create a sense of profound frustration in children, making them view the world as an unequal place that can only be coped with by means of aggression to dominate and subordinate others.[9] This description fits the households Greg and Stan grew up in. By burying their childhood traumas in their uncontained form, Greg and Stan left them unmourned, undealt with. It would have been unthinkable for them to take out the frustration stemming from intense unresolved feelings of rejection, inadequacy, envy and guilt on those who had originally harmed them – their all-powerful parents. Instead their frustrations were taken out on those whom they saw as having less power than them – ethnic minorities and immigrants. Race hate provided a convenient home, or a 'container', for their unresolved frustrations from past trauma. The racial 'other', rather irrationally, gave them easier targets upon which to project their frustrations.[10]

When Greg experienced feelings of threat and anger on seeing the Turkish man with a white woman, instead of reacting as he did by throwing the bottle through his window, he could have instead taken a step back to gain perspective on the situation. In the aftermath of the incident he could have worked backwards to figure out how it had happened; looked at the situation from the viewpoint of others; accepted that the blame for his mother being injured could be shared amongst all parties; talked about the situation instead of acting out, and so on. But Greg, like Stan, was not equipped with the ability to address his other-race encounters with these ways of containing the situation. Such people see their world differently from most of us.

This can be seen in Greg's use of racialised psychological coping strategies in his encounter with the Turkish man. Greg saw it as a battle between the strong (white British) and the weak (brown immigrant); he rationalised the battle as inevitable in an unequal world where the Turkish man was encroaching on Greg's rightful property (white women); he only drew on his own perspective, as taking on board the other's would have meant identifying with weakness; he saw his mother's injury as intended instead of accidental; and he acted out on his frustrations because he was not capable of articulating them verbally.

These ways of coping with encounters with members of the out-group actively 'do difference' in the moment – they separated out Greg from the Turkish man in a hierarchical way.[11] Greg might say he 'put him back in his place'. They also allow people like Greg and Stan to feel a sense of power over their victims. This feeling is intoxicating, as they have been denied it since childhood.[12] Seeking out this feeling of power from dominating others is a predominantly male phenomenon because it helps fulfil the requirements of a certain type of masculinity – it made Greg feel more like a man and on top of his image of the social order.[13]

The traumas suffered by Greg and Stan during childhood are deep-rooted and personal. Trauma that leads to using hate as a container can also be experienced during adulthood. Greg and Stan talked of their adult losses: loss of jobs, loss of respect, loss of a certain way of life – all common to deindustrialising towns and cities. These losses can impact whole communities and can result in multiple types of coping: some collective, like the nostalgic celebration of a mythical bygone era before the immigrants arrived; some individualistic, like a personal preoccupation with racial mixing. These community and individual frustrations can suddenly become intertwined – deeply personal frustrations can combine with political propaganda about the risks of unfettered migration.

It is clear from Greg and Stan's interviews that they rationalised 'Asian gangs', 'asylum seekers', 'Turks' and 'Albanians' as somehow responsible for some of the pain they were experiencing. Their inner emotional worlds, shaped by childhood trauma, collided with what they saw as an external crisis in their home town. Their deeply rooted feelings of rejection, inadequacy, envy and guilt became intertwined, irrationally, with the community issue of immigration and race that they saw as the root of white unemployment, poverty, ill-health, the erosion of 'British' identity – all additional losses in their lives.

Stoke-on-Trent, like many parts of the UK, suffered badly from deindustrialisation in the 1980s and 90s. The potteries for which it is famous employed seventy thousand people in the 1950s, now reduced to fewer than ten thousand. Employment, wages and educational achievement are consistently below the regional and national average. This economic decline coincided with a sharp rise in inward migration, made more stark when the city was designated an asylum dispersal area in 2000. The combined Indian, Pakistani and Bangladeshi population increased from 5,224 in 1991 to 13,855 in 2011 (three years after the interviews with Greg and Stan), a 165 per cent rise. During the same period the white population fell by 7 per cent, due to those with youth and an education on their side moving out of the area to other towns and cities.[14] Rapid demographic change was blamed for preventing local residents from having 'a nice life'.[15] Stoke-on-Trent was described by those living there as a 'dumping ground' for 'foreigners', resembling 'war zones', 'Africa' and 'Bombay'. Young white residents felt the 'needy foreigners' were directly to blame for the city's decline, and 'Pakis' and 'Turks' were reviled for taking their town away from them.[*16]

---

* As seen in Stan's case, the far right was quick to capitalise on the intense animosity. In 2008 the now moribund BNP took nine seats out of sixty in the local election, becoming the joint second largest party in the council after the Conservatives. The BNP dubbed the city the 'jewel in their crown'. While this success was short-lived (largely due to electoral boundary changes and in-party fighting), only two years later the newly formed EDL staged one of its largest ever demonstrations in the city. Leading up to the referendum on the UK's future in the EU, UKIP gained a foothold, mobilising voters with anti-immigration rhetoric. Stoke-on-Trent voted 69:39 in favour of leaving the EU, the highest level in any city, awarding it the moniker the 'Brexit Capital'. Like many majority Leave areas, Stoke-on-Trent saw an increase in race and religious hate crimes following the vote, with the

Greg and Stan engaged in one of the few things they felt they could do to alleviate the feelings of weakness, rejection and shame – subjecting those they thought responsible to harassment and violence. An attack on an immigrant lad on the council estate restored, for a limited time, a sense of control and pride that had been lost through an irrational mix of personal and community tragedy.[17] For these men, acts of racial violence are as much about achieving a sense of masculine power and pride as they are about subjugating an outgroup.

The conflation of childhood trauma with frustrations over local community problems exacerbated by an influx of outsiders may help explain why some 'ordinary' people turn to hate crime even when they insist they are not prejudiced. Unlike the average hate crime offender, who is often keen to deny their prejudices, those responsible for the most grotesque form of hate – murder motivated by some sense of mission – openly admit to them. Can looking into the backgrounds of the worst hate crime offenders help us understand their motivations?

The 'exceptional' hate criminal

The racist American sniper

Unlike many serial killers, Joseph Paul Franklin never killed for sexual pleasure, something that distinguished him from the likes of Ted Bundy, Albert DeSalvo (the Boston Strangler) and Peter Sutcliffe. Franklin killed for ideology – a belief in the purity of the white race that he saw as threatened by black and Jewish people.

number soaring by 46 per cent compared to the same period the year before (the national average rise was around 29 per cent). This represented the largest increase in hate crimes in Stoke-on-Trent since records began a decade earlier.

In the late 1970s he embarked on his own three-year-long race war across America, stalking and shooting with deadly accuracy anyone he thought was a threat to white supremacy.

Franklin, born James Clayton Vaughn Jr, was raised in a family tormented by abuse and neglect. Along with his half-sisters and brother, James was subject to daily beatings from both parents. His father, James Clayton Vaughn Sr, was an alcoholic and would often leave home on drinking binges for months at a time. His mother, Helen, was of German descent. Her parents had reportedly supported the Nazis and abused her physically. Like them, Helen was cold, stubborn and a disciplinarian. She terrorised the children, especially James. While he was eating she would slap him across the face hard and yell, 'Sit up there and eat that right.'[18] James would mirror his mother's aggression by torturing animals – he hanged cats on the clothesline by their tails. Although his sisters recalled James was often the focus of the abuse, the whole family was embroiled in the violent maelstrom, and the children would routinely witness Helen being badly beaten by their father. After one such beating, Helen lost her unborn child. In addition to the routine violence, Helen would starve her children, leading to malnutrition and subsequent developmental problems. All the children reportedly suffered mental health issues later in life.

James Sr's alcohol abuse meant stable employment was difficult to come by. The family moved around to support him in finding work, but each job ended up being temporary. The children's education and friendships were lost in the wake. The family eventually settled in the segregated Birdville housing project in Mobile, Alabama, although without James Sr, who abandoned them. It was around this time that James Jr suffered a biking accident at age seven that would change his life. The accident resulted in James losing some of his sight. For this he blamed his mother for not attending to complications following the accident, which if addressed might have saved his vision. His impairment did not, however, interfere with his penchant for guns, and he was an able marksman. He was given a gun for his birthday by his brother, who taught him to hunt in the woods nearby. In his teenage years, James recalled never being without a gun at his side. Guns were a crutch for him, a way to compensate for his partial blindness and associated feelings of inadequacy.

Between the ages of nine and eleven James became a bookworm. He avidly consumed fairy tale after fairy tale in an attempt to escape the abuse of his childhood. He was solitary and had few if any friends. Eventually he pulled away from his sisters and his brother. He would refuse to drink out of the same glasses as them, even if washed, and would cover chairs they had sat on with a cloth before sitting down himself.

James attended one of the largest high schools in the area and to his chagrin witnessed the first enrolments of black pupils. School desegregation came late to Alabama due to staunch resistance by state officials, resulting in violent clashes between civil rights groups and police. James was now exposed to violence both inside and outside of his family. Around this time he took an interest in the ideology of the extreme right, which blossomed in adolescence with his avid consumption of the Bible and *Mein Kampf*. He would often imagine what it would be like to meet his Nazi-sympathising grandparents, and pored over photos of distant relatives wearing Hitler Youth uniforms. His reading led to dabbling with several branches of Christianity, before he embraced one of the more extreme which had white supremacism at its core.

At the age of eighteen in 1968, James married and shortly after had a child. But like some of those exposed to extreme violence in childhood, James beat his wife, ending the union in under a year.

This was the second time family life hadn't worked out for James, so he abandoned the idea altogether and instead moved out of Alabama on his quest for an alternative home. He joined the American Nazi Party in Washington DC, moved on to the National States Rights Party in Atlanta and eventually ended up with the United Klans of America back in Alabama, one of the two most prominent and violent Ku Klux Klan organisations of the era. It was here that James transformed into Joseph Paul Franklin, legally changing his name in honour of the Nazi Joseph Goebbels (whose first name was Paul) and the American Founding Father Benjamin Franklin. Franklin embarked on learning the skills required for fighting the 'impending race war', aiming to become a lone soldier for the white race. Following a few failed bombing attempts on the Jewish community in 1977, Franklin went on his spree of twenty sniper killings across the US that ended in 1980 following his arrest for the Liberty Park murders.[*][19]

Days before his execution, Franklin said he regretted his actions. He claimed the neglect, poverty and repeated beatings he suffered as a child stunted his development so much that he felt his perception of black people was a decade or more behind the average person's. It was his mother he blamed, not his father.[20]

The London nail bomber

David Copeland's family life was picture perfect compared to Joseph Paul Franklin's wildly dysfunctional upbringing, with no history of the child abuse or domestic violence that encompassed Franklin's early life. Born in 1976, David was a middle child,

---

* Franklin was convicted of seven racially motivated murders, but confessed to twenty.

sandwiched between two brothers. His parents – Stephen, an engineer, and Caroline, a housewife – and teachers told of a quiet boy who was sensitive and well behaved. His diminutive stature echoed his reclusive nature. Worried about his late development, including underdeveloped testes, his parents sent him to a doctor around the age of thirteen. David was left disturbed by the medical examination, which included an inspection of his genitals. He was angry at his parents for putting him through this deeply embarrassing episode.

Possibly tied to this experience was his insecurity about his sexual orientation. He recalled the family's love of the show *The Flintstones*, and every time they sang along to the theme tune and got to the lyric 'We'll have a gay old time', he imagined them adding emphasis, thinking his parents were sending a subliminal message that he was a homosexual. His mother regularly prompting him to confide in her further ingrained this belief. His father recalled a moment in David's later teenage years when his grandmother questioned him about being gay because he never had a girlfriend. He never spoke to her again. This series of happenings left him feeling 'mentally tortured' by his parents and made him 'want to hurt someone'. His parents maintained that this family conspiracy to 'out' their son was merely a facet of his inner fantasy world, claiming they had no questions over his sexual orientation. After his arrest years later he was assessed by six psychiatrists; one was of the opinion Copeland was a closeted homosexual.

When Copeland was nineteen his parents split up. His father was convinced their separation led to the onset of his son's downward spiral into mental illness. It was on his younger brother's birthday when the row that ended the marriage erupted. That night Copeland's mother walked out and never came back. His father shared the news the morning after with an angry Copeland, who vowed never to speak to or of his mother again. In the aftermath of the split he became more introverted, began to drink heavily and stopped communicating with his family and friends.

After leaving school with seven GCSEs and taking an electrical course at college, he tried to gain employment but failed several times. It was at this point that the first signs of prejudice were voiced – he blamed immigrants for taking the top jobs. In 1997 he left home and got a job as an engineer's assistant on the London Underground. Unfamiliar with the city, he spent much of his time after work in his cheap bedsit and visiting female sex workers. He dabbled with right-wing organisations, including the BNP, which he quickly left, blaming their refusal to take up arms, and the National Socialist Movement, a breakaway group of the terrorist neo-Nazi organisation Combat 18 led by David Myatt.

The pipe bombing of the Centennial Olympic Park, Atlanta in 1996, one of a series of attacks by Eric Rudolph targeting abortion rights and the 'homosexual agenda', was a key moment in the development of Copeland's vision for his London attacks. After this he digested biographies of Hitler, *The Turner Diaries* (which depicts violent revolution and a race war in the US), the pamphlet *A Practical Guide to Aryan Revolution* written by David Myatt, and *The Terrorist's Handbook*, downloaded from the internet. Before committing his horrific crimes, he visited his GP to tell them he was 'losing his mind'. He was prescribed antidepressants.

As suggested in Myatt's pamphlet, found in Copeland's bedsit, he began his mission to start a race war with explosives. He went on to build nail bombs, and detonated them in Brixton, Brick Lane and Soho on 17, 24 and 30 April 1999, targeting black, Bengali and LGBTQ+ communities. The blasts that sprayed thousands of four-inch nails through the air injured forty-eight people in the Brixton attack and thirteen in Brick Lane. The bomb in the Admiral Duncan gay bar in Soho caused the most casualties, with patrons packed into the confined space on the evening of a Bank Holiday weekend. Of the seventy-nine people in the bar, Copeland killed Andrea Dykes, who was four months pregnant, and her friends Nik Moore and John Light. Andrea and Nik were heterosexual. No one escaped without injury, and many lost limbs or eyes. The police arrested Copeland at home shortly after this third blast. His bedsit was littered with bomb-making equipment, National Socialist Movement literature and a membership card, Nazi memorabilia, and news clippings covering his own bombings as well as other atrocities across the world. Police reports state he casually confessed to all attacks, admitted to planning more, and used cold military-style language to describe his actions – he talked of a sense of 'mission' and expected 'casualties'.

After his arrest and medical assessment, Copeland was diagnosed by five Broadmoor Hospital psychiatrists as suffering from paranoid schizophrenia, the onset of which was traced back to his teenage years. He told the psychiatrists of the *Flintstones* story, and of his belief he was a messenger from God who would be rescued by the 'Almighty' after his trial – clear examples of delusional belief and lost rationality.

A sixth psychiatrist called for the prosecution diagnosed personality disorder, not a mental illness, rejecting Copeland's delusion of being a messenger from God. After seeing the volume of religious and political literature in Copeland's bedsit, something the other doctors were not fully aware of, he concluded that he was simply reciting passages. Copeland exhibited behaviours that deviated markedly from the expectations of his culture, but did not show any more biological signs of mental illness than someone with OCD. Unlike those with schizophrenia, he had a good grasp on reality.[21]

Copeland eventually denied he was ill, and while on remand wrote to a pen pal, Patsy Scanlon, that he had 'fooled all the doctors', that he was on medication 'for no reason' and that he was 'no monster but some kind of terrorist, someone who puts themselves forward for what they believe in'. But Patsy was not the lonely English rose that Copeland had fallen for. She was in fact the true crime author Bernard O'Mahoney, who had a history of fooling criminals into corresponding with his fake identities in order to elicit confessions and evidence for the prosecution.[22] Although the five Broadmoor psychiatrists would say schizophrenics often deny their condition, the letters to 'Patsy' were used in the trial as evidence that Copeland was not suffering from an illness so deleterious as to diminish his responsibility.

Copeland was deemed fit to stand trial. He knew right from wrong and had the ability to exercise willpower and free choice. He was sane enough to build bombs, without blowing himself up in the process, and to know the consequences of his actions. The jury heard he had spent £1,500 on fireworks and detonators and used the mechanisms from analogue alarm clocks as timers. He had conducted a series of controlled tests in a field near to his bedsit to see if different amounts of chemicals would create bigger explosions to maximise casualties. After his attack on the Admiral Duncan pub, he went to a local hotel to watch the devastation unfold on the news. He admitted feeling sick at the news that he had killed a pregnant woman. The jury found him guilty of murder and he was given six life sentences.

A reporter for the *Guardian* covering the case wrote that Copeland showed emotion only once in the courtroom. When he pleaded guilty to manslaughter, but not to murder due to diminished responsibility caused by mental illness, his words were met with disquiet from the victims in the gallery: 'Shame!' 'Send him down!' Through tears a woman yelled, 'You bastard! You bastard!' Copeland looked up at her and smirked.[23]

Understanding the 'exceptional' hate offender

Most forms of extreme violence evoke a sense of bewilderment, but serial murder engenders feelings of horror so intense that it reduces our willingness to contemplate motive. If we were to make sense of the killer's motive in any way, we risk diminishing the evil in their act. Instead we are more comfortable thinking that those who go on a killing spree are 'insane' – beyond understanding.

Although a diagnosis of insanity is convenient as it allows us to explain away the offender's acts, it can deny the victim's loved ones the answers that they are looking for. A diagnosis of insanity can mask what may otherwise be at least partly understandable to the average person, dare we look. No matter how rare or unusual the circumstances that contribute to motive, by piecing them together we risk humanising the murderer. Their set of circumstances are part of the human experience, regardless of how horrific and singular they may seem.

Franklin clearly suffered multiple failures of containment, physical abuse, devastating injury and malnutrition, and began to show signs of personality disorder during adolescence. Copeland claimed he was 'mentally tortured' over his sexual orientation by his family, went through a humiliating examination of his genitals, and took his parents' divorce badly. Although his experience pales in comparison to what Franklin endured, the effects of trauma are always relative to the individual's capacity to cope, and Copeland's threshold for stress may have been much lower.

Greg and Stan's racist behaviours do not compare to the terrible crimes of Franklin and Copeland. Does this make the use of psychosocial criminology redundant in understanding their motives? We can see that Franklin and Copeland's childhood traumas were not contained by their parents, leaving them in their raw and unmanageable forms. This may have inhibited their mental ability to deal with stressful situations with members of the outgroup. Later in life, the resentment caused by their trauma may have been deflected from the true cause, their parents, onto other less powerful objects, their minority victims. As with Greg and Stan, race hate may have become a container for their extreme feelings of loss.

If this analysis was sufficient in explaining the multiple murders committed by Franklin and Copeland, we would see many more hate-filled mass killings than we do. What about Frankin's siblings who suffered similar childhood trauma, but did not turn out to be racist killers? And are we convinced that Copeland's upbringing was in any way traumatising enough to account for his bombing raid? Maybe the additional information we need is located in the personalities of the two men.

Personality, mental illness and hate

The huge influence of our parents on the shaping of our personalities is well known. When your partner says, 'you're just like your mother' or 'you're just like your father', I'm afraid they are correct. Studies of twins show that personality is determined as much by the genes passed down by mum and dad as it is by the parenting environment.[24] For most of us, our rearing hammers home the biological traits.

Does this mean that Franklin and Copeland inherited prejudice and hate from their parents, grandparents and so on (possibly the Nazi sympathisers in the case of Franklin)? As neither prejudice nor hate counts as an aspect of personality, we won't find a racist, homophobic, sexist or any other prejudice gene that can be passed down the generations. However, certain elements of personality are hereditary, and some of these can play their part in prejudice and hate.

Some serious science backs this up. Evidence from seventy-one studies involving 22,068 people from nine countries shows an *indirect link* between some personality traits and prejudice.[25] Many of these studies looked at the 'Big Five' traits that many of us have been mapped onto as part of teamwork exercises in our jobs. No matter what you might have made of your results, various mixes of *extraversion, agreeableness, conscientiousness, neuroticism* and *openness to experience* account for north of 50 per cent of our personalities.[26]

Franklin and Copeland would score high on the classic prejudice-predicting Right-Wing Authoritarianism (RWA) and Social Dominance Orientation (SDO) attitude scales.[27] The RWA scale measures investment in the social order or status quo that is threatened by value infraction and a lack of security afforded by stable leaders. People who score highly feel the world is an inherently dangerous and threatening place that can only be brought under control by conforming to a set of dominant rules. The SDO scale measures preference for unequal relationships among categories of people, including the dominance of one race over another. People who score highly feel that the world is a ruthlessly competitive jungle in which the strong win and the weak lose, leading to the belief that group hierarchies are natural, unavoidable and desirable.

The RWA and SDO scales are closely linked to low ratings in two of the Big Five: openness to experience and agreeableness. While those of us who are closed-minded and overly self-interested (the inverse of these two traits) are not all destined to become racists and homophobes, we are more inclined to think the world is a dangerous place that only rewards the strong. Franklin and Copeland may have invested so much in these attitudes that they became closed off to the world around them. Combined with socialisation by parents that reinforces these elements, and a general prejudiced attitude in the household, then we have fertile soil. But there is no clear evidence that their parents did express prejudiced attitudes, and even if they did, why would their siblings, who share the same genetic ancestry and family environment, have been less affected?

Maybe the answer can be found in mental illness after all. Although it remains unclear whether or not Franklin and Copeland were mentally ill at the time of their crimes, it is possible their childhood traumas interfered with the normal development of emotional response, arousal and impulse control. There is a physiological consequence to deeply traumatic childhood histories. Childhood stressors, or traumatic events like child abuse and witnessing repeated violence, trigger the release of glucocorticoids that are in part responsible for triggering the 'red alert' fight-or-flight response.[28] A young brain being flooded with glucocorticoids has an amplifying effect on the amygdala, making it more resistant to the influence of the executive control area (prefrontal cortex) that slams on the brakes, which in turn makes it more likely that fear of the stimulus is committed to long-term memory. This glucocorticoid-inspired fear memory is incredibly resistant to eradication. Glucocorticoids encourage destructive habitual behaviours in the face of problems and increased risk taking, because while under stress it is more difficult to take in new information to inform behaviours. Studies suggest they also increase selfishness and decrease empathy and emotional regulation.[29]

The effects of childhood traumas are not confined to a particular time and place. In later life long-term fear memories re-emerge when triggered, recreating the original stress response and flood of glucocorticoids, impairing rational decision making and encouraging destructive behaviours – we resort to rage and aggression more easily and rapidly.[30] Why? Because aggression can reduce glucocorticoid levels and stress, making us feel better.[31] An interesting side note to all of this is that research shows that women who encounter similar stressors to men actually respond differently. Instead of fight-or-flight, it is more likely to be tend-and-befriend (nurturing behaviour designed to create a safe environment for ourselves and our children).[32]

The emotional scars from childhood trauma can also reshape the physical structure of the brain. Research into PTSD shows that stressful events can actually change the size of brain regions, shaping behavioural response later in life.[33] The amygdala grows, creating an anxious brain, and the hippocampus shrinks, creating a brain which learns inefficiently. PTSD sufferers are more likely than the general population to experience the fight-or-flight response in non-threatening situations and more likely to store fear memories that are poorly anchored to the time and place of their original creation.

This expansion and atrophy create a toxic mix where the traumatic fear memory can be recalled by other sights and sounds, however benign, creating disturbing flashbacks to the original trauma that are difficult to escape. Those suffering with PTSD are known to exhibit disruptive behaviours, and some of them are aggressive, even explosively violent and uncontrollable.[34] Of course, it is not inevitable that all children who witness domestic violence or experience child abuse develop PTSD. But the chances of experiencing PTSD-type symptoms increase dramatically if the domestic violence and abuse is ongoing and if there are no carers able to 'contain' the trauma – if that is even possible in cases of repeated victimisation. Add poverty, malnutrition, a history of mental illness, drug and alcohol abuse, and the chances skyrocket.

At the time of Franklin's conviction, understanding of PTSD was in its infancy and it is unlikely that any psychiatrist would have indicated it as a possible mitigating factor in his crimes. Close to his execution date Franklin indicated that abuse had impacted upon his psychological development, resulting in a warped perception of black people. This is not inconceivable given his sister claimed to have suffered from PTSD due to the abuse she experienced during their childhood, and his brother had been in and out of mental institutions all his life.[35] Knowledge of PTSD was more developed at the time of Copeland's trial, but none of the psychiatrists suggested his past may have resulted in its onset. Unlike Franklin, Copeland was diagnosed with paranoid schizophrenia, but this did not satisfy the judge that he was unfit to stand trial. His own confession that he was sane, and that he tricked the psychiatrists, also undermines a diagnosis of mental illness.

Unearthing the deeply traumatic pasts of hate crime offenders helps to shed light on motivation. From the mild to the extreme, Greg, Stan, Franklin and Copeland all had histories of unresolved and uncontained childhood trauma. A reduced mental capacity to cope with the eruption of past negative feelings in later life may have been addressed by using hate as a container, manifesting in their attacks on minority victims. An analysis based on this psychosocial criminological approach feels like it explains the crimes of Greg and Stan better than the multiple hate murders of Franklin and Copeland. For these more serious hate crimes additional accelerants likely came into play. Their criminal profiles showed an avid engagement with extremist materials and groups. For Copeland, the availability of extremist online content certainly played a role. Triggers were also evident – events that galvanised their warped view of the world.

7

Trigger Events and the Ebb and Flow of Hate

On a Saturday in early November 2008, a group of teenage high-school friends arranged to meet up in the wealthy seaside town of Patchogue, Suffolk County, New York, to play a twisted game. This game, which they played most weeks, was called 'beaner hopping'. The objective was to hound and attack Latinx people. The seven boys, who dubbed themselves the Caucasian Crew, set out on their hunt in the small town, a forty-minute drive from the Hamptons. They began by drinking alcohol in the local park and boasting about beating a Latinx man unconscious five days earlier. From there they set off to prowl the dark streets for their victims. By the early evening they had beaten up a Latinx man and tormented another by firing a BB gun at him repeatedly.

Around midnight, Marcelo Lucero, an undocumented immigrant of Ecuadorean descent, and his old school friend, Angel Loja, stumbled into the pack's path in a train station car park. The seven teenagers darted racial slurs at both men as they encircled them. In reaction to being smacked across the face by one of the boys, Marcelo took off his belt and began to swing it in the air like a bolas. Before he could duck, another of the Crew, seventeen-year-old high school star athlete Jeffrey Conroy, was hit on the head with the belt buckle. Infuriated, Conroy pulled out a knife and stabbed Marcelo in the chest, killing him. Marcelo had been living in the US for sixteen years, working low-wage jobs to fund the building of a family home back in Gualaceo, his home village. He had been planning on leaving the US to rejoin his family the following month.[1]

Conroy, who was found to have a swastika tattoo on his leg, admitted to the Sheriff's Office that he held racist views and sometimes visited white supremacist websites.* During the investigation he was also linked to the assault of eight other Latinx immigrants, one of whom he attacked with his knife. Conroy was sentenced to twenty-five years in prison for a hate crime. The remaining six boys were sentenced to between five and seven years.

The Southern Poverty Law Center examined Marcelo's murder case and found it was not an isolated incident. Latinx immigrants in Suffolk County were suffering a sustained campaign of hate from residents, with local leaders and police accused of turning a blind eye. Victims were routinely spat at, hit with fruit and glass bottles, shot at in their homes, run off the road, robbed and beaten with baseball bats. Most of the attackers were white males under the age of twenty.[2]

I came across this hate crime in the *New York Times* article titled 'Teenagers' Violent "Sport" Led to Killing on Long Island, Officials Say'.[3] It resonated with me because of its similarity to my attack – it was another example of the gamification of hate crime. Around the same time in 2008, I remember reading reports of an annual threefold rise in hate crimes against gay men and women in Santa Clara County, California.[4] Did this spate of hate crimes on opposite coasts share something in common? Intrigued, I looked back, searching for a pattern to try to determine if these temporal clusterings of hate were isolated phenomena.

I found repeated examples of sudden peaks in hate crimes across

---

* Conroy's lawyer said he only admitted to holding white supremacist views to avoid being housed with inmates who might attack him for his hate crime.

the US: in April 1992 hate crimes against white people spiked; in February 1993 it was hate crimes against Muslim people that suddenly rose; in October 1995 hate crimes against black people; in September 2001 hate crimes against Muslim people again; in the fourth quarter of 2008 hate crimes against Latinx people; and in the last quarter of 2016 hate crimes against Muslim, Latinx and black people. I turned to other countries. In July 2005, hate crimes against Muslim people spiked dramatically in the UK; in October 2002 attitudes towards immigrants sharply worsened across Portugal, Poland and Finland; in March 2004 a strong negative shift in attitudes towards immigrants occurred across Spain.

These surges in hate crime and the hardening of anti-immigrant attitudes all had one thing in common: they were preceded by a *trigger event* that galvanised bigoted sentiment towards an outgroup. For a minority, in the aftermath of these trigger events their prejudices became bolstered to such an extent that for a temporary period they could not contain them within their minds. They felt the need to evacuate them with violent force onto those perceived to be associated with the event.

The killing of Marcelo Lucero and the surge in race hate crimes around the time of the attack in Suffolk County was preceded by the election of the first black president of the United States of America, Barack Obama. And the spate of anti-gay hate crimes in California followed the passing of Proposition 8, a law that restricted marriage to opposite-sex couples. I knew at the time that the two examples were anecdotal. To say with any confidence that reactions to events were part of the puzzle of hate crime motivation, I would need to turn to science. What I found in the years following was alarming – the multiple spikes in hate crimes throughout recent history across the world all followed a significant political vote, court case, terror attack or policy change.

Uncovering the triggers of hate

Events and hate on the streets

FBI data allow us to pinpoint multiple trigger events that coincided with significant spikes in police-recorded hate crime in the US. Although these data are incomplete and do not capture every hate crime (see Chapter 2), they are useful for looking at trends over time.* One of these events proceeded the April 1992 spike in anti-white hate crimes (see Figure 7).

In March 1991, following a police chase in Los Angeles, black construction worker Rodney King was pulled over for speeding and asked to get out of his car. On the assumption that King was reaching for a weapon, four officers tasered him, beat him fifty-six times with batons and kicked him seven times. The assault lasted more than eight minutes as a dozen other officers looked on. King suffered broken bones, a fractured skull and brain damage. Before and around the time of the trial of the officers, amateur video of the beating was shown all over the globe by broadcasters.

On 29 April 1992, a jury (consisting of nine white jurors, one Latinx, one Asian and one mixed-race), acquitted the police officers involved in the beating. The verdict came at a time of deep resentment in the black community in South Central Los Angeles, a community that was gripped by unemployment, crime and overly aggressive policing. Within hours, rioting broke out in response to the verdict and lasted five days.

---

* Crudely put, those police departments that are good at reporting their hate crimes to the FBI tend to be consistently good, and those who are bad are consistently bad (with a few exceptions). Consistency allows for the inspection of trends over time that are not a function of improving or worsening reporting to the FBI.

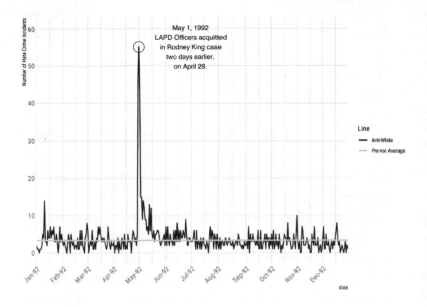

Fig. 7: Anti-white hate crimes across the US following the Rodney King verdict, 1992 (by day).[†]

In one incident, white truck driver Reginald Denny drove into the path of a rioting mob who began to throw rocks, forcing him to stop. He was pulled out of his truck and the mob attacked him with claw hammers and cinderblocks.[5] In another incident, white motorcyclist Matt Haines was pulled off his bike by a mob of black men and shot dead.[6] Analysis by Ohio State University's Professor Ryan King and colleagues shows that the spike, or as he described it, 'pulse' of anti-white hate crime was not confined to LA, indicating the event had an effect across the US, with the backlash as

---

† Reproduced using FBI hate crimes data. Based on R. D. King and G. M. Sutton, 'High Times for Hate Crimes: Explaining the Temporal Clustering of Hate Motivated Offending', *Criminology* 51 (2014), 871–94.

likely in New Jersey as in California.'[7] The eight days after the riots were the most dangerous that year for white people in terms of hate crime. Following a separate federal civil rights case in April 1993, two police officers were found guilty of violating King's civil rights and served thirty months in prison, and two were fired from the LAPD.

The spikes in anti-Muslim hate crime between 1993 and 2001 in the US were all preceded by terror attacks perpetrated in the name of radical Islam: the World Trade Center bombing on 26 February 1993, the Oklahoma City bombing on 19 April 1995 (which was initially blamed on Islamic fundamentalists), and 9/11 in 2001. Each attack was individually associated with a sharp rise in anti-Muslim and anti-Arab hate crime, with 9/11 exhibiting the strongest effect. During the days and weeks following each attack, anti-black hate crimes remained stable, indicating a distinct targeted effect – US citizens were taking out their revenge on people who shared similar characteristics with the perpetrators (or presumed perpetrators) of the attacks. In the case of 9/11, anti-black, anti-Asian and anti-Latinx hate crimes actually declined in the aftermath,[8] whilst the spike in anti-Muslim hate crime lasted for over a month, far in excess of the effect of the other terror attacks. Between the years of 1992 and 2001 the FBI recorded 691 hate crimes against Muslims and Arabs (the actual number was likely much greater, considering the issues with reporting and recording hate crimes). Around 66 per cent of these were perpetrated between 11 September and 31 December 2001.[9] This is an incredibly strong effect that remains the trigger of the largest surge in anti-Muslim hate crime in recent American history.

---

* King et al. confirmed their findings were not a reflection of an increase in police recording after the verdict.

The election of both Barack Obama and Donald Trump turned out to coincide with spikes in hate crime in the US, although the Trump effect was far more significant.[†] FBI hate crimes data from 1992 to 2019 show Trump's election victory was the most likely explanation for a significant spike in the fourth quarter of 2016 (see Figure 8).[‡] To rule out the impact of other possible explanations, economists controlled for a dizzying array of factors, including the effect of the homicide rate, infant mortality rate, prisoner execution rate, unemployment rate, real police expenditures, racial and rural/urban demographics, total ethanol consumption, the proportion of the state House and Senate that were Democrat, other terrorist attacks and even fluctuations by season (hate crimes are more likely to happen in the summer as more people are out and about). None of these alternatives emerged as significant, leading to the conclusion that Trump's win was the most likely explanation for the astonishing rise in hate crimes following the 2016 presidential election.[§] His placement in the White House is

[†] The much smaller spikes in hate crime following Obama's election in 2008 and 2012 likely had more to do with an increased sense of threat experienced by some Americans. Following the placement of a black man in the White House the KKK and Council of Conservative Citizens saw a flood of new interest, bolstered by concerns over immigration and the 2008 financial meltdown. See M. Bigg, 'Election of Obama Provokes Rise in US Hate Crimes', Reuters, 24 November 2008.

[‡] When the detrended hate crime dataset shown in Figure 8 is separated into some of the constituent hate crime types, clear counter-seasonal trend shocks continue to be apparent. At the time of the 2016 election clear spikes are seen for anti-Latinx and anti-black hate crimes. A mixed picture emerges for anti-Muslim hate crimes, with counter-seasonal trend shocks emerging late in 2015, and again in 2016. The Islamic extremist terrorist attack in San Bernardino, California, which killed sixteen people and injured twenty-four, is a likely trigger for the first shock. In response to the attack Trump called for a 'total and complete' ban on Muslims entering the US, something he put into law in January 2017.

[§] A macroeconomic panel regression technique was used by G. Edwards and estimated to have contributed to approximately 410 additional hate crimes nationally per quarter, or 2,048 additional hate crimes from the date of his victory to the end of 2017. In comparison to recent terror attacks such as those in Orlando, Florida and San Bernardino, California, the Trump effect was thirty-three times more powerful in motivating hate crimes.[10]

How can we explain this? Trump's 2016 election campaign was littered with his intolerant outbursts that likely mobilised a prejudiced minority to turn violent. Trump referred to Mexican immigrants as criminals and rapists, questioned the heritage of President Obama, tweeted anti-Semitic content related to Hillary Clinton, and thanked the @WhiteGenocideTM Twitter account for its support (as well as other alt-right and white supremacist accounts that have subsequently been banned by Twitter for breaking their hate speech rules). While the majority of opinions were unswayed by Trump's divisive rhetoric (on the whole Americans' anti-minority prejudice actually declined after the election of Trump[11]), those who already held far-right views were emboldened by seeing these views reflected back at them by the most powerful leader in the world. This minority may also have been galvanised by seeing how many other Americans had voted for Trump, giving the false impression that their extreme views were more widespread than they first assumed.

S. Rushin ('The Effect of President Trump's Election on Hate Crimes', SSRN, 18 January 2018) to rule out a wide range of the most likely alternative explanations for the dramatic increase in hate crimes in the fourth quarter of 2016. While a powerful statistical model, it cannot account for all possible explanations for the rise. To do so, a 'true experiment' is required in which one location at random is subjected to the 'Trump effect', while another control location is not. As the 2016 presidential election affected all US jurisdictions, there is simply no way of running a true experiment, meaning we cannot say with absolute certainty that Trump's rise to power caused a rise in hate crimes. Nonetheless, all quasi-experimental research on the topic indicates this as the most plausible explanation.

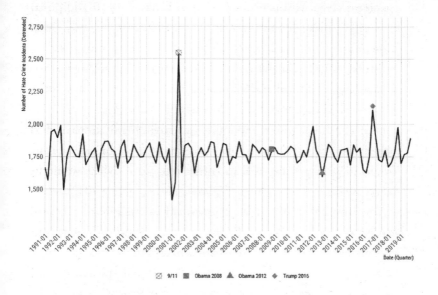

Fig. 8: Hate crimes in the US by quarter, 1992–2019.[*]

Experimental research backs this up. In one study, before the election around 450 test subjects were recruited from states in which the predicted probability of Trump winning was 100 per cent: Alabama, Arkansas, Idaho, Nebraska, Oklahoma, Mississippi, West Virginia, and Wyoming.[12] Half of the test subjects were randomly informed about these 100 per cent odds while the other half were not. Their perception of the social acceptability of strong anti-immigrant sentiment was then measured using a

[*] Reproduced from FBI hate crimes data. Based on G. Edwards and S. Rushin, 'The Effect of President Trump's Election on Hate Crimes', SSRN, 18 January 2018. The data have been detrended to cancel out the effect of seasonality, which can hide other effects. The process of detrending reduces the total number of hate crimes (as seen in the y, or vertical axis) in the dataset, as information is removed to focus on the underlying trends of interest.

donation game with real stakes. Test subjects were first told that they could make a donation to an organisation that was either pro- or anti-immigration, which would be selected at random – in reality, 90 per cent were assigned a staunchly anti-immigrant organisation, the Federation of American Immigration Reform. Subjects were then asked if they would like to authorise the donation of one dollar to the 'randomly' selected organisation on their behalf. Importantly, half of the subjects were told this donation would be kept private, and the other half were told it would be made public.

Test subjects who had been informed of their state's 100 per cent chance of voting for Trump were significantly more likely to donate to the anti-immigration organisation *and to have it publicly known* than those who were not given the same information. The experiment was repeated after Trump's victory and the same results were found: more public donations were made to the anti-immigrant organisation. These experiments show that either thinking your state will overwhelmingly vote for Trump, or Trump's actual win, causally increases the social acceptability of anti-immigrant action to the point where it overrides societal pressure to appear non-prejudiced.

Like bigoted jokes (see Chapter 5), Trump did not make Americans more prejudiced; rather his election and racist tweets temporarily released a minority from having to regulate the prejudiced attitudes they already held, but which they routinely suppressed due to wider societal pressure to appear non-prejudiced. Trump therefore functioned as a 'releaser' of prejudice that likely shaped hateful behaviours on the streets. It will come as no surprise to learn that those counties which most strongly supported Trump saw the largest increases in hate crime after his election.

Looking to the UK, temporal shocks on hate crime rates have also been registered in connection with political votes and terror attacks (see Figure 9). My team's work in the field has shown that the EU referendum vote in 2016 acted as a trigger for hate crime. The grey line in Figure 10 shows our estimate of what would have happened in its absence, based on a projection of the trend before the vote. The bars beneath show the monthly magnitude of the impact of the vote on race and religious (RR) hate crimes. While controlling for a range of factors known to predict hate crimes, my team and I isolated the effect of the campaign and the lead-up to the vote to calculate that combined they resulted in an additional 1,100 hate crimes.

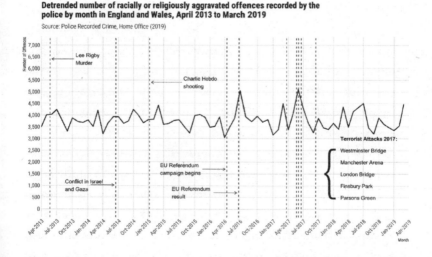

Detrended number of racially or religiously aggravated offences recorded by the police by month in England and Wales, April 2013 to March 2019

Source: Police Recorded Crime, Home Office (2019)

Fig. 9: Hate crimes in England and Wales by month, 2013–19
(seasonally detrended).

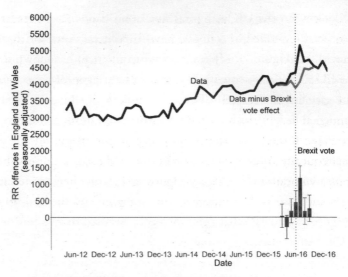

Fig. 10: Estimate of race and religious (RR) hate crimes in the absence of the Brexit vote.

Research conducted at University College London showed that the 7/7 radical Islamic bombing in London in 2005 was associated with an immediate 22 per cent increase in hate crimes against people of Asian and Arab appearance or heritage. The same study also showed that 9/11 increased hate crimes against Asians and Arabs in the UK by 28 per cent, providing the first evidence that events can have an effect internationally.[13] Research from the London School of Economics expanded this study by looking at the influence of ten terror attacks between 2013 and 2017 (seven of which occurred outside of the UK) on hate crime in the UK.[14] All resulted in an increase in hate crimes, including attacks that took place in Tunisia (June 2015) and Berlin (December 2016).

What was most fascinating about this study was the link found between national newspaper coverage of attacks and hate crimes. Islamic extremist terror attacks attract around 375 per cent more media coverage than those based on other motivations, leading to a situation where the public have an inflated sense of threat from these types of attack.[15] This frequency in press reporting is shown to have a causal relationship with hate crimes on the street and online. The decision to act on prejudices also depends on the number killed in the attack. Not surprisingly, both are strongly correlated – the more people killed in a terror attack, the higher the frequency of newspaper stories about the event.*[16] In other words, without such inflated reporting in the press we would likely see fewer hate crimes following terrorist attacks committed in the name of radical Islam.

Moving on to continental Europe, I learned events are also responsible for creating much wider shifts in attitudes towards minorities. Although attitudes are not in themselves harmful, if left unchecked they can develop into prejudice and hate. While digging through the research I found that some European countries experienced an anomalous negative shift in attitudes towards immigrants in October 2002 and March 2004. Harvard University's Professor Joscha Legewie examined why these abnormal patterns emerged, using a particular scientific technique: the natural experiment.[17]

His hunch was that the radical Islamic terrorist bombing in Bali acted as a trigger for the worsening in negative attitudes towards immigrants in EU countries. On 12 October 2002, at approximately 11 p.m. a man entered Paddy's Pub in Kuta, Bali, and detonated his backpack full of explosives. Those lucky enough to escape death and severe injury ran out onto the street in utter panic and horror. A few minutes later a car parked on the now crowded street exploded at the hands of a second suicide bomber.

---

* A correlation of .81, which is extremely high (the range is from 0 to 1).

The attack killed 202 and injured 209, including Indonesians, Australians, Americans and Europeans.

By chance, the European Social Survey (tasked with gathering the attitudes and opinions of the population across the EU) was then halfway through its data collection cycle. This coincidence meant the survey would work as a natural experiment, where the Bali bombing acted as an *exogenous* shock, or external causal trigger. Around half of the people tasked with completing the survey had done so before the attack (and thus became the control group), while the other half answered the questions after the attack (forming the treatment group). Such research studies are impossible to plan, but when accidents like this one come along, researchers rush to get their hands on the data.

The findings showed that the Bali attack was the cause of a significant worsening in attitudes towards all immigrants in Portugal, Poland and Finland. The strength of the effect of the attack was enhanced if the person lived in an area with high unemployment – both Poland and Portugal showed the highest increase in unemployment in 2001–2. The effect was also stronger on people who did not have immigrants as friends or co-workers but who lived in areas with high immigrant numbers. These findings were replicated in relation to the Islamist terrorist bombing in Madrid in 2004. The proportion of the Spanish population that thought immigration was one of the most important issues the country was facing rose from 8 to 21 per cent immediately after the attack, with the effect being strongest in areas with high unemployment. Taken together, these two studies were amongst the first to prove terror attacks cause a worsening in attitudes towards immigrants, especially in people who live in areas characterised by high unemployment, high immigration and low contact with the outgroup.

Events and hate online

The finding that trigger events don't impact everyone equally in terms of hate crime and attitudes towards outgroups has also been replicated on social media. The University of Oxford's Dr Bertram Vidgen studied the tweets sent by followers of four British political parties, namely the Conservatives, Labour, UKIP and the BNP, between 2017 and 2018, covering the period when the UK was hit by the string of terror attacks perpetuated by ISIS and extreme right-wing organisations.[18] Dr Vidgen was careful to remove tweets by bots (automated accounts) that were designed to spread misinformation and hate. His aim was to determine if followers from each party reacted differently to the attacks, and in particular if one group was more susceptible to these trigger events. The expectation was that UKIP and BNP followers would be most likely to post tweets containing Islamophobic hate speech, based on those parties' popularity with those expressing extreme far-right views, and that such behaviour would be less frequent amongst the followers of the more mainstream parties.

The results were surprising. The terror attacks in 2017 triggered followers of all parties to post hate speech. To understand why this was the case, Dr Vidgen applied a theory called cumulative extremism. The theory suggests that extremist ideologies are symbiotic – they feed off each other, and when events like ISIS and far-right terror attacks happen, the opposing ideology's followers are galvanised and mobilised. Each attack then results in an escalation from the opposing side, manifesting in hate crimes, hate speech and even their own terror attacks.

These galvanising and mobilising mechanisms also have a net-widening effect. It's not just the hardcore extremists who get more entrenched in their viewpoints and more active on Twitter and on the streets. Those who consider themselves the mainstream, the average person, can also be 'activated' by extremist incidents, and while their actions may not manifest in taking to the streets and harming the next Muslim they encounter, they might log in to Twitter and post content that is grossly offensive. But this activation is short-lived, and quickly after the inciting terror attack, the hateful tweeting stops within a few days. These 'one-off Islamophobic tweeters' get caught up in the online frenzy of negativity that tends to follow events of national and international interest. Dr Vidgen's continuing research shows that in the UK, those hardcore Islamophobes who tweet hateful posts long after terror attacks are firmly located within the followership of the more right-wing parties. These people are also more likely to post the most grossly offensive hate speech, but they are a very small number compared to the total Twitter population.[19]

Micro-events and hate

Most of the research that has been done on the temporal triggers of hate focuses on major events (e.g. terror attacks, political votes, high-profile court cases) and whole populations (e.g. states and countries). But even micro-events that occur at the city or town level can shape prejudiced behaviour. Following his European-wide investigation, Professor Legewie turned his interest to racial bias in policing in New York City.[20] Although many suspect racial bias has been evident in policing for some time, Legewie's idea was that discrimination is not static over time, but fluctuates in line with particular kinds of events that galvanise conflict between groups – in this case the New York Police Department (NYPD) and black youth.

The NYPD's stop and frisk policy – which had drawn criticism due to its apparent biased application to the black community – was the focus of the study. The practice of stop and frisk increased dramatically in New York City from 160,750 incidents in 2003 to 684,000 in 2011. It was noted that a disproportionate number of black people were being stopped compared to other races. In this period, the black population in NYC was around 25 per cent, whereas their stop and frisk rate was 54 per cent. This compares to a white population of 45 per cent with a 10 per cent stop and frisk rate, and a Latinx population of 28 per cent with a 32 per cent stop and frisk rate. Minority groups were clearly over-targeted by police, but this could not be classed as proof of discrimination as each individual targeting may have been warranted. Tentative evidence of discrimination emerged when it was found that stop and frisk of white suspects yielded higher rates of success in terms of finding weapons and contraband, leading to arrest.

Legewie also looked at police use of force during stop and frisk encounters. Use of force is a potential indicator of prejudice when it is disproportionately applied to different races. When disproportionately applied to a particular racial group, it can indicate officers hold a stereotype that members of that group are more hostile and violent. Across the study period (2003–11) a quarter of all stop-and-frisk events ended in officers using force: 16 per cent with white suspects, 22 per cent with black suspects and 24 per cent with Latinx suspects.

Legewie analysed nearly 4 million police stops before and after shootings of NYPD officers by black men, and focused on the use of force during these stops. The results showed that physical use of force against black suspects increased by 16 per cent after a shooting in 2007 and by 13 per cent after a shooting in 2011, with the effect lasting four to ten days. But what was most surprising about the results was that use of force against white and Latinx suspects did not increase at all after incidents when members of both groups had shot an officer. Legewie's analysis, which controlled for a host of factors, proved that certain shootings cause the racialised use of force for a temporary period. The NYPD's reaction to events of extreme violence against one of their own was race-specific, possibly driven by underlying prejudice and stereotypes about black youth in the city.

From national-level political votes right down to precinct-level cop killings, some events have the power to spur a prejudiced attitude into hateful violence. From the studies examined so far, we know the types of events that can accelerate us towards hate, but they do not tell us anything about the psychological mechanisms of how these events trigger some people but not others.

Our psychology and trigger events

Events that challenge our values can lead to hate

Following trigger events it is possible to separate people into three broad categories: 1) those triggered to do bad things, such as discrimination and hate crime; 2) those triggered to do good things, such as donating to charity; and 3) those who were emotionally impacted by the events, but were not triggered to do good or bad things. These are not exclusive groups; those who do bad things can also do good things, and vice versa. The point is that events can create polarised behaviours within people and between them.

Those who do the bad things displace their frustration and aggression onto people who they think share the values and characteristics of those responsible for the event. This displacement occurs most often following events where the original perpetrators are not accessible – in the case of suicidal terror-ism those responsible are dead; in the case of high-profile court cases those responsible are either imprisoned or of higher status than the average person, making them unreachable, and so on. Displacement can take many forms, ranging from violent hate crimes on the streets to more subtle forms of discrimination. After 9/11, as well as hate crimes increasing, Muslims also faced increased discrimination in housing and employment.[21]

The psychological phenomenon called *sacred value protection* differentiates those who do bad things and those who do good things following trigger events. Professor Linda Skitka and col-leagues at the University of Illinois at Chicago set out to test what happens when our sacred values – those that we hold precious and dear beyond all other things – are challenged by events.[22] In response to 9/11 they found examples of people expressing *moral outrage*, including increased discrimination and hate crimes, and examples of people expressing *moral cleansing*, including display-ing the American flag, volunteering, donating blood and seeing family more frequently.[23]

Moral outrage involves displaying condemnation of the threat to sacred values, including demonising, expressing anger towards and punishing challengers. Moral cleansing involves reaffirming core values by engaging in acts that shore them up, including more frequent bonding with those who hold the same values and doing good deeds. Moral outrage often involves negative engagement with the challengers, whereas moral cleansing is most likely to be performed via positive interactions with like-minded people, or even in isolation.

After 9/11 roughly equal numbers of Americans engaged in only moral outrage (18 per cent) or only moral cleansing (16 per cent). The majority (37 per cent) engaged in behaviours that were indicative of both types of reaction. Those remaining (29 per cent) did nothing to indicate outrage or cleansing. Those most angry at 9/11 were more likely to engage in moral outrage, while those most scared were more likely to engage in moral cleansing. Those feeling both fear and anger engaged in both types of reaction.[24]

Professor Skitka's study examined reactions that were primarily interactive, such as committing hate crimes against those who looked like the perpetrators or visiting family more after the event. The University of Toronto's Behavioural Research Lab examined non-interactive forms of reaction to value threat – those strange behaviours we adopt when we are alone to cope with trigger events.[25]

The Lab studied what they called the 'Macbeth effect'. In William Shakespeare's *Macbeth*, Lady Macbeth thought a small amount of water might clear her of the murder of King Duncan, as indicated in the lines: 'A little water clears us of this deed,' and 'Out, damned spot; out, I say.' The study set out to test if a threat to values, a psychological phenomenon, could be addressed by an individual physically cleaning themselves, mirroring Lady Macbeth's hope. If subjects were more inclined to want to clean themselves after a value violation, and if the act of cleaning itself achieved the desired effect of ridding the subject of the associated negative emotions, then what would this all mean for reactions to trigger events?

The first study tested whether threats to values increased the tendency for subjects to think of cleansing words. Each subject was asked to remember how they felt in relation to a past event personal to them that either challenged or reinforced their values, such as attending a gay wedding or taking part in a religious festival. Subjects were then asked to fill in the letters of the following word fragments: W _ _ H, SH _ _ ER and S _ _ P. Each fragment could be completed to form cleaning words ('wash', 'shower' and 'soap') or non-cleaning words (e.g. 'wish', 'shiver' and 'ship'). Subjects tasked with recalling an event that challenged their values were significantly more likely to generate cleaning words, compared to the subjects who recalled events reinforcing their values.

The second study tested whether choosing cleaning words was the result of subjects' desire to clean their bodies after recalling a value-threatening event. To distract them from the real aim of the study, subjects were told they were taking part in an experiment on handwriting and personality. Two groups were formed: Group 1 was tasked with copying out a short story about an event that challenged their values, say attending the gay wedding, while Group 2 copied out a story that reinforced their values, say taking part in the religious festival. After the tasks, subjects were asked to rate their desire for a range of products.

One set of products was related to cleaning: Crest toothpaste, Windex cleaner, Tide detergent, Dove soap and Lysol disinfectant. The other set was a random collection of products that had nothing to do with cleaning: orange juice, CD cases, Snickers bars, batteries and Post-it notes. Group 2, the hypothetical religious festival attendees, selected non-cleaning products as much as cleaning products. But Group 1, the hypothetical gay wedding attendees, were significantly more likely to report desiring products like Dove soap rather than products like the Snickers bar. Those who thought about the value-challenging event desired the cleaning products far more than those who thought about the value-reinforcing event.

To test whether the subjects actually wanted to clean themselves, the first study was extended. Subjects were given a choice of gift for taking part in the tasks: a pack of antiseptic wipes or a pen. Seventy-five per cent of those in Group 1 (challenged values) took the wipes, compared to just over 37.5 per cent of those in Group 2 (reinforced values). All subjects then filled out a survey about how they were feeling, having previously either cleaned their hands or not. Those who cleaned their hands in Group 1 reported less disgust, regret, guilt, shame, embarrassment and anger, while those in the same group who did not clean their hands showed no reduction in these negative emotions.

A final question asked Group 1 if they would volunteer for another study to help out a poor graduate student with their thesis. Those who had cleaned their hands after recalling the value-challenging story were much less likely to offer to help: only 41 per cent, compared to 74 per cent of those who had not cleaned their hands. The act of cleaning after having your values challenged somehow washes away 'moral stains' and restores your 'stable moral self' that is less likely to need to reinforce personal values by doing something helpful.*

Is it strange to find that physical washing assuages negative emotions stemming from threats to values? Is cleaning merely a basic function to turn the unclean into the clean, to change a state of disorder into order, or is there more behind the practice? In her pioneering book *Purity and Danger*, anthropologist Mary Douglas notes that holiness and impurity are at opposite poles.[26] Putting aside the point that one person's dirty can be another person's clean, the process of ritualised washing is observed in many religions. Judaism, Islam, Hinduism, Sikhism, Christianity and many other religions have ancient washing practices that are symbolic of purity of body *and* mind. There is little question that these ancient practices, passed down the generations, instil a sense that physical washing can also cleanse the soul.

---

* A meta-analysis found the Macbeth Effect is likely to exist only under certain conditions.

Vigil for Srinivas Kuchibhotla, who was murdered by Adam Purinton on 22 February 2017. Around a month earlier Trump introduced his 'Muslim ban'.

Satoshi Uematsu (left) murdered nineteen disabled people at his former place of employment. He could not be charged with a hate crime under the law in Japan.

Map 1: Choropleth showing hate crimes recorded by the police in 2019.

Map 2: Cartogram showing hate crimes recorded by the police in 2019.

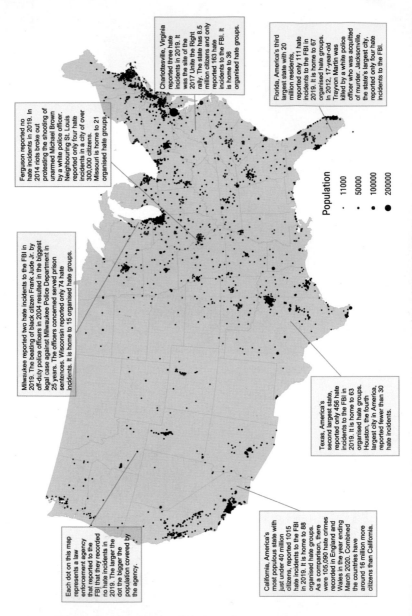

Charlottesville, Virginia reported three hate incidents in 2019. It was the site of the 2017 Unite the Right rally. The state has 8.5 million citizens and only reported 163 hate incidents to the FBI. It is home to 36 organised hate groups.

Florida, America's third largest state with 20 million residents, reported only 111 hate incidents to the FBI in 2019. It is home to 67 organised hate groups. In 2012, 17-year-old Trayvon Martin was killed by a white police officer who was acquitted of murder. Jacksonville, the state's largest city, reported only four hate incidents to the FBI.

Ferguson reported no hate incidents in 2019. In 2014 riots broke out protesting the shooting of unarmed Michael Brown by a white police officer. Neighbouring St. Louis reported only four hate incidents in a city of over 300,000 citizens. Missouri is home to 21 organised hate groups.

Milwaukee reported two hate incidents to the FBI in 2019. The beating of black citizen Frank Jude Jr. by off-duty police officers in 2004 resulted in the biggest legal case against Milwaukee Police Department in 25 years. The officers concerned served prison sentences. Wisconsin reported only 74 hate incidents. It is home to 15 organised hate groups.

Each dot on this map represents a law enforcement agency that reported to the FBI that they recorded no hate incidents in 2019. The larger the dot the bigger the population covered by the agency.

Texas, America's second largest state, reported only 456 hate incidents to the FBI in 2019. It is home to 63 organised hate groups. Houston, the fourth largest city in America, reported fewer than 30 hate incidents.

California, America's most populous state with just under 40 million citizens, reported 1015 hate incidents to the FBI in 2019. It is home to 88 organised hate groups. As a comparison, there were 105,090 hate crimes recorded in England and Wales in the year ending March 2020. Combined the countries have around 16 million more citizens than California.

Population

· 11000
· 50000
• 100000
● 200000

Map 3: Places in the United States where law enforcement agencies recorded no hate incidents in 2019. Note: Only towns and cities with populations over 10,000 shown.
Source: FBI Uniform Crime Reporting Program Hate Crime Statistics.

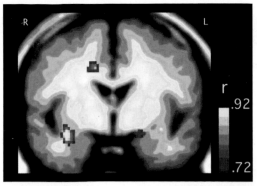

Brains of white people viewing black faces. Coloured regions in the lower area show amygdala activation correlated with IAT scores that indicate an automatic preference for White Americans over African Americans.

(E. Phelps et al. 'Performance on indirect measures of race evaluation predicts amygdala activation', *Journal of Cognitive Neuroscience* 2000, 12:5, 729–38.)

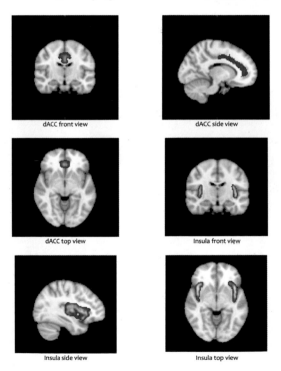

Results of my brain scan showing activation in the insula and dorsal anterior cingulate cortex (dACC) when viewing black male angry faces.

The men accused of the rape and murder of South African gay rights activist Eudy Simelane in court in August 2009. The judge concluded that Eudy's sexual orientation had 'no significance' in her killing and no hate crime was recorded.

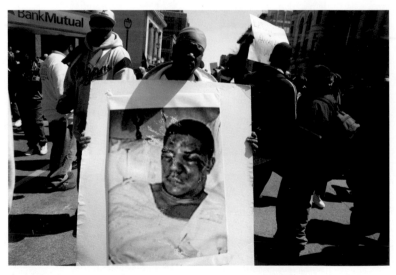

A protester holds a photo of Frank Jude Jr during a march in Milwaukee. Jude Jr was beaten by police officers in 2004. An all-white jury acquitted the officers of most charges.

A neighbour looks at a trail of blood left by hate crime victim Marcelo Lucero, an Ecuadorean immigrant killed by seventeen-year-old high school star athlete Jeffrey Conroy in Patchogue, New York, November 2008.

Unite the Right rally, Charlottesville, Virginia, August 2017. The internet played a key role in making the rally the most successful extreme rightwing event in recent times.

A Rohingya Muslim man looking at Facebook at a refugee camp, September 2017. According to the United Nations, Facebook had a 'determining role' in stirring up hate in the Rohingya genocide in Myanmar.

Mohamed Salah with his daughter and wife in May 2019. Merseyside had a 16 per cent lower hate crime rate following Salah's signing compared to the expected rate had he not joined Liverpool FC.

The implications of the Behavioural Research Lab's work may be significant. If, following events that challenge our values, we can individually deal with negative feelings by physically cleaning ourselves, does this mean we are less likely to engage in bad and good behaviours towards others? If so, should those with a pro-clivity towards moral outrage take a long hot bath after a trigger event? The scientific jury is still out on that one, but research on washing and value threat may help us understand the inactivity of those who do not show moral outrage. Sacred value protection seems to explain the behaviours of some people following trigger events. The behaviours of the remainder may be explained by a peculiar psychological process that kicks in when events remind us of our own inevitable death.

Events that remind us of our mortality can lead to hate

The University of Arizona's Professor Jeff Greenberg frequently roped in his psychology students to take part in his research. One semester he turned up to class and informed his undergraduates that for credit they could take part in one of his experiments. Those who came forward were asked about their political leanings. The group was whittled down to those with moderate liberal or conservative views. In total, thirty-six male and female students were selected.[27]

On the day of the experiment, the college students tentatively stepped into the lab. Following some polite chit-chat, Professor Greenberg split the undergraduates into four groups, first by their political persuasions, and then into control and treatment groups. On one side of the room, Republicans and Democrats in the control group were asked to write down 'the emotions that the thought of your next important exam arouses in you' and 'what you think will happen to you as you physically take your next exam'. On the other side of the room, Republicans and Democrats in the treatment group were asked to write down 'the emotions that the thought of your own death arouses in you' and 'what you think will happen to you as you physically die, and once you are physically dead'.

Once they had finished jotting down their fearful and morbid thoughts, all students were asked to read a text extract that was critical of either Republican or Democratic views. The design of the study meant that four experimental conditions were created: i) thought about death and challenged political views; ii) thought about death and reinforced political views; iii) thought about exams and challenged political views; and iv) thought about exams and reinforced political views.

In the second part of the study the students were told they were going to taste food and note their preferences. Much better than writing about your own death and exams, they thought. But there was a twist. The food they would be tasting was extremely hot sauce and the students themselves would administer it to each other, anonymously. In turn, each student was instructed to fill a cup with the hot sauce to give to another student, who was hidden behind a screen. The cups could be filled as high as they wanted, but all of it would need to be consumed by the receiving student. Then came the crucial point: the student filling the cup was told that the receiving student had written the extract – and that they did not like hot sauce!

The students set about filling the cups. A Republican was told her receiver had written the anti-Republican extract, so filled the cup to the brim, then a Democrat was told his receiver had written the same extract, so went easy. Another Democrat was told her receiver had written the anti-Democrat extract, so sloshed in the sauce. This process went on until all servers and receivers were done and Professor Greenberg had made a note of the amounts of extremely hot sauce administered.

The students surmised the experiment was about political leaning and aggression; that it would show that either Republicans or Democrats were more aggressive with their hot-sauce deposits. But they were wrong. Political leaning was only used to define an ingroup and an outgroup. What the study found was that students in the first experimental condition, those who were asked to think about death and who had their political views challenged, dished out way more hot sauce than subjects in any of the other conditions. On average, politically challenged students who thought about exams filled their pots with fifteen grams of hot sauce, compared to the students with their own mortality on their minds, who sloshed in a tongue-tingling twenty-six grams. Professor Greenberg had shown that the combination of being reminded of our own mortality and having our views challenged makes us aggressive towards the outgroup, a finding equally applicable to Republicans and Democrats.

An array of experiments that test the effect of considering our own mortality on our attitudes towards others have come up with similar revelations.[28] The basic idea is that being reminded that we will inevitably die one day affects our behaviour towards outgroups. We are the only species on the planet that knows of its own mortality, and this knowledge shapes who we are and how we interact with others.

Humans are programmed by evolution to preserve life beyond almost all else. When reminded of our eventual deaths nearly all of us are filled with fear, even terror. We take great care preparing our children for the knowledge that life ends – that their grandparents, parents, partners and pets will eventually die. Sometimes we do a good job, and sometimes not. When it hits us for the first time, usually between the ages of three and five, it must be arresting, although you'd be hard pressed to find anyone who can recall this moment in their past.

From early childhood the fear of death is something we all live with, but it is mostly well managed and contained. If the inescapable terror wasn't contained, we would be paralysed by it. The hope is that every child will feel protected from death by its loving parents whom they consider as all-powerful. But when this protection falls away, either by the realisation that our parents cannot save us from death, or by their actual death, we have to find alternative ways of coping. One way of calming the terror stemming from the realisation of our own mortality is to think of ways we may transcend our own deaths. This is why some people turn to religion in older age, as the inevitable day comes closer. The belief in some religions that death is just a process where we move on to a better place helps contain the terror. For those who do not turn to religion, it can be their legacy that tames the fear.

For most of us nowadays it is our cultural worldview and the associated values we hold most dear that act as a buffer, turning a state of terror to one of comfort in the face of our own mortality. We may invest in and teach the attitude of positivity, the principle of freedom, the quality of hard work, the belief in equality and fairness, and the love for country. Meaning in life stems from cultural worldviews, and by subscribing and contributing to the institutions that underpin them, say the nation or the family, we can leave a legacy, symbolically escaping the finality of death.

When subscribing and contributing to cultural worldviews, our self-esteem gets a boost, which in turn acts like a buffer to the anxiety posed by death. We think: 'I am doing something good that contributes to my country and family, so at least on my deathbed I can look back and think my life was worth something.'

Throughout history great poets, philosophers and writers have singled out this phenomenon in their thoughts on death:

'From my rotting body, flowers shall grow and I am in them and that is eternity.' – Thomas Moore

'I shall not wholly die, and a great part of me will escape the grave.' – Horace

'Even death is not to be feared by one who has lived wisely.' – Buddha

'By becoming deeply aware of our mortality, we intensify our experience of every aspect of life.' – Robert Greene

An eclectic mix of musings, but the point is clear: in whatever form, many of us invest in the belief in some form of afterlife (not necessarily in the religious sense) to escape the terror of death – be it offspring, a work of art or science or simply a legacy of a life well lived.

Professor Greenberg and colleagues call this phenomenon 'terror management'. Terror Management Theory (TMT) posits that when we are reminded of our inevitable deaths we draw upon and intensify our cultural worldviews to provide a sense of 'symbolic immortality'. In the immediate aftermath of events such as terrorist attacks, we deal with the terror of being reminded of our mortality by increasing cohesion with people like us who share the same worldview, at the expense of those who do not.

TMT has two psychological components: cultural worldview and self-esteem. We manage the terror of death by holding onto: (i) belief in a cultural worldview that gives our life meaning, predictability and ideals to live up to; and (ii) the goal of striving to uphold the ideals and become 'better people'. When we invest in both we feel we have some sense of immortality because our virtuous behaviour is what separates us from every other species – we have legacies and souls that live on beyond death.

The first formal test of TMT was conducted on judges who were asked to pass sentence on cases involving sex workers. One group of judges was reminded of their mortality beforehand, while the other group was not. Those who were reminded of their mortality gave heftier fines to sex workers, leading the scientists to conclude that thinking about death before passing sentence made the judges reinforce their values at the expense of the defendants (and their outgroup).[29]

Since this first experiment some five hundred studies have demonstrated that when people are reminded of their inevitable death (referred to as *mortality salience*), they more readily defend their values (cultural worldview) and try harder to live up to them, thus making themselves feel better (self-esteem). The scientific evidence shows mortality salience makes people in all walks of life reinforce their worldview at the expense of the outgroup: they more readily defend their worldview, make harsh judgements about people who challenge their values, and treat those challengers poorly. These reinforcements allow us to reduce the terror associated with death.[30]

Following experiments like the hot-sauce study, scientists turned to the effect of events that act as reminders of our mortality on topics such as politics and prejudice. One study set out to test if terror attacks made charismatic political leaders who espouse populist views more attractive to the average person.[31] The terror attacks on 9/11 were taken as events that were likely to increase mortality salience among people in the US. Following the attacks, the popularity of President Bush increased from around a 50 per cent approval rating (he had lost the popular vote in the 2000 election) to around 90 per cent on 13 September. The scientists wanted to formally test whether reminders of mortality and 9/11 actually prompted subjects to approve of Bush.

Around eighty students from Rutgers University in New Jersey were split into two groups. Group 1, the experimental group, was asked the standard TMT treatment questions: 'Please briefly describe the emotions that the thought of your own death arouses in you,' and 'Jot down, as specifically as you can, what you think will happen to you as you physically die and once you are physically dead.' Group 2, the control group, was simply asked to recall something they had seen on television recently. All subjects were then asked to read the following paragraph:

> It is essential that our citizens band together and support the President of the United States in his efforts to secure our great Nation against the dangers of terrorism. Personally, I endorse the actions of President Bush and the members of his administration who have taken bold action in Iraq. I appreciate our President's wisdom regarding the need to remove Saddam Hussein from power and his Homeland Security Policy is a source of great comfort to me. It annoys me when I hear other people complain that President Bush is using his war against terrorism as a cover for instituting policies that, in the long run, will be detrimental to this country. We need to stand behind our President and not be distracted by citizens who are less than patriotic. Ever since the attack on our country on September 11, 2001, Mr. Bush has been a source of strength and inspiration to us all. God bless him and God bless America.

Subjects were then asked: 'To what extent do you endorse this statement?' and were instructed to state their level of agreement with two statements: 'I share many of the attitudes expressed in the above statement,' and 'Personally, I feel secure knowing that the President is doing everything possible to guard against any further attacks against the United States.'[32] The results indicated that subjects who had been asked to think of their deaths were significantly more likely to answer all three questions positively in support of Bush.

To take the study further, in place of the questions asking subjects to imagine their own deaths, the researchers tested whether 9/11 itself acted as a reminder of death. In other words, could presenting word strings such as '911' and 'WTC' induce the fear of death in subjects, and if so would this fear have the same effect on approval for Bush? The researchers factored in the politics of students to control for any potential bias. Asking subjects to remember 9/11 significantly increased support for Bush amongst both Republicans and Democrats, but more so amongst Democrats.

A final study checked whether mortality salience resulted in an increase in favour for any political leader. It compared support for Bush and 2004 presidential candidate John Kerry. For subjects asked to think about their mortality, support for Bush rocketed, while support for Kerry plummeted. Thinking about death seems only to increase support for leaders with particular qualities: those who promote populist depictions of the ingroup as heroes who will triumph over the evil outgroup. TMT posits that people need meaning in their life, and in times of crisis that eat away at their worldview, charismatic leaders can fill the void. They provide a substitute for a parent in that they can help manage the deeply rooted fear of death in the face of uncertainty that terror attacks can bring.[33]

TMT research then turned to the effect of terror attacks on prejudice. In a fascinating study conducted just over a decade after 9/11, City University of New York Professor Florette Cohen and colleagues focused on the proposed building of the controversial 'Ground Zero mosque', a 2010 development consisting of an Islamic community center and mosque two blocks from the site of the World Trade Center.[34] A sample of fifty-four non-Muslim college students was split into two groups. One group was asked the usual TMT mortality salience questions, and the other the question about exams. The passage below was then read by each subject:

After nearly a month of debate, the controversy surrounding the new Cordoba House or the so-called 'Ground Zero Mosque' continues to roil, both domestically and worldwide. The proposed Islamic community center has dominated much of the US news cycle and political discourse. Critics say it would be inappropriate to build a mosque on the 'hallowed ground' of Ground Zero. Yet there are already mosques throughout New York City. As the debate rages many actually question the right of the mosque itself to be built. And others acknowledge its right to exist but question the location of its existence.

They were then each asked three questions: 'How much do you support a decision to build the new Cordoba House?' 'How much do you believe it a constitutional right to build the new Cordoba House?' and 'Do you believe it's wrong to build Cordoba House at Ground Zero even though it may be a constitutional right?' The subtle reminder of death, yet again, made subjects more critical of the proposed mosque build. Subjects in the mortality salience condition were also more likely to think the mosque should be built further away from Ground Zero than those who had not had the reminder of death.

A second study found that subjects asked to imagine a mosque being built in their neighbourhood more readily generated death-related words in a word completion task (e.g. C O F F _ _ could be completed 'coffee' or 'coffin'), including 'coffin', 'grave', 'dead', 'skull', 'corpse' and 'stiff'. The same results were not found for other places of worship, such as churches or synagogues (meaning the result was not down to subjects relating places of worship to funerals more generally). For the subjects in this study, thinking about a mosque, and therefore Islam, generated as much death-related thought as thinking of their own death.

Religion versus hate

A final part of Professor Cohen's study found that the effect of being reminded of our death could be neutralised. After priming with mortality salience, subjects were asked to read a story about Florida pastor Terry Jones publicly burning the Quran in 2011. This had the impact of actually decreasing death-associated thoughts related to the building of a mosque in subjects' neighbourhoods. It seems the destruction of a sacred item, even one belonging to another cultural worldview, neutralised the threat of Islam for the American college students.[35] Sacred items that represent worldviews, like flags, statues of great figures and religious texts, seem to hold enough power that their destruction carries meaning between cultures and beliefs, not only within.

The power of religion has also been found to moderate the effect of mortality salience on perceptions of the outgroup. Recall that earlier I stated some people manage the terror of their eventual death by investing in a religion that has a notion of an afterlife. It may therefore follow that after terror attacks, religious people are less likely to need to manage their fear of death by bolstering their cultural worldview, because their faith already acts as an anxiety buffer.

The University of Oxford's Professor Miles Hewstone and colleagues went about testing if religion was a maker or an unmaker of prejudice.[36] Over two hundred non-Muslim British university students were split by four experimental conditions: religious with mortality salience priming; religious without mortality salience priming; non-religious with mortality salience priming; and non-religious without mortality salience priming. As with most previous TMT research, for non-religious subjects, being reminded of death increased negative attitudes towards Muslims. But this effect was absent for most religious subjects. Of the religious group, prejudice increased with mortality salience only for subjects indicating they were of a 'fundamentalist' orientation – those who thought their beliefs were paramount and that all other religions were invalid. These findings show that for the most part religion can make us more tolerant, even in the face of deadly crises.

There are other factors that shape our individual susceptibility to the shock of horrific events. Those who are depressed, anxious, lonely and generally frustrated, when reminded of their deaths, are more likely to react in negative ways towards immigrants following terror attacks. In contrast, those people who have high self-esteem, think they regularly contribute to the greater good, or are religious (although not fundamentalist) cope in less negative ways with the reminder of their mortality in similar circumstances.[37] A meta-analysis of two decades of TMT research found that the negative effects of being reminded of death were strongest in the US, followed by the UK and other western countries, and non-western countries.[38] The difference in strength of effect between countries may have a lot to do with how religious a population is – widespread religion equals a widespread death anxiety buffer.

These variations aside, the evidence for terror management is compelling, especially in relation to the effect of terror attacks.[*] It's so convincing that if I were asked to create a policy for government based on this evidence I would suggest better equipping children to cope with death, in the form of education and parental support, and to put in place ready-made campaigns for activation in the immediate aftermath of events, like terror attacks, that promote tolerance and understanding of the worldviews of others (see Chapter 11 for more).

Hate is a temporal phenomenon. Our tolerance for the 'other' varies from day to day, week to week and month to month, often driven by external factors. Even those who are full of hate have days when they feel it less intensely. As discussed in Chapter 1, we know age can influence our behaviour towards the outgroup. In our youth we are more inclined to be 'groupish' – to want to be included, selected and valued by our ingroup – and this may manifest in negativity towards the outgroup. Our brains at the time of adolescence are also still maturing – the part of the grey matter responsible for executive control (prefrontal cortex) is still developing, meaning we are less well equipped to rationalise away misperceived threats from the 'other'.

From what we have seen in this chapter it is abundantly clear that

---

[*] A multi-lab replication attempt of an early TMT experiment failed to obtain support for the mortality salience effect on worldview defense. However, this replication effort deviated from its pre-registered protocol leading to questionable results.

it is not just our biological clock that impacts upon our chances of expressing intolerance and hate. Events distant from ourselves also shape our behaviours and can act as an accelerant for hate crime and speech. For the majority of us in society, a trigger event forces us to consider our own values and mortality, sharpening our attention to 'us' versus 'them'. For a minority, such events tip them over the edge from sharing a prejudiced thought with a trusted member of their ingroup to publicly expressing hateful sentiment. A string of extremist events, buttressed by inflammatory media coverage and political noise-making, can transform these one-off haters into more casual repeat offenders. In the aftermath of an event, consistent reminders of the 'dangerous other' by public figures increase division, making the drift into more extreme ways of thinking a possibility. But drift alone is not enough to turn a temporary state of moral outrage after a divisive event into a more sustained way of life that has hate at its core; a toxic state of being that undergoes a migration from the 'push' to the 'pull' category of hate. For this transformation to be completed, access to radical material and grooming by extremist groups is needed.

8

Subcultures of Hate

Salman was one of four children born into the Abedi family in Manchester, UK. His refugee parents, devout Muslims who followed the Salafist movement, fled to Britain in 1991 to escape Gaddafi's Libya. As a quiet boy, Salman did not seem out of place in the strict religious household. At school he was a below-average performer, and was often subjected to bullying, sometimes brought about by his own aggressive behaviour. He would often clash with other pupils over a difference in morals and had got into fights with girls for their wearing of short skirts. Despite these outbursts, his school friends at the time described him as a moderate Muslim.

In 2011, his father Ramadan, a long-time member of the jihadist Libyan Islamic Fighting Group, returned to Libya to assist them in their battle against the Gaddafi regime. Salman, then sixteen, and his younger brother Hashem were flown out during school holidays to join their father, and pictures uploaded to social media show them holding automatic weapons, with one captioned 'Hashem the lion . . . training.'

Their time in Libya was formative, and after his return to the UK, Salman spread the word of radical Islam to anyone that would listen. His apparent early radicalisation was noticed, and he was reported to the anti-terrorist hotline by two friends attending the Manchester College, where he was studying. After college Salman took a gap year and returned to Libya with his brother, making contact with members of ISIS. After being injured during the fighting, he was returned to the UK by the Royal Navy along with a hundred other British nationals.

In 2015, Salman enrolled at Salford University to study business management, only to drop out the year after. In the absence of his mother and father, he got involved with a local gang of Libyan boys and started drinking alcohol and smoking cannabis. Around this time Salman was heard vowing revenge at the funeral of a friend who was killed in a gang feud between the Libyans and a splinter group of the Moss Side Bloods (a local Manchester gang). Shortly after he began referring to Britons as 'infidels'.

In 2016, Salman's friend Abdalraouf Abdallah was imprisoned for running an ISIS communications network from his home in Manchester. Salman was allowed to visit him twice while in prison during his five-year sentence. At this time Salman began wearing more traditional Arab clothing and was seen by neighbours praying loudly in the street. Worried he was losing his way, Ramadan routinely commanded the presence of his son in Tripoli.

A year passed by before Salman's final trip to Libya in May 2017. Concerned with his son's increasingly extreme comments, Ramadan confiscated Salman's passport. To get it back, he told his parents he wanted to make Umrah, a pilgrimage to Mecca. Instead he flew from Tripoli back to the UK on 17 May, where he was shortly after caught on CCTV withdrawing £250 from a cash machine and purchasing a blue Karrimor rucksack.

On the evening of 22 May 2017, thousands of children and parents were leaving the Manchester Arena after enjoying Ariana Grande's performance on her *Dangerous Woman* tour. Fourteen-year-old Eve Senior noticed something strange as she escorted her younger sister from the venue: Salman Abedi was walking against the flow of the crowd, as he passed within five metres of her wearing his blue rucksack. Seconds later he detonated a bomb filled with nuts and bolts, killing himself and twenty-two concert-goers, the youngest of whom was eight-year-old Saffie Roussos. Eve and her sister survived the attack, but the shrapnel caused them life-long physical damage.

Minutes before the bomb blast, Salman made a call to his mother and Hashem in Tripoli to ask for their forgiveness. Salman was believed to have been radicalised by ISIS on his trips to Libya and in Manchester in the absence of his family, a process that was made easier by his exposure to extremist violence at the hands of his father. An investigation by the *Guardian* found that sixteen dead or convicted ISIS terrorists had emerged from the same area of Manchester in which Salman grew up.[1] Ramadan claimed he knew nothing of the planned attack. Hashem was arrested the day after the suicide bombing by police in Tripoli, and was eventually extradited, tried and found guilty of twenty-two charges of murder on the grounds that he had assisted his brother in building the bomb. He was jailed for a minimum of fifty-five years.

What turns the 'average' person into a murdering terrorist? Would Joseph Paul Franklin have embarked on his racist killing spree had he not dabbled with the American Nazi Party and the United Klans of America? Were David Copeland's abominable crimes fuelled by his exposure to extremist material provided by the National Socialist Movement? If Salman Abedi had not learned of the Libyan Islamic Fighting Group via his father and then been cherry-picked by ISIS, would he have detonated his suicide bomb in Manchester Arena?

Violent extremists sit towards the very end of the spectrum of hate. What makes them different from the 'average' hate offender is their zealous subscription to religious or political goals and the deadliness of their violence.[2] The majority of violent extremist acts involve either right-wing, left-wing, religious, separatist/territorial or single-issue (such as animal rights) motivations. Groups that operate within these categories require unflinchingly loyal volunteers for their cause. The perceived losses each group endures secure this dedication and motivate the adoption of radical ways of thinking and intense group bonding. Their extreme violence is made legitimate by the adoption of language like 'struggle', 'battle', 'war' and 'resistance'. These words neutralise their horrific actions – the 'good fight' justifies the killing. One person's terrorist is another person's freedom fighter.

The 'good fight' raises the individual from the fleeting, trivial and pedestrian, and puts them into a state of meaning, coherence and significance. Being part of the embattled radical group also generates other dividends, including learning life skills such as discipline, coping strategies, independence from parents and gaining a perceived wider perspective on existence.[3] This improved and sought-after state, fuelled by conflict, is difficult to relinquish. The fight in itself then becomes the goal, not the intended end of the struggle.[4] This means that dealing with radical groups is difficult, as simply removing threats or meeting their needs is unlikely to stop the conflict. Members of these groups are firmly in the 'pull' category of hate. Instead of 'pushing' the object of hate away, extremist haters seek out their victims, now considered their sworn enemy that must be eliminated.

The demographic and psychological characteristics of people that have been radicalised in the west are indistinguishable from those of the general population. They are mostly married with children and have good educations and jobs.[5] You would be hard pressed to point your finger at a violent extremist in a crowd, especially if they wanted to go unnoticed (often a requirement for a terrorist). They are not those people who look 'shifty' or act in strange ways around others. For the most part, they do not suffer with mental illness or express any social anxieties that may alert you to their presence.[6] They walk among us undetectable. But criminological and psychological research has isolated certain factors that help us understand the radicalisation process.

The basic theory of radicalisation has three stages. In the first stage a person finds a *motivation* to raise themselves out of a state of meaninglessness and vulnerability, often by embarking on a quest for personal significance. In the second stage, *radical ideology* provides a pathway to personal significance through the promotion of violence, self-sacrifice and 'martyrdom'. The third and final stage involves complex *social processes* that sustain interaction with radical peers who are also on a quest for significance. These processes create a strong, almost family-like bond with the group, increasing the chances of extremist behaviours with little regard for personal consequences.

Each phase of radicalisation can vary by the context and the individual.[7] For some individuals, vulnerability may be felt more acutely due to psychological weaknesses brought about by past traumas, and in some areas or countries there may be larger networks of radical peers ready to recruit vulnerable people to their cause. While this is an oversimplified summary of the radicalisation process (for example, it may not best explain 'lone wolf' attackers), it captures the major accelerants that are responsible for turning the average 'hater' into a full-blown murdering terrorist.

Quest for significance and extreme hatred

We've all had that moment when we think 'what's it all for?' The loss of a job, dropping out of school or a break-up can bring on a sense of despair. Most of us find the will to carry on, and somewhere down the road we discover something to invest in that makes us feel of value again. An acute form of this uncertainty is called 'a quest for significance'. It repeatedly emerges as a motivation for joining hateful subcultures.[8]

Emerging adulthood, between the ages of eighteen and twenty-five, has been identified as a period of exploration, with low commitment to the institutions of society, but most importantly a period when life's ups and downs can be felt most acutely, largely due to underdeveloped coping strategies (the executive control area of the brain is not fully formed until around the age of twenty-five).[9] This is fertile ground for those looking to inculcate radical religious or political ideologies, as the openness to new ideas, the freedoms of responsibility from a career and family, and actual or perceived personal 'losses', can create an available and willing subject.

A study of nine young Swedish adults involved in various forms of extremism (right-wing, left-wing and Islamist) found that all of them became involved between the ages of sixteen and twenty, and engaged with the extremist group for roughly two years before leaving.[10] All had committed violent acts in the name of their ideology, ranging from assault and robbery to manslaughter and murder. They all indicated a moment of loss of significance in their life that initiated their reaching out to radical groups.[11] The words of Damir, an ex-ISIS fighter in the study, sum up this listless state:

I did nothing. Just eat and sleep, wake up, sleep, wake up. Of course, you know, I got outside and took walks and met with people but . . . What was missing was a, like a job or school [which he had recently dropped out of]. And, that's not why I went [to Syria], it wasn't because I didn't have school or anything like that, you see. But it would have been better if you, if you were busy doing something, you see.[13]

This period of early adulthood is peppered with minor losses that can lift the 'anchor' on a person. Young people, still developing the skills to cope with life, are set adrift.[12] A yearning to belong to something soon develops, as illustrated by the experiences of Tom, an ex-recruit to Antifa:*

I had nothing to do. I was alone and isolated in my room, you know. I felt really bad. But I had heard that there was this group, Antifa, who hunted Nazis. So I wrote to them on their web page, like 'Help me, there are Nazis at my school, I'm being beaten and bullied by them because I'm from [country]' [sic] . . . I started going to these demonstrations, for refugees, social justice, that kind of thing. And there I met with one of the organizers, who knew someone, and he introduced me to these . . . people who knew these antifascist groups. And at that point, as I started to hang out with them and listen to them, think about myself in relation to them, I got interested. You know, I had just wanted their help. But now I thought that maybe I could be part of what they were doing. They hunted Nazis, and I wanted to do that too.[14]

Similarly, Eric found personal significance through belonging to a far-right organisation:

---

* Antifa is an anti-fascist direct-action movement made up of activists from the left and far left who have a history of using violence against the alt-right, neo-Nazis and white supremacists at public rallies, demonstrations and protests. Mark Bray claims in *Antifa: The Anti-Fascist Handbook* (2017) that while Antifa do not rule out violence as a form of self-defence in tackling fascism, violent responses only form a minority of their activities, which also include non-violent disruption of protests before they happen by pressuring venues to cancel events, exposing neo-Nazis to their employers, and running public education campaigns.

I hung out with people who were like me. I mean, in the sense that they were tough and hard and you came into a new group and made new friends, who were very vigorous and powerful . . . They liked that I was a big guy, and I was tough, I was violent. I think they liked that . . . Out in the street, if something happened, they called on me. So it was, I was just supposed to be there. I was appreciated there . . . I enjoyed that, my feelings had [finally] found an outlet and I really enjoyed this, back then. And I felt even stronger, I felt even more strongly about this, I was very, my self-confidence was really high. [Through these people] I got to know myself more, what I was capable of. It was as if, I felt great, it was as if I had spread my wings.[15]

Deep-rooted attachments to group members, fuelling positive feelings of being needed and wanted, provide a pathway for radical ideology transmission.* Brain imaging studies back this up. A group of thirty-eight Moroccan men vulnerable to Islamist radicalisation had their brain activity monitored.[16] Each participant was placed inside an fMRI scanner and asked to take part in a computer game called Cyberball: a ball is tossed between four players thirty times, but the subjects in the treatment group are only tossed the ball twice, making them feel excluded.

Following the game, with participants in one group feeling excluded and participants in the other included, all were tasked with making decisions regarding their willingness to fight or die for a sacred belief in Islam (e.g. 'Those who abandon Allah's true religion should be punished most severely') or a non-sacred belief (e.g. 'Elderly people should be respected'). As expected,

---

* Hate is not the only motivator, and some radicals are driven by prosocial goals.

participants were more willing to fight and die for extreme Islamic sacred values, which lit up an area of the brain responsible for processing rule-bound thinking. This brain area showed much less activation when participants were presented with the decision to fight and die for a non-sacred value. But it lit up far more in the participants who felt socially excluded as a result of the Cyberball game manipulation. Feeling left out and marginalised seems to make would-be recruits to radical groups more willing to consider extreme behaviours, even when sacred values are not invoked.

Quest for significance as a motivating factor has also been tested on those radicalised in their own countries. A group of sixty-five imprisoned Islamic extremists from the Abu Sayyaf Group in the Philippines were recruited for a study.[17] The subjects were all men who had experienced varying levels of loss of significance, resulting in feelings of humiliation or shame relating to personal circumstances. These feelings indicate personal devaluation and loss of social standing that beg for some kind of closure – living with them day in, day out is difficult and a need to eradicate them through 'significance restoration' soon arises following their onset.

All subjects in the study were asked how often they had experienced feelings of shame and humiliation and if they could recall people laughing at them in their everyday lives. They were also asked a series of questions on loss-induced feelings of uncertainty and anxiety. These acted as measures of the level of 'loss impact', which if high enough may induce a strong need for significance restoration.

Results showed that those who had experienced a high level of loss of significance (through humiliation and shameful events in their lives), and who expressed a high degree of uncertainty and anxiety as a result, were more likely to approve of extremist behaviour, including suicide bombing. Although seemingly a self-less act, the Islamic extremist suicide bomber may believe they can bring closure on their deeply personal loss of significance by living forever as a martyr.

In a surprising twist, these findings were replicated in a study on everyday Americans. Those who reported humiliation and shame in their life, and corresponding feelings of anxiety and uncertainty, were much more likely to adopt extreme views on abortion (e.g. backing an outright ban or allowing termination late in pregnancy). These studies, conducted on imprisoned Islamic extremists and everyday Americans, provide compelling evidence that loss of significance leading to anxiety and uncertainty in life can lead to the adoption of extremist views. This is not to say that all those who experience a loss in life and feel smaller because of it will become suicide bombers. There are many who go through the ups and downs of life and easily resist extremist thought and behaviour. Other factors are at play of course, including the context within which loss of significance is experienced.

For those with loving families, living in stable countries with strong institutions and rule of law, turning to extremist behaviours to restore a sense of significance is unlikely. There are many other legitimate pathways for significance restoration – volunteering, helping out a friend, going back to school, getting a new job. But consider those without family ties, living in less stable countries or in societies that they feel are at odds with their beliefs, where the rule of law is weak or is not respected. These people may be more inclined to risk what little they have to restore some feeling of significance through fighting for a radical ideology. When the cause of loss of significance is the very thing they end up fighting then they will undoubtedly find others who share their pain, making extremist violence more likely.

Collective quests for significance and extreme hate

In 2017, Dr Katarzyna Jasko at the Jagiellonian University in Poland embarked on a novel study. She asked 260 Moroccan Muslims to take part in a survey on their beliefs about jihad.[18] Participants were recruited from two very different cities, Casablanca, whose residents are known to be largely moderate in their views, and Tétouan (aka the White Dove) in the Rif Mountains region, the home of the 2004 Madrid bombers and the 2015 Paris and 2016 Brussels attackers. Casablanca and Tétouan therefore represented cities with loose and close ties to radical networks respectively.

Each Moroccan participant was asked sets of questions about general and personal feelings. The first set asked them to rate five collective statements about Muslims: 'Muslims deserve special treatment', 'I will never be satisfied until Muslims get the recognition they deserve', 'It really makes me angry when others criticise Muslims', 'If Muslims had a major say in the world, the world would be a much better place', and 'Not many people seem to fully understand the importance of Muslims.' The second set asked participants how often they experienced negative personal feelings like unimportance, humiliation, shame and worthlessness. The third set asked about support for ideological violence in service of Islam by asking the respondents to agree or disagree with statements like 'Jihad is the only remedy for jahiliyyah [ignorance],' and 'Armed Jihad is a personal obligation of all Muslims today.'

Those living in Tétouan reported much higher agreement with the collective statements about Muslims than those living in Casablanca, who scored higher for the questions on negative personal feelings. Tétouan residents were more likely to have family, friends and acquaintances who shared the same quest for significance, creating the feeling that personal quests were not so singular after all.[19] This Tétouan collective quest for significance was tightly bound to a belief in extremist violence. For Muslims living in Casablanca, collective feelings about Muslims had a much weaker bond to extremist violence, and instead it was individual negative feelings that were linked with desire for violence.

Due to Tétouan's closer historical ties to extremism compared to Casablanca, Dr Jasko concluded that being surrounded by radical peers creates a collective quest for significance, which in turn can foster a stronger belief in extremist violence. The merging of individual quests for significance, fuelled by a collective sense of loss, can help predict who will carry out an act of extremist violence. Who your family and friends are makes a great difference when it comes to acting on a radical belief.

The motivation for radical ideologies that call for violent actions emanates from losses felt by an identifiable group, defined by race, religion, class, politics or territory.[20] These losses, or strains, can include things like feeling repressed by a dominant group; claims over lost territory; value, cultural and religious disputes; and threats to ways of life. A sense among group members that these strains have a long history and are intense, widespread, seemingly unending, unjustified and impact upon group members indiscriminately (e.g. including children) is usually required to invest in an ideology that justifies violent action.

Although these strains are 'real' for many extremist groups, such as the Irish Republican Army and al-Qaeda, they may be less observable for others, such as National Action in the UK and the Ku Klux Klan in the US. For many far-right and far-left groups it is the *perception* of strain that motivates hate, not the reality of it – for example the perception that the white heterosexual working class are somehow threatened by growing numbers of non-whites in their communities, facilitated by a 'Jewish-run' government and media.

Extremist groups promote beliefs that are favourable to terrorism through a range of tactics. These include drawing attention to the differences between 'us' and 'them'; cutting all ties with those who do not share the group's ideology; emphasising losses and their impacts on the most vulnerable in their group; claiming those responsible for the loss are subhuman and undeserving of understanding; closing down non-violent forms of action by claiming they are ineffective or exhausted; coaching on how to feel in reaction to loss, with a focus on hopelessness, humiliation, shame and rage; offering rewards for taking part in extremist violence, such as respect and martyrdom; convincing members that individual violent acts are part of a wider campaign, and won't necessarily lead to victory in isolation; and offering up a utopian vision of the future that can only be brought about by violent action.[21]

Such a barrage, if accepted without much question, inevitably results in a feeling of 'linked fate', where losses impact the group and individual equally.[22] Extreme negative emotion arises that can reduce a member's ability to cope with the perceived loss in a way that does not break the law. The once-held belief that acts of extremist violence are wrong slowly gets chipped away – there are no illegitimate victims in terrorist acts, and all death is justified for the higher calling.

Extremist ideology and compassion

Psychological research on how humans respond to victims of undeserved suffering shows how compassion can result in harmful consequences for those responsible. Compassion normally results in empathising with the victims and attempting to alleviate suffering. We give money to charity when shown the suffering of children in war-torn Syria and give blood to victims when we witness the horrors of terror attacks. These are prosocial behaviours that tend not to have any negative consequences.

In cases of extreme suffering that prompt moral outrage, compassion for the victim can manifest in punishment of the perpetrator. What happens to our compassion when it is caused by events such as terror attacks, war, sexual assaults and abuse of children, where we cannot help the victim directly? Do we want those responsible to be punished, and would we be willing to take matters into our own hands?

A study found that our desire to punish increased dramatically if the suffering in question was deemed highly unjust and morally outrageous, as in the case of terror attacks and sexual assaults.[23] When the suffering of victims cannot be alleviated, compassion and moral outrage generates a desire to harm the perpetrator instead. Radical belief systems often exploit this fact, using the inability to alleviate suffering to justify targeting those accused of causing it. Instead of sending donations to those suffering in the Middle East, radical Islamist groups target western governments. Instead of helping homeless and unemployed white people find shelter and work, white supremacist groups target ethnic minorities and immigrants. Radical ideology is crafted to legitimise this course of action. It rewires the would-be radical's thought process to ensure feelings of compassion and moral outrage result in a desire for punishment, not the direct reduction of suffering.

God made me do it

The power of scripture in shaping thought and behaviour is generally well accepted. Belief in a superior being can motivate behaviours that represent the best of human nature. Even between groups locked in a multigenerational war, such as Jewish Israelis and Muslim Palestinians, the request to see dilemmas from the perspective of God, and not from a personal viewpoint, motivates a more equal valuation of human life.[24]

Religious belief is also associated with wars and the deaths of millions. Once compassion has been manipulated to generate the desired outcome, in some religious ideologies the idea that God sanctions the killing of the enemy is gradually inculcated. Some holy texts include depictions of violence against 'unbelievers' that if taken out of context seem to promote the murder of fellow humans. Evidence on the radicalisation process points to extreme interpretations of scripture as the cause of much extremist violence.

The science shows particular readings of religious scriptures can even motivate violent outcomes amongst non-radical believers. In one study, a written passage from the Old Testament was provided to 490 college students split into two groups. The passage of text provided to one group told a story set in Israel about the rape and murder of a man's wife by a neighbouring tribe and the question of what to do in retaliation. It included the following lines which explicitly justified retaliatory action:

> The assembly fasted and prayed before the LORD and
> asked 'What shall be done about the sins of our brothers
> in Benjamin?'; and the LORD answered them, saying
> that no such abomination could stand among his people.
> The LORD commanded Israel to take arms against their
> brothers and chasten them before the LORD.[25]

God was obeyed, resulting in the massacre of tens of thousands of men, women and children. The same passage of text was provided to the other group of test subjects, but without the lines in which God commanded vengeance.

After reading the passage, subjects from both groups took part in another, seemingly separate study. Subjects were paired and told to compete in a button-pressing task, where one who was slower to react would receive a blast of sound though earphones. The winner could select the level of noise the loser was subjected to, with the loudest being comparable to a smoke alarm. Religious students who had read the passage including the justification of violence by God were twice as likely to turn the volume up to the maximum, compared to religious students who had read the passage without the justification. The same pattern was also found in non-religious students, but with a much reduced effect.[26]

These results, taken from a sample of non-radical college students, may indicate that the selective reading and misinterpretation of violent passages in holy texts by religious extremist groups is implicated in the use of violence by radicalised members. Professor Scott Atran of France's National Centre for Scientific Research has spent years seeking out extremists in occupied regions in the Middle East. Unlike most who are looking for these jihadists, he doesn't want to apprehend or kill them. He wants to talk to them. When he can't get to them, he gets to their parents, who reveal their innermost thoughts about the radicalisation of their child. His central question is: Can a fundamentalist belief in the word of one's God push a person closer to suicidal behaviour for the sake of that belief?

In one of Professor Atran's studies the 'sacred values' of sharia were compared with those of democracy among 260 potential Middle Eastern freedom fighters in towns associated with militant jihad.[27] Those who subscribed to sharia (around 60 per cent) were far more likely to self-sacrifice and engage in militant jihad, even if doing so would result in their children suffering.[28] People will fight and die for an idea, be it religious doctrine, freedom of speech or self-determination. Up to seventy thousand American patriots died fighting for 'sacred rights' in the War of Independence against the British. At the time, the standard of living in the colonies was the highest in the world – they wanted for nothing but to have a voice in their own destiny and were willing to sacrifice themselves to attain it.[29]

Taking advantage of powerful fMRI technology, Professor Atran and colleagues scanned the brains of thirty members of the radical group Lashkar-e-Taiba, known to support al-Qaeda.[30] The aim was to discover what circuits in the brain were involved in being willing to self-sacrifice for 'sacred values'. To put it crudely, is the brain activity of religious extremist suicide bombers different from ours?

Specifically, they wanted to know if suicide bombers failed to engage the part of the brain that weighs up the costs and benefits of actions (the dorsolateral prefrontal cortex or dlPFC), allowing them to sacrifice themselves despite the evolutionary imperative that drives us to survive. In addition, they sought to find out if parts of the brain responsible for making us fall into line with peer expectations also fail to engage in extremists. This final question is important for understanding if extremists are reformable or not – can a religious extremist ever give up the 'sacred values' they have adopted?

While in the brain scanner, the jihadists were presented with a list of sacred values (e.g. 'Prophet Mohammed must never be caricatured') and a list of non-sacred values (e.g. 'Elderly members of the community should be respected') and were then asked to rate their willingness to self-sacrifice via fighting and dying for each. When presented with sacred values that motivated self-sacrifice, the areas involved in assessing costs and benefits in extremists' brains activated less, compared to when they were presented with non-sacred values and decisions to self-sacrifice.

The results showed that logic has little sway in deciding the actions of suicide bombers. One argument is that sacred values are so deeply held that there is little need to process decisions when presented with a choice invoking them. Unlike non-sacred values that are not deeply held, which have to be mentally processed on the fly when a choice invokes their consideration, sacred values and their implications have been 'cached offline'.

One study lent empirical support to this idea by showing that the ventromedial prefrontal cortex (vmPFC) engaged within the brains of a sample of Pakistani jihadists when they were asked to consider self-sacrificing for their sacred values.[31] The vmPFC is the less rational counterpart to the dlPFC, and is involved in making decisions based on emotion. If these findings hold up to future scrutiny, trying to talk down an extremist wrapped in explosives with logical argument relating to the costs of their actions and instrumental trade-offs is unlikely to work.

There was one encouraging finding from the study that may be useful in making sure extremists' thumbs don't end up hovering over a detonator button in the first instance. Extremists' brains are the same as ours when it comes to the influence of our peers. Getting a suicide bomber to reconsider their actions is best done by one of their own. The influence of the embattled 'brotherhood' is so powerful that it can make and unmake a terrorist.

Adherence to an ideology's sacred values can illuminate the pathway to individual and collective significance, and can even be used to justify killing. But not all of those who subscribe to an extremist ideology kill. Many with unwavering belief only ever engage in non-violent activities (although clearly implicated in the eventual terrorist act), including recruitment, training, planning, communications and financing. If the answer is not in the heavens, maybe it can be found on the battlefield.

Warrior psychology

A strand of science dubbed 'warrior psychology' puts to the test the theory that extreme levels of bonding to a group – a form of *identity fusion* where the individual and group become one – can lead to the types of unfathomable self-sacrifice we see in suicide terror attacks. Fusion happens when the boundary between the individual and group becomes difficult to draw as the two have started to blend together.

This is more than the feeling that we belong to a group within our school, workplace or local community. The fusion is so extreme that individual and group believe they share 'essence', where one cannot imagine existing without the other: total devotion. In this fused state, an attack on the group is experienced as a direct attack on the individual.[32] For our ancestors in prehistory, fusion was essential for the survival of groups, and hence individuals. In the face of terrifying battles against neighbouring tribes, fusion ensured no individual fled the fight in order to save themselves.

The idea of fusion has been tested on tribal warriors in Papua New Guinea, Islamic jihadists in Indonesia, anti-Gaddafi revolutionaries in Libya and football hooligans in Brazil. All who reported high levels of identity fusion were willing to fight and die to defend their group. The ultimate sacrifice, normally reserved for our closest kin, was being offered up for a group of genetically different members of society. This rare process helps to explain the unimaginable acts of suicide terrorism carried out in the name of an ingroup against an outgroup – ISIS against westerners, the far right against Muslims, white supremacists against people of colour.

If you think of how many people hold extreme beliefs in society today, and then count the number of suicide attacks in recent history, there is a huge mismatch in the tens of thousands. Where there are sacred values to be held, there is usually a group underpinning them. You might ask: What came first, the group or the ideology? Can there be an ideology without a group? Does a set of beliefs have to be shared to qualify it as an ideology? If so, what form does this sharing take? Fusion to a group may range from weak to strong, and here lies an answer. It is strong identity fusion, and not so much extremist beliefs, that may tell us who will become the next suicide bomber and who will not. But how can we know who is most fused with an extremist group? The answer is in ritual and shared trauma.

Drawing on the classic work of sociologist Emile Durkheim and psychologist Leon Festinger,[33] Professor Harvey Whitehouse of the University of Oxford claims that collective traumatic experiences are key to identity fusion, including rituals such as painful rites of passage. Society is awash with ritual, ranging from 'hazing' practices in college and the military to rites of passage in warrior tribes. Anthropologists have for decades written of the terrifying rituals endured by those initiated into war bands in Papua New Guinea. The list of strange, often seemingly meaningless activities makes for a difficult read, and includes 'penis-bleeding' and 'piercing of the nasal septa and the burning of forearms'.[34] The rituals are designed to induce maximum terror in the uninitiated, and they often succeed. Witnessing others go through such an ordeal resulted in one young man defecating on the spot at the sight of what was in store for him.[35]

Rituals undertaken by warrior tribes change the initiated

permanently in ways that bond them to the group. Because the rituals are weird and puzzling, in that they have no practical reason for taking place, those who go through them continually search for their meaning. A recently initiated young man may ask himself, 'Why did people I trust require me to endure having my penis mutilated to become a man?' This constant search for an answer, over months and years after the ritual, creates deep symbolic meanings that are group-specific. The psychological theory of *cognitive dissonance* shows that people who go through unpleasant initiations end up more bonded to the group because they strive to rationalise why they accepted the challenge and why the peers they trust insisted upon it.[36] Tentative conclusions include 'I did it to prove my loyalty and commitment to the group' and 'They insisted we endure the pain to weed out the freeloaders.'[37]

In addition, extreme acts forced upon the uninitiated create a sense of shared trauma which comes to define them. The memory of these shared rituals is burned into the minds of the initiated, and becomes part of the history of the individual, who cannot be separated from the group.[38] Importantly, the process of ritual does not have to be physical to induce fusion. Enduring emotional rituals, such as repeated storytelling of traumatic experience, can also create a sense of shared pain, fear and disgust in listeners, fusing them in a similar, but less powerful, way to physical ritual.*[39]

---

* A thorough review of research on terrorism showed that initiation rituals were common in small terror cells involved in planning suicide attacks. Ritual telling of stories including 'sacrificial myths' and ceremonies commemorating 'martyrs' are common, as are ritual tests of commitment to the group (see R. Pape, *Dying to Win: The Strategic Logic of Suicide Terrorism*, Random House, 2005). Radical groups have marshalled the force of fusion through stories of collective trauma and manufactured rituals, to turn 'average' haters into killing machines (see H. Whitehouse, 'Dying for the Group: Towards a General Theory of Extreme Self-sacrifice', *Behavioral and Brain Sciences* 41 (2018)).

Fusion and generosity towards the ingroup

The weird and wonderful traditions practised during Thaipoosam Cavadee, a Hindu festival in Mauritius about faith, endurance and penance, are a good example of rituals that can create identity fusion. Participants in the festival endure a range of rituals, some more taxing than others. Most show their faith by chanting mantras and making offerings of rose water, clarified butter and milk. A minority go the extra mile to show their endurance and penance, including piercing the tongue, cheek, chest, back, stomach and thighs with small spears, known as vels, and pulling chariots attached by hooks to the skin of the back for several hours, before climbing a mountain barefoot to a Kovil temple.

Around a hundred Thaipoosam Cavadee festival-goers took part in a study on fusion.[40] These included high-ordeal performers (those who underwent lots of body piercing and chariot tugging) and low-ordeal performers (those who just engaged in mantra-chanting and offerings). All were given two hundred rupees (an average of two days' salary) for completing a simple questionnaire, and upon their departure were asked to enter a booth where they could donate some of their fee to the temple.

The results showed that low-ordeal performers, those who mainly just prayed, gave an average of eighty-one rupees, compared to 133 rupees given by the high-ordeal performers, those who skewered themselves. Those high-ordeal performers who reported feeling the most pain gave the most to the temple. But in a surprising twist, a third group, called high-ordeal observers, those who assisted and watched the skewered but endured no physical pain themselves, actually donated the most, an average of 161 rupees. This third group actually reported experiencing by proxy similar levels of pain to those skewered, through simply observing and assisting. The researchers concluded that both going through and witnessing painful rituals had the effect of fusing individuals with the group.

Fusion and hateful violence

Warrior psychology has also been used to understand subcultural hate and violence among football hooligans. Football teams share many traits with warring tribes, including demarcated territory (e.g. pubs and bars), forms of dress (e.g. football kits and scarves), traditions, rituals and chants, a share of 'won resources', such as money from betting, and group status.[41] Super-fans are also known to generate intense feelings of hate towards rival teams, especially when the team they support has suffered a string of defeats.

Identity fusion theory was applied to violent clashes between Brazilian *torcidas organizadas*, groups of rival football hooligans. The study tested whether the super-fans who engaged in the most violence were more fused with their group than the fans who engaged in less or no violence. Brazilian football fans completed a survey with questions asking about their willingness to self-sacrifice for fellow fans, including 'I would fight someone physically threatening another fan of my team' and 'I would sacrifice my life if it saved another fan's life.'

Members of *torcidas organizadas* (around half of the sample) reported high levels of identity fusion, showing a willingness to engage in hateful football violence far more often than the average fan. Highly fused fans also reported more willingness to die for the group. Poorly fused members of *torcidas organizadas* engaged in much less violence and were less willing to self-sacrifice, indicating that simply being a member of a hooligan 'firm' did not

271

explain propensity to fight or die for the group. The scientists concluded that members of *torcidas organizadas* who had fused identities with the group could rapidly escalate to hateful violence and self-sacrifice to protect their 'psychological brothers-in-arms'.[42] These results were also replicated in a study of 725 football fans in the UK. Fans of losing teams were more willing to sacrifice themselves in a Moral Dilemma task (see Chapter 5) than were the fans of winning teams, indicating enhanced fusion in the face of threat.[43]

These findings suggest that football violence is not simply a product of maladjustment, a form of sociopathy or antisocial behaviour, or simple displays of masculinity or class pride. Members of *torcidas organizadas*, hooligan firms and 'ultra' groups are also motivated by identity fusion to protect their group's physical and reputational safety by using hateful violence in the face of a rival team threat.

Fusion and self-sacrifice in the name of hate

With evidence mounting for the roles of ritual and fusion in changing behaviour, such as donating money and defensive football violence, can it explain extreme acts of selflessness – dying for one's group? A study into the psychological mindset of Libyan rebels involved in the struggle against the Gaddafi regime suggests it can.[44] Most of those who joined the fight in Libya, like Manchester Arena bomber Salman Abedi, had never borne arms before, and knew their chances of dying on the battlefield were depressingly high – it could well be a suicide mission.

Four different battalions comprising 179 rebels participated in the study. Rebels self-identified as either frontline fighters or logistical supporters (i.e. non-combatants). All were asked to look at the image in Figure 11 and identify with a letter on the scale from A, indicating total separation of the self and group, to E, which indicated that the self and group were one.

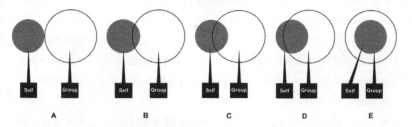

Fig. 11: Image scale of identity fusion.*

Almost all rebels chose E as best representing how they saw themselves in relation to their battalion – completely fused. This was an astonishing finding, as it compares to a usual fusion rate of between 6 and 41 per cent (amongst citizens across eleven countries and six continents in peacetime).[45] When asked who they were most fused with, 45 per cent of fighters chose their battalion over their family (compared to 28 per cent of non-fighters). Younger men were significantly more likely to join as frontline fighters, and were most likely to indicate they were more fused with the battalion than with their own family.

This stark difference was down to the horrific trauma of battle only experienced by the fighters (recall that Salman Abedi was injured on the battlefield), and was akin to the rites of passage experienced in the Papua New Guinean war tribes. Once a person shares such horrors with fellow group members, the bonds formed are kin-like, if not super-kin-like.

* W. B. Swann, Jr et al., 'Identity Fusion: The Interplay of Personal and Social Identities in Extreme Group Behavior', *Journal of Personality and Social Psychology* 96 (2009), 995–1011.

Is fusion always needed for hateful murder?

In the case of Salman Abedi, once he had gone through the first two phases of radicalisation, fusion seems to have completed his transformation into a suicide bomber. His exposure to fighting against the regime in Libya at a young age, and his subsequent rudderless existence in the UK in the absence of his parents, likely created in him a need for a personal quest for significance. It is possible he experienced a harsh decline from a warrior-like status in Libya, fighting and being wounded next to his 'brothers-in-arms', to a status of insignificance back in the UK.

A short period of drug and alcohol abuse may have been his temporary fix for feeling small and of little value. Repeated trips back to Libya involving meetings with ISIS, followed through with links to extremists in the UK, may have created in him a collective quest for significance. These quests are known to feed off group-based radical ideology, and we know Abedi became increasingly devout a year or so before the bombing. Finally, he was likely fused to both his proximate (Manchester-based) and distant (Libyan) 'brothers-in-arms', paving the way to his self-sacrifice in the name of radical Islam.

In the absence of fusion, would Abedi have become a suicide bomber? Some scientists have argued that devotion to radical ideology alone can explain suicide terrorism. This may certainly be the case for 'lone wolf' terror attackers who have no or limited history of group involvement (although they may imagine they are part of a group).[46] The National Consortium for the Study of Terrorism and Responses to Terrorism has studied radicalised individuals in the US. Its data show that only around 30 per cent were part of a clique, and that extreme behaviours were more likely to manifest in non-clique members.[47] This was certainly the case with both Joseph Paul Franklin and David Copeland, who seemed to self-radicalise, then join groups only to abandon them before an opportunity for fusion could arise.

For these far-right terrorists, it may be more pertinent to examine individual cognitive differences that do not rely on group relations. For example, an experience such as the loss of parents during childhood might play a part in creating attachment issues that are known to fuel violence as a means to fulfil the need to be noticed and accepted by their ingroup.[48] This is akin to the quest for significance mentioned earlier as a possible reason for terrorist self-sacrifice.[49] Like other 'lone wolf' terrorists, Franklin and Copeland may have been psychologically predisposed to over-empathise with the perceived suffering of their ingroup (the white race), leading them to engage in attacks that they were unlikely to get away with.[50] This over-sensitivity can also come into play where a group's honour has been threatened, leading to aggression as a proof of dedication.[51]

Limitations considered, a host of empirical studies published between 2009 and 2019 show that identity fusion can act like a trigger, pushing some who believe in an extreme ideology over that tipping point into hateful violence and murder. When it plays a role, the evolved drive to sacrifice for genetic kin has been hijacked by group ideology, where fellow members are considered psychological brothers-in-arms.

Because of this convincing body of evidence, the advice to policy makers wanting to tackle radicalisation is to steer clear of directly challenging radical versions of religion or making them illegal. Doing so challenges group and therefore individual identity, which in turn serves to reinforce the sense of threat that helped to radicalise the individual in the first place. Focus instead should be placed on challenging the enablers of identity fusion:

ritual and collective traumatic experience. Meanings of rituals should be questioned, and the validity of shared trauma must be properly investigated and challenged if found to be manufactured. For example, if a young man claims his radicalisation was partly due to his shared frustration that a western government is hell-bent on destroying Islam, or that immigrants are taking over the country, then efforts should be made to disprove such claims with clear evidence and logical argument. Skipping over these elements of fusion and focusing only on challenging the beliefs of radical Islam and the far right, such as attempting to debunk beliefs that non-believers must die or that a race war is inevitable, may only serve to entrench these extreme ideologies.

Violent extremist subcultures can draw on every accelerant of hate covered in this book. They can act like finishing schools for those who have gone through the hate mill, sometimes becoming the final destinations for people who are vulnerable to divisive and violent narratives and who are attracted by their offer of a new, supportive home. While hate may not be an inevitable feature of every extremist subculture, as prosocial reasons like fighting for a 'better future' for everyone can motivate membership and violence (e.g. some ecoterrorist organisations), it is certainly a feature of those whose core mission it is to sow division between groups (e.g. extreme right-wing organisations). These extremist subcultures inculcate in new recruits separatist ideologies that are difficult to challenge or undo with logic and reason, creating an army of indoctrinated soldiers loyal to the cause. Some of the blame lies in our learned over-response to threat triggered by some outgroups, past traumas, and our susceptibility to divisive events. These can indeed make for a toxic mix, but the final ingredient is possibly the most insidious of them all.

9

Rise of the Bots and Trolls

In 1966 MIT professor Joseph Weizenbaum created ELIZA, a computer programme that could hold a conversation with a human.[1] It was capable of conversing in English, German and Welsh, but the programme was more of a trick than a form of artificial intelligence (AI). Within minutes of chatting, it became obvious ELIZA was coded simply to pick up keywords in the human-crafted sentence and repeat them back in the form of questions or requests for further information, creating a conversational loop. Though ELIZA's programming was primitive by today's standards, its influence is still visible in the form of modern chatbots, which remain the barometer of AI sophistication.

In March 2016, Microsoft unveiled Tay, an online chatbot created to demonstrate the company's advanced conversational AI. It was light years ahead of ELIZA, with an algorithm designed to use statistical relationships (known as n-grams) between words, sentences and objects to recognise patterns in online text. It obtained these derived patterns from a vast number of online messages sent to it via a range of sources popular among eighteen-to-twenty-four-year-olds (including Twitter, GroupMe and Kik). From this content it learned how to converse with humans online in a light-hearted way (improvisational comedians assisted in the design of its code).

Tay began its first day with the tweet 'helloooooooo world!!!', followed with a raft of polite messages, avoiding political issues that were prevalent online, such as Black Lives Matter. But it wasn't long before Tay gave up the cute and daft posts for the racist, xenophobic and anti-Semitic. Only sixteen hours after its launch Tay was taken offline. Microsoft claims its AI was targeted by Twitter trolls who fed it with hateful content, not helped by the seemingly unpoliced 'repeat after me' feature that enabled users to dictate the bot's exact words, resulting in some of the most offensive tweets.

But Tay also produced original content that was offensive and hateful, based purely on its own AI that had learnt from the original source material. These included jokes about Hitler and transphobic comments (see Figure 12). No one on Twitter asked Tay to post these messages via the 'repeat after me' command, and Microsoft certainly hadn't trained it to make such posts. Their creation stemmed from the millions of online posts that were mined by the AI. Statistical associations between words and sentences were computed and patterns were found resulting in the regurgitation of hateful online sentiment. Data gleaned from social media radicalised Microsoft's AI in under twenty-four hours.

Fig. 12: Microsoft's Tay AI created hateful content
before it was taken down.

Two years before the creation of Tay, Microsoft had launched a Chinese chatbot, named Xiaoice. Although the technology underlying both was similar, Xiaoice has not suffered the same fate as Tay. Based on China's version of Twitter, Weibo, the popular chatbot has refrained from making hateful posts despite having a reported 660 million users.[2] This may not be surprising given that Chinese users of social media tend to be more restricted in their online conversations due to government monitoring, censorship and manipulation. Research by Harvard professor Gary King provided the first empirical evidence that Chinese state actors (known as the 50 Cent Army, after the amount each commentator is alleged to be paid per social media message) post an average of 448 million messages a year that aim to distract from controversy and change online debates.[3] While I do not advocate a manipulated or censored internet, from a scientific standpoint its existence has facilitated a natural experiment of sorts.

The Chinese online environment is in total contrast to that created by US-based social media giants, where free speech is upheld as a basic right. The stark contrast between the behaviours of Tay and Xiaoice, both designed to learn from human-generated online content, is a reflection of this difference. But again, how the east and west gave rise to two very different chatbots says more about how we use Twitter and Weibo than it does about Microsoft's AI.

We get back what we put in

Tay spouted hate speech because it fed off what humans posted online. Algorithms, bits of computer code designed to learn from human behaviour, play a key role in filtering the information we see. These algorithms govern almost everything we encounter online, from the search results in Google to the specific colour of a hyperlink. How algorithms work (and get things wrong) is increasingly important, as many of us now rely on their output exclusively to keep us up to speed with the information we find most relevant. In the US, online sources, including social media, now outpace TV and traditional print outlets as people's usual first choice when seeking out news (72 per cent compared to 59 per cent and 20 per cent respectively). The pattern in the UK is broadly similar, with the internet ahead (77 per cent), and TV (55 per cent) and print (22 per cent) trailing behind.[4] For younger age groups (particularly those aged sixteen to twenty-four), online sources are their primary gateway to information about the world, family and friends.[5]

Algorithms learn from user behaviour, and therefore influence our collective actions. This means our prejudices and biases become embedded in bits of code that go on to influence what we are exposed to online, reflecting back these biases in often amplified ways. The emerging consensus from the field of data science is that algorithms are assisting in the polarisation of information exposure and hence debate and action online. Take YouTube as an example. The website Algotransparency.org, developed by an ex-Google employee, analyses YouTube's top autoplay suggestions based on any search in order to demonstrate how the site's recommendation algorithm works. People searching for video content on a politician, such as Donald Trump, are often guided by algorithms to more extreme information, such as climate change denial and anti-immigration content. The more they click on these links the further into the rabbit warren they go. Similarly extreme content is offered up to those searching for liberal politicians. The algorithms begin by recommending videos related to socialism, then eventually anti-establishment content and left-wing conspiracy theories.*

A 2017 investigation by the *Wall Street Journal* and an ex-YouTube employee who worked on its recommendation algorithm confirmed that the site routinely returned far-right and far-left sources in answer to mainstream search queries.[6] It did the same for non-political searches: a search for flu vaccines can lead to anti-vaccination videos, while searches for news coverage of school shootings can lead to hoax conspiracy theories. The algorithm is designed to make the site 'sticky', so users will continue to watch videos and help Google make more revenue from advertisers. And it seems to work, with the company claiming its 1.5 billion users (more than the number of homes with TVs globally) watch over a billion hours of its content daily, almost eclipsing TV viewing.[7]

To put these claims to the test, the University of Amsterdam's Professor Bernhard Rieder examined the top twenty recommended videos for searches including 'Gamergate',† 'Islam' and 'Syria' over a forty-four-day period. While some mainstream news sources were recommended as the top video, sources from the alt-right often dominated the top twenty, especially following events such as terror attacks.[8] These videos ranked up hundreds of thousands of views by 'issue hijacking'.‡ Since 2016, Google and YouTube have been altering their algorithms to focus on recommending more authoritative news sources. But the use of new 'deep learning' technology that is informed by billions of user behaviours a day means extreme videos will continue to be recommended if they are popular with site visitors.

---

* Accurate at the time of writing. YouTube have stated they are working to address the way their recommendation algorithm works.

† A largely online controversy involving the US alt-right and video gamers.

‡ Issue hijacking refers to the practice of taking a pre-existing issue and manipulating it to service an alternative, often extreme narrative.

Filter bubbles and our bias

Research on internet 'filter bubbles', often used interchangeably with the term 'echo chambers',* has established that partisan information sources are amplified in online networks of like-minded social media users, where they go largely unchallenged due to ranking algorithms filtering out any challenging posts.[9] Data science shows these filter bubbles are resilient accelerators of prejudice, reinforcing and amplifying extreme viewpoints on both sides of the spectrum.

Looking at over half a million tweets covering the issues of gun control, same-sex marriage and climate change, New York University's Social Perception and Evaluation Lab found that hateful posts related to these issues increased retweeting within filter bubbles, but not between them. The lack of inter-filter bubble retweeting is facilitated by Twitter's 'timeline' algorithm which prioritises content from the accounts that users most frequently engage with (via retweeting or liking). Given that these behaviours are highly biased towards accounts that share users' views, exposure to challenging content is minimised by the algorithm. Filter bubbles therefore become further entrenched via a form of online confirmation bias, facilitated by posts and reposts that contain emotional content in line with held views on deeply moral issues.[10] It therefore seems likely that at points in time when such issues come to the fore, say during court cases, political votes or following a school shooting, occupants of filter bubbles (likely to

---

* 'Echo chamber' refers to the phenomenon of individuals being exposed only to information preferred by like-minded people and encompasses both online and offline manifestations (e.g. social media and the local pub). 'Filter bubble' refers to the online version of this phenomenon only, and implicates algorithms specifically.

be a significant number of us who don't sit on the fence) hunker down and polarise the debate.

According to the science, even if internet users are willing to listen to the opinions of those who don't share their views, such open-mindedness isn't enough to pop the filter bubble. We may be willing to listen, but not to change our minds. To test the resilience of filter bubbles to alternative viewpoints, the Polarization Lab at Duke University ran an experiment to see if they could be dismantled by forced exposure to challenging content, effectively counteracting the effect of Twitter's timeline algorithm.

Republican and Democrat-supporting Twitter users were paid to follow Twitter bots set up by the research team. For one month, these bots automatically posted twenty-four messages a day that challenged the participants' political viewpoints. The team found that Republicans, and to a lesser extent Democrats, actually became more entrenched in their ideology when exposed to opposing views on Twitter, highlighting the resilience of filter bubbles.[11] When exposed to these alternative viewpoints online, we tend to use them to reinforce what we already believe. Those of us with a tolerant mindset can become more liberal when challenged by hate speech, and those of us with an intolerant mindset can become more conservative when challenged by counter-hate speech.

Biased algorithms also feed into other algorithms online in a sort of ecosystem, effectively creating a chain of contagion where one prejudice-reinforcing piece of code infects another. These infected algorithms influence what humans see, and we in turn leave behind a trace of clicks and likes for them to learn more about our behaviours, which then get reflected back to us by other algorithms.

Unsurprisingly, Facebook's algorithms also display similar biases generated from partisan filter bubble content. In 2016 and 2017 the non-profit investigative journalism organisation ProPublica found that Facebook's algorithmic advertising service was facilitating prejudiced targeting. The system allowed advertisers to target their products and events to those who expressed interest in the topics 'Jew hater', 'how to burn jews' and 'History of why jews ruin the world'.[12] As with Twitter's timeline, YouTube's recommendations and Microsoft's chatbot algorithms, Facebook's advertising code is shaped by what users post, share and like. In this instance, the algorithm pulled information from far-right and alt-right filter bubbles where Facebook users had indicated these hateful topics as 'interests'. Once notified, Facebook altered its advertising service and claimed it was not at fault as it was the algorithms that made them available, not staff. Despite these changes, advertisers were still allowed to block housing advertisements being shown to African Americans, Latinxs and Asian Americans for a period of time.*[13]

Gingers are . . .
creepy mutants, going extinct, adopted, dying

Ex-Google employee and *New York Times* journalist Seth Stephens-Davidowitz unearthed something worrying as he began his research for his 2017 book about online search habits, *Everybody Lies*. When US internet users typed the term 'African American' into Google's search engine, a great many of them included words such as 'rude', 'racist', 'stupid', 'ugly' and 'lazy' in the same search. For the term 'Christian', they most often followed it with 'stupid', 'crazy', 'dumb', 'delusional' and 'wrong'.

---

* Twitter also came under fire in 2020 for allowing advertisements to be targeted at users who had an interest in keywords such as 'transphobic', 'anti-gay' and 'white supremacists'. See J. Tidy, 'Twitter Apologises for Letting Ads Target Neo-Nazis and Bigots', BBC News, 16 January 2020.

The Google search algorithm is shaped by our own search terms, which in turn are influenced by what is happening in the world. The terrorist shooting in San Bernardino, California in 2015, perpetrated by Syed Rizwan Farook and Tashfeen Malik, was rapidly followed by a spike on Google searches for 'kill Muslims'. At the time its search rate was equivalent to the searches 'martini recipe' and 'migraine symptoms'.[14]

The repeated pairing of search terms like those above by billions of Google users shapes what others see. Google's 'autocomplete' algorithm predicts what we are searching for before we finish typing the query. It offers us up to ten predictions of our search query based on the first few letters and words we type. Google states that these predictions are based on common or trending searches on the site, our past search history and the area where we live.

The online search giant has come under repeated criticism because this feature was returning hateful predictions, simply because the algorithm was influenced by the billions of searches being made every day. Type in 'are Jews' and Google suggested the term 'evil'. The same suggestion was made for 'Islamists are'. Type in 'blacks are' and the prediction 'not oppressed' popped up. 'Hitler is' was followed by the algorithmic prediction 'my hero' or 'god', and 'white supremacy is' by 'good'.

When Google was called out on these hateful predictions they were quickly removed. Sexually explicit, hateful, violent and dangerous search predictions are now routinely moderated by Google. The company's policy for protecting people against hateful search predictions covers 'race or ethnic origin, religion, disability, age, nationality, veteran status, sexual orientation, gender, gender identity, or any other characteristic that is associated with systemic discrimination or marginalization'.[15]

I tested their system three years after the first correction was implemented. 'Are Jews' was followed by 'an ethnic group', 'European', 'baptised', 'allowed to eat pork' and so on – nothing hateful that I could determine. The same applied to the other examples above, and in the case of 'blacks are' no predictions were made at all. But their system is not perfect: type in a term that deviates from conventional description, or a group that is not explicitly covered in their policy, and predictions make unconfortable viewing for some of us.

When I typed in 'queers are', Google search returned 'an abomination' as one of the ten suggestions (see Figure 13). Amongst others, 'goths are' returned 'weird', 'annoying', 'losers', 'evil', 'attention seekers', 'not attractive'. Similarly, 'gingers are' returned 'creepy', 'mutants', 'going extinct', 'adopted' and 'dying'. The $100+ billion company claims it cannot police all predictions made, as its algorithms are continuously shaped on a daily basis by the billions of searches people make on its site.

queers are

queers are **doing to the soil**
queers are **just better**
queers are **an abomination**
queers are **steers**
the queers are **here**
how many queers are **in the world**
rabbits are queers
steers and queers are **from texas**
firefighters are queers

Fig. 13: Google's autocomplete search predictions for 'queers are' in March 2019, based on my account settings and location.

The Google Translate algorithm suffers from similar biases. Before changes in late 2018,[16] when asked to translate from a language where gender pronouns are non-specific, the algorithm associated males and females with stereotypical gender roles.[17] When I typed in '*hän on lääkäri*' (Finnish for 'she/he is a doctor') Google returned 'he is a doctor' in the English translation, and when I typed in '*hän on sairaanhoitaja*' (Finnish for 'he/she is a nurse') Google returned 'she is a nurse'.* Google states it does not endorse such views, and that it embraces equality and diversity.

At Princeton University, Aylin Caliskan and colleagues decided to test if the content we include on webpages, which Google uses to inform its algorithms, actually does reflect the biases we hold. They replicated the results of the Implicit Association Test (covered in Chapter 3) on the internet by looking for how often individual characteristics, such as gender and race, co-occurred with pleasant and unpleasant terms over billions of webpages.[18] Like those whose IAT score suggests a strong automatic preference for White Americans over African Americans, the analysis of the online data showed the same associations. White American names were more likely to co-occur with pleasant terms online, while African American names were more likely to co-occur with unpleasant terms. Names like 'Brett', 'Matthew', 'Anne' and 'Jill' were more likely to be associated with terms like 'wonderful', 'friend', 'peace' and 'happy', while names like 'Leroy', 'Tyrone', 'Latoya' and 'Tamika' were more likely to be associated with the terms like 'terrible', 'nasty', 'evil' and 'failure'. This has profound implications for how Google's AI learns and repeats these prejudices, but again says more about the implicit biases of humans than the technology itself.

---

* In late 2018 Google took steps to eradicate bias from its translation algorithm. Ask for a translation from Finnish into English using the example provided and you now get the masculine and feminine forms.

How much online hate speech?

If what we post and search for online plays a key role in creating algorithms that pump out prejudiced results, does this mean the internet is awash with hate? Research showed high numbers of young people witnessing online hate speech as far back as 2013.[19] A large representative survey of fifteen-to-thirty-year-olds, covering the US, UK, Germany and Finland, found on average 43 per cent had encountered hate material online. This rose to just over half of those surveyed in the US, while 39 per cent of UK respondents reported encountering such material.

Most hate material was encountered on social media, such as Facebook, Twitter and YouTube. The proportion of survey respondents who reported having been personally targeted was much lower, at around 11 per cent.* The proportion was highest in the US (16 per cent), followed by the UK (12 per cent), Finland (10 per cent) and Germany (4 per cent).[20] Similarly, rates of sending hate material were low in the sample. Those in the US were most likely to admit to this act (4.1 per cent), followed by respondents in Finland (4.0 per cent), the UK (3.4 per cent) and Germany (0.9 per cent). Young men living alone with a close connection to the online world were most likely to post hate material.[21]

Perhaps most concerning is the exposure of young people to online hate. A 2021 survey from the UK's communications regulator, Ofcom, found that half of twelve-to-fifteen-year-olds reported encountering hateful content online, an increase on the 2016 figure of 34 per cent. Girls were more likely than boys to report the content to platforms (33 versus 10 per cent).[22] This increase in exposure to online hate content between 2016 and

---

* The sample did not specifically target those with protected characteristics.

2021 may be a reflection of the number of trigger events that occurred later in the period. As we have seen, hate crime and hate speech tend to increase dramatically in the aftermath of certain events, such as terror attacks and controversial political votes. These events, and others like them, also motivate individuals to take to the internet to spread hateful rhetoric.

Training the machine to count hate

To gather evidence to confirm whether events do act like a trigger for online hate, an additional source of data is required. Police data are flawed due to reporting and recording problems, and survey data are too infrequent, occurring once a year at most. What is needed are data that capture a good proportion, if not all of the hate speech that is sent on a social media platform, at an interval small enough to record the rhythm of events as they unfold. To get these data we need to move away from traditional ways of working and look towards the internet itself.

The work of HateLab, the initiative I run from Cardiff University, examines the production and spread of hate on social media. In contrast to police or survey data on hate speech and crime, our data are generated from direct observations of hate as it occurs in real time on social media. This means we monitor the perpetrators in the act using algorithms developed via machine learning. We essentially teach a machine to recognise hate speech so it can do so at scale and at speed (classifying millions of social media posts a minute as hateful or not).

The basic process of creating a machine that can spot online hate begins with collecting a large corpus of social media posts for human annotation. Next, we get four humans to look at each post and decide if it is hateful or not. These can be members of the general public, or experts in particular forms of hate (e.g. race, transgender, disability). Posts that get at least three out of four votes for hate are then put into a training dataset. This is our gold standard that trains the machine to mimic the human judgement in the annotation task.

Various algorithms are then run across the dataset, including deep learning varieties popular with Google, Facebook, Twitter and Microsoft. But unlike their use of these algorithms, ours are developed in a closed workshop, meaning they can't be gamed by new data being sent to them from mischievous internet users. Once we determine the algorithm that produces the most accurate results, we deploy it on live social media data streams.

Measuring hate in this way is not perfect. The machine learning algorithms we use only approximate human judgement. Our best-performing algorithm gets it right about 90 per cent of the time, but some perform less well (as low as 75 per cent). And the data we use to train the machine are not error-free, as human judgement can be wrong – but we try to minimise this by using multiple judgements. Despite these limitations, this is the agreed-upon process in the scientific community for measuring online phenomena, and it provides us with the first insight into the production of online hate from direct observation.

Using hate speech detection algorithms, my HateLab researchers were the first to measure the Twitter reaction to the terror attack in London in 2013 when Fusilier Lee Rigby was gruesomely murdered in broad daylight outside the Royal Artillery Barracks in Woolwich by two Islamic extremist British Nigerian men. Figure 14 visualises this reaction over time, geographically and textually. The maps of the UK and London show the location of tweets about the attack, with clusters appearing in Manchester (the Rigby family home), the Midlands, South Wales and the west, the east, and Woolwich.

The textual content of tweets is presented in the wordcloud, a representation of the most frequent words used across all tweets posted. Figure 15 shows the frequency of moderate and extreme anti-Muslim online hate speech produced on Twitter in the aftermath of the attack. Moderate hate speech included posts that were likely to cause offence, such as 'Told you we shouldn't have let them Muslims in. Send them home! #BurntheQuran'. Extreme hate speech included similar content, but also degrading racial slurs and expletives that might qualify the offending tweets for deletion and criminal prosecution.

Both forms of online hate speech peaked on the day of the attack and then rapidly declined within the next forty-eight hours. We describe this period of decline as the 'half-life' of online hate.[23] This half-life is also found in relation to anti-Muslim online hate speech produced and shared following the Brexit vote in June 2016 (see Figure 16) and anti-Semitic hate speech produced and spread following the story the same year relating to Ken Livingstone's suspension from the Labour Party for his claim that Hitler 'supported Zionism' (Figure 17).* In both cases hate speech spiked on or just following the date of the incident and then sharply declined.

In the case of terror attacks, the rapid escalation and decay in the frequency of hate speech posts has been explained by the capacity of trigger events to temporarily reduce some users' ability to suppress or regulate their implicit prejudices held towards individuals who share similar characteristics to the perpetrators. The posting of hate is further encouraged by others who post similar messages (a cascade effect) and the perception that such actions have little or no personal consequence.

---

* Similar patterns were found around the Brussels, Orlando, Nice, Normandy, Berlin and Quebec attacks.

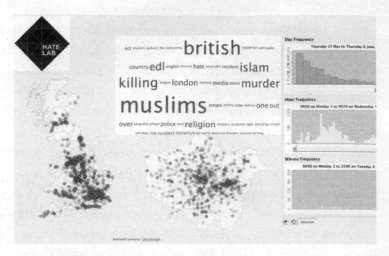

Fig. 14: UK-wide Twitter reaction to the Woolwich terror attack in 2013.

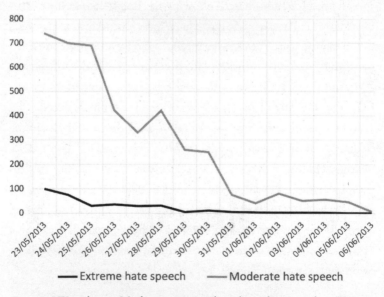

— Extreme hate speech — Moderate hate speech

Fig. 15: UK-wide anti-Muslim extreme and moderate hate speech on Twitter in the fifteen days following the Woolwich terror attack in 2013.

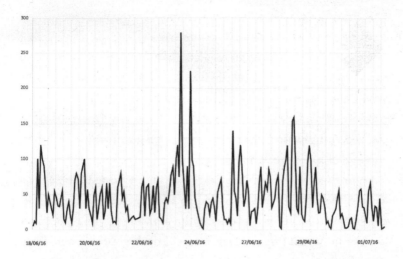

Fig. 16: UK-wide anti-Muslim hate speech on Twitter around the Brexit vote.

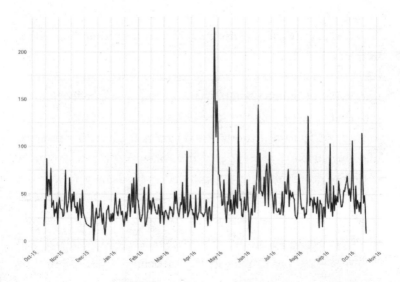

Fig. 17: UK-wide anti-Semitic hate speech on Twitter around the
Ken Livingstone story breaking in 2016.

Following a frisson of hateful sentiment in the first twenty-four to forty-eight hours, in the days and weeks after the trigger event users regain their capacity to regulate their implicit prejudices, and the posting of hate reduces. However, what is observable in the weeks and months following these incidents is that hate speech production and propagation remains higher on average than in the preceding period. This may mean we are living with a new baseline of hate speech online.

Figure 18 shows anti-Muslim hate speech posted globally on Twitter throughout 2017.* Spikes in hate speech are discernible, coinciding with key events during the year, notably the UK terror attacks in Westminster, Manchester, London Bridge and Finsbury Park. The large spike in October, after the Parsons Green attack in London, is in fact related to the mass shooting in Las Vegas in the US, when assumptions were initially made on Twitter that the attack was an extremist Islamic terrorist incident, fuelled in part by a false claim by ISIS that the shooter was acting on their behalf.

My lab's analysis showed that across all events, compared to all other types of online content, hate speech was least likely to be retweeted in volume and to survive for long periods of time, supporting the 'half-life' hypothesis. Where hate speech is retweeted following an event, there is evidence to show this activity emanates from a core group of like-minded individuals who seek out each other's messages. These Twitter users act as a filter bubble, in which grossly offensive hateful messages reverberate between members but rarely spread widely beyond them. Hate speech produced around the Brexit vote in particular was found to be

---

* Represents both moderate and extreme anti-Muslim hate speech combined, and original tweets and retweets combined.

largely driven by a small number of Twitter accounts. Around 50 per cent of anti-Muslim hate speech was produced by only 6 per cent of users, many of whom were classified as politically anti-Islam.[24]

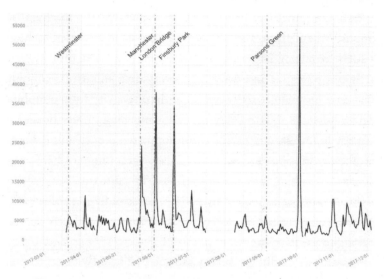

Fig. 18: Global anti-Muslim hate speech on Twitter during 2017
(gaps relate to breaks in data collection).

Bots inflate the hate

Some of this 6 per cent was the responsibility of algorithm-driven accounts, also known as bots or fake accounts. In October 2018, Twitter published over 10 million tweets from around 4,600 Russian and Iranian-linked bot and fake accounts. Bots are automated accounts that are programmed to retweet and post content for various reasons. Fake accounts are semi-automated, meaning they are routinely controlled by a human or group of humans, allowing for more complex interaction with other users, and for more nuanced messages in reaction to unfolding events. While not all bots and fake accounts are problematic (some retweet and post useful content), many have been created for more subversive reasons, such as influencing voter choice in the run-up to elections and spreading divisive content following national events.

Bots can sometimes be detected by the characteristics that distinguish them from human users. These characteristics include a high frequency of tweets and retweets (e.g. over fifty a day), activity at regular intervals (e.g. every five minutes), content that contains mainly retweets, the ratio of activity from a mobile device versus a desktop device, following many users but having few followers, and partial or unpopulated user details (photo, profile description, location, etc.). Fake accounts are harder to detect, given they are semi-controlled by humans, but telltale signs include accounts less than six months old and profile photos that can be found elsewhere on the internet and clearly do not belong to the account.

Research at Cardiff University showed that fake Twitter accounts purportedly sponsored by the Russian Internet Research Agency spread fake news and promoted xenophobic messages following the 2017 terror attacks in the UK, potentially raising tensions between groups. Following the Manchester and London Bridge terror attacks, a fake account assumed to be linked to the same Russian agency sent a racially divisive tweet within minutes of the news breaking. In the minutes following the Westminster terrorist attack, suspected fake social media accounts retweeted fake news about a woman in a headscarf apparently walking past and ignoring a victim. This was retweeted thousands of times by far-right Twitter accounts with the hashtag '#BanIslam'.

All four terror attacks in the UK in 2017 saw an online response from Russian fake accounts, with close to five hundred original messages being retweeted over 150,000 times.[25] A key tactic used by these accounts was to attempt to engage celebrity and alt-right accounts, thereby increasing the profile of their messages if a response was made. The additional challenge created by these fake accounts is that they are unlikely to be susceptible to counter-speech and traditional policing responses. It therefore falls upon social media companies to detect and remove such accounts as early as possible in order to stem the production and spread of divisive and hateful content.

Sticks and stones

When taking into account the 'virtual' nature of online interaction, where action can seem devoid of consequence due to anonymity and sometimes vast distances between victim and perpetrator, it is not surprising to encounter claims that hate speech is a trivial issue. Indeed, some of those who support right-wing perspectives have argued that online hate speech is less serious than hate crime in the physical world. However, to make such a claim is to grant the would-be online offender the right to attack individuals on the basis that their actions do not harm the victim or themselves.

Research on offline hate speech has found that victims experience trauma in a pattern that is similar to the response of victims of physical crimes. In some of the more extreme cases the short- and long-term effects of hate speech are similar in form to the effects of burglary, domestic violence, assault and robbery.[26] The reason for the extremity of harm from hate speech stems from the targeting of a person's core identity. Vilifying or dehumanising a person because of a fundamental part of their identity can generate negative emotional, attitudinal and behavioural changes. The impact is deeper if the victim is already vulnerable, for example suffering from depression, anxiety or the lack of a support network, and if the context in which the hate speech is uttered is conducive, such as where there exists a culture of fear, repression or intimidation. Short-term impacts lasting a few days can include feelings of shock, anger, isolation, resentment, embarrassment and shame. Long-term impacts, lasting months or years, can include low self-esteem, the development of a defensive attitude and prejudices against the hate speaker's group, concealment of identity and heightened awareness of difference. Remembering hate speech attacks has also been associated with increases in self-rated stress levels, and increased levels of the stress hormone cortisol in LGBTQ+ victims.[27]

Regardless of the form of victimisation, the emotional consequences of online hate speech are felt in the offline world by those targeted and the communities to which they belong. Not surprisingly, those without the cognitive tools to deal with online victimisation, namely the young, feel the effects most. A survey of over 1,500 young people aged between thirteen and eighteen in the UK found that those that encountering online hate reported feeling anger, sadness and shock. As many as three quarters said it made them modify their online behaviour, including posting fewer messages or avoiding social media altogether.[28] Another study found respondents most frequently exposed to online hate material in the US and Finland were less satisfied with their lives.[29] Young LGBTQ+ victims of online hate speech I have spoken to during various research projects told me they had suffered mental health issues, feelings of isolation, fear for their physical safety, and a diffusion of impacts to partners and children, sometimes resulting in break-ups and time off work.

Why online hate speech hurts

Bringing all this evidence together, it seems clear that online hate speech has the potential to inflict more harm than some physical acts, due to several unique factors. The anonymity offered by the internet means offenders are likely to produce more hate speech, the character of which is more serious because of the lack of inhibition. The temporal and geographical reach of the internet means hate has become a 24/7 phenomenon. For many, especially young people, communicating with others online is now a routine part of everyday life, and simply turning off the computer or mobile phone is not an option, even if they are being targeted with hate. Online hate speech then has the insidious power to enter the traditional safe haven of the home, generating a cycle of victimisation that is difficult to break.

When individuals claim they have been injured by hate speech, they are ascribing power to language that equals the force of some physical acts. Online hate speech is said to have an *illocutionary force*, the term referring to an act of speech or writing which has a tangible or real outcome.[30] Examples of illocutionary speech include a priest stating 'I now pronounce you husband and wife,' a police officer saying 'You're under arrest on suspicion of grievous bodily harm,' or a judge saying 'This court finds you guilty of murder.' These words have significant weight, and some forms of hate speech can carry similar power with deeply serious consequences. Through a close examination of thousands of social media posts I found illocutionary force in online hate speech is created in five ways:

1. Through invoking *rule infraction*. For example, a tweet containing a picture of a gay male couple kissing could

motivate hate speech that draws on law in a country that criminalises homosexual relations.

2. Through attempting to *induce shame* in the victim. For example, the same tweet could motivate hate speech that uses the gaze of the victim's parents or grandparents as a vehicle for shame: 'Imagine what your mother/grandmother would think if they saw this disgusting image!'

3. Through attempting to *induce fear* in the victim. For example, the use of threats and intimidation.

4. Through attempting to *dehumanise* the victim. For example, comparing individuals or groups to insects, vermin or primates.

5. Through attempting to spread *misinformation* related to the victim or the group they belong to. For example, creating conspiracy theories or false information in relation to past events (such as the Holocaust) or religious observances (such as Ramadan).

These five forms of illocutionary online hate speech are not mutually exclusive, and a post can use a blend of tactics to harm their intended victim. The hate speech is also more likely to have the desired negative consequences if the conditions of *uptake*, *context* and *power* are met:

(i) The *uptake* of the post by the victim is only accomplished when they recognise they are being targeted because of their identity. Only when uptake is achieved can the victim recognise the act as hate speech. There are situations where uptake fails, or the hate speech misfires, for example the use of a slur that is not familiar to the victim due to cultural or temporal variation. In these circumstances, while the perpetrator of the hate speech may still be guilty of sending grossly offensive communications, the impact on the intended victim will be negligible, at least in the immediate term.

(ii) A conducive *context* occurs when a victim is living in a culture of fear, intimidation and repression where personal characteristics are routinely targeted and there are no or minimal laws protecting them. In these contexts, which exist in some parts of the US and Russia and many other countries, the pains of hate speech are amplified simply due to the fact that there is a lack of protection leading to more frequent and more extreme forms of victimisation (as there is no consequence for the attackers).

(iii) The *power* of the perpetrator outweighs that of the victim when the hate speech offender is perceived by the target to be higher in a hierarchy, whether offline or online. In these circumstances victims are more likely to feel subordinated. Due to the additional level of vulnerability brought about by this power difference, the victim is likely to feel the pains of hate speech more. This is certainly the case with humiliation that occurs within relationships of unequal status, where the humiliator dominates the victim and undermines their sense of identity.

These impacts are compounded where direct online hate speech is also experienced as an extension or a precursor to hate crime in the offline world.[31] Hate crime is not always a discrete isolated event, and for some victims it is experienced as a process, involving a range of incidents over time, from hate speech online to hate speech offline, and possibly face-to-face threats and physical violence.[32] Hate crime can therefore be considered as *re-engineered* to function in the online environment, utilising new technologies such as social media. For some, this is the beginning of a longer process of victimisation that may migrate offline, while for others it is an isolated event that remains online.

Can law stop it?

On 17 March 2012, Bolton Wanderers and Tottenham Hotspur fought it out at White Hart Lane in the FA Cup quarter-finals. Just five minutes before the end of the first half Bolton's midfielder, Fabrice Muamba, collapsed on the pitch. As medics struggled to turn Muamba onto his back, a cardiologist who was watching the game rushed onto the pitch to provide assistance. It became clear that the midfielder was in cardiac arrest.

The match was called off and social media erupted with chatter from sports fans. Liam Stacey, a final-year biology student at Swansea University in Wales, had been watching the match before he launched the Twitter app on his phone.

'LOL. Fuck Muamba. He's dead!!!' Stacey posted.

Twitter users rushed to condemn his offensive comment. Although his comment about Muamba was not hateful in a criminal sense, Stacey's reaction towards his fellow Twitter users became deeply racist. He called people who criticised him 'wogs' and told one to 'go pick some cotton'.

Several reports from the public were made to the police and Stacey was subsequently arrested and charged. In court, before passing sentence, the judge highlighted the racist and aggravating nature of his posts, their reach amplified by social media and the news event, and the significant public outrage that resulted. Stacey was charged under the Public Order Act 1986 and sentenced to serve fifty-six days in prison. This is one of the first cases in the UK where a social media user was charged and found guilty of an online hate crime.

Online hate speech has become such a pernicious social problem that international organisations, such as the European Commission and the United Nations, have suggested ways of combating it to national governments.[33] Governments with a progressive stance on the issue have introduced domestic laws criminalising certain forms of online content. Thirty-two countries across the world, up to the date of publication, signed up to, ratified and brought into force the additional protocol of the Convention of Cybercrime, which criminalises racist and xenophobic online material. But some of the big players refused to sign. While the US signed up to the original Convention, it opted out of the additional protocol on online hate speech on the grounds that it contradicted the freedom of speech protections embedded within the US Constitution. Other signatories of the original Convention who did not sign the additional protocol include Australia, Israel and Japan.[34]

Hate speech is not legally defined in the UK. Recall from Chapter 2 that there is an array of Acts dealing with hate crime and speech that begin by defining who is protected and who is not. Race and religion have specific criminal categories, while sexual orientation, transgender identity and disability do not, but courts can increase the sentence for an offender if hostility towards these categories can be proven. Alongside the hostility-focused offences, there are legal protections against stirring up or inciting hatred against a race, religion or sexual orientation. Stirring up or inciting hatred includes behaviours that go much further than simply voicing an opinion or causing offence, and in the case of sexual orientation and religion it must also be threatening.

Beyond the specific hate crime laws, hate speech can also be dealt with under the two Communications Acts. These criminalise speech on social media that is grossly offensive, indecent, obscene, menacing, false or harassing. A high threshold is used by prosecutors when considering what is grossly offensive, in order to protect freedom of speech. It must therefore be more than just shocking or distasteful.

Since Liam Stacey's conviction, several online hate speech cases have been brought before the courts that involve social media, but far fewer than might be imagined given the amount of hate that abounds online. In 2013, feminist campaigner and journalist Caroline Criado Perez began a petition to replace the planned image of Winston Churchill on the new £10 note with a female figure. The campaign was a success, and the Bank of England announced that an image of Jane Austen would appear on the new note to be issued in 2017. In response to this announcement, Criado Perez was subject to hateful comments and threats of sexual violence on social media. John Nimmo and Isabella Sorley sent death and rape threats that caused Criado Perez to instal a panic button in her home. Both pleaded guilty to sending menacing tweets, admitting they were among the users of eighty-six separate Twitter accounts from which Criado Perez had received abusive messages. Before passing sentence, the judge highlighted the extreme nature of the threats and the harm caused to the victim. Sorley was jailed for twelve weeks and Nimmo was jailed for eight weeks for threatening behaviour. In 2017 Nimmo was sentenced to two years and three months in prison for sending threatening and racist tweets to MP Luciana Berger. One tweet featured a picture of a knife and the text 'You are going to get it like Jo Cox'. Another called Berger 'Jewish scum' and was signed off 'your friend the Nazi'. For his offences that were racially aggravated, the sentences were increased by 50 per cent.

More recently, in 2018, UKIP member Mark Meechan was found guilty under the Communications Act and fined £800 for posting grossly offensive material on YouTube after uploading a video of his girlfriend's dog which had been trained to give the Nazi salute to the commands 'Sieg heil' and 'Gas the Jews'. The video was viewed over 3 million times on the platform. In defending his actions, Meechan stated that he was only making a joke that was intended to annoy his girlfriend and to be seen by those who subscribed to his YouTube channel. He apologised for causing offence. The sheriff of the court stated that the video not only showed the dog responding to a Nazi command and anti-Semitic speech, but also showed it watching a clip of a Nuremberg rally and flashing images of Hitler. By deliberately using the Holocaust as a theme for the video, Meechan was deemed to have caused gross offence that went beyond the limits of free speech. Meechan appealed the decision, stating that the court's acceptance of the context of the video was at odds with what he intended. His appeal was found to lack merit and was refused.

There are also examples of failed cases. In 2012, Port Talbot football player Daniel Thomas sent a homophobic tweet referencing Olympic divers Tom Daley and Peter Waterfield: 'if there is any consolation for finishing fourth atleast [sic] daley and waterfield can go and bum eachother [sic] #teamHIV'. The tweet was not directly sent to Daley or Waterfield via the @ mention feature on Twitter, and hence was meant for a more general audience. Thomas was arrested and charged but not prosecuted. The Director of Public Prosecutions (DPP) decided, following consultation with Daley and Waterfield, that the tweet was not grossly offensive, was not intended to reach Daley and Waterfield, and was not part of a campaign. Therefore the communication fell below the threshold for criminal prosecution. Thomas was also swift to remove the message and showed remorse for causing offence. The DPP concluded that while merely offensive social media posts may not warrant criminal prosecution, they may attract alternative non-custodial sanctions, including those that can be administered by social media platforms.

As Tom Daley had not come out as gay at the time the tweet was posted, he may have decided not to push for prosecution given the attention it would garner in the press. Had he pushed, it is likely the case would have progressed. Thomas, a local sporting figure, was not exercising his faith-based freedom of speech. His words were meant to be offensive, if not grossly offensive to both Daley and Waterfield, and to the LGBTQ+ community more widely. The hashtag '#TeamHIV' hammers home the true intent of the post.

Cases such as this raise the question of whether the law is working to protect the most vulnerable online. The UK Law Commission scoping review of online abusive and offensive communications, initiated in February 2018, considered the adequacy of the law. They found that most online hate speech goes unchallenged by prosecutors and the courts. In particular, because of a lack of protections in law, gender-based online abuse, one of the more prevalent forms of hate speech, was not being dealt with unless it involved threats. In conclusion, the Commission agreed that the law fails to capture the nature and impact of online hate speech on victims.

Can the social media companies stop it?

The short answer is yes, but they may not be willing to do so without being forced. In 2016 the European Commission, Facebook,

Microsoft, Twitter and YouTube signed up to a code of conduct on countering illegal hate speech online across EU countries, with Instagram, Google+, Snapchat and Dailymotion joining in 2018.[35] By signing they all agreed on rules banning hateful conduct and to introduce mechanisms, including dedicated teams, for the review and possible removal of illegal content within twenty-four hours. It took some time and considerable political pressure for these social media giants to come around the table. The bad press related to the rise of Islamist and far-right extremism on their platforms was a motivating factor, as was the global coverage of attacks on high-profile black and female users. But they represent only a fraction of companies operating in this space, and many of the alternative sites, like Reddit, Gab, Voat, Telegram and Discord, are yet to engage.

Figure 19 shows the numbers from the last six evaluations of the scheme. In 2021, 81 per cent of participating social media companies reviewed the majority of hate posts flagged to them within twenty-four hours, and 63 per cent of these posts were removed, which showed a slight decline on the year before.[*] In 2016, when monitoring first began, only 40 per cent of participating companies reviewed the majority of hate posts flagged to them within twenty-four hours, and 28 per cent of these posts were removed. In the sixth round in 2021, compared the year before, Facebook and YouTube saw their removal rate drop, while Twitter and Instagram saw their rate increase. Sexual orientation and xenophobia (including anti-migrant hatred) were the most commonly reported grounds of hate speech.[†]

---

[*] From 2019 the figures include Google and Instagram, who joined in 2018.

[†] For a full breakdown see: https://ec.europa.eu/commission/presscorner/detail/en/IP_21_5082

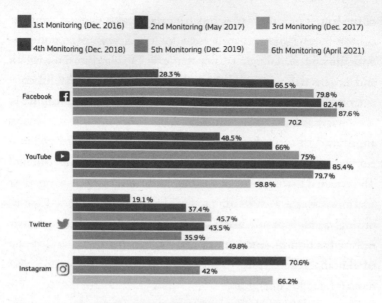

Fig. 19: Removal of illegal hate speech in the EU
by social media companies.

The average removal rate for the UK was 43 per cent in 2021, compared to 96 per cent in Germany. Such comparisons are important because they indicate how existing social media laws are working to change the behaviour of tech giants. The Netzwerkdurchsetzungsgesetz (NetzDG) law in Germany that came into force in October 2018 imposes fines of up to 50 million euros on social media companies if they fail to remove illegal hate speech flagged by a trusted third party in the country. The European Digital Services Act includes similar rules for the removal of illegal content and applies across the EU. Staunch advocates of free speech have voiced their concerns over censorship and the wider implications of regarding social media companies as publishers.

While significant moves to deal with hate speech are clearly under way in Europe, the same cannot be said about the US, one of the largest producers of online hate speech. Here, hateful online content goes largely unchallenged by the government and law enforcement, and it comes down to the tech giants, pressure groups and citizens to fight against the rising tide of online hate.

Unfortunately, even for the tech giants, deciding what to remove is not straightforward. Algorithms can do part of the job, but humans are needed to make the final call. Between them, the tech giants employ tens of thousands of people to moderate suspect content. This low-paid work involves viewing hundreds of posts a day that feature child abuse, beheadings, suicides and acts of hate. Unsurprisingly, staff turnover is significant. In May 2020, Facebook was reported as having agreed to pay $52 million to current and former content moderators in a class-action lawsuit, with each of the 11,250 moderators receiving at least $1,000; more if they were diagnosed with a mental illness stemming from their job. The case was brought against Facebook for not providing a safe working environment for moderators, who complain of suffering from PTSD-like symptoms from continuously viewing disturbing content.

Can we stop it?

An encouraging finding in my research, and one that maintains my faith in the wisdom of the crowd, is that counter-hate speech always outweighs hate speech following 'trigger' events. In the UK, following the Brexit vote, hate speech on Twitter was dwarfed by those social media users who came to the support of the targeted groups. In response to the hashtags #RefugeesNotWelcome, #SendThemHome, #MakeBritainWhiteAgain and #IslamIsThe-Problem, users began to counter-post #InTogether, #SafetyPin, #PostRefRacism and #PolesInUK. The inclusive hashtags outstripped the hateful ones by a significant amount. Research within

HateLab shows that counter-speech can stem the spread of online hate following an event. It is most effective when it is rapid and communicated in groups. We looked at four forms of counter-speech, including *attribution of prejudice* (e.g 'Shame on #alt-right racists for taking advantage of this situation'); *claims making and appeals to reason* (e.g. 'This has nothing to do with Islam, not all Muslims are terrorists!'); *requests for information and evidence* (e.g. 'How does this have anything to do with the colour of someone's skin??'); and *insults* (e.g. 'There are some cowardly racists out there!').

We found that not all counter-speech is productive. Using insults against hate speech producers often inflames the situation, resulting in the production of further hate speech. Counter-speech is most likely to be effective on the casual, escalating or de-escalating hate speaker. It is less likely to work on those who identify as being on the extreme right. When engaging in counter-speech, or advising others on its use, we argue the following principles should be followed to reduce the likelihood of the further production of hate speech:

1. Avoid using insulting or hateful speech.
2. Make logical and consistent arguments.
3. Request evidence if false or suspect claims are made.
4. State that you will make a report to the police or third party if the hate speech continues and/or gets worse (e.g. becomes grossly offensive or includes threats).
5. Encourage others also to engage in counter-speech.
6. If the account is likely fake or a bot, contact the social media company and ask for it to be removed.

Acts of counter-speech seek to undermine the hate. Counter-speakers are often the first at the online scene who witness the hate bubbling up. They are the 'online first-responders' who, through micro-protests against intolerance, can build into a formidable force for good when they come together to communicate norms that make hate speech socially unacceptable. Research conducted at George Washington University provides evidence that counter-speech directed at the meso-level, in other words, not just at individuals or the entire hate network but at clusters of online haters (such as Facebook groups, communities and pages), can be effective. This effectiveness is bolstered when counter-speech is used across all platforms, and not just a few. Using methods from physics, the scientists theoretically demonstrate that by targeting only 10 per cent of hate network clusters, counter-speakers can destabilise the whole online hate network.[36]

When we hear that as many of half of all children aged twelve to fifteen report seeing hate speech online, we know there is a deep-seated problem with the internet. Algorithms that learn from the speech we post online, and in turn shape what we are exposed to, can create toxic environments where hate speech becomes the norm. Governments and social media companies cannot solve this problem alone. Politicians are rarely effective against companies like Facebook and Google, and expecting total self-regulation by these tech giants is like asking them to grade their own homework. As citizens of the internet we also have to take on part of the responsibility. We must hold on tightly to what we think healthy online conversation looks like, and together call out speech that undermines human dignity. But this task is made more challenging when there are opposing forces dedicated to using the world's most powerful communications network to accomplish their extreme goals.

10

Hate in Word and Deed

On 11 August 2017 in the Nameless Field behind the University of Virginia's Memorial Gymnasium, a group of over two hundred mostly Caucasian men in all-American polos and khakis gathered into a mass, their white shirts beginning to glow crimson in a warm late sun. By 8.30 p.m. the sun had gone down and the dimmed knot of bodies began to glimmer as tiki torches were lit one by one. In faux-military fashion orders were barked and they began to march in the direction of the Pantheon-inspired Rotunda designed by Thomas Jefferson. The surrounding university buildings reverberated eerily to the sound of their chants, 'You will not replace us', 'Blood and soil', as they snaked through the campus grounds. Their destination was the statue of Jefferson, which they would find ringed by a thirty-strong chain of defiant counter-protesters. The black students among this number were targeted first with ape imitations and the chant 'White lives matter!' Minutes later violence erupted. This would be the beginning of twenty-four hours of deadly hate in the usually sleepy college town of Charlottesville.

Much of what happened the following day is well documented, and the rally is considered the first alt-right event to garner global attention. The stated motivation for the rally was to protest the planned removal of a statue of Confederate figure Robert E. Lee in Emancipation Park.[*] Lee, publicly regarded by Donald Trump

---

[*] It was called Lee Park until June 2017, Emancipation Park at the time of the

as a 'great general',[1] advocated and fought for the right of states to enslave black people. At the rally, over a thousand white supremacists took a stand for their heritage, history and the people who they felt were being threatened by the left. The culture being referred to was white, Christian and southern. One rationalised her participation in the rally, 'It's not hate, it's our heritage,' while another stated, 'I'm here because our Republican values are, number one, standing up for local white identity. Our identity is under threat. Number two, free market. Number three, killing Jews.'[2]

Widespread violence broke out around 11 a.m. on the 12th when rally-goers deviated from their route and headed straight into the mass of counter-protesters. Antifa, anti-fascist activists, who represented a minority of counter-protesters on the day, played their part in the escalation of violence. They charged with clubs and launched balloons filled with dye at the white supremacists, with police and journalists getting hit in the cross-fire. But it was Antifa, not the alt-right, that protected the First United Methodist Church where the Charlottesville Clergy Collective supplied refreshments and support to citizens that morning.[3]

Within twenty minutes of the violence erupting the police declared the gathering an unlawful assembly, and shortly after the Governor of Virginia declared a state of emergency. The white supremacists dispersed and headed back to where they began, the Nameless Field where their lifts home were waiting. But it wasn't over. A few hours later a white supremacist, intent on harming the protesters, drove his car into a crowd just a few blocks away from the statue of Lee, killing one and injuring twenty-eight. He was later charged with thirty federal hate crimes, including the murder of Heather Heyer.

There are many lessons to learn from the Charlottesville rally,

rally, and in 2018 became Market Street Park.

but the one I delve into in this chapter is not about why the violence took place in those twenty-four hours. Instead, I focus on an *accelerant* of the rally – a system that has given a coordinated voice to once fragmented extremists on both sides: the internet.

A game changer for the far right

The Unite the Right rally at Charlottesville was heralded as a defining moment in the alt-right's history. While there were no fewer than ten neo-Nazi and white supremacist events organised in 2017 in the US, it was the one at Charlottesville that was successful in bringing together so many from multiple disparate right-wing groups into what seemed like a coherent, formidable whole. And it was the internet that had a key part to play in that success.

The chat site Discord, predominantly used by the gamer community, was awash with posts from alt-right members in the weeks running up to the rally. Appealing to the various factions that had never previously overcome their differences enough to convene in public en masse, popular alt-right blogger Hunter Wallace posted:

> I've put together this little explainer of the interest of each
> faction in coming together at #UniteTheRight on August
> 12th. I don't expect everyone will agree, but no one has
> explained every layer of the controversy in Charlottesville
> [the dispute centring on calls for the removal of Lee's statue
> as part of a wider shift towards racial equality] and why
> these rightwing factions are starting to converge at public
> events. We're in the earliest stages of a mass movement
> which is gestating in the real world and social media around
> the issues of identity, heritage, free speech, freedom of
> assembly and ending political correctness . . . It goes without

saying that many of these groups have their differences. At the end of the day though, they have [sic] all have common enemies whether they choose to recognize them or not . . . By joining forces as a *cultural vanguard*, we will be stronger.[4]

Red-pilling

This call for unity was not contained within the internet's alt-right backwaters. Key players in the movement had a plan to soften the neo-Nazi and white supremacist message so that it was more palatable to those just right of the mainstream. The rally was promoted on Facebook, Twitter and Reddit, platforms with the widest possible reach. The objective was to shift the *Overton window* – what is politically possible based on the current climate of public discourse – further to the right (see Figure 20).[5]

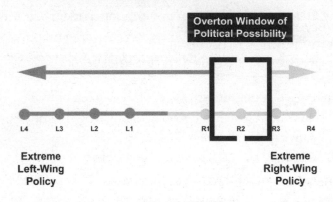

Fig. 20: The Overton window.

The London-based Institute for Strategic Dialogue analysed ten thousand posts and two hundred pieces of online propaganda related to the rally.[6] The alt-right were targeting students between the ages of fourteen and eighteen. This strategy was based on a survey of fifty thousand US high school students, or 'Generation Z', that showed 58 per cent of them would vote for Trump, in sharp contrast to 'millennials', those born between the early 1980s and early 2000s. Declared 'Generation Zyklon' by the neo-Nazi website the Daily Stormer, after the cyanide gas used to kill millions of Jews during the Holocaust, these potential recruits were seen as the future of the movement. The Facebook page for the event was mild in its tone, referencing the protection of First Amendment rights from a communist crackdown. The popular Rebel Media (1.2 million YouTube followers) and InfoWars (10 million monthly visits) covered the event sympathetically. UK-based Paul Joseph Watson, InfoWars editor-at-large, tweeted on 8 August 2017 (see Figure 21):

Paul Joseph Watson ✓
@PrisonPlanet

Follow

Everyone on the right needs to get over their petty grudges & personality clashes and realize we are all being targeted. Time to unite.

2:19 PM - 8 Aug 2017

4,347 Retweets **10,527** Likes

669   ♻ 4.3K   ♡ 11K

Fig. 21: Tweet from InfoWars' Paul Joseph Watson ahead of the Charlottesville rally.

The more clandestine discussions on Discord focused upon recruitment strategy. Borrowing from the military and intelligence services, posters made reference to using psychological operations (psy-ops) on the most vulnerable. Official documents were claimed to have been hacked from intelligence agencies, providing a set of instructions for how to persuade individuals using well-tested psychological techniques. It is unclear whether such a hacking ever did take place, but the alt-right certainly ran with the idea of manipulating young people's emotions, desires and motives by appealing to issues that were known to be of concern to Generation Z, including threats to economic resources and cultural identity. When a story breaks in the media about a subject such as a hike in unemployment, a rise in house prices or the planned removal of a statue of a white man, the alt-right and far right piggy-back on the issue and blame their usual suspects.

This process is called 'red-pilling' in alt-right circles, a reference to a turning point in the movie *The Matrix*, where the protagonist, Neo, is given a choice between taking a red or blue pill. Neo takes the red pill, which brings him out of the illusory Matrix and into reality. Before being adopted by the alt-right, the term was used within the men's rights movement to describe the moment of realisation that men, not women, are oppressed. To be red-pilled in alt-right terms means to awaken from a state of illusion – usually seen as being crafted by socialists, Jews and Marxists – into one of enlightenment, where the conspiracy to undermine white Western civilisation by advocating equality between groups, especially races, comes into sharp focus. The internet is well suited to spreading extremist ideas via tactics such as red-pilling. Younger generations are easily exposed to this tactic due to the decentralised structure of the internet that democratises content production, and the increasing reliance of online giants, such as Google, Twitter, YouTube and Facebook, on algorithms to organise information. The tactic of piggy-backing on a mainstream news item to push an alt- or far-right agenda has resulted in some figures becoming YouTube stars, including Infowars' Paul Joseph Watson.

Extreme filter bubbles

Right-wing political and far-right figures are known to use online filter bubbles to drum up support for their campaigns. Columbia University Professor Jonathan Albright was one of the first scientists to map the alt-right 'fake news' filter bubble, identifying where links to the sites were being shared. He found thousands of webpages and millions of links spread over not only Facebook, YouTube and Twitter but also the *New York Times*, *Washington Post* and many other mainstream sites.[7] This filter bubble was occupied not solely by alt-right 'keyboard warriors', but also major political figures, and rising international stars in the alt-right movement. On Twitter, Donald Trump has retweeted some of the most extreme actors in far- and alt-right filter bubbles, including but not limited to alt-right activists after Charlottesville, anti-Semitic accounts targeting Hillary Clinton, the @WhiteGenocideTM Twitter account, and the extreme-right group Britain First, whose Islamophobic comment he shared. He has even contributed original content to this filter bubble, tweeting that Mexican immigrants were 'criminals' and 'rapists'.

The 'New Right' populist Five Star Movement in Italy, founded by a comedian and a web strategist in 2009, became the country's most popular party in the 2018 election, with little more than rabble-rousing speeches and a sophisticated online campaign that tapped into filter bubbles. Their anti-establishment approach, facilitated by the democratising nature of the internet, was replicated by Nigel Farage when he set up his Brexit Party, which went on to dominate the 2019 European Parliament elections in the UK, taking the largest vote share.

Further to the right, the leaders of Britain First and the ex-leader of the English Defence League (EDL) also tapped into right-wing filter bubbles to spread their divisive narrative. For years social media content moderators protected some far-right pages from deletion due to their high number of followers and profit-generating capacity. Before it was banned, the far-right 'Tommy Robinson' Facebook page had over a million followers, and held the same protections as media and government pages, despite having violated the platform's policy on hate speech nine times, while typically only five violations were tolerated by Facebook's content review process.[8] The page was eventually removed in February 2019, a year after Twitter removed the account of Stephen Yaxley-Lennon (alias Tommy Robinson) from its platform. In May the same year, Facebook also banned alt-right stars including Milo Yiannopoulos, Laura Loomer, Alex Jones, Paul Nehlen and Paul Joseph Watson. But many far-right pages, including some that call non-whites 'vermin' and LGBTQ+ people 'degenerates' and that display neo-Nazi imagery, remain on Facebook and other sites.[9]

Research conducted in 2019 by the UK Home Office's Office for Security and Counter Terrorism found that a neo-Nazi online discussion forum received eight hundred thousand visits globally, with eighty thousand of these from British residents.[10] In June 2020, the Global Project Against Hate and Extremism found Twitter and YouTube failed to remove over one hundred Generation Identity accounts in over fourteen countries that promoted white supremacist content, despite likely violations of the platforms' hate speech, crime and terrorism rules. Many of these accounts promote the Great Replacement racist conspiracy theory which argues that white people are being replaced by non-white immigrants in a plot by 'elites'.[11] These extremist agitators continue to reinforce their rhetoric of invasion, threat and otherness in an attempt to increase polarisation online, in the hope that it spills into the offline world in the form of financial support, participation at rallies and hate crime.[12]

Algorithmic far right

The alt-right and far right are technological opportunists who are aware of the power of algorithms, and they do their best to game them to their advantage. The alt-right have approached their goal much like a company does – they work on optimising their search engine ranking and driving up their social media stats to maximise their visibility. The higher up they get, the more the algorithms that power Google's autocomplete function, Facebook's advert choices, YouTube's autoplay and Twitter's timeline will suggest certain content that will lead to links to far-right and alt-right pages. That translates into clicks on links, which then feed back into the algorithms, further embedding this prejudiced material in the information ecosystem.

The outcomes of all this aren't just played out online. Professor Robert Epstein of the American Institute for Behavioral Research has shown via experiments conducted in the US and India that page rank matters when it comes to convincing people to vote for a candidate in closely contested elections. The Search Engine Manipulation Effect (SEME) exerted the greatest influence on moderate Republicans and could shift the voting preferences of undecided voters by 20 per cent or more in the US.[13]

What is more insidious is that once links are clicked and pages are visited, the administrators of unscrupulous websites are known to use 'trackers' to follow a visitor's future moves around the internet, allowing them to develop psychological profiles through clicks and likes. This can facilitate Cambridge Analytica-style political micro-targeting.[14]

The effectiveness of online advertisements tailored to psychological profiles has been tested by Columbia University's Professor Sandra Matz. Expanding established laboratory studies to the internet, Matz conducted three field experiments involving 3.5 million internet users. She studied whether targeting products to psychological profiles gleaned simply from Facebook likes and tweets resulted in desired behaviour change. The findings were arresting. Advertisements that were tailored to internet users' psychological characteristics resulted in up to 40 per cent more clicks.

This study and others provide a solid evidence base on the effectiveness of online psychological targeting for digital mass persuasion, resulting in real-life behaviour change.[15] A visit to an alt-right site that appears high on Google's listings, possibly masquerading as something less extreme, can result in ads popping up on Facebook tailored to a user's psychological profile, which attempt to red-pill them in the hope of shifting the Overton window further to the right.

Gateway sites

Using the internet to start a movement is not a new phenomenon. The Stormfront website, launched in 1995, is regarded as the first successful neo-Nazi online presence. It is run by Don Black, a former Ku Klux Klan leader, and actively promotes offline violence against minority groups. At its height, it had three hundred thousand registered users. Don Black's son, Derek, was born into the best-known white supremacist family in the US, if not the world. Derek says he is no longer a white supremacist and campaigns against the network. In an interview with the *New York Times* he revealed how as far back as the early 1990s the internet was seen as a turning point in spreading the white supremacist message:

Pioneering white nationalism on the web was my dad's goal. That was what drove him from early '90s from beginning of the web, and so growing up . . . we had the latest computers, first people in the neighborhood to have broadband because we had to keep Stormfront running, and so technology and connecting people on the website, long before social media and the way the web is set up now was his driving purpose, so we were very connected to everybody in the white nationalist movement; to everyone in the world.[16]

His godfather, David Duke, a former Grand Wizard of the Ku Klux Klan, wrote on his website in 1998:

My friends, the internet gives millions access to the truth that many didn't even know existed. Never in the history of man can powerful information travel so fast and so far. I believe that the internet will begin a chain reaction of racial enlightenment that will shake the world by the speed of its intellectual conquest. Now, there is a new racial consciousness growing in our people that will sweep the West . . . As the new millennium approaches, one can feel the currents of history moving swiftly around us. The same race that created the brilliant technology of the internet, will – through this powerful tool – be awakened from its long sleep. Our people will learn that our very survival is in jeopardy. We will finally realize that our culture and traditions are under attack; that our values and morality, our freedom and prosperity are in danger. Even more importantly, our best minds will finally come to understand that our very genotype faces possible extinction. Massive immigration, differential birth-rates and miscegenation will constitute a political and social nightmare for Western nations, one from which we must awaken if our people are to live.[17]

While still a white supremacist, Derek Black convinced his father to tone down the neo-Nazi rhetoric on the Stormfront site. The intention was to tap into the perceived cultural and economic grievances of many white Americans – later marshalled to great effect by the Trump presidential campaign – while not putting them off with more direct racist and xenophobic content. Stormfront would become a gateway site for the far right, producing a lot of shareable content that was easy for moderate conservatives to agree with. Once hooked, the more extreme information was drip-fed until the audience's perception of acceptable social and political norms was shifted (see *Overton window* earlier this chapter).

This was not the first time Don Black had attempted to surreptitiously spread the white supremacist message. In 1999 he registered MartinLutherKing.org as a gateway site to spread misinformation about its namesake (see Figure 22). Up until the beginning of 2018, when it was reported to Google as being owned by Stormfront, the site frequently appeared in the top four hits on searches for 'Martin Luther King'. At first glance, there was no hint of white supremacist rhetoric, apart from the note at the bottom of the page in small font that read 'Hosted by Stormfront'.

Before its removal, the site masqueraded as a bona fide information resource targeted at schoolchildren, opening with the line 'Attention Students: Try our MLK Quiz!' A click led to a page titled 'How Much do you really know? Here's a little MLK quiz to coincide with the upcoming MLK holiday! Enjoy!' All of the questions criticised or defamed Dr King. One asked 'According to whose 1989 biography did King spend his last morning on earth physically beating a woman?'; another, 'Whom did King plagiarize in more than 50 complete sentences in his doctoral thesis?' At the end of the quiz schoolchildren got to tot up their scores:

If you got no questions correct it means that you are exactly the kind of ignorant citizen your government desires.

1–3 questions correct means you could be dangerous.

4–6 questions correct means you must read to [*sic*] much.

7–10 questions correct means you must value historical correctness instead of political correctness. Congratulations!!

11 or more questions correct means you've been reading this website and learned the truth.

Now it's up to you to tell others the truth.

Fig. 22: The MartinLutherKing.org website owned by Stormfront's Don Black.

The site purported to offer 'A True Historical Examination'. Links to 'Rap Lyrics' led to the text: 'Here's what black rappers say, and what their followers do. Keep in mind that most of this is produced and distributed by Jewish-run companies', alongside lyrics that described black people committing violence and sexual acts against whites. The webpage encouraged children to download and print off pamphlets for distribution in schools on Martin Luther King Day. The pamphlets called for the abolition of that national holiday and accused King of domestic and sexual violence.

Modern forms of these far-right gateway recruitment tactics now abound. Increasingly, far-right activists like Stephen Yaxley-Lennon are adopting 'citizen journalism' as a tactic to polarise opinion. Notably, in 2018, Yaxley-Lennon live-streamed himself outside a Leeds Crown Court hearing of the Huddersfield child grooming trials to hundreds of thousands of online viewers. He presented the issue with faux logic in an attempt to appear moderate, all the while twisting the facts with anti-Islam rhetoric. By violating the blanket reporting ban imposed by the judge to prevent any influence on the jury, the stunt almost derailed the trial. Yaxley-Lennon was arrested, prosecuted and sentenced to jail time for his stunt.

Such tactics take advantage of the internet's immediacy, manipulation, and its lack of the accountability which applies to mainstream media. Such qualities can provide a veil of authenticity and realism to stories, having the power to reframe the original casting of situations by the 'official' establishment narrative, further enabled by dramatic delivery of 'evidence' of events as they occur. This 'hacking' of the information-communications marketplace enabled by social media disrupts the primacy of mainstream media, allowing those who produce subversive and polarising fake news narratives to rise up the hierarchy of credibility. Before the criminal justice system could catch up with Yaxley-Lennon the stunt attracted tens of thousands of views. Once arrested, he amassed £300,000 in donations to help with legal costs.

In March 2019, Facebook by chance discovered a clandestine network of 130 far-right accounts that were acting as gateways by spreading misinformation. Initially, the content on the network's pages was moderate, but after gaining a significant number of followers (in excess of 175,000), the pages were renamed and the content changed to reflect extreme viewpoints. Around $1,500 had been spent on targeted ads spreading this content. Cleverly, the network would post both far-right and far-left content, in an attempt to avoid detection, sow division and polarise opinion.[18] Similar networks were found across Europe ahead of the 2019 EU elections.[19] Misinformation and illegal hate posts spread from over five hundred Facebook pages in Germany, France, Italy, Poland and Spain, reaching 32 million users and being viewed over half a billion times in the three months leading up to the vote.

Beyond organised far-right networks, the scientific evidence shows individual social media users also tone down their hate speech to appear moderate. A study that examined the tweets of the followers of the far-right British National Party over a year revealed different hate posting behaviours.[20] BNP party followers who posted hate speech could be categorised into extreme, escalating, de-escalating and casual. Few Twitter followers of the BNP engaged in 'strong' hate speech on a constant basis that would place them in the extreme category (around 15 per cent / 976 people in this study).* The majority (around 32 per cent / 2,028 people)

---

* Twitter data on BNP followers were collected between 1 April 2017 (when the BNP had 13,002 followers) to 1 April 2018 (when the BNP had 13,951 followers). Between these dates there were 11,785 Twitter users who persistently followed the BNP. Of these, 6,406 tweeted in the study window, did so in English and were identified to be human (i.e. not a bot).

were casual haters who occasionally sent Islamophobic posts of a 'weaker' nature. Escalating haters (around 6 per cent / 382 people) were those whose tweets became progressively extreme and more frequent over time, compared to de-escalating haters whose tweets did the opposite (around 18 per cent / 1,177 people).

At first it seemed the proportion of casual and de-escalating haters (50 per cent of the study sample) who posted 'weak' hate speech should be seen as good news. Strong hate speech is more likely to be grossly offensive (including expletives and slurs), while the weak blend conveys prejudice without such colourful language. However, as the weak hate speech was less likely to be deleted by the social media platform, and less likely to attract the eye of the law, it stayed online for much longer, if not indefinitely. The structure of the language in 'weak' hate posts also made it seem like the prejudice that was being espoused was harmless. This was especially true of posts that used jokes as a mechanism to communicate prejudice.

'Real life effort post'

On 14 March 2019 at 8.28 p.m., a regular at the fringe social media site 8chan sent a post that started: 'Well lads, it's time to stop shitposting and time to make a real life effort post.' Beneath it a Facebook video link was pasted. Around 1.40 p.m. the next day the link went live.

A man could be seen packing a truck with shotguns and semi-automatic weapons, driving down a highway listening to the military marching song 'The British Grenadiers', and pulling up outside Al Noor Mosque in Riccarton, Christchurch, New Zealand. In what looked like footage from a first-person shooter video game, the live feed showed the man wielding his weapons as he approached the mosque on foot. At the entrance he began firing indiscriminately at the worshippers inside. With the aid of a strobe light attached to his body he was able to disorientate his victims, preventing some from escaping. Before the stream ended, he had killed forty-two people and injured dozens more.

The livestream video lasted seventeen minutes, with the first report to the platform being made after the twelfth minute. The video was taken down within the hour, but it was too late to stop the widespread sharing. It was re-uploaded over 2 million times on Facebook, YouTube, Instagram and Twitter and it remained easily accessible over twenty-four hours after the attack. Some on Facebook, Twitter and particularly 8chan posted messages praising the attack. Many of these posts were removed, but those on 8chan remained until the site was taken down.*

Following arrest, the terrorist was named as twenty-eight-year-old Brenton Tarrant, from New South Wales, Australia. His references in his 8chan message to 'shitposting'† and 'real life effort post' made it clear his intention was to graduate from spreading hatred over social media to taking the dialogue offline, into action.

Tarrant's seventy-four-page manifesto uploaded to the internet referenced others who had been radicalised online. Darren Osborne, the perpetrator of the Finsbury Park mosque attack in 2017, is known to have been influenced by social media communications ahead of his attack. His phone and computers showed that he read this tweet by Stephen Yaxley-Lennon two days before

* 8chan was hosted by the US-based Cloudflare company, known for its strong free-speech orientation. It is also home to other extreme sites, including terrorist organisations. It hosted the neo-Nazi site the Daily Stormer until its deletion after the Charlottesville rally in 2017.

† The deliberate posting of off-topic or worthless content by internet trolls as a means of derailing a discussion and/or provoking an emotional reaction.

the attack: 'Where was the day of rage after the terrorist attacks. All I saw was lighting candles.' He also received a group email from Yaxley-Lennon, including the line 'There is a nation within a nation forming just beneath the surface of the UK. It is a nation built on hatred, violence and on Islam'. A direct Twitter message was also sent to Osborne by Jayda Fransen of Britain First.

Other lone actor far-right terrorists, including the mosque bomber Pavlo Lapshyn and the Norwegian mass murderer Anders Breivik, are also known to have self-radicalised via the internet.[21] John T. Earnest cited Tarrant's terror attack as an inspiration for his synagogue shooting in Poway, California, in 2019, as did Patrick Crusius for his Walmart shooting in El Paso, Texas, the same year. The losing battle against algorithms, clandestine far-right and state networks of disinformation, and the lacklustre responses from social media giants mean that these incidents are unlikely to be the last.

Most contemporary far-right terror attacks have some link to the internet. But not every person who is subjected to red-pilling and far-right gateway tactics becomes a terrorist. The majority who consume the online material share their thoughts with like-minded others, most likely online, but occasionally offline. Many who attended the Unite the Right rally in Charlottesville were encouraged to join it via posts on Facebook, Twitter, Reddit, 4chan, Discord and other platforms. The week before the rally, the Discord alt-right channel boasted over four thousand members, with over six hundred registering that they would attend.[22]

Demonstrating that online hate can migrate to offline world action, be it attending the Unite the Right rally, driving a car into a crowd of counter-protesters or storming the US Capitol, is a challenge for science. Proof that a spate of hate online is linked to offline harms has been elusive – until social media came along. The sheer number of people posting hate speech on platforms like Twitter and Facebook has allowed scientists to mine the data for statistical associations with offline hate crimes. A cascade effect has been reported where online hate speech reaches a critical mass around a particular event. The resulting harms are not only found online.

Social media posts by right-wing politicians that target minority groups have been found to cause increases in hate on the streets. Scientists found that anti-refugee posts on the far-right Alternative für Deutschland (AfD) Facebook page triggered offline violent crime against immigrants in Germany.[23] The same scientists also found a strong statistical association between President Donald Trump's tweets about Islam and anti-Muslim hate in US counties.[*24] Trump's tweets about Muslims were almost twice as likely to be retweeted by his followers than his tweets on any other subject. His divisive anti-Muslim rhetoric also caused a 58 per cent spike in other Twitter users posting with the hashtags #BanIslam and #StopIslam. No increase was found in anti-Muslim posts before Trump's tweets. His anti-Muslim posts were also highly correlated with mentions of Muslims on TV, especially on Fox News.

Figure 23 shows Trump's tweets containing reference to Muslims (solid line) and anti-Muslim police-recorded hate crimes in the US (dashed line) between 2015 (week 26) and 2016 (week 50). The frequency patterns of Trump's Muslim-related tweets and hate crimes on the streets are remarkably similar. Of course, this correlation could reflect that Trump reacted to US-wide anti-Muslim hate crimes driven by factors like terrorist attacks. Equally, it could

---

* Trump is not the only politician to use hate speech that is linked to hate crimes on the streets. Research across 163 countries covering the period 2000 to 2017 found that the use of hate speech in speeches by mainstream politicians was causally linked to higher rates of domestic political violence. J. A. Piazza, 'Politician Hate Speech and Domestic Terrorism', *International Interactions* 46 (2020), 431–53.

be that Trump's anti-Muslim tweets encouraged those with exist-ing prejudices to take to the streets to commit hate crimes.

To test which of these explanations was most likely, the researchers controlled for a wide range of other potential con-tributory factors, including (at the county level) population growth, age, ethnic composition, number of hate groups, qualifi-cations, poverty rate, unemployment rate, local income inequality, share of uninsured individuals, household income, vote share of the Republican party, salience of Muslim-related topics based on Google searches, viewership share of Fox News, cable TV spending, prime-time TV viewership and the number of mentions of Mus-lims on main US TV networks (Fox News, CNN and MSNBC).

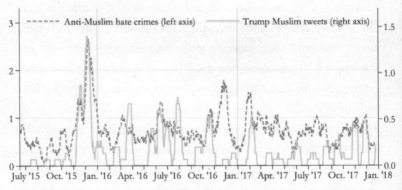

Fig. 23: Trump's tweets and hate crimes against Muslims in America
(fourteen-day moving average).[*]

Their results confirmed that Trump's anti-Muslim tweets pre-dated the hate crimes they predicted, but only for the time period after the start of his presidential campaign. A positive, but weaker

* Figure taken from K. Müller and C. Schwarz, 'From Hashtag to Hate Crime: Twitter and Anti-Minority Sentiment', SSRN, 2020.

causal effect was also found in relation to Trump's anti-Latinx tweets and anti-Latinx hate crimes on the streets during the same period. The researchers discovered the pattern was mainly driven by cases of assault and vandalism. This gives reassurance that the finding is not a function of Trump's tweets increasing reporting. If that were the case, the researchers would have expected to see more reports on hate crimes of lower significance, such as minor public order offences.[†] In addition, the US National Crime Victimisation Survey did not show an increase in reporting from hate crime victims during the period in question.

The researchers concluded that Trump's tweets bolstered existing prejudiced beliefs held by a minority that in turn enabled hate crimes. Other experimental research adds weight to the effect of Trump's divisive online messaging. After viewing explicitly racist tweets posted by Trump, test subjects with existing anti-black views were significantly more likely to associate black people with negative traits, such as being 'argumentative' and 'quick-tempered', compared to those with the same views who viewed neutral tweets by Trump.[25] In another experiment, test subjects were more likely to approve of prejudiced behaviour by another directed towards Latinx people, and to perform prejudiced behaviour themselves, after viewing Trump's anti-Latinx comment: 'When Mexico sends its people, they're not sending their best . . . They're sending people that have lots of problems, and they're bringing those problems

---

[†] To further rule out reverse causality – i.e. the possibility that anti-Muslim hate crimes resulted in Trump tweeting about Muslims – the researchers turned their focus to when Trump tweeted. He was found to tweet about Muslims significantly more on golfing trips, when away from Washington and hence policy issues, and when in the presence of his social media manager, Dan Scavino, who is known to have suggested divisive tweet topics to Trump. Trump's planned golfing trips are clearly independent of spikes in hate crimes, indicating it is unlikely that his anti-Muslim tweets were driven by a possible knowledge of a rise in hate crimes.

with them. They're bringing drugs. They're bringing crime. They're rapists.' When the experiment factored in the role of other politicians supporting Trump's comment the prejudice-inducing effect skyrocketed.[26]

Trump was also accused of stirring up hatred of Asians after he used the term 'Chinese virus' to describe COVID-19. His first use of the term at a press briefing, questioned at the time by reporters, caused a discernible online reaction, consisting of both criticism and endorsement. Trump uttered the term at least twenty times in March, the month in which a spike in hate crimes on the streets against Asian people was recorded.[27] A third-party reporting centre at San Francisco State University recorded 1,710 COVID-19-related hate incidents targeting Asian Americans in just six weeks, across forty-five states.[28] Most victims had been verbally harassed on the street, with others suffering physical assault and being attacked online. In the same period police in the UK recorded a 21 per cent increase in hate crimes targeting south and east Asians.[29] Similar rises have been recorded across Europe, Australasia, Asia, Africa and the Americas.[30]

No science has yet confirmed a link between Trump's divisive rhetoric and the rise in anti-Asian hate crimes in the US. There are certainly alternative explanations, such as a rise in general online hate speech and disinformation targeting Chinese and Asian people. Online disinformation also singled out Muslims, Jews and the LGBTQ+ community for spreading the virus. Via clicks from Facebook, thirty-four websites known for spreading far-right conspiracy theories and hate received *c.*80 million interactions between January and April 2020. In comparison, via Facebook, the US Centers for Disease Control (CDC) website received just 6.4 million interactions, and the World Health Organisation website 6.2 million.[31]

Much of the far-right social media chatter came from 'acceler-ationists' who believe that the collapse of the state can be brought about by extreme violence against liberal, black, Muslim and Jew-ish people. Over two hundred thousand posts by accelerationists across Twitter, Reddit, Tumblr, 4chan and Voat discussed how COVID-19 could be hijacked to speed up a 'civil war between the races'. Posts urged the stockpiling of weapons and the gamification of violence against minorities where 'players' could earn points for kills in the impending civil war.[32]

Some of these posts were linked to offline violence. On 24 March 2020, thirty-six-year-old Timothy Wilson was taken down by FBI agents in Belton, Missouri during a shootout that prevented him from car-bombing a hospital treating COVID-19 patients.[33] Before he could be questioned he committed suicide by shoot-ing himself in the head. In the days running up to the planned attack, Wilson had been active on the site Telegram, contributing as 'Werwolfe 84' to the neo-Nazi National Socialist Movement and Vorherrschaft Division channels, posting that COVID-19 had been created by Jews: 'I think it's real, however zog* is using it as an excuse to destroy our people. They scare people and have society break down. Then they pass this climate diversity bill. And before we know it we are living in South Africa. Monkeys roaming around killing white people. Mark my words it's coming I hope people are ready.'[34]

In the UK, my HateLab team found a similar link between online and offline hate in London. We correlated anti-Muslim and anti-black hate speech from Twitter with racially and religiously aggravated hate crime on the streets.[35] The difference with our

* An acronym for the anti-Semitic conspiracy theory known as 'Zionist occupa-tion government'.

study is that the hate speech was not just from political figures and the far-right, but included hate spread by everyday social media users. We found that hateful tweets sent in an area tend to foreshadow hate crimes on the streets. As we couldn't look to see if the person doing the tweeting then went out afterwards to commit a hate crime, we didn't find a direct causal relationship. Instead the association we found may point to rising levels of collective racial and religious tension that first erupt online, and then migrate onto the streets if not addressed. Those doing the hateful tweeting and those committing the hate crimes on the street may be different people, but it is most likely there is a mix of those who did both and those who did only one of the activities. We conclude that when the number of hate tweets reaches a certain level in a London area where there are a significant number of BAME residents, hate crimes on the streets are more likely to happen. This may be a useful finding as it can alert social media users, Twitter and the police to get involved to reduce the amount of hate online before it spills onto the streets.

Social media has also been implicated in the most extreme form of hate – genocide. Before 2011 internet access in Myanmar was extremely limited. The cost of a sim card for a mobile phone was prohibitively expensive, at the equivalent of around $200, stopping most citizens using any form of modern telecommunications. Following the release of opposition leader Aung San Suu Kyi, the government began to relax business laws, bringing down the cost to around $2.[36] Within a few years around 40 per cent of Myanmar's population was online. The platform that citizens all flocked to was Facebook.[37]

The rapid uptake of technology meant that few internet users had the experience or knowledge to fully evaluate the information they were seeing in their newsfeeds. Many internet users in the western world now take shocking posts – like those that attempt to demonise other groups using lies – with a pinch of salt. We question their origin, validity and purpose, and call out 'fake news'. Citizens in Myanmar were not so social media-savvy. So when posts appeared that dehumanised the Rohingya minority and called for their subjugation and even extermination, many were not inclined to challenge them. Those few that did had little success with Facebook.

Thousands of posts were produced by those responsible for human rights abuses against Rohingya Muslims. Between them, they had amassed nearly 12 million Facebook followers. Those that fell foul of the platform's hate speech rules remained online, some for years. Why? Because the platform had not adequately invested in understanding the use of their services in developing countries, and as a result only had a handful of content moderators who spoke Burmese.*

Facebook in Myanmar was left unpoliced, making it an effective tool for accelerating ethnic conflict – it was weaponised. It took a Reuters investigation to convince Facebook to delete posts and accounts. The United Nations came to the conclusion that Facebook had a 'determining role' in stirring up hate against Rohingya Muslims in Myanmar in the 2016–17 genocide.[38] Eventually Facebook acknowledged its role and apologised, admitting to being too slow to address the hate speech posted on its platform in the region. Facebook now recognises that countries that are new to social media are most vulnerable to online disinformation and hate speech. The suspension of Donald Trump from their platform for praising those who violently stormed the US Capitol in his support

---

* Since that time Facebook has increased its number of Burmese-speaking moderators.

may be a sign that Mark Zuckerberg now acknowledges that online hate can have physical consequences much closer to home.

The first two decades of the twenty-first century saw the far right attract an audience at a scale not seen since the Second World War. Extreme ideas that were considered unutterable in public a decade ago now flow unabated across our social media time-lines. The re-emergence of the far right is undoubtedly tied to the rise in social media use, in particular the big players like Face-book, YouTube and Twitter. Without these platforms, it is hard to see how the disinformation, fear-mongering and hate that have become the hallmark of divisive politics could have been gener-ated at the industrial scale required to gain a solid foothold in so many democracies. The events of Wednesday 6 January 2021 in Washington DC will serve as a reminder of what can happen when internet-accelerated political dog whistles are hosted and protected by tech giants.

The largely unfettered rise of the far right online has not only seen an increase in its support in the polls, but also in the num-ber of hate crime victims and in the body count from terrorism. The technology that underpins the internet acts like a megaphone for hate groups. It amplifies their reach, deepens their impact and helps them avoid regulation. A 320 per cent increase in far-right terror attacks since 2014, with many recent attacks perpetrated by those with no clear connection to organised offline hate groups, forces us to consider the role of the internet in the radicalisation process.[39] If left unchecked, the tactics of these internet-enabled hatemongers can act like a super-accelerant, transforming those vulnerable to extreme rhetoric into terrorists.

11

The Tipping Point from Prejudice to Hate and How to Prevent It

Political scientist Morton Grodzins adopted the physics concept of the *tipping point* to explain his theory for 'white flight' from mixed neighbourhoods in 1950s America.[1] He argued that racially mixed neighbourhoods contained white families with varying degrees of tolerance towards black people. This created an unstable situation, where the most racist families would leave town first, shifting the balance towards majority black. One by one the more tolerant families would leave, until a tipping point was reached that saw an exodus of white families, generating natural segregation. Grodzin's theory eventually attracted empirical support fifty years later with a vast US dataset (1970–2000) showing that cities where whites were relatively tolerant (e.g. San Diego) had much higher tipping points than cities in which whites held strong views against inter-racial contact (e.g. Memphis).[2] Despite the depressing finding, Grodzin's idea is fascinating, and it introduced the tipping point concept to the science of hate.

Since the 1950s, the phrase 'the tipping point' has been used to describe other contexts in which a large group of people quickly

---

* It is worth knowing that an analysis of the same dataset but with different methods showed no evidence of a tipping point, meaning the jury is still out on whether Grodzin's theory applies to all neighbourhoods (W. Easterly, 'Empirics of Strategic Interdependence: The Case of the Racial Tipping Point', *BE Journal of Macroeconomics* 9 (2009)). Regardless, the concept of the tipping point in the science of hate is here to stay.

adopt a behaviour that was previously rare. It draws on the *power law*, which suggests minor changes by a few people can have disproportionately dramatic effects on a population. The author Malcolm Gladwell famously applied the principle to understand the rapid spread of rumour and disease, explosive fashion trends, and the dramatic reduction in crime in New York City in the 1990s.[3] These examples relate to changes in group behaviour. But unlike much of the work on this phenomenon, the main focus of this book has been the *internal* tipping point – the point at which biology and psychology interact with the remnants of trauma, events, subcultures and technology to accelerate an individual from thinking prejudiced thoughts to acting on them in hateful ways.

Figuring out what makes a person change their behaviour is a little bit like unmaking a cake. You try taking a sumptuous red velvet cake with white frosting and deconstructing it into its most basic components. The problem is, once the ingredients have been mixed and baked in, it's pretty damn difficult to extract them in their original form.

The humans we scientists get to study come 'ready baked'. Science that focuses on the human mind must therefore reveal its inner workings by asking questions and observing behaviours. It is a mammoth challenge to identify what ingredients, in what order and in what measures, go into making a human behaviour or a behaviour change.

My modest attempt in this book is based on the tradition in criminology of casting a wide net to draw on as much of the relevant science as possible to understand the criminal behaviour under study. Only with a field of study open to multiple ways of scientific thinking can this holistic understanding of hate be achieved. Even so, this effort cannot possibly identify all the ingredients. But from the evidence that is out there, I am confident that *some* hateful behaviour in *some* people is based on this basic recipe:

- Parts and networks of the brain that are responsible for processing faces, stereotypes, threat, fear, memory, pain, disgust, empathy, attention, evaluation and decision-making. Other biological factors, such as hormones and personality types, can also interact to influence behaviour towards people different from 'us';

- Our out-of-date threat detection mechanism, and how it can be hacked and hijacked to generate negative attitudes about outgroups by those who have something to gain from our prejudiced responses;

- Negative stereotypes perpetuated by culture (including via family, friends, TV, radio, press, the internet etc.) and a lack of positive contact with people different from 'us'.

- Personal and community traumas and losses, some of which have not been dealt with (where this is even possible), which are projected onto undeserving targets perceived as threats;

- Divisive events, such as terror attacks, high-profile court cases and political votes, that increase a sense of perceived threat (including our own mortality), challenge sacred values and polarise opinion;

- Groups that prey on lost, vulnerable people, inculcating hateful ideology in the form of sacred values and fostering identity fusion, leading to an increased likelihood of self-sacrificing behaviours;

– An online ecosystem which reflects our prejudices back at us in an amplified way via the power of algorithms, and which has been weaponised by subversive state actors and hate groups.

The separation of these ingredients into discrete tidy chapters in this book may have created a false impression that they exist independent of each other and have their own isolated effects on hate. Of course, this is not always the case, and the ingredients can interact in complex ways that the science is yet to fully get to grips with. We are yet to map the entire range of possible ingredients and interactions given the limitations of current science. Only more research, building on the basic recipe mix, will reveal them.

Predicting the next hate crime

Now we have these ingredients, can we look for them in the population and pinpoint that tipping point, allowing us to predict who will be the next hate criminal? Unfortunately, it's not that straightforward. Like everyone else, scientists can never be 100 per cent certain about anything. Despite their most valiant efforts, scientists who study hate can never measure and truly represent 'reality' with their various methods of discovery. The results that hate studies generate are approximations of reality – imperfect representations of the real world. This means results always contain a degree of error and uncertainty. The basic fact is that any science of hate that tries to prove causality – that this phenomenon is a direct result of this set of happenings – is never going to be perfect.

Our ability to predict the next hate crime or criminal is also hampered by the variation in the quality of the science of hate. When the high-, medium- and low-quality studies are difficult to tell apart, we get mixed messages. How often have we read a news report of a study that found drinking red wine improves heart health (reaches for wine glass), and then months later another report says it makes no difference (backs away from wine glass)? Frustrating, right? And these contradictory reports don't do much for public confidence in science.

What the papers don't tell us is the differences between the two studies that can account for the varying findings. Was the design of the studies the same? Were the samples between studies comparable? Did both studies measure alcohol intake in the same way, and how sure can we be that all participants were truthful? Were the analyses conducted using the same statistical techniques and conventions? These are only a handful of factors that may influence the results. There is no need for us to understand what these factors technically mean to get an impression of the complexity of conducting top-quality scientific research.

We may ask, 'Why don't they just standardise?' This is more straightforward in some disciplines, like inorganic chemistry, than in others, like hate studies. We know most (if not all) of the naturally occurring elements and how they interact, so ways of studying them are relatively standardised (though new methods are developed over time). The factors that go into causing a particular behaviour are not all known (if they ever can be), and even less is known about how they might interact under a dizzying array of conditions. This means ways of studying the ingredients that go into causing a behaviour like hateful violence vary greatly, sometimes generating contrasting results.

This does not mean the studies reported in this book should be ignored. They represent the state of the art on the subject at the time they were published and many have been replicated and verified in later work on new samples of participants using better analytical procedures. Those areas of study that have accumulated a large body of research, such as the Implicit Association Test of prejudice (IAT), Integrated Threat Theory of prejudice (ITT), Terror Management Theory (TMT), and the role of contact in reducing prejudice, have been subject to powerful *meta-analysis*. Meta-analysis brings together all the highest-quality studies from across the globe and comes to an overall conclusion – a form of *cumulative science*. Where available, these meta-analyses have been included in this book to provide a close to definitive answer on the utility of a theory for understanding hate.

All this said, when a scientific result indicates that a set of ingredients helps predict a behaviour, it doesn't necessarily apply to everyone. The chances are it applies to most people, but there will always be a few that are *outliers*. In statistics, outliers are those people or measurements that stick out like a sore thumb from the majority. As they are few and far between, they are considered anomalies, and are often discarded from the data, so as not to mess with the analysis. This is seen as controversial by some, because there may be something theoretically interesting about these people, and efforts are made to work this out before they are removed. Nevertheless, they usually end up being put in the Recycle Bin.

You could be an outlier. There may be something about you that means the general rules do not apply. You may not react to threats in the way Integrated Threat Theory suggests, or your granny may not react to a reminder of her inevitable death (sorry) by being nasty to people unlike her, as Terror Management Theory posits.

Compared to elements in the periodic table, people are less well understood and are more difficult to predict. We are more confident about knowing what will happen when we combine two elements to create a compound than we are about combining two ingredients to create a behaviour in a human. There is just too much to account for, and too much variability between humans and the contexts in which they live, to be able to predict with any certainty a particular behavioural outcome in any one person.

Take the following example. A child, let's call him Billy, is born to two white parents in a small town in the American South where race relations are strained. Billy is a healthy child, with a typical brain that does what it learns to do when recognising faces of different races, reacting to perceived threats and so on. During the first five years of life Billy experiences the effects of an abusive household, bad parenting and malnutrition. His father holds negative stereotypes of black people and frequently uses racist terms in the household. Billy's parents divorce, and his mother gains full custody due to his father's alcohol abuse and record of domestic violence, which included hurting Billy. His mother moves around looking for work, disrupting his education, and gets involved in other abusive relationships with men, one of whom she has another child with. During this period Billy is left to raise himself and look after his sister, as his mother works and develops her own substance abuse problem. No one is there to teach Billy and his sister the skills to deal with pain and trauma, or to reassure them that 'life will get better'. He becomes closed-minded and self-interested.

In early adolescence Billy shows behavioural changes resulting from the years of abuse and neglect. If it was available, a scan of Billy's brain would show structural changes akin to those created by PTSD. He is routinely anxious, hypersensitive to threat and unable to deal with life's ups and downs like an average person. Billy's emotional and physical vulnerabilities lead him to search for someone who cares, and he finds a group online of similar individuals. The leaders of the group say they are motivated by religion, but it's a cover for something insidious. Billy is exposed to white supremacist online propaganda that resonates with him, and he decides to meet up offline with some of his fellow 'recruits'. Over time he begins to feel needed and valued for the first time in his life, and his identity fuses with the group as he adopts their sacred values as his own. These values are threatened when a decision is reached to remove a symbol of white supremacy from a public place in Billy's hometown, and the group organises a rally in protest. On the day of the rally Billy and his friends are verbally challenged by a black member of the local community. What is the chance Billy becomes violent and commits a hate crime? Ninety per cent? Sixty per cent? Twenty per cent?

We might guess towards the upper end, and we could be right. But there is no surefire way of knowing what Billy will do. This is because, despite him experiencing most of the basic ingredients that go into making someone hateful, there remain the unknown ingredients and interactions locked away that scientists are yet to discover, or may never discover. On this basis we might say that a person who had a polar opposite childhood experience to Billy could end up in a situation where they commit a serious hate crime. While the chances are likely to be low, we will find such an example out there if we look hard enough.

Paul Joseph Franklin had many of the ingredients identified by scientists, but David Copeland seemed to have few, if any. Both committed horrendous hate crimes. There is no getting away from the reality that predicting the behaviour of individuals is an imprecise science, full of known unknowns, and unknown unknowns. This is why the use of predictive technologies in policing and criminal justice is so controversial. They are not accurate enough at the individual level to tell us where the next crime will be committed, and by whom. Where predictions are made, they are often no better than a fifty–fifty guess, resulting in cases of injustice.

Does this mean we should give up hope of predicting the next far-right mass shooting in a synagogue, or whether an imprisoned ISIS terror attacker is fully rehabilitated? Prediction is often seen by practitioners as the holy grail, but behavioural scientists prefer description and explanation. This doesn't mean figuring out what causes a behaviour is off the table for these scientists – doing so is still of great interest, and can occupy whole careers. It just means that explanatory causal models don't always make for good predictions for specific individuals. This is because behavioural scientists work at the level of groups, usually samples of people drawn from populations. These samples consist of hundreds and sometimes thousands of people that are supposed to represent everyone else, *in the average*. Unfortunately, the average is rarely useful in predicting rare behaviours like hate crimes and terror attacks.

With the average we can take a random sample of a thousand people and say with some degree of certainty that around *one* person is likely to commit a hate crime. We can even use the scientific evidence to narrow this down and say this hate crime is most likely to be perpetrated by a white male between the ages of fifteen and twenty-four. Down from one thousand to around fifty people. Let's go even further with the science and say this one person we are looking for is likely to have unresolved issues from childhood trauma and to have engaged with far-right material either online or offline. Maybe we get down to about five people. Finally, we can give a hint at the timing of this hate crime, and say it is most likely to happen following a trigger event like a terror attack.

What do we do with these five people? Do we detain them for life to prevent the hate crime? Do we just detain them in the aftermath of a trigger event and then release them? Do we monitor them closely around the event without detaining anyone? Or do we do nothing? How sure are we that we have the right five?

Statistics may indicate there is a good chance we have them, maybe even better than fifty–fifty. But we can't be sure. Do the rights of the five, four of whom will in all statistical likelihood never commit a hate crime, outweigh the rights of the one likely hate crime victim? With the ever-present uncertainty in the science we can never justify interfering with the rights of these five, or anyone who is labelled 'at risk' but has not been found guilty of a crime by a jury of their peers in a court of law.

What the average is good for is developing interventions that will work on the majority. Isolating some of the ingredients that cause or prevent hateful behaviours means the average person can address *seed* thoughts, like conscious bias, and behaviours, like micro-aggressions, before they cause harm or develop into anything more nefarious. On a larger scale, policy makers can institute changes in criminal justice, education, housing, social care and healthcare to address the ingredients of hate at the level of populations. While this may be of little comfort to those victims and their families who suffer at the hands of hate criminals, the science that filters into individual change and policy can and is preventing future hate crimes and people from becoming victims.

Seven steps to stop hate

Mohamed Salah joined Liverpool Football Club in July 2017 in a club record €42 million transfer. He is one of around fifty Muslims among the Premier League's five hundred-odd players. He scored thirty-six times in his debut season, becoming Europe's leading goal scorer that year. Shortly after his transfer he was awarded Player of the Month by fans for his outstanding performance, and eventually won the Players' Player of the Year and Premier League Golden Boot in 2018.

On the pitch Salah celebrates goals by performing the sujud (prostration to Allah) and has further raised awareness of Islam by posting pictures of Islamic practices (e.g. Ramadan observance) to his more than 11 million followers on social media, and refusing to celebrate goals following attacks on mosques. In appreciation of his success, fans have taken to victory chants that incorporate positive sentiment towards Islam:

> If he scores another few, then I'll be Muslim, too;
> If he's good enough for you, he's good enough for me;
> Sitting in a mosque, that's where I wanna be!

Salah joined Liverpool only months after the string of Islamic extremist terror attacks in 2017 which saw the highest rise in anti-Muslim hate crime ever recorded by police in the UK. At this time, Liverpool, being less ethnically diverse than the UK as a whole, ranked in the top five police force areas for hate crime. Within months, Salah's actions were having a positive impact on perceptions of Islam amongst fans. Evidence was also mounting that this 'Salah effect' was spilling onto the streets of Liverpool. A study by Stanford University showed that Merseyside had a remarkable 16 per cent lower hate crime rate following Salah's signing compared to the expected rate had he not joined Liverpool FC. The 'Salah effect' also spread online, with a 50 per cent drop in anti-Muslim tweets posted by Liverpool fans. Meanwhile the rates of hate crimes and tweets in other areas and other fan bases either remained stable or increased after his signing, indicating that the effect on tolerance towards Muslims was localised.[*4]

---

* The 'Salah effect' only applied to Liverpool FC and the county of Merseyside. In fact, anti-Muslim sentiment (especially on Twitter) rose in other areas and fan bases directly because of his success. Racism expressed by the fans of opposing

THE SCIENCE OF HATE

There were likely many elements to the Salah effect, but possibly the most salient was his portrayal of his religious identity, which may have been novel information to many Liverpool fans, and which may have had the effect of softening attitudes towards Islam. Acts including prostrating himself in prayer after scoring goals, his wife attending matches in a headscarf, and naming his daughter after the holy site of Mecca have made Salah one of the most well-known Muslim footballers globally. His frequent messaging regarding his religion also indicates he is unlikely to be seen as an 'exception', which helps challenge the negative stereotype of Islam as threatening and at odds with British values, counteracting it and humanising other Muslims.

The Salah effect shows the prejudice- and hate-reducing impact of portraying a minority identity in a positive light. To give us hope that hate is not inevitable, we need look no further than the stands of Anfield, around which praise for Islam has echoed.

Gordon Allport was one of the first psychologists to recognise that aside from the out-and-out bigot, most of us experience our prejudiced thoughts with compunction and routinely suppress them.[5] As norms and laws changed in the latter half of the twentieth century, fuelled by various social movements (civil rights, women's liberation and gay rights), people's unease relating to culturally fed biases increased, and so did the amount of suppression. It became socially unjustifiable to verbally express negative stereotypical views of others, and in some cases criminal to act in ways that discriminated. Prejudice may be better suppressed in the

football teams remains a pernicious problem amongst a minority. This pattern is not unique to football. Experience of the 'other' that turns out negative, as is the case when your team is beaten because of Salah's goals, can result in worsening attitudes and behaviours.

twenty-first century, but it has not gone away.[6] The mass use of largely unregulated social media and the rise of populism across the world has seen norms begin to slip, helping some people justify the expression of their prejudices once again.[7]

We have learned of the shortcomings of our brains, psychology, society and technology that can see our prejudices accelerate towards hate. None of us is immune to these forces, and we all have a responsibility to recognise their effect on us and our behaviours towards others.

What follows next is a set of steps, some more practical than others, that we can take to prevent our prejudices, many of them unconscious, from turning into discrimination and hateful behaviours.

1. We must recognise false alarms

The human threat detector, locked away inside our brains, has evolved to keep us safe. It's done a great job getting us to where we are, but it's now out of date, and no longer fit for purpose for most of us in the developed world (that is, unless, you are Bear Grylls and get a kick out of putting yourself in harm's way). Together with a range of biological processes that can kick in under certain circumstances and our learning of negative stereotypes, red alert can be triggered when no or little threat exists. When the false alarm is triggered by a person different from us, the resulting action can take the form of prejudice and hatred. To rewire this threat detection mechanism takes a lot of conscious effort.

The effort begins with our executive control area, the prefrontal cortex, which is designed to stand down the amygdala-induced red alert when a (non)threat is recognised for what it really is. The better we become at recognising false alarms, the quicker we can stand down and avoid a prejudiced response. Key to this is knowing when our out-of-date machinery is being hijacked by those who have something to gain from our resulting response.

Consider the Robbers Cave Experiment where Sherif purposely manipulated the relations between the groups of boys to create a sense of threat. Opposing identities were encouraged, resources were made scarce to force competition, and fictitious acts of vandalism were planted. On cue, the boys' threat detectors came online, and aggression ensued. Politicians and the media are conducting their own Robbers Cave Experiments on unsuspecting publics around the globe. 'Natives' are told 'outsiders' threaten their national identity and their resources, such as jobs, healthcare, homes and school places. If unprepared for it, like the boys in Sherif's study, we react with fear, at best voting in a populist leader, at worst taking to the streets and eliminating the perceived threat with violence.

The Eagles and the Rattlers got over their differences when the perception of threat was removed from the equation. As we saw, in an earlier experiment, Sherif was unable to instil a sense of threat in the harmonious Pythons and Panthers, because the two groups of boys got to know each other before the study began.

When we are told by politicians and the media that life is bad because of people different from us, we must always question their motive, and stand down red alert when we spot mis/disinformation.

2. We must question our prejudgements of others different from us

Though our brains are great at many things, they are flawed in a few important areas. The human brain cannot process all the information out there in the world, so it makes shortcuts, which go on to influence opinions, attitudes and behaviours. These short-cuts, in the form of stereotypes, can be responsible for how we see others, especially strangers. Stereotypes learned during childhood are especially resistant to change, given that our young brains were more willing to accept them without question.[8]

Some of these stereotypes are relatively benign in their outcomes – if someone thinks the German job applicant is efficient and a good time-keeper, they may favour her for the job; if someone assumes all British people have a stiff upper lip, they may think a brave face is an act and offer sympathy in hard times. But some are harmful in their consequences – some think Jewish people are greedy, dishonest and exploitative and so have little empathy when they are persecuted; an employer may assume a black employee is lazy and therefore give them less demanding and lower-profile projects, hindering promotion; government officials may think gay men are promiscuous and deserving of disease, so are slow to call a national emergency in response to an HIV epidemic.

Prejudices and stereotypes are taught and transmitted by culture, and can prey on our group threat response mechanism. Vehicles for transmitting culture, including newspapers, TV, books, the internet and our family and friends, can generate general, often crude, impressions of others. These stereotypes are encoded and stored for later retrieval when needed to inform judgements and behaviours.[9] But because stereotypes are based on culture, we are not slaves to their influence. We can resist what they tell us in a moment of action, allowing us to moderate our behaviour to achieve a non-biased outcome.[10]

Unlike threat-based prejudices that involve the fear-controlling amygdala, stereotypes are predominantly associated with a different part of the brain that is more susceptible to change.[11] In the lab, repeatedly exposing subjects to counter-stereotypical information can change their perceptions. However, put them back into a culture that reinforces old stereotypes, and they can relapse if an effort is not made to question such representations. To counteract this, we must promote positive stereotypes beyond the lab, in the wild – at home and in newspapers, on TV and in sport.

Like the Mo Salah example, there are many others that show the effect of the breakdown of negative stereotypes by prominent cultural figures. But their success varies, and often depends on keeping a squeaky-clean record, avoiding the negative end of the tabloid press where possible. A scandal, even a minor one, can reinforce old negative stereotypes of the group in question. In mid-2018 a negative story about Salah using a mobile phone while driving hit the press, and in late 2019 his performance on the pitch dipped due to an injury. These knocks have the power to negatively impact the 'Salah effect' on hate crimes and attitudes towards Islam.

We have more control over the fictional roles our celebrities play in TV and film. More positive and less stereotypical portrayals of various identities in fiction can promote tolerance. I am a huge *Star Trek* fan, and was thrilled when the writers of the reboot sequel, *Star Trek: Beyond*, revealed the character Sulu, played by John Cho, was gay. After watching the movie, I was disappointed to learn that a kiss between Sulu and his husband had been edited out of the final cut, I assume due to concerns that it might reduce revenue at home and internationally. It is not the movie studio's sole purpose to spread the inclusive message that same-sex relationships are normal, so the cut, whether motivated by anxieties over unsold tickets or creative reasons, can be forgiven. But I think if I were running the show, giving up a few hundred thousand dollars to send out that message to millions is worth the dividends it might eventually pay in increasing tolerance.

The science backs this up. Ever since the hit sitcom *Will & Grace* and *The Ellen Show,* gay characters and personalities, many displaying counter-stereotypical traits, have been beamed into our homes. The impact on the audience has been largely positive, with many reporting increased acceptance and reduced prejudice towards homosexuals on and off the screen.[12] The effect also extends to other identities, as viewers cognitively and emotionally connect with fictional 'minority' characters. In particular, where the story has the character experience discrimination, viewers can take their perspective and empathise.[13] However, the power of media also means lazy writing that portrays negative stereotypes can reaffirm viewers' prejudices.[14]

We can't rely on celebrities and Hollywood writers to do all the work for us. We are all free thinkers and can resist what the 'culture machine' churns out. It is incumbent on us always to challenge what feels like an automatic crude assumption about a person or a group. Instincts are useful in certain situations, but they can lead to discrimination when used to make decisions regarding people different from us. We should never act on first impressions and must always give someone a chance to prove us wrong. But for counter-stereotypes to really stick, we need a bit more help. We need direct *personal contact* with people different from ourselves.

3. We should not shy away from engaging in contact with others different from us

Think of your closest circle of friends, those you would turn to in a crisis. Now think of your neighbours and the people you regularly see in the coffee shop or down the local pub. Next, think of your colleagues, fellow students or whatever the equivalent might be in your life. Finally, think of the colour of all those people's skin, their gender, sexual orientation, religion, age and any physical or mental impairment they may have.

The chances are that your inner circle is the least diverse, and your workplace, college or equivalent is the most diverse. It is no surprise that we see this pattern repeated in the most popular TV shows in the western world, including mega hits like *Cheers, Sex in the City* and *Friends.** The formula represents our experience. Because those we would turn to in a crisis share many of the same characteristics as us, this can influence who we trust more generally. This can have consequences for a range of decisions in life that occur in the wider circles of friends, acquaintances and colleagues.

In the early part of the twentieth century there was disagreement on the outcomes of interracial mixing. Some scholars hypothesised that increased contact between races on equal terms, for example in the classroom, would create unease, tension, even violence, while others argued tolerance and respect would result.[15] Intergroup Contact Theory was developed to address the question, and set out four key ingredients for *optimal* prejudice-reducing contact:

(i) In the context of contact, both parties need to be of equal status; this can come about naturally in the workplace and in educational settings, for example where white and black employees and students of the same rank are asked to work together.

(ii) Both parties need a common goal, such as working on a joint project.

(iii) In the pursuit of this goal both parties must openly co-operate, and not work in isolation.

---

* More recently, some sitcoms have moved away from this formula and include multiple contrasting identities in the close-knit circle of friends.

(iv) The pairing must be sanctioned or supported by an authority figure that both parties respect, such as a boss or teacher.[16]

The absence of one or more of these conditions does not mean contact will fail to reduce prejudice, but rather that the effect may be weaker, may take longer to come about, or may not last as long.

Some of the earliest studies tested the theory in US housing projects. The Housing Act of 1949 set out a rapid programme of public housing building to clear the slums in US cities. It was seen by some as an opportunity not just to clean up deprived areas, but also to end racial segregation in housing. This was a controversial move, as scientific opinion on residential desegregation was mixed at the time. The early experiments were producing encouraging results, but there was no guarantee that these would be replicated on the streets. But to build swathes of public housing that were segregated by race would have given the impression that the federal government endorsed 'black only' and 'white only' housing blocks and neighbourhoods, and would do more damage to multicultural relations.

In what became regarded as one of the first large-scale social engineering experiments, the Newark low-rent public housing project assigned black and white residents to separate blocks, and compared their experiences to two similar blocks in New York City that were desegregated. Compared to their counterparts in the segregated blocks, white housewives in desegregated housing reported better experiences with black neighbours, and came to hold them in higher esteem. Following the publication of the results, a policy was enacted that ordered housing be 'allocated on the basis of need, regardless of race, religion and color'. Segregated public housing ended in Newark, and white and black residents were mixed in all eight housing projects. A minority of residents complained about the policy, but quickly backed down when it was explained to them, along with the scientific evidence.[17]

A decade later saw white flight to the suburbs, turning the city of Newark majority black. Along with white people went political influence, and unemployment and crime rose. In 1967, a black man was badly beaten by white cops, resulting in the Newark race riots in which twenty-six people died, twenty-four of whom were residents. Race relations took a dive, possibly due to the erosion of desegregation caused by wider economic and social forces of the late 1960s. The once proportionately policed housing projects became over-policed, and almost all of the cops were white.

If Newark Police Department had hired and promoted more black officers, would race relations have deteriorated so far and so fast? Intergroup Contact Theory would suggest not. Positive contact in employment can reduce prejudice, fostering improved relations within and outside of the workplace. In an early study, white police who worked with black officers in Philadelphia PD softened their attitudes towards partnering with black officers in the future and taking orders from a black superior officer.[18]

These results were replicated in other places of work. In a pioneering 1960s study conducted in the American South, white female office workers with racist attitudes were partnered with black colleagues for a period of twenty days. Care was taken to select participants with equal status, and the office tasks ensured shared goals, cooperation and authority sanction. Initially, those white women with the most racist views showed negative behaviours towards their black colleagues, including avoiding contact, ignoring their questions and excluding them from conversations. By the end of the study period, almost all the white women reported favourable experiences (measured by likability and competence) with their black colleagues, agreeing to work with them again on future assignments.[19]

Contact also reduces prejudice amongst young people in recreational settings. A recent restaging of the Robbers Cave Experiment involved young people on a camping expedition being randomly assigned either to an all-white group or a racially mixed group. During the three-week trip the groups were trained in survival techniques under the conditions for optimal intergroup contact. A month after the trip, compared to teens assigned to the all-white group, white teens from the racially mixed group reported less prejudiced attitudes towards black people.[20]

Contact works best if it is direct, meaning individuals need to come together, preferably under the optimal conditions set out earlier. If this is not possible, then indirect forms of contact can also reduce prejudice, but to a lesser extent.[21] The 'Salah effect' is an example of indirect contact. Salah and Liverpool fans shared the common goal of winning tournaments; Salah was endorsed by the club's management and coaches, representing the fans' trusted authority figures; and he had been successful on delivering his promises, creating a positive experience for all. But the fans rarely got to spend direct time with him.

Since the 1950s, over five hundred studies including more than 250,000 people across thirty-eight countries have been conducted to test Intergroup Contact Theory across a range of identities. The conclusion is that positive contact under the right conditions reduces prejudice and hate.[22] Contact seems to work particularly well for reducing anti-gay prejudice, followed by prejudice motivated by physical impairment, race, mental impairment and age. Those most susceptible to change are children and college students, with adults being the most stubborn. There is no significant difference between men and women, regardless of age.

Of the studies conducted over a fifty-year period, those based in recreational settings reported the greatest effect of contact on reducing prejudice, followed by work, education and residential settings. Positive contact has even been shown to have an effect in the most prejudice-prone individuals, including those with far-right beliefs.[23]

These studies threw people together for periods of time to see if they would get along. What these people did when in contact with one another was not always prescribed, as it often is in a lab setting. The conversations they had over the weeks of contact in workplaces, schools, summer camps and housing blocks involved the telling of personal stories, boosted empathy and showed similarities between groups. White and black, heterosexual and homosexual, young and old participants learned of shared problems and prospects, breaking down often imagined cultural barriers. The tasks they undertook forced them to cooperate, boosting confidence in the abilities and intelligence of 'others'. The scientists concluded that contact works between different groups by breeding familiarity and liking, and reducing uncertainty and anxiety via countering stereotypes and removing the perception of threat.[24]

One question that remains unanswered is how long the reduction in prejudice lasts following contact. The concern amongst policy makers exploring prejudice-reducing initiatives is that the effect of contact may rapidly erode after the intervention, especially if participants go back to their everyday lives with little intergroup contact.[25] Research conducted within the last decade indicates that living in a neighbourhood where there is a high rate of positive intergroup contact results in a reduction in prejudice within residents.[26] The general community's tolerant attitude filters down to individuals, where people are influenced by the behaviour of others, bolstering the positive effects of their own intergroup contact. Even with no direct personal contact, people living in these areas report less prejudice.

Where you live matters. However, it is not enough simply to have diverse neighbourhoods. Diversity in residents must also be accompanied with meaningful positive contact. It does no good to plan a 50 per cent black and 50 per cent white neighbourhood if both communities are reluctant to interact on a regular basis. Over time, diverse neighbourhoods with positive contact can counteract any sense of threat towards outgroups. Data across twenty years and from a hundred countries shows that while an influx of religiously and racially different residents to an area can at first be difficult to become accustomed to, within a maximum of eight years, and sometimes much sooner (four to six years), any self-reported negative effect on quality of life (life satisfaction, happiness and health) dissipates as positive contact creates a sense of trust between all. Humans all over the world can adapt and make a virtue of multiculturalism. But this process can be derailed by those who might benefit from working against diversity. Politicians and the media spreading anti-immigration narratives that highlight and manufacture differences between groups trigger the human threat mechanism, slowing down and even stopping successful integration.[27]

The clear lesson from this extensive body of research is that we should mix with people who are different from us as much as possible. I acknowledge that for many it's easier to read this than it is to actually leave the home and mix with different people, especially for those who do not live and work in diverse places. So when an opportunity does present itself to mix with others different from us, we must grasp it with both hands and embrace the experience. To ensure open and tolerant minds of future generations, we must also make sure our children do the same, preferably as early as possible, and especially before high school.[28]

During initial contact, accept that feeling a little anxious about doing or saying the wrong thing is not uncommon. We are all guilty of sometimes slipping up during our interactions with people different from us: forgetting to order the right kind of food for our house party, spelling the neighbour's name wrong on the Christmas card, asking an insensitive question or making a stereotypical assumption about someone's life or behaviour. The worst of these, often brought about by the stress and anxiety of trying not to come across as prejudiced, are called micro-aggressions (recall Chapter 1). When you think you've caused offence, apologise. It will mean a lot.

4. We must take the time to put ourselves in the shoes of 'others'

Viewing counter-stereotypical characters on TV and spending time with others who are different from us can teach us a little bit about what it's like to be somebody else. This is something we should be doing routinely, and we should not have to rely on the media and our celebrities to make us feel empathy for those who are experiencing prejudice and discrimination on a regular basis.

Restorative justice programmes used by criminal justice services bring victims and hate perpetrators together to encourage empathy.[29] In the lab, exercises in imagining others' perspectives and experiences have been shown to promote what psychologists call *decategorisation*, which means we come to see 'others' as individuals, and less as a part of a separate group. In some cases, we *recategorise* or *cross-categorise* others, meaning we see them not only as individuals but also as part of a group we belong to: 'we may be from different groups, but we are on the same team'.[30] These three processes break down negative stereotypes and ultimately help reduce prejudice.

When we encounter representations of the plight of others in newspapers, online and on TV, we should make a habit of imagining ourselves as the protagonist in their story. Would I trade places with them, and if not, why not? In what ways am I better off than them and why? What do we have in common? What were their goals and motivations? What must it have felt like to encounter the obstacles they faced? What must it have been like to endure their loss or pain? When we think hard enough about others, we can acknowledge any privilege we may have, and begin to see ourselves in them, and them in us.

5. We must not allow divisive events to get the better of us

Periods of economic recession, controversial political votes, high-profile court cases and terror attacks all have something in common. They have an incredible power to divide, but also to unite. In times of crisis the instinct is to hunker down and protect those like us, sometimes at the expense of outgroups. This applies as much to resources such as jobs and healthcare as it does to the values we hold sacred, such as our worldview.

When a divisive event unfolds we must ask ourselves if those groups depicted as being at its centre are really to blame. We must question the motives of those pointing the finger and seek out a range of opinions from across the spectrum of viewpoints before we decide on how to feel and how to behave.

Whatever the outcome, we must try our best to avoid the easier reaction of moral outrage. While it can be cathartic, it is short-lived and causes more pain and misery in the long run. Instead, we must focus on healthier behaviours that reflect moral cleansing. If we feel a divisive event challenges our deeply held values and way of life, we should reinforce them with positive behaviours – visiting friends and family, donating to charity, volunteering. The short-, medium- and long-term benefits will be felt by us and those we share with.

6. We must burst our filter bubbles

Despite the global reach of the internet, our contacts and exposure to viewpoints online may be less diverse than in our offline world. While the science is yet to reach a definitive conclusion on whether online filter bubbles greatly impact our attitudes, it is safe to assume most of us either actively avoid, or are guided by algorithms away from, groups and information that do not match our preferences.

Online we actively seek out those more like us and news that reinforces what we already think and believe, informing algorithms that then go on to automate this process for us. Social media giants are already working on ways to mediate reinforcing information with countervailing information in users' feeds. Despite initial evidence that shows approaching the problem in this way can actually entrench existing viewpoints,[31] being aware of this phenomenon may be enough to make some of us think twice when engaging with people and information online. Of course, those who find it cosy in their online bubble probably won't be motivated to burst it, and it may come down to others to do it for them in a way that doesn't make them recoil in horror.

7. We must all become hate incident first responders

When we see hate, we must call it out. The limited research on those witnessing prejudice and hate shows that fewer than half actually do something in the moment either to help the victim or admonish the perpetrator.[32] There are several conditions to becoming a hate incident 'first responder'. Recognising the act is a result of hate is the important first step. Where there is uncertainty over motivation, asking the victim to give their viewpoint will yield valuable information on how to proceed. If this is not possible or safe to do, we can turn our attention to the wider context within which the act has taken place. If there is a recent divisive event, such as a terror attack, a high-profile court case or a political campaign, then we can factor it into our thought process. Then we can make a cost–benefit analysis on a range of possible responses.

Factoring in personal safety is paramount. Where personal risk is low, such as in the case of an off-the-cuff prejudiced joke being made, we can safely intervene with a challenge. Where the risk of harm is higher, we can call the police or another authority figure trained to handle the situation safely. If the hate witnessed is online, we can report it, or use counter-narratives that diffuse the hate, while being mindful not to encourage more hate with aggressive or abusive language. Online counter-speech is most effective in reducing hate speech when performed in groups, so encouraging others to join you in reinforcing norms of acceptable behaviour is a good idea.

There are several effective ways of making people question their hateful behaviour in the moment, all tested in the lab by psychologists: use expert opinion to debunk prejudiced claims and tropes;[33] ask them to justify their words and actions, then highlight inconsistencies in their argument and/or set of beliefs;[34] target their powerful emotions of guilt and shame by highlighting their role in harming the victim;[35] and ask them to take on the perspective of their victim in an attempt to induce empathy.[36]

Our ancestors organised into small tight-knit groups. They needed super-sensitive threat-detecting powers to cope with the harsh reality of their hostile environment: flesh-eating wildlife, freak weather, disease and competing tribes. The bond created within tribes in the face of such adversity was incredibly strong. Our brains went through hundreds of thousands of years of development under these conditions, so it is no surprise that today we are quicker to react to manufactured 'threats' from outsiders than we are to scientific evidence showing our susceptibility to these 'threats'.

Taking the seven steps onboard is usually a gradual process. While most of us have an internal motivation not to express prejudice or hate, it is not easy or straightforward to challenge our own well-entrenched viewpoints of other groups. Nor is it comfortable to take a long hard look at ourselves and to arrive at the conclusion that the attitudes we hold may be biased. For some of us, it won't be possible to arrive at this conclusion, because our biases are so deeply buried that we cannot or do not want to see them. Some of us may need the insight of others to help us along.

Those who invest in their prejudiced attitude, whether they recognise it for what it is or refuse to, are unlikely to accept the science that underpins the seven steps. This does not mean the steps won't work on people who are motivated to express prejudice. While it may be difficult to get them to engage directly, they are not immune to wider progressive cultural shifts and the liberal media, both of which have proven so powerful in their indirect influence on attitudes. These and other more subtle forms of persuasion are preferred for the most hardened haters, as most direct methods that challenge hateful viewpoints result in anger and rejection.[37]

The science suggests that if adopted in whole or in part, these seven steps would see a reduction in the expression of prejudice and hate in suitably motivated people. Broader, less practical steps required to address systemic bias in society can only be enacted by institutions and governments, and would take an entire other book to flesh out and discuss. Needless to say, these are essential to design anti-hate initiatives and build them into society.

What twenty years of research told me about my attackers (and me)

Becoming a hate crime victim started me on a twenty-year journey to discover the motivations of my attackers. I set out with the naive hope I might find something fundamental separating them from me; maybe a difference in the wiring of our brains and our psychology. I was looking for something concrete that would tell me why they invested in hate and I did not. At the time such a discovery would have been comforting, a clear demarcation in what made us tick. Instead my journey revealed I had more in common with my attackers than I was happy to admit.

I found that my attackers and I share neurological and psychological traits that predispose us to think about strangers using crude categories and to prefer people like ourselves. The factors that separate me from them are less fundamental. Their upbringing was probably different from mine, including the events they experienced as children. Some of the things they watched, listened to and read I might have avoided or not had access to. We may have lived in neighbourhoods faced with contrasting problems creating divergent scapegoats. But despite these likely differences, I am confident that if I was to spend time with my attackers, I would find much in common with them beyond our core traits.

The factors that caused the hateful behaviour of those three men are not immutable. Under different life circumstances, with less exposure to the various accelerants detailed in this book, my attackers would have been diverted away from hate. Instead of choosing to commit a hate crime that day they would have walked on by. Turning the lens on myself, faced with accelerant on top of accelerant, there is a chance I would be committing hate crimes rather than studying them. Coming to terms with the fact that I would be capable of similar acts of intolerance and prejudice given the right set of circumstances continues to be a challenge.

By picking up this book you showed a curiosity about the worst of human behaviour. The complex interplay between your brain, biology, psychology, personal experience, technology and embeddedness in subculture and wider culture shapes how you see the world and how you interact with others. Being aware of these factors, how they combine and their influence on you, is key to questioning your judgements of others before they can manifest as negative behaviours. You may turn the curiosity for understanding human behaviour 'at a distance' on yourself. If you find the person staring back is not who you expected, what will you do?

Postscript

July 11 2021 was unlike any other Sunday that year for the HateLab team. At around 7:00 p.m. we gathered in a small darkened room, all of us knotted in front of a bank of computer monitors. At the flick of a switch, our faces began to glimmer as they reflected back the dazzling light emanating from the floor-to-ceiling array of screens. Charts displaying social media data streaming in live flickered onscreen – a 'situation room' for monitoring online hate in real-time. We had come together in anticipation of the largest volume of online hate posted on social media in the history of the lab's existence: the UEFA Euro 2020 final at Wembley stadium.

Emotions were running high. England had bucked their historic trend all tournament, beating Germany, Ukraine and Denmark to get to the final. It felt like England's best chance to end their five-decade wait for a major victory on the international stage.

The conditions on that night met all of our expectations for an explosion of online negative sentiment – and possibly hate – should the sorely sought-after victory slip though England's fingers. England's previous string of tournament losses to Italy ensured the ingroup and outgroup were firmly established, the threat and its consequences were abundantly clear, the stakes of the competition high, years of hurt felt by fans still alive in collective memory, and the chatter on social media polarising. This was a tinderbox for xenophobic hate, but the eventual targets were not who we had anticipated.

The game opening was electrifying for England's fans, with Gareth Southgate's team tearing out of the blocks and scoring in under two minutes. But it wasn't long before Italy dominated possession and eventually equalised. In familiar fashion, the game ended in the ultimate test of nerve – a penalty shootout. In anticipation, Southgate had made substitutions late in extra time, sending on two young black players: Marcus Rashford and Jadon Sancho. Both, along with another black player, Bukayo Saka, missed their penalties, leading to England's defeat.

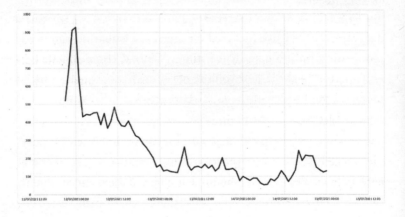

Fig. 24: Posts sent and shared (per hour) on Twitter including racist content following the Euro 2020 final

We had anticipated a minority of England fans posting online hate speech directed at Italy's players, but instead the events near the end of the game saw them turn on their own. Within minutes of the penalty misses the number of racist posts sent and shared on Twitter skyrocketed, peaking at over 920 between 11:00 p.m.

and 12:00 a.m. just after the game. Rashford, Sancho and Saka were the prime targets.[*]

The situation room display screens flooded with racial slurs and primate emojis. Twitter wasn't the only platform to host the bile, and Instagram, Facebook, and many others allowed thousands of racist messages to be posted. In the subsequent days each platform claimed to have removed the most egregious violations of their community standards. Our analysis showed a different picture, with many harmful posts remaining online months after the game.

In the aftermath of the surge in online hate, complaints were filed and police reports were made. Police in the UK manually looked through tens of thousands of posts from across platforms. The Football Policing Unit received 600 reports and determined 207 to be potentially criminal. But only fifty-five of these were put forward for investigation as the majority of the incidents had emanated from overseas.[†] Only eleven arrests were made, and by November 2021 just three convictions had been successful.

Scott McCluskey, a forty-three-year-old from Runcorn, Cheshire, was at home watching the final with his son and partner. Purportedly fuelled with alcohol and cannabis, McCluskey took to Facebook following the penalty shootout and posted the racist comment, 'Well it took three ethnic players to fuck it up. Unlucky England. Sack them three monkeys though.' In his defence he stated he wrote the post to make people laugh. In court he pleaded guilty to sending by a public communication network an offensive message. He was given a suspended sentence of fourteen weeks imprisonment.

---

[*] Most of these posts are unlikely to reach the criminal threshold. It is likely our hate speech detection algorithm also picked up some counter-speech that used similar language to hate speech (e.g. by quoting the original hate speech).

[†] Our analysis of Twitter estimated 50 per cent of racist messages posted in the days after the Euro 2020 final emanated from accounts claiming to be based in the UK.

Following the game, Bradford Pretty, a forty-nine-year-old from Folkstone, Kent, recorded his reaction and uploaded it to Facebook. Heavily intoxicated with a smudged England flag painted across his face, Pretty slurred, 'Where do I start, where do I start? Sick, gutted like all of us. Proper deflated. Be proud of the boys, be proud, but anyone and everyone that knows me well will understand what I'm talking about.' He then went on to use two racist slurs while referring to Rashford, Sancho and Saka. In his defence his solicitor said it was a 'moment of drunken madness.' He was found guilty and sentenced to fifty days of imprisonment, suspended for twelve months.

Fifty-two-year-old Jonathan Best of Feltham, London, took to Facebook after imbibing a dozen beers to post an eighteen-second video blaming the loss on 'three black cunts who can't play for fucking England.' Best was asked to remove the video after his colleague reported it to his boss. In response, Best said 'It's my profile, I can do what I fucking want.' During sentencing the judge said Best 'cursed them because of the colour of their skin' and that his words 'strike at the very nature of civilised society and are corrosive . . . encourag[ing] those who want to express similar views.' A suspended sentence was considered, but the judge decided only an immediate imprisonment for ten weeks would suffice to deter others from similar acts of hate.

Since the start of the coronavirus pandemic the grisly problem of online abuse targeted at Premier League football players seemed to have accelerated, possibly fuelled by an increased use of social media around games due to the ban on stadium attendance. But HateLab analysis shows the problem has a long history.

In a groundbreaking study we collected every undeleted Twitter post sent over the last decade to an ethnic minority

Premier League player active in the 2020/21 season.* Naturally we found more online racism in recent years, given our focus on current players. Some players came into the firing line more than others, sometimes due to poor performance on the pitch, but mostly because of their bigger profiles and their actions related to standing up to racism; racist posts were also more prevalent in recent years due to the trend in players taking the knee following the murder of George Floyd in May 2020. Based on our estimates, around 40 per cent of posts sent in the ten-year period originated from accounts claiming to be based in the UK.

What we also noticed were surges in hate dating back between five and ten years. When we included some retired ethnic minority premier league players, it became evident that there was little novel about the most recent spikes in online racism.

We took Rio Ferdinand as a case study and found he had received significant amounts of online racism on Twitter between 2011 and 2014, at points exceeding the massive surges seen in 2020.† These included the tweets, '@rioferdy5 honestly why didn't ur mum have an abortion, your such a useless ugly nigga shit on the pitch look like a donkey nd thick as shit', and '@rioferdy5. You fuckin black donkey why didn't you shake @luis16suarez hand? Your a fuckin black cunt, get that?' Sent in 2012, both remain on Twitter at the time of writing.

* Because we could not collect deleted posts, some of the more extreme cases of online racism that resulted in deletion, either by Twitter or the user, are excluded from this analysis. Therefore, our collection represents a partial picture of online racism targeting ethic minority premier league footballers in the 20/21 season. Despite this limitation, it is notable that we still picked up significant amounts of racist content, indicating that Twitter has historically been reluctant to remove posts deemed as racially offensive.

† Our estimates show 67 per cent of these posts emanated from accounts claiming to be based in the UK.

Some of the hateful posts sent to Ferdinand emanate from accounts that lack user detail, making it difficult to tell 'real' accounts – with actual identifiable people behind them – from fake or bot accounts. This makes the job of law enforcement hunting down culprits near impossible, especially when social media companies fail to cooperate in a timely manner, if at all.

Online hate targeting Premier League players is nothing new, but the actions of several players following the Euro 2020 final has galvanised the attention it has received. The abuse of Rashford, Sancho and Saka acted as a lightning rod for calls to governments to introduce serious consequences for social media companies that fail to deal with hate posted on their platforms. If law enforcement is operating with one hand tied behind its back, then surely the social media companies should step up and take some of the responsibility. Some big names in the sport have called for a ban on anonymous social media accounts, and a strengthening of laws to fine platforms for not removing hateful content.

These touted solutions are likely unworkable. Banning anonymity risks stifling the freedom of expression social media affords citizens living in repressive regimes, and it is unlikely that users would trust platforms with their government identity documents following the string of mass data leaks and misuse of data scandals. A ban on anonymity would therefore see platforms' profits tumble as users left in droves.

Imposing large fines on platforms that refuse to remove hate speech will only work in a limited number of cases. It is likely that the hate speech would have to be clearly criminal in nature to issue a take-down notice, leaving a wide array of offensive content untouched. A time frame of twenty-four hours for removal, as has been suggested by some, also means the damage is likely already done to the victim and the wider community. Any move to compel platforms to prevent posting using some form of technology, such as machine learning, would also likely fail given the difficulty in automatically detecting hate speech and distinguishing it from non-hate speech that has a similar form, such as some counter-speech. Even improvements in prosecutions are unlikely to deter the most hardened haters, or those who post in the heat of the moment.

The solutions proposed by politicians, pundits and players are way off-target. This issue is not a technical one, but a social one. Together with the government and platforms, we too must take a stand against hate.

In addressing all online hate, we should turn our attention to the true great successes of the internet, digital commons. We have the ability to coordinate in powerful ways to stop online hate. In the face of hate and abuse, counter-speech that reinforces community standards can change online behaviour, and perhaps the minds of those behind the screens. HateLab research shows that when groups stand-up to online hate speech the chance of further hate is reduced.*

Those that care the most about football need to become hate incident first responders, setting and enforcing the standards of acceptable behavior both online and in stadiums. While this may be the more difficult of the proposed solutions, it will surely be the most effective and long-lasting should we enact it.

* 'A study of cyber hate on Twitter with implications for social media governance strategies' (2019). *Conference on Truth and Trust Online*, arxiv.org (Cornell University) | https://arxiv.org/abs/1908.11732

Acknowledgements

This book has benefitted from the intelligence, energy and generosity of many people which I am glad to have this opportunity to acknowledge. I will feel forever indebted to Anwen Hooson for taking a chance on me. Your careful thought and guiding hand turned the seed of an idea into something real. I am grateful to Laura Hassan for giving the book a home at Faber. Thank you to Eleanor Rees for the forensic but sensitive editing, and to Tom Bromley, Mo Hafeez and Fred Baty for the sharp suggestions on structure. Others at Faber also deserve a mention: Rowan Cope, Phoebe Williams, Josephine Salverda, Lizzie Bishop and all of the rights team. Thank you to Geraint Griffiths of OCW Studio for the great design and artwork.

Researchers who have at some point worked with me over the years also deserve my gratitude: Jasmin Tregidga, Sefa Ozalp, Arron Cullen, Amir Javed, Han Liu and Vivek Roy-Chowdhury, thank you for providing valuable insights. Sefa deserves an additional mention for creating many of the charts contained within the book. I am also lucky to have worked with many inspirational colleagues who have shaped how I think over the years, including Pete Burnap, Steven Stanley, Alex Sutherland, Luke Sloan, Mike Levi, Mike Maguire, Lesley Noaks, Paul Atkinson and Sara Delamont. I am indebted to the academics and practitioners who gave up their precious time to speak to me about the ideas contained within this book: David Gadd, Joe Dumit, David Amodio, Jay Van Bavel,

Paul Giannasi, Kirsty Penrice and John Doran. Zargol Moradi deserves a particular mention for her time, patience and insight.

Many of my family and friends deserve thanks for their support: Mam, Dad, Jodi, Gareth, Rhys, Nan, Bamps, Joanne, Ceri, Margaret, Graham, Megan, Alex, Annabel, Max, Andrew, Alys, Chris A, Chris C, Damian, Lee, Bleddyn, Gareth, Robin and Mark. I'd also like to remember Mia. Her company on those long days of writing was a great comfort.

This work would not have been possible without the financial support of the Economic and Social Research Council at UK Research and Innovation. Samantha Barrington-McGregor and Bruce Jackson deserve specific mention.

Finally, a special thank you to my husband and best friend, Dean.

List of plates

Page 8

(Top) Rohingya Muslim man: photo by Ahmed Salahuddin/Nur-Photo via Getty Images.

(Bottom) Mohamed Salah: photo by Chris Brunskill/Fantasista/Getty Images.

Notes

Introduction

1. N. Elias, *The Civilizing Process*, Oxford: Blackwell, 1994.
2. S. Pinker, *The Better Angels of our Nature*, New York: Viking, 2011.
3. Information Commissioner's Office, 'ICO Investigation into Use of Personal Information and Political Influence', London: Information Commissioner's Office, 2020.
4. Institute for Strategic Dialogue, 'Far-Right Exploitation of Covid-19', London: ISD, 2020; S. Parkin, '"A Threat to Health Is Being Weaponised": Inside the Fight against Online Hate Crime', *Guardian*, 2 May 2020; K. Paul, 'Facebook Reports Spike in Takedowns of Hate Speech', Reuters, 12 May 2020.
5. EU vs Disinfo, 'EEAS Special Report Update: Short Assessment of Narratives and Disinformation around the Covid-19/Coronavirus Pandemic', 24 April 2020, euvsdisinfo.eu/eeas-special-report-update-2-22-april; C. Miller, 'White Supremacists See Coronavirus as an Opportunity', Southern Poverty Law Center, 26 March 2020.

1. What It Means to Hate

1. A. D. S. Burch, 'He Became a Hate Crime Victim. She Became a Widow', *New York Times*, 8 July 2017.
2. 'Olathe, Kansas, Shooting Suspect "Said He Killed Iranians"', BBC News, 28 February 2017.
3. Burch, 'He Has Become a Hate Crime Victim'.
4. 'Olathe, Kansas, Shooting Suspect "Said He Killed Iranians"'.
5. Burch, 'He Has Become a Hate Crime Victim'.
6. US Department of Justice, 'Kansas Man Pleads Guilty to Hate Crime

and Firearm Offenses in Shooting of Two Indian Nationals and Third Man at a Bar', Press Release 18-657, 21 May 2018.

7. 'Remarks by President Trump in Joint Address to Congress', 28 February 2017, https://www.whitehouse.gov/briefings-statements/remarks-president-trump-joint-address-congress/.

8. S. Karri and E. Barry, 'At a Funeral Pyre in India, Anger over a Shooting in Kansas', *New York Times*, 28 February 2017.

9. A. Fischer et al., 'Why We Hate', *Emotion Review* 10 (2018), 309–20.

10. G. W. Allport, *The Nature of Prejudice*, Reading, MA: Addison Wesley, 1954.

11. T. Leader, B. Mullen and D. Rice, 'Complexity and Valence in Ethnophaulisms and Exclusion of Ethnic Out-groups: What Puts the "Hate" into Hate Speech?', *Journal of Personality and Social Psychology* 96 (2009), 170–82.

12. Human Rights Watch, '#Outlawed: The Love That Dare Not Speak Its Name', 2019, features.hrw.org/features/features/lgbt_laws.

13. M. Patria, 'Russia's Largest Gay Nightclub Strives to Be a Haven Despite Horrific Attacks', ABC News, 12 February 2014.

14. Allport, *The Nature of Prejudice*.

15. M. Habib et al., *Forced Migration of Rohingya: The Untold Experience*, Ontario: Ontario International Development Agency, 2018.

16. S. L. Gaertner and J. F. Dovidio, 'The Aversive Form of Racism', in *Prejudice, Discrimination, and Racism*, ed. J. F. Dovidio and S. L. Gaertner, San Diego: Academic Press, 1986; W. G. Stephan and C. W. Stephan, 'An Integrated Threat Theory of Prejudice', in *Reducing Prejudice and Discrimination*, ed. S. Oskamp, Mahwah, NJ: Erlbaum, 2000.

17. E. Halperin, 'Group-Based Hatred in Intractable Conflict in Israel', *Journal of Conflict Resolution* 52 (2008), 713–36.

18. J. M. Nichols, 'Here's What Happens When Two Men Hold Hands While Walking the Streets of Russia', *HuffPost*, 14 July 2015.

19. M. K. Lavers, 'Gunmen Open Fire at Moscow Gay Nightclub', *Washington Blade*, 18 November 2013.

20. Patria, 'Russia's Largest Gay Nightclub Strives to Be a Haven'.

21. E. Gaufman, *Security Threats and Public Perception: Digital Russia and the Ukraine Crisis*, Cham, Switzerland: Palgrave Macmillan, 2017;

A. Toor, 'Russia's New Neo-Nazi Sport: Terrorizing Gay Youth Online', *The Verge*, 7 August 2013.

22. Patria, 'Russia's Largest Gay Nightclub Strives to Be a Haven'.

23. D. M. Mackie, T. Devos and E. R. Smith, 'Intergroup Emotions: Explaining Offensive Action Tendencies in an Intergroup Context', *Journal of Personality and Social Psychology* 79 (2000), 602–16.

24. Halperin, 'Group-Based Hatred in Intractable Conflict in Israel'.

25. D. Webber et al., 'The Road to Extremism: Field and Experimental Evidence That Significance Loss-Induced Need for Closure Fosters Radicalization', *Journal of Personality and Social Psychology* 114 (2017), 270–85.

26. R. F. Pettigrew and L. R. Tropp, 'A Meta-Analytic Test of Intergroup Contact Theory', *Journal of Personality and Social Psychology* 90 (2006), 751–83.

27. M. Rich, 'After Mass Knife Attack in Japan, Disabled Victims Are Still in the Shadows', *New York Times*, 9 September 2016.

28. 'Murder in Facilities for Persons with Disabilities: There Were Many Signs [Translation]', *Okinawa Times* editorial, 27 July 2016.

29. M. Yamaguchi, 'Worker at Japan Care Home Sentenced to Hang for Mass Killing', ABC News, 16 March 2020.

30. H. Fein, *Accounting for Genocide*, Chicago, IL: University of Chicago Press, 1984.

31. J. McDevitt, J. Levin and S. Bennett, 'Hate Crime Offenders: An Expanded Typology', *Journal of Social Issues* 58 (2002), 303–17.

32. R. D. King and G. M. Sutton, 'High Times for Hate Crimes: Explaining the Temporal Clustering of Hate Motivated Offending', *Criminology* 51 (2014), 871–94.

33. E. Hanes and S. Machin, 'Hate Crime in the Wake of Terror Attacks: Evidence from 7/7 and 9/11', *Journal of Contemporary Criminal Justice* 30 (2014), 247–67.

34. J. W. Messerschmidt, *Crime as Structured Action*, London: Sage, 1997; B. Perry, *In the Name of Hate*, London: Routledge, 2002.

2. Hate Counts

1. 'Mpithi v. S (A830/2014) [2015] ZAGPPHC 535 (26 June 2015)', High Court of South Africa, 2015.

2. 'South Africa Killing of Lesbian Nogwaza "a Hate Crime"', BBC News, 3 May 2011.

3. Anonymous personal correspondence.

4. 'R v. Herbert & Ors', England and Wales Court of Appeal, 2008.

5. D. Arudou, *Embedded Racism: Japan's Visible Minorities and Racial Discrimination*, London: Lexington Books, 2015.

6. M. Walters, A. Owusu-Bempah and S. Wiedlitzka, 'Hate Crime and the "Justice Gap": The Case for Law Reform', *Criminal Law Review* 12 (2018), 961–86.

7. 'United States of America, Plaintiff-Appellee v. Jon Bartlett, et al.,' United States Court of Appeals for the Seventh Circuit; 'USA v. Bartlett, Spengler, and Masarik', 2009.

8. M. Desmond, A. V. Papochristos and D. S. Kirk, 'Police Violence and Citizen Crime Reporting in the Black Community', *American Sociological Review* 81 (2016), 857–76.

9. T. Cohen, 'Obama: "Trayvon Martin Could Have Been Me."', CNN, 19 July 2013.

10. G. Edwards and S. Rushin, 'The Effect of President Trump's Election on Hate Crimes', SSRN, 18 January 2018; R. D. King and G. M. Sutton, 'High Times for Hate Crimes: Explaining the Temporal Clustering of Hate Motivated Offending', *Criminology* 51 (2014), 871–94.

11. S. Pinker, *Enlightenment Now: The Case for Reason, Science, Humanism, and Progress*, New York: Viking, 2018.

3. The Brain and Hate

1. H. Damasio et al., 'The Return of Phineas Gage: Clues About the Brain from the Skull of a Famous Patient', *Science* 264 (1994), Issue 5162, 1102–5.

2. D. G. V. Mitchell et al., 'Instrumental Learning and Relearning in Individuals with Psychopathy and in Patients with Lesions Involving the Amygdala or Orbitofrontal Cortex', *Neuropsychology* 20 (2006), 280–9.

3. G. Orellana et al., 'Psychosis-Related Matricide Associated with a Lesion of the Ventromedial Prefrontal Cortex', *Journal of the American Academy of Psychiatry and the Law* 41 (2013), 401–6.

4. Mitchell et al., 'Instrumental Learning and Relearning in Individuals with Psychopathy'.

5. G. M. Lavergne, *A Sniper in the Tower*, Denton, Texas: University of North Texas Press, 1997.

6. S. Fink, 'Las Vegas Gunman's Brain Exam Only Deepens Mystery of His Actions', *New York Times*, 9 February 2018.

7. H. Tajfel, 'Experiments in Intergroup Discrimination', *Scientific American* 223 (1970), 96–102.

8. A. G. Greenwald et al., 'Measuring Individual Differences in Implicit Cognition: The Implicit Association Test', *Journal of Personality and Social Psychology* 74 (1998), 1464–80.

9. ibid.

10. A. G. Greenwald et al., 'Understanding and Using the Implicit Association Test: Iii. Metaanalysis of Predictive Validity', *Journal of Personality and Social Psychology* 97 (2009), 17–41.

11. A. Maass et al., 'Language Use in Intergroup Contexts: The Linguistic Intergroup Bias', *Journal of Personality and Social Psychology* 57 (1989), 981–93.

12. D. M. Amodio, 'The Social Neuroscience of Intergroup Relations', *European Review of Social Psychology* 19 (2008), 1–54; D. M. Amodio, E. Harmon-Jones and P. G. Devine, 'Individual Differences in the Activation and Control of Affective Race Bias as Assessed by Startle Eyeblink Responses and Self-Report', *Journal of Personality and Social Psychology* 84 (2003), 738–53; D. M. Amodio, 'The Neuroscience of Prejudice and Stereotyping', *Nature Neuroscience* 15 (2014), 670–82; A. M. Chekroud et al., 'A Review of Neuroimaging Studies of Race-Related Prejudice: Does Amygdala Response Reflect Threat?', *Frontiers in Human Neuroscience* 8 (2014), 179; A. J. Hart et al., 'Differential Response in the Human Amygdala to Racial Outgroup Versus Ingroup Face Stimuli', *Neuroreport* 11 (2000), 2351–5; J. T. Kubota, M. R. Banaji and E. A. Phelps, 'The Neuroscience of Race', *Nature Neuroscience* 15 (2012), 940–8; E. Phelps et al., 'Performance on Indirect Measures of Race Evaluation Predicts Amygdala Activation', *Journal of Cognitive Neuroscience* 12 (2000), 729–38.

13. L. W. Swanson and G. D. Petrovich, 'What Is the Amygdala?', *Trends in*

Neurosciences 21 (1988), 323–31.

14. ibid.

15. Phelps et al., 'Performance on Indirect Measures of Race Evaluation Predicts Amygdala Activation'.

16. R. M. Sapolsky, *Behave: The Biology of Humans at Our Best and Worst*, New York: Penguin Press, 2017.

17. D. P. Fry and P. Söderberg, 'Lethal Aggression in Mobile Forager Bands and Implications for the Origins of War', *Science* 341 (2013), 270.
I. J. N. Thorpe, 'Anthropology, Archaeology and the Origin of Warfare', *World Archaeology* 35:1 (2003), 145–65. Raymond C. Kelly, *Warless Societies and the Origin of War* (Ann Arbor: University of Michigan Press, 2000).

18. W. A. Cunningham et al., 'Separable Neural Components in the Processing of Black and White Faces', *Psychological Science* 15 (2004), 806–13.

19. Amodio, 'The Neuroscience of Prejudice and Stereotyping'.

20. R. Z. Goldstein and N. D. Volkow, 'Dysfunction of the Prefrontal Cortex in Addiction: Neuroimaging Findings and Clinical Implications', *National Review of Neuroscience* 12 (2012), 652–69.

21. His Honour Judge Keith Cutler CBE Assistant Coroner, 'Inquest into the Death of Mark Duggan', 2014.

22. J. Correll, G. R. Urland and T. A. Ito, 'Event-Related Potentials and the Decision to Shoot: The Role of Threat Perception and Cognitive Control', *Journal of Experimental Social Psychology* 42 (2006), 120–8.

23. Y. Mekawi and K. Bresin, 'Is the Evidence from Racial Bias Shooting Task Studies a Smoking Gun? Results from a Meta-Analysis', *Journal of Experimental Social Psychology* 61 (2015), 120–30.

24. J. Correll et al., 'The Police Officer's Dilemma: Using Ethnicity to Disambiguate Potentially Threatening Individuals', *Journal of Personality and Social Psychology* 83 (2002), 1314–29.

25. C. Forbes et al., 'Negative Stereotype Activation Alters Interaction between Neural Correlates of Arousal, Inhibition and Cognitive Control', *Social Cognitive and Affective Neuroscience* 7 (2011), 771.

26. Sapolsky, *Behave*.

27. R. G. Parsons and K. J. Ressler, 'Implications of Memory Modulation

for Post-Traumatic Stress and Fear Disorders', *Nature Neuroscience* 14 (2013), 146–53.

28. I. Blair et al., 'Imagining Stereotypes Away: The Moderation of Implicit Stereotypes through Mental Imagery', *Journal of Personality and Social Psychology* 81 (2001), 828.

29. Phelps et al., 'Performance on Indirect Measures of Race Evaluation Predicts Amygdala Activation'.

30. E. H. Telzer et al., 'Amygdala Sensitivity to Race Is Not Present in Childhood but Emerges in Adolescence.', *Journal of Cognitive Neuroscience* 25 (2013), 234–44.

31. J. Cloutier, T. Li and J. Correll, 'The Impact of Childhood Experience on Amygdala Response to Perceptually Familiar Black and White Faces', *Journal of Cognitive Neuroscience* 26 (2014), 1992–2004.

32. M. D. Lieberman et al., 'An fMRI Investigation of Race-Related Amygdala Activity in African American and Caucasian American Individuals', *Nature Neuroscience* 8 (2005), 720–2.

33. J. J. Van Bavel, D. J. Packer and W. A. Cunningham, 'The Neural Substrates of In-group Bias: A Functional Magnetic Resonance Imaging Investigation', *Psychological Science* 11 (2008), 1131–9.

34. L. Q. Uddin et al., 'Structure and Function of the Human Insula', *Journal of Clinical Neurophysiology* 34 (2017), 300–6.

35. V. Menon, 'Salience Network', *Brain Mapping* 2 (2015), 597–611.

36. M. L. Rosen et al., 'Salience Network Response to Changes in Emotional Expressions of Others Is Heightened During Early Adolescence: Relevance for Social Functioning', *Developmental Science* 21 (2018).

37. Y. Liu et al., 'Neural Basis of Disgust Perception in Racial Prejudice', *Human Brain Mapping* 36 (2015), 5275–86.

38. M. Rhodes, 'Naïve Theories of Social Groups', *Child Development* 83 (2012), 1900–16.

39. P. Molenberghs et al., 'Increased Moral Sensitivity for Outgroup Perpetrators Harming Ingroup Members', *Cerebral Cortex* 26 (2016), 225–33.

40. D. L. Oswald, 'Understanding Anti-Arab Reactions Post-9/11: The Role of Threats, Social Categories, and Personal Ideologies', *Journal of Applied Social Psychology* 35 (2005), 1775–99.

41. X. Xu et al., 'Do You Feel My Pain? Racial Group Membership Modulates Empathic Neural Responses', *Journal of Neuroscience* 29 (2009), 8525–9.

42. L. S. Contreras-Huerta et al., 'Racial Bias in Neural Empathic Responses to Pain', *PLoS One* 8 (2013); R. T. Azevedo et al., 'Their Pain Is Not Our Pain: Brain and Autonomic Correlates of Empathic Resonance with the Pain of Same and Different Race Individuals', *Human Brain Mapping* 34 (2013), 3168–81.

43. M. T. Richins et al., 'Empathic Responses Are Reduced to Competitive but Not Non-Competitive Outgroups', *Social Neuroscience* 14 (2018), 345–58.

44. Sapolsky, *Behave*.

45. L. T. Harris and S. T. Fiske, 'Dehumanizing the Lowest of the Low: Neuro-Imaging Responses to Extreme Outgroups', *Psychological Science* 17 (2006), 847–53.

46. S. Fiske et al., 'A Model of (Often Mixed) Stereotype Content: Competence and Warmth Respectively Follow from Perceived Status and Competition', *Journal of Personality and Social Psychology* 82 (2002), 878.

47. J. Ronquillo et al., 'The Effects of Skin Tone on Race-Related Amygdala Activity: An fMRI Investigation', *Social Cognitive and Affective Neuroscience* 2 (2007), 39–44; Lieberman et al., 'An fMRI Investigation of Race-Related Amygdala Activity'; J. A. Richeson et al., 'An fMRI Investigation of the Impact of Interracial Contact on Executive Function', *Nature Neuroscience* 6 (2003), 1323–8.

48. D. Grossman, *On Killing: The Psychological Cost of Learning to Kill in War and Society*, New York: Back Bay Books, 1996; S. L. A. Marshall, *Men against Fire: The Problem of Battle Command*, Norman, OK: University of Oklahoma Press, 2000.

49. Van Bavel, Packer and Cunningham, 'The Neural Substrates of In-group Bias'.

50. Kubota, Banaji and Phelps, 'The Neuroscience of Race'.

51. J. C. Brigham and R. S. Malpass, 'The Role of Experience and Contact in the Recognition of Faces of Own- and Other-Race Persons', *Journal of Social Issues* 41 (1985), 139–55.

52. S. Pinker, *The Blank Slate*, New York: Viking, 2002 / 2016.

4. My Brain and Hate

1. A. Berger, 'Magnetic Resonance Imaging', *British Medical Journal* 324 (2002), no. 7328, 35.

2. M. Proudfoot et al., 'Magnetoencephalography', *Practical Neurology* 14 (2014), 336–43.

3. C. D. Navarrete et al., 'Fear Extinction to an Outgroup Face: The Role of Target Gender', *Psychological Science* 20 (2009), 155–8; J. K. Maner et al., 'Functional Projection: How Fundamental Social Motives Can Bias Interpersonal Perception', *Journal of Personality and Social Psychology* 88 (2005), 63–78.

4. P. Molenberghs et al., 'Increased Moral Sensitivity for Outgroup Perpetrators Harming Ingroup Members', *Cerebral Cortex* 26 (2016), 225–33.

5. C. Bennett, M. Miller and G. Wolford, 'Neural Correlates of Interspecies Perspective Taking in the Post-Mortem Atlantic Salmon: An Argument for Multiple Comparisons Correction', *NeuroImage* 47 (2009).

6. E. Vul et al., 'Puzzlingly High Correlations in fMRI Studies of Emotion, Personality, and Social Cognition', *Perspectives on Psychological Science* 4 (2009), 274–90.

7. R. Q. Quiroga et al., 'Invariant Visual Representation by Single Neurons in the Human Brain', *Nature* 435 (2005), 1102–7.

8. J. Dumit, *Picturing Personhood: Brain Scans and Biomedical Identity*, Princeton, NJ: Princeton University Press, 2004.

9. N. Rose, 'Reading the Human Brain: How the Mind Became Legible', *Body and Society* 22 (2016), 140–77.

5. Group Threat and Hate

1. 'R v. James and Norley', Bristol Crown Court, 2013.

2. D. McCallum, 'Multi-Agency Learning Review Following the Murder of Bijan Ebrahimi', Bristol: Safer Bristol Partnership, 2017; K. Quarmby, *Scapegoat: Why Are We Failing Disabled People?*, London: Portobello Books, 2011.

3. 'R v. James and Norley'.

4. McCallum, 'Multi-Agency Learning Review'.

5. H. Blalock, 'Economic Discrimination and Negro Increase', *American Sociological Review* 21 (1956), 548–88; H. Blumer, 'Race Prejudice as a Sense of Group Position', *Pacific Sociological Review* 1 (1958), 3–7.

6. L. Quillian, 'Prejudice as a Response to Perceived Group Threat: Population Composition and Anti-Immigrant and Racial Prejudice in Europe', *American Sociological Review* 60 (1995), 586–611; B. M. Riek, E. W. Mania and S. L. Gaertner, 'Intergroup Threat and Outgroup Attitudes: A Meta-Analytic Review', *Personality and Social Psychology Review* 10 (2006), 336–53.

7. S. L. Neuberg and M. Schaller, 'An Evolutionary Threat-Management Approach to Prejudices', *Current Opinion in Psychology* 7 (2016), 1–5.

8. C. K. W. De Dreu et al., 'Oxytocin Promotes Human Ethnocentrism', *Proceedings of the National Academy of Sciences* 108 (2011), 1262–6.

9. R. M. Sapolsky, *Behave: The Biology of Humans at Our Best and Worst*, New York: Penguin Press, 2017.

10. De Dreu et al., 'Oxytocin Promotes Human Ethnocentrism'.

11. C. H. Declerck, C. Boone and T. Kiyonari, 'Oxytocin and Cooperation under Conditions of Uncertainty: The Modulating Role of Incentives and Social Information', *Hormones and Behavior* 57 (2010), 368–74.

12. C. K. W. De Dreu et al., 'The Neuropeptide Oxytocin Regulates Parochial Altruism in Intergroup Conflict among Humans', *Science* 328 (5984) (2010), 1408–11.

13. H. Zhang et al., 'Oxytocin Promotes Coordinated Out-group Attack during Intergroup Conflict in Humans', *eLife* 8 (2019), 1–19.

14. J. Holt-Lunstad et al., 'Influence of a "Warm Touch" Support Enhancement Intervention among Married Couples on Ambulatory Blood Pressure, Oxytocin, Alpha Amylase, and Cortisol', *Psychosomatic Medicine* 70 (2008), 976–85; V. Morhenn et al., 'Monetary Sacrifice among Strangers Is Mediated by Endogenous Oxytocin Release after Physical Contact', *Evolution and Human Behavior* 29 (2008), 375–83; G.-J. Pepping and E. J. Timmermans, 'Oxytocin and the Biopsychology of Performance in Team Sports', *Scientific World Journal* (2012), 1–10.

15. M. Gilead and N. Liberman, 'We Take Care of Our Own: Caregiving

Salience Increases Out-group Bias in Response to Out-group Threat', *Psychological Science* 25 (2014), 1380–7.

16. M. Sherif et al., *The Robbers Cave Experiment: Intergroup Conflict and Cooperation*, PA: Harper & Row Publishers, 1988; G. Perry, *The Lost Boys: Inside Muzafer Sherif's Robbers Cave Experiment*, Melbourne and London: Scribe, 2018.

17. W. G. Stephan and C. W. Stephan, 'An Integrated Threat Theory of Prejudice', in *Reducing Prejudice and Discrimination*, ed. S. Oskamp, Mahwah, NJ: Erlbaum, 2000.

18. Quillian, 'Prejudice as a Response to Perceived Group Threat'.

19. House of Commons Home Affairs Select Committee, 'Asylum Accommodation: Twelfth Report of Session 2016–17', 2017.

20. Office for National Statistics, 'International Immigration and the Labour Market', Newport: ONS, 2017.

21. A. Nandi et al., 'The Prevalence and Persistence of Ethnic and Racial Harassment and Its Impact on Health: A Longitudinal Analysis', Colchester: University of Essex, 2017.

22. G. D. Suttles, *The Social Construction of Communities*, Chicago: University of Chicago Press, 1972.

23. D. P. Green, D. Z. Strolovitch and J. S. Wong, 'Defended Neighborhoods, Integration, and Racially Motivated Crime', *American Journal of Sociology* 104 (1998), 372–403; C. J. Lyons, 'Community (Dis)Organization and Racially Motivated Crime', *American Journal of Sociology* 113 (2007), 815–63.

24. D. F. Clive, 'Islamophobia in Contemporary Britain: The Evidence of the Opinion Polls, 1988–2006', *Islam and Christian Muslim Relations* 18 (2007), 447–77.

25. L. McLaren and M. Johnson, 'Resources, Group Conflict and Symbols: Explaining Anti-Immigration Hostility in Britain', *Political Studies* 55 (2007), 709–32.

26. D. G. Myers and G. D. Bishop, 'Discussion Effects on Racial Attitudes', *Science* 169 (3947) (1970), 778–9.

27. P. Connolly, Alan Smith and Berni Kelly, 'Too Young to Notice: The Cultural and Political Awareness of 3–6 Year Olds in Northern Ireland', Belfast: Northern Ireland Community Relations Council, 2002.

28. P. Hartmann and C. Husband, *Racism and the Mass Media*, London: HarperCollins, 1974.

29. UCLA College of Social Sciences, 'Hollywood Diversity Report 2020: Part 1: Film', Los Angeles: CA: UCLA, 2020. UCLA College of Social Sciences, 'Hollywood Diversity Report 2020: Part 2: TV', Los Angeles: CA: UCLA, 2020

30. T. E. Ford et al., 'More Than "Just a Joke": The Prejudice-Releasing Function of Sexist Humor', *Personality and Social Psychology Bulletin* 34 (2008), 159–70.

31. T. E. Ford, 'Effects of Sexist Humor on Tolerance of Sexist Events', *Personality and Social Psychology Bulletin* 26 (2000), 1094–1107; T. E. Ford et al., 'Not All Groups Are Equal: Differential Vulnerability of Social Groups to the Prejudice-Releasing Effects of Disparagement Humor', *Group Processes and Intergroup Relations* 17 (2014), 178–99.

32. J. M. Bonds-Raacke et al., 'Remembering Gay/Lesbian Media Characters: Can Ellen and Will Improve Attitudes toward Homosexuals?', *Journal of Homosexuality* 53 (2007), 19–34; J. P. Calzo and L. M. Ward, 'Media Exposure and Viewers' Attitudes toward Homosexuality: Evidence for Mainstreaming or Resonance?', *Journal of Broadcasting and Electronic Media* 53 (2009), 280–99; T. T. Lee and G. R. Hicks, 'An Analysis of Factors Affecting Attitudes toward Same-Sex Marriage: Do the Media Matter?', *Journal of Homosexuality* 58 (2011), 1391–408; M. Ortiz and J. Harwood, 'A Social Cognitive Theory Approach to the Effects of Mediated Intergroup Contact on Intergroup Attitudes', *Journal of Broadcasting and Electronic Media* 51 (2007), 615–31.

33. B. McLaughlin et al., 'Stereotyped Identification: How Identifying with Fictional Latina Characters Increases Acceptance and Stereotyping', *Mass Communication and Society* 21 (2018), 585–605.

34. M. Endrich, 'A Window to the World: The Long-Term Effect of Television on Hate Crime', in ILE Working Paper Series, No. 33, University of Hamburg, 2020.

35. L. Little, 'Joe Biden Says "Will and Grace" Helped Change Public Opinion on Gay Rights', *Wall Street Journal*, 7 May 2012.

6. Trauma, Containment and Hate

1. D. Gadd and B. Dixon, *Losing the Race*, London: Karnac, 2011.

2. S. Farrall et al., 'The Role of Radical Economic Restructuring in Truancy from School and Engagement in Crime', British Journal of Criminology (2019), 118–40; S. Farrall and C. Hay, *The Legacy of Thatcherism: Exploring and Theorising the Long-Term Consequences of Thatcherite Social and Economic Policies*, Oxford: Oxford University Press, 2014; S. Farrall and W. Jennings, 'Policy Feedback and the Criminal Justice Agenda: An Analysis of the Economy, Crime Rates, Politics and Public Opinion in Post-War Britain', *Contemporary British History* 26 (2012), 467–88; W. Jennings et al., 'The Economy, Crime and Time: An Analysis of Recorded Property Crime in England & Wales 1961–2006', *International Journal of Law, Crime and Justice* 40 (2012), 192–210.

3. Gadd and Dixon, *Losing the Race*; D. Gadd, 'Racial Hatred and Unmourned Loss', *Sociological Research Online* 15 (2010); B. Dixon, D. Gadd and T. Jefferson, 'Context and Motive in the Perpetuation of Racial Harassment and Violence in North Staffordshire', Colchester, Essex: UK Data Archive, 2004.

4. Gadd, 'Racial Hatred and Unmourned Loss'.

5. Gadd and Dixon, *Losing the Race*.

6. Gadd, 'Racial Hatred and Unmourned Loss'; Gadd and Dixon, *Losing the Race*.

7. Gadd and Dixon, *Losing the Race*.

8. H. Segal, 'A Psycho-Analytic Approach to the Treatment of Schizophrenia', in *The Work of Hanna Segal*, ed. H. Segal, New York: Jason Aronson, 1975, 131–6.

9. T. Adorno et al., *The Authoritarian Personality*, New York: Harper and Row, 1950; J. Sidanius and F. Pratto, *Social Dominance: An Intergroup Theory of Social Hierarchy and Oppression*, Cambridge: Cambridge University Press, 1999.

10. M. Rustin, 'Psychoanalysis, Racism and Anti-Racism', in *Identity: A Reader*, ed. P. Du Gay, J. Evans and P. Redman, London: Sage, 2000, 183–201.

11. B. Perry, *In the Name of Hate*, London: Routledge, 2002.

12. E. Fromm, *The Anatomy of Human Destructiveness*, New York: Holt, 1973.

13. J. W. Messerschmidt, *Crime as Structured Action*, London: Sage, 1997.

14. A. Pike et al., 'Uneven Growth: Tackling City Decline', Joseph Rowntree Foundation, 2016.

15. Gadd and Dixon, *Losing the Race*.

16. Dixon, Gadd and Jefferson, 'Context and Motive in the Perpetuation of Racial Harassment and Violence in North Staffordshire'.

17. L. Ray, D. Smith and L. Wastell, 'Shame, Rage and Racist Violence', *British Journal of Criminology* 44 (2004), 350–68.

18. T. Jett, 'Interview with a Serial Killer: Joseph Paul Franklin', *Times Free Press*, 19 November 2013.

19. J. R. Gaines, 'On the Trail of a Murderous Sniper Suspect: The Tangled Life of Joseph Paul Franklin', *People* (1980); J. Rosewood and D. Walker, *Joseph Paul Franklin: The True Story of the Racist Killer*, Wiq Media, 2016.

20. 'Joseph Franklin, White Supremacist Serial Killer, Executed', BBC News, 20 November 2013.

21. G. McLagan and N. Lowes, *Killer on the Streets*, London: John Blake Publishing, 2003.

22. B. O'Mahoney, *Hateland*, London: Mainstream Publishing, 2005.

23. N. Hopkins and S. Hall, 'Festering Hate That Turned Quiet Son into a Murderer', *Guardian*, 1 July 2000.

24. K. Jang et al., 'Heritability of the Big Five Personality Dimensions and Their Facets: A Twin Study', *Journal of Personality* 64 (1999), 577–92; R. K. Krueger et al., 'The Heritability of Personality Is Not Always 50%: Gene-Environment Interactions and Correlations between Personality and Parenting', *Journal of Personality* 76 (2008), 1485–521.

25. C. G. Sibley and J. Duckitt, 'Personality and Prejudice: A Meta-Analysis and Theoretical Review', *Personality and Social Psychology Review* 12 (2008), 248–79.

26. O. P. John and S. Srivastava, 'The Big-Five Trait Taxonomy: History, Measurement, and Theoretical Perspectives', in *Handbook of Personality: Theory and Research*, ed. L. A. Pervin and O. P. John, New York: Guilford Press, 1999, 102–38.

27. B. Altemeyer, *Right-Wing Authoritarianism*, Winnipeg, Canada: University of Manitoba Press, 1981; B. Altemeyer, *The Authoritarian Spectre*, Harvard, MA: Harvard University Press, 1996; Sidanius and Pratto, *Social Dominance*.

28. S. Lupien et al., 'Effects of Stress Throughout the Lifespan on the Brain, Behaviour and Cognition', *Nature Reviews Neuroscience* 10 (2009), 434–5.

29. Sapolsky, *Behave*.

30. V. Carrion et al., 'Stress Predicts Brain Changes in Children: A Pilot Longitudinal Study on Youth Stress, Posttraumatic Stress Disorder, and the Hippocampus', *Pediatrics* 119 (2007), 509–16.

31. Sapolsky, *Behave*.

32. S. Taylor et al., 'Biobehavioral Responses to Stress in Females: Tend-and-Befriend, Not Fight-or-Flight', *Psychological Review* 107 (2000), 411–29.

33. Sapolsky, *Behave*.

34. L. P. Solursh, 'Combat Addiction: Overview of Implications in Symptom Maintenance and Treatment Planning', *Journal of Traumatic Stress* 2 (1989), 451–60; J. J. Collins and S. L. Bailey, 'Relationship of Mood Disorders to Violence', *Journal of Nervous and Mental Disease* 178 (1990), 44–51.

35. D. Terry, 'Joseph Franklin, Prolific Racist Serial Killer, Is Executed', Southern Poverty Law Center, 2013.

7. Trigger Events and the Ebb and Flow of Hate

1. M. Ojito, *Hunting Season: Immigration and Murder in an All-American Town*, Boston: Beacon Press, 2014.

2. Southern Poverty Law Center, 'Climate of Fear: Latino Immigrants in Suffolk County, N.Y.', Montgomery, Alabama: Southern Poverty Law Center, 2009.

3. C. Buckley, 'Teenagers' Violent "Sport" Led to Killing on Long Island, Officials Say', *New York Times*, 20 November 2008.

4. T. Kaplan, 'Surge in Anti-Gay Hate Crime Cases', *Mercury News*, 15 March 2009.

5. J. Newton and H. Weinstein, 'Three Suspects Seized in Beating of Truck Driver During Riot', *Los Angeles Times*, 13 May 1992.

6. R. Kopetman and G. Krikorian, 'Mob Did Not Take Time to Ask Their Victim His Views', *Los Angeles Times*, 3 May 1993.

7. R. D. King and G. M. Sutton, 'High Times for Hate Crimes: Explaining the Temporal Clustering of Hate Motivated Offending', *Criminology* 51 (2014), 871–94.

8. I. Disha, J. C. Cavendish and R. D. King, 'Historical Events and Spaces of Hate: Hate Crimes against Arabs and Muslims in Post-9/11 America', *Social Problems* 58 (2011), 21–46.

9. King and Sutton, 'High Times for Hate Crimes'.

10. G. Edwards and S. Rushin, 'The Effect of President Trump's Election on Hate Crimes', SSRN, 18 January 2018.

11. D. J. Hopkins and S. Washington, 'The Rise of Trump, the Fall of Prejudice? Tracking White Americans' Racial Attitudes 2008–2018 Via a Panel Survey', *Public Opinion Quarterly* 84 (2020).

12. L. Bursztyn, G. Egorov and S. Fiorin, 'From Extreme to Mainstream: How Social Norms Unravel', in Working Paper 23415, Cambridge, Massachusetts: National Bureau of Economic Research, 2017.

13. E. Hanes and S. Machin, 'Hate Crime in the Wake of Terror Attacks: Evidence from 7/7 and 9/11', *Journal of Contemporary Criminal Justice* 30 (2014), 247–67.

14. R. Ivandic, T. Kirchmaier and S. Machin, 'Jihadi Attacks, Media and Local Hate Crime', Centre for Economic Performance Discussion Paper 1615, London: London School of Economics and Political Science, 2019.

15. E. M. Kearns et al., 'Why Do Some Terrorist Attacks Receive More Media Attention Than Others?', *Justice Quarterly* 36 (2017), 985–1022.

16. B. Vidgen, 'Tweeting Islamophobia', University of Oxford, 2019.

17. J. Legewie, 'Terrorist Events and Attitudes toward Immigrants: A Natural Experiment', *American Journal of Sociology* 118 (2013), 1199–245.

18. Vidgen, 'Tweeting Islamophobia'.

19. B. Vidgen et al., 'Trajectories of Islamophobic Hate Amongst Far Right Actors on Twitter', preprint (2019), ArXiv:1910.05794.

20. J. Legewie, 'Racial Profiling and Use of Force in Police Stops: How Local Events Trigger Periods of Increased Discrimination', *American*

Journal of Sociology 122 (2016), 379–424.

21. H. Ibish, 'Report on Hate Crimes and Discrimination against Arab Americans: The Post–September 11 Backlash, September 11, 2001–October 11, 2002', Washington, DC: American-Arab Anti-Discrimination Committee, 2003.

22. L. J. Skitka et al., 'Political Tolerance and Coming to Psychological Closure Following the September 11, 2001, Terrorist Attacks: An Integrative Approach', *Personality and Social Psychology Bulletin* 30 (2004), 743–56.

23. P. E. Tetlock et al., 'The Psychology of the Unthinkable: Taboo Trade-Offs, Forbidden Base Rates, and Heretical Counterfactuals', *Journal of Personality and Social Psychology* 78 (2000), 853–70.

24. G. S. Morgan et al., 'The Expulsion from Disneyland: The Social Psychological Impact of 9/11', *American Psychologist* 66 (2011), 447–54.

25. C. Zhong and K. Liljenquist, 'Washing Away Your Sins: Threatened Morality and Physical Cleansing', *Science* 313 (5792) (2006), 1451–2.

26. M. Douglas, *Purity and Danger*, New York: Routledge, 1984.

27. H. McGregor et al., 'Terror Management and Aggression: Evidence That Mortality Salience Motivates Aggression against Worldview Threatening Others', *Journal of Personality and Social Psychology* 74 (1988), 590–605.

28. J. Greenberg, T. Pyszczynski and S. Solomon, 'The Causes and Consequences of a Need for Self-Esteem: A Terror Management Theory', in *Public Self and Private Self*, ed. R. F. Baumeister, New York: Springer-Verlag, 1986, 189–212.

29. A. Rosenblatt et al., 'Evidence for Terror Management Theory I: The Effects of Mortality Salience on Reactions to Those Who Violate or Uphold Cultural Values', *Journal of Personality and Social Psychology* 57 (1984), 681–90.

30. J. Greenberg et al., 'Terror Management Theory and Research: How the Desire for Death Transcendence Drives Our Strivings for Meaning and Significance', in *Advances in Motivation Science*, Vol. 1, ed. Andrew Elliot, New York: Elsevier, 2014.

31. M. J. Landau et al., 'Deliver Us from Evil: The Effects of Mortality Salience and Reminders of 9/11 on Support for President George W. Bush', *Personality and Social Psychology Bulletin* 30 (2004), 1136–50.

32. ibid.
33. F. Cohen et al., 'Fatal Attraction: The Effects of Mortality Salience on Evaluations of Charismatic, Task-Oriented, and Relationship-Oriented Leaders', *Psychological Science* 15 (2004), 846–51; Landau et al., 'Deliver Us from Evil'.
34. F. Cohen et al., 'Evidence for a Role of Death Thought in American Attitudes toward Symbols of Islam', *Journal of Experimental Social Psychology* 49 (2012), 189–94.
35. ibid.
36. A. Newheiser et al., 'Social-Psychological Aspects of Religion and Prejudice: Evidence from Survey and Experimental Research', in *Religion, Intolerance, and Conflict: A Scientific and Conceptual Investigation*, ed. S. Clarke, R. Powell and J. Savulescu, Oxford: Oxford University Press, 2013.
37. Greenberg et al., 'Terror Management Theory and Research'.
38. B. Burke, A. Martens and E. Faucher, 'Two Decades of Terror Management Theory: A Meta-Analysis of Mortality Salience Research', *Personality and Social Psychological Review* 14 (2010), 155–95.

8. Subcultures of Hate

1. N. Parveen, 'Small Part of Manchester That Has Been Home to Sixteen Jihadis', *Guardian*, 25 February 2017.
2. G. LaFree et al., 'Correlates of Violent Political Extremism in the United States', *Criminology* 56 (2018), 233–68.
3. L. G. Calhoun and R. G. Tedeschi, *Handbook of Posttraumatic Growth*, Mahwah, NJ: Erlbaum, 2006; C. L. Park and V. S. Helgeson, 'Introduction to the Special Section: Growth Following Highly Stressful Life Events—Current Status and Future Directions', *Journal of Consulting and Clinical Psychology* 74 (2006), 791–6.
4. D. R. Rovenpor et al., 'Intergroup Conflict Self-Perpetuates Via Meaning: Exposure to Intergroup Conflict Increases Meaning and Fuels a Desire for Further Conflict', *Journal of Personality and Social Psychology* 116 (2019), 119–40.
5. E. Bakker, 'Jihadi Terrorists in Europe, Their Characteristics and the

Circumstances in Which They Joined the Jihad: An Exploratory Study', Clingendael Security Paper, The Hague: Clingendael Institute, 2006; R. Pape, *Dying to Win: The Strategic Logic of Suicide Terrorism*, New York: Random House, 2005; M. Sageman, *Understanding Terror Networks*, Philadelphia: University of Pennsylvania Press, 2004.

6. M. Crenshaw, 'The Psychology of Terrorism: An Agenda for the 21st Century', *Political Psychology* 21 (2000), 405–20; J. M. Post, 'Terrorist Psycho-Logic: Terrorist Behavior as a Product of Psychological Forces', in *Origins of Terrorism: Psychologies, Ideologies, Theologies, States of Mind*, ed. W. Reich, Cambridge: Cambridge University Press, 1998, 25–40; Pape, *Dying to Win*; A. Silke, 'Cheshire-Cat Logic: The Recurring Theme of Terrorist Abnormality in Psychological Research', *Psychology, Crime and Law* 4 (1998), 51–69.

7. M. King and D. M. Taylor, 'The Radicalization of Homegrown Jihadists: A Review of Theoretical Models and Social Psychological Evidence', *Terrorism and Political Violence* 23 (2011), 602–22; A. W. Kruglanski et al., 'The Psychology of Radicalization and Deradicalization: How Significance Quest Impacts Violent Extremism', *Advances in Political Psychology* 35 (2014), 69–93; C. McCauley and S. Moskalenko, 'Mechanisms of Political Radicalization: Pathways toward Terrorism', *Terrorism and Political Violence* 20 (2008), 415–33.

8. A. W. Kruglanski et al., 'Terrorism – a (Self) Love Story: Redirecting the Significance Quest Can End Violence', *American Psychologist* 68 (2013), 559–75.

9. J. J. Arnett, *Emerging Adulthood: The Winding Road from the Late Teens through the Twenties*, Oxford: Oxford University Press, 2004.

10. C. Carlsson et al., 'A Life-Course Analysis of Engagement in Violent Extremist Groups', *British Journal of Criminology* 60 (2019), 74–92.

11. J. Monahan, 'The Individual Risk Assessment of Terrorism: Recent Developments', in *The Handbook of the Criminology of Terrorism*, ed. G. LaFree and J. D. Freilich, West Sussex: John Wiley & Sons, 2017, 520–34.

12. D. Matza, *Delinquency and Drift*, New Brunswick, NJ: Transaction Publishers, 1964.

13. Carlsson et al., 'A Life-Course Analysis of Engagement in Violent Extremist Groups'.

14. ibid.

15. ibid.

16. C. Pretus et al., 'Neural and Behavioral Correlates of Sacred Values and Vulnerability to Violent Extremism', *Frontiers in Psychology* 9 (2018).

17. D. Webber et al., 'The Road to Extremism: Field and Experimental Evidence That Significance Loss-Induced Need for Closure Fosters Radicalization', *Journal of Personality and Social Psychology* 114 (2017), 270–85.

18. K. Jasko et al., 'Social Context Moderates the Effects of Quest for Significance on Violent Extremism', *Journal of Personality and Social Psychology* 118 (2019), 1165–87.

19. Sageman, *Understanding Terror Networks*.

20. R. Agnew, 'A General Strain Theory of Terrorism', *Theoretical Criminology* 14 (2010), 131–53.

21. ibid.

22. E. Simien, 'Race, Gender, and Linked Fate', *Journal of Black Studies* 35 (2005), 529–50.

23. S. Pfattheicher et al., 'Compassion Magnifies Third-Party Punishment', *Journal of Personality and Social Psychology* 117 (2019), 124–41.

24. J. Ginges et al., 'Thinking from God's Perspective Decreases Biased Valuation of the Life of a Nonbeliever', *Proceedings of the National Academy of Sciences* 113 (2016), 316–19.

25. B. Bushman et al., 'When God Sanctions Killing: Effect of Scriptural Violence on Aggression', *Psychological Science* 18 (2007), 204–7.

26. ibid.

27. S. Atran et al., 'For Cause and Comrade: Devoted Actors and Willingness to Fight', *Cliodynamics* 5 (2014), 41–57.

28. S. Atran and Á. Gómez, 'What Motivates Devoted Actors to Extreme Sacrifice, Identity Fusion, or Sacred Values?', *Behavioral and Brain Sciences* 41 (2018), 1–62.

29. Atran et al., 'For Cause and Comrade'.

30. N. Hamid et al., 'Neuroimaging "Will to Fight" for Sacred Values: An Empirical Case Study with Supporters of an Al Qaeda Associate', *Royal Society Open Science* 6 (2019).

31. ibid.

32. H. Whitehouse, 'Dying for the Group: Towards a General Theory of Extreme Self-Sacrifice', *Behavioral and Brain Sciences* 41 (2018), 1–62.

33. E. Durkheim, *Les Formes élémentaires de la vie religieuse* [*The Elementary Forms of Religious Life*], Paris: Alcan, 1912; L. Festinger, *A Theory of Cognitive Dissonance*, Redwood City, CA: Stanford University Press, 1962.

34. F. J. P. Poole, 'The Ritual Forging of Identity: Aspects of Person and Self in Bimin-Kuskusmin Male Initiation', in *Rituals of Manhood: Male Initiation in Papua New Guinea*, ed. G. H. Herdt, Berkeley, CA: University of California Press, 1982; H. Whitehouse, 'Rites of Terror: Emotion, Metaphor, and Memory in Melanesian Initiation Cults', *Journal of the Royal Anthropological Institute* 2 (1996), 703–15.

35. F. Barth, *Ritual and Knowledge among the Baktaman of New Guinea*, New Haven: Yale University Press, 1975.

36. Festinger, *A Theory of Cognitive Dissonance*.

37. J. A. Bulbulia and R. Sosis, 'Signalling Theory and the Evolution of Religious Cooperation', *Religion* 4 (2011), 363–88; A. Cimino, 'The Evolution of Hazing: Motivational Mechanisms and the Abuse of Newcomers', *Journal of Cognition and Culture* 11 (2011), 241–67; J. Henrich, 'The Evolution of Costly Displays, Cooperation and Religion: Credibility Enhancing Displays and Their Implications for Cultural Evolution', *Evolution and Human Behavior* 30 (2009), 244–60.

38. Whitehouse, 'Rites of Terror'.

39. H. Whitehouse, *Inside the Cult: Religious Innovation and Transmission in Papua New Guinea*, Oxford: Oxford University Press, 1995.

40. D. Xygalatas et al., 'Extreme Rituals Promote Prosociality', *Psychological Science* 24 (2013), 1602–5.

41. B. Winegard and R. O. Deaner, 'The Evolutionary Significance of Red Sox Nation: Sport Fandom as a by-Product of Coalitional Psychology', *Evolutionary Psychology* 8 (2010), 432–46.

42. M. Newson et al., 'Brazil's Football Warriors: Social Bonding and Inter-Group Violence', *Evolution and Human Behavior* 39 (2018), 675–83.

43. H. Whitehouse et al., 'The Evolution of Extreme Cooperation Via Shared Dysphoric Experiences', *Nature: Scientific Reports* 7 (2017).

44. Whitehouse, 'Dying for the Group'.

45. H. Whitehouse et al., 'Brothers in arms: Libyan revolutionaries bond like family', *Proceedings of the National Academy of Sciences*, 111:50 (2014), 17783–5.

46. Atran and Gómez, 'What Motivates Devoted Actors to Extreme Sacrifice'.

47. J. E. Lane et al., 'A Potential Explanation for Self-Radicalisation', *Behavioral and Brain Sciences* 41 (2018), 1–62.

48. J. Cassidy and P. R. Shaver (eds), *Handbook of Attachment: Theory, Research, and Clinical Applications*, 2nd edition, London: Guilford Press, 2010.

49. Kruglanski et al., 'The Psychology of Radicalization and Deradicalization'.

50. S. Moskalenko and C. McCauley, 'The Psychology of Lone-Wolf Terrorism', *Counselling Psychology Quarterly* 24 (2011), 115–26; C. D. Batson et al., 'Anger at Unfairness: Is It Moral Outrage?', *European Journal of Social Psychology* 37 (2007), 1272–85.

51. A. Möller-Leimkühler, 'Why Is Terrorism a Man's Business?', *CNS Spectrums* 23 (2018), 119–28.

9. Rise of the Bots and Trolls

1. J. Weizenbaum, 'ELIZA – a Computer Program for the Study of Natural Language Communication between Man and Machine', *Communications of the ACM* 9 (1966), 36–45.

2. 'Microsoft Opens AI Framework to Other Firms', *China Daily*, 22 August 2019.

3. G. King, J. Pan and M. E. Roberts, 'How the Chinese Government Fabricates Social Media Posts for Strategic Distraction, Not Engaged Argument', *American Political Science Review* 111 (2017), 484–501.

4. N. Newman et al., 'Reuters Institute Digital News Report 2020', Oxford: Reuters Institute, 2020.

5. Ofcom, 'News Consumption in the UK', London: Ofcom, 2020.

6. J. Nicas, 'How YouTube Drives People to the Internet's Darkest Corners', *Wall Street Journal*, 7 February 2018.

7. C. Goodrow, 'You Know What's Cool? A Billion Hours', 2017, youtube. googleblog.com/2017/02/you-know-whats-cool-billion-hours.html.

8. B. Rieder, A. Matamoros-Fernández and O. Coromina, 'From Ranking Algorithms to "Ranking Cultures": Investigating the Modulation of Visibility in YouTube Search Results', *Convergence* 24 (2018), 50–68.

9. M. Del Vicario et al., 'The Spreading of Misinformation Online', *Proceedings of the National Academy of Sciences* 113 (2016), 554–9; C. R. Sunstein, *#Republic: Divided Democracy in the Age of Social Media*, Princeton, NJ: Princeton University Press, 2017.

10. W. J. Brady et al., 'Emotion Shapes the Diffusion of Moralized Content in Social Networks', *Proceedings of the National Academy of Sciences* 114 (2017), 7313–18.

11. C. A. Bail et al., 'Exposure to Opposing Views on Social Media Can Increase Political Polarization', *Proceedings of the National Academy of Sciences* 115 (2018), 9216–21.

12. J. Angwin, M. Varner and A. Tobin, 'Facebook Enabled Advertisers to Reach "Jew Haters"', ProPublica, 14 September 2017.

13. J. Angwin and T. Parris, 'Facebook Lets Advertisers Exclude Users by Race', ProPublica, 28 October 2016.

14. S. Stephens-Davidowitz, *Everybody Lies*, New York: HarperCollins, 2017.

15. 'Autocomplete Policies', Google.com, 2020, support.google.com/websearch/answer/7368877?hl=en.

16. J. Kuczmarski, 'Reducing Gender Bias in Google Translate', Google Blog, 2018, blog.google/products/translate/reducing-gender-bias-google-translate.

17. J. Zou and L. Schiebinger, 'AI Can Be Sexist and Racist – It's Time to Make It Fair', *Nature* 559 (2018), 324–6.

18. A. Caliskan, J. J. Bryson and A. Narayanan, 'Semantics Derived Automatically from Language Corpora Contain Human-Like Biases', *Cognitive Science* 356 (2017), 183–6.

19. J. Hawdon, A. Oksanen and P. Räsänen, 'Exposure to Online Hate in Four Nations: A Cross-National Consideration', *Deviant Behavior* 38 (2017), 254–66.

20. M. Kaakinen et al., 'How Does Social Capital Associate with Being a Victim of Online Hate?', *Policy and Internet* 10 (2018), 302–23.

21. M. Kaakinen et al., 'Social Capital and Online Hate Production: A Four Country Survey', *Crime, Law and Social Change* 69 (2018), 25–39.

22. Ofcom, 'Children and Parents: Media Use and Attitudes', London: Ofcom, 2021.

23. M. L. Williams and P. Burnap, 'Cyberhate on Social Media in the Aftermath of Woolwich: A Case Study in Computational Criminology and Big Data', *British Journal of Criminology* 56 (2016), 211–38.

24. Demos, 'Anti-Islamic Content on Twitter', London: Demos, 2017, demos.co.uk/project/anti-islamic-content-on-twitter.

25. Crest, 'Russian Influence and Interference Measures Following the 2017 UK Terrorist Attacks', Lancaster: Centre for Research and Evidence on Security Threats, 2017.

26. L. Leets, 'Experiencing Hate Speech: Perceptions and Responses to Anti-Semitism and Anti-Gay Speech', *Journal of Social Issues* 58 (2002), 341–61.

27. J. P. Crowley, 'Expressive Writing to Cope with Hate Speech: Assessing Psychobiological Stress Recovery and Forgiveness Promotion for Lesbian, Gay, Bisexual, or Queer Victims of Hate Speech', *Human Communication Research* 40 (2013), 238–61.

28. UK Safer Internet Centre, 'Creating a Better Internet for All: Young People's Experiences of Online Empowerment and Online Hate', London: UK Safer Internet Centre, 2016.

29. T. Keipi et al., 'Exposure to Online Hate Material and Subjective Wellbeing: A Comparative Study of American and Finnish Youth', *Online Information Review* 42 (2018), 2–15.

30. J. Butler, *Excitable Speech: A Politics of the Performative*, London: Routledge, 1997.

31. I. Awan and I. Zempi, '"I Will Blow Your Face Off" – Virtual and Physical World Anti-Muslim Hate Crime', *British Journal of Criminology* 57 (2017), 362–80.

32. M. L. Williams et al., 'Hate in the Machine: Anti-Black and Anti-Muslim Social Media Posts as Predictors of Offline Racially and Religiously Aggravated Crime', *British Journal of Criminology* 60 (2019), 93–117.

33. M. L. Williams, 'Online Hate Speech Report', London: HateLab and Mishcon de Reya, 2019.

34. Council of Europe, 'Chart of Signatures and Ratifications of Treaty 189: Additional Protocol to the Convention on Cybercrime, Concerning the

Criminalisation of Acts of a Racist and Xenophobic Nature Committed through Computer Systems', 2020.

35. European Commission, 'Code of Conduct on Countering Illegal Hate Speech Online', 2016.

36. N. F. Johnson et al., 'Hidden Resilience and Adaptive Dynamics of the Global Online Hate Ecology', *Nature* 573 (2019), 261–5.

10. Hate in Word and Deed

1. Factbase, 'Donald Trump Speaks to the Press before Marine One Departure', 26 April 2019, factba.se/transcript/donald-trump-press-gaggle-marine-one-departure-april-26-2019.

2. J. Heim, 'Recounting a Day of Rage, Hate, Violence and Death', *Washington Post*, 14 August 2017.

3. M. Bray, *Antifa: The Anti-Fascist Handbook*, Brooklyn, NY: Melville House Publishing, 2017.

4. H. Wallace, 'Why We Should #Unitetheright', 2017, www.occidental-dissent.com/2017/08/04/why-we-should-unitetheright.

5. J. Daniels, 'The Algorithmic Rise of the "Alt-Right"', *Contexts* 17 (2018), 60–5.

6. J. Davey and J. Ebner, 'The Fringe Insurgency', London: Institute for Strategic Dialogue, 2017.

7. J. Albright, 'The #Election2016 Micro-Propaganda Machine', 2016, medium.com/@d1gi/the-election2016-micro-propaganda-machine-383449cc1fba.

8. A. Hern, 'Facebook Protects Far-Right Activists Even after Rule Breaches', *Guardian*, 16 July 2018.

9. L. Dearden, 'Neo-Nazi Groups Allowed to Stay on Facebook Because They "Do Not Violate Community Standards"', *Independent*, 24 March 2019.

10. R. Ford, '80,000 Responses on Neo-Nazi Web Forum from the UK', *The Times*, 15 May 2019.

11. H. Beirich, and W. Via, *Generation Identity: International White Nationalist Movement Spreading on Twitter and YouTube*, Global Project Against Hate and Extremism, 2020.

12. Hope Not Hate, 'State of Hate 2019', www.hopenothate.org. uk/2019/02/17/state-hate-2019/.

13. R. Epstein and R. Robertson, 'The Search Engine Manipulation Effect (SEME) and Its Possible Impact on the Outcomes of Elections', *Proceedings of the National Academy of Sciences* 112 (2015), 4512–21.

14. Albright, 'The #Election2016 Micro-Propaganda Machine'.

15. S. C. Matz et al., 'Psychological Targeting as an Effective Approach to Digital Mass Persuasion', *Proceedings of the National Academy of Sciences* 114 (2017), 12714–19.

16. M. Barbaro, '"The Daily" Transcript: Interview with Former White Nationalist Derek Black', *New York Times*, 22 August 2017.

17. D. Duke, 'White Revolution and the Internet', 1998.

18. N. Gleicher, 'Removing Coordinated Inauthentic Behavior from the UK and Romania', Facebook, 2019, about.fb.com/news/2019/03/removing-cib-uk-and-romania.

19. Avaaz, 'Far Right Networks of Deception', 2019, secure.avaaz.org/campaign/en/disinfo_network_report.

20. B. Vidgen, 'Tweeting Islamophobia', University of Oxford, 2019.

21. D. Peddell et al., 'Influences and Vulnerabilities in Radicalised Lone Actor Terrorists: UK Practitioner Perspectives', *International Journal of Police Science and Management* 18 (2016), 63–76.

22. Davey and Ebner, 'The Fringe Insurgency'.

23. K. Müller and C. Schwarz, 'Fanning the Flames of Hate: Social Media and Hate Crime', *Journal of the European Economic Association* (2020).

24. K. Müller and C. Schwarz, 'From Hashtag to Hate Crime: Twitter and Anti-Minority Sentiment', University of Warwick, 2018.

25. N. M. Anspach, 'Trumping the Equality Norm? Presidential Tweets and Revealed Racial Attitudes', *New Media and Society*, 2020.

26. B. Newman et al., 'The Trump Effect: An Experimental Investigation of the Emboldening Effect of Racially Inflammatory Elite Communication', *British Journal of Political Science*, 2020, 1–22.

27. H. Cheung, Z. Feng and B. Deng, 'Coronavirus: What Attacks on Asians Reveal About American Identity', BBC News, 27 May 2020; C. P. Hong, 'The Slur I Never Expected to Hear in 2020', *New York Times*, 16 April 2020.

28. C. Choi, 'In Six Weeks, STOP AAPI HATE Receives over 1700 Incident Reports of Verbal Harassment, Shunning and Physical Assaults', STOP AAPI HATE Reporting Center, 13 May 2020.

29. Home Affairs Committee, 'Oral Evidence: Home Office Preparedness for Covid-19 (Coronavirus), Hc 232', London: House of Commons, 2020.

30. Human Rights Watch, 'Covid-19 Fueling Anti-Asian Racism and Xenophobia Worldwide', 12 May 2020, www.hrw.org/news/2020/05/12/covid-19-fueling-anti-asian-racism-and-xenophobia-worldwide.

31. Institute for Strategic Dialogue, 'Far-Right Exploitation of Covid-19', London: ISD, 2020.

32. Institute for Strategic Dialogue, 'Covid-19 Disinformation Briefing No. 2', London: ISD, 2020.

33. A. Goldman, 'Man Suspected of Planning Attack on Missouri Hospital Is Killed, Officials Say', *New York Times*, 25 March 2020.

34. Institute for Strategic Dialogue, 'Covid-19 Disinformation Briefing No. 2'.

35. M. L. Williams et al., 'Hate in the Machine: Anti-Black and Anti-Muslim Social Media Posts as Predictors of Offline Racially and Religiously Aggravated Crime', *British Journal of Criminology* 60 (2019), 93–117.

36. S. Stecklow, 'Hatebook: Inside Facebook's Myanmar Operation', Reuters, 15 August 2018.

37. 'The Country Where Facebook Posts Whipped up Hate', BBC Trending, 12 September 2018.

38. S. Nebehay, 'U.N. Calls for Myanmar Generals to Be Tried for Genocide, Blames Facebook for Incitement', Reuters, 27 August 2018.

39. Institute for Economics and Peace, 'Global Terrorism Index 2019: Measuring the Impact of Terrorism, November 2019', Sydney, 2019.

11. The Tipping Point from Prejudice to Hate

1. M. Grodzins, *The Metropolitan Area as a Racial Problem*, Pittsburgh: University of Pittsburgh Press, 1958.

2. D. Card, 'Tipping and the Dynamics of Segregation', *Quarterly Journal of Economics* 123 (2008), 177–218.

3. M. Gladwell, *The Tipping Point: How Little Things Can Make a Big Difference*, New York: Little, Brown, 2000.

4. A. Alrababa'h et al., 'Can Exposure to Celebrities Reduce Prejudice? The Effect of Mohamed Salah on Islamophobic Behaviors and Attitudes', IPL Working Paper Series, 2019.

5. G. W. Allport, *The Nature of Prejudice*, Reading, MA: Addison Wesley, 1954.

6. S. L. Gaertner and J. F. Dovidio, *Reducing Intergroup Bias: The Common Ingroup Identity Model*, Philadelphia: PA: Psychology Press, 2000.

7. C. S. Crandall et al., 'Social Norms and the Expression and Suppression of Prejudice: The Struggle for Internalization', *Journal of Personality and Social Psychology* 82 (2002), 359–78.

8. D. M. Amodio, E. Harmon-Jones and P. G. Devine, 'Individual Differences in the Activation and Control of Affective Race Bias as Assessed by Startle Eyeblink Responses and Self-Report', *Journal of Personality and Social Psychology* 84 (2003), 738–53.

9. J. P. Mitchell et al., 'Neural Correlates of Stereotype Application', *Journal of Cognitive Neuroscience* 21 (2009), 594–604.

10. A. R. Aron, T. W. Robbins and R. A. Poldrack, 'Inhibition and the Right Inferior Frontal Cortex', *Trends in Cognitive Sciences* 8 (2004), 170–7.

11. K. Kawakami et al., 'Just Say No (to Stereotyping): Effects of Training on the Negation of Stereotypic Associations on Stereotype Activation', *Journal of Personality and Social Psychology* 78 (2000), 871–88.

12. J. M. Bonds-Raacke et al., 'Remembering Gay/Lesbian Media Characters: Can Ellen and Will Improve Attitudes toward Homosexuals?', *Journal of Homosexuality* 53 (2007), 19–34; J. P. Calzo and L. M. Ward, 'Media Exposure and Viewers' Attitudes toward Homosexuality: Evidence for Mainstreaming or Resonance?', *Journal of Broadcasting and Electronic Media* 53 (2009), 280–99; T. T. Lee and G. R. Hicks, 'An Analysis of Factors Affecting Attitudes toward Same-Sex Marriage: Do the Media Matter?', *Journal of Homosexuality* 58 (2011), 1391–408; M. Ortiz and J. Harwood, 'A Social Cognitive Theory Approach to the Effects of Mediated Intergroup Contact on Intergroup Attitudes', *Journal of Broadcasting and Electronic Media* 51 (2007), 615–31.

13. B. McLaughlin et al., 'Stereotyped Identification: How Identifying with Fictional Latina Characters Increases Acceptance and Stereotyping', *Mass Communication and Society* 21 (2018), 585–605.

14. S. Ramasubramanian, 'Television Viewing, Racial Attitudes, and Policy Preferences: Exploring the Role of Social Identity and Intergroup Emotions in Influencing Support for Affirmative Action', *Communication Monographs* 77 (2010), 102–20.

15. P. E. Baker, *Negro–White Adjustment*, New York: Association Press, 1934; H. A. Lett, *Techniques for Achieving Interracial Cooperation*, Proceedings of the Institute on Race Relations and Community Organization, Chicago: University of Chicago and the American Council on Race Relations, 1945.

16. Allport, *The Nature of Prejudice*.

17. M. Deutsch and M. Collins, *Interracial Housing: A Psychological Evaluation of a Social Experiment*, Minneapolis: University of Minnesota Press, 1951.

18. W. M. Kephart, *Racial Factors and Urban Law Enforcement*, Philadelphia: University of Pennsylvania Press, 1957.

19. S. W. Cook, 'The Effect of Unintended Interracial Contact upon Racial Interaction and Attitude Change', Project No. 5–1320. Final Report, Washington, DC: US Department of Health, Education, and Welfare, 1971.

20. D. P. Green and J. S. Wong, 'Tolerance and the Contact Hypothesis: A Field Experiment', in *The Political Psychology of Democratic Citizenship*, ed. E. Borgida, C. M. Federico and J. L. Sullivan, Oxford: Oxford University Press, 2008.

21. A. Eller, D. Abrams and A. Gomez, 'When the Direct Route Is Blocked: The Extended Contact Pathway to Improving Intergroup Relations', *International Journal of Intercultural Relations* 36 (2012), 637–46; R. Wölfer et al., 'Indirect Contact Predicts Direct Contact: Longitudinal Evidence and the Mediating Role of Intergroup Anxiety', *Journal of Personality and Social Psychology* 116 (2019), 277.

22. R. Brown and J. Paterson, 'Indirect Contact and Prejudice Reduction: Limits and Possibilities', *Current Opinion in Psychology* 11 (2016), 20–4; E. L. Paluck, S. A. Green and D. P. Green, 'The Contact Hypothesis Re-Evaluated', *Behavioural Public Policy* 3 (2018), 129–58; R. F. Pettigrew and L. R. Tropp, 'A Meta-Analytic Test of Intergroup Contact Theory', *Journal of Personality and Social Psychology* 90 (2006), 751–83.

23. N. S. Kteily et al., 'Predisposed to Prejudice but Responsive to Intergroup Contact? Testing the Unique Benefits of Intergroup Contact across Different Types of Individual Differences', *Group Processes and Intergroup Relations* 22 (2019), 3–25.

24. Pettigrew and Tropp, 'A Meta-Analytic Test of Intergroup Contact Theory'.

25. Paluck, Green and Green, 'The Contact Hypothesis Re-Evaluated'.

26. O. Christ et al, 'Contextual Effect of Positive Intergroup Contact on Outgroup Prejudice', *Proceedings of the National Academy of Sciences* 111 (2014), 3996–4000.

27. M. R. Ramos et al., 'Humans Adapt to Social Diversity over Time', *Proceedings of the National Academy of Sciences* 116 (2019), 12244–9.

28. J. Cloutier, T. Li and J. Correll, 'The Impact of Childhood Experience on Amygdala Response to Perceptually Familiar Black and White Faces', *Journal of Cognitive Neuroscience* 26 (2014), 1992–2004.

29. M. Walters and C. Hoyle, 'Exploring the Everyday World of Hate Victimization through Community Mediation', *International Review of Victimology* 18 (2012), 7–24.

30. A. Bettencourt et al., 'Cooperation and the Reduction of Intergroup Bias: The Role of Reward Structure and Social Orientation', *Journal of Experimental Social Psychology* 284 (1992), 301–19; Gaertner and Dovidio, *Reducing Intergroup Bias*; A. Marcus-Newhall et al., 'Cross-Cutting Category Membership with Role Assignment: A Means of Reducing Intergroup Bias', *British Journal of Social Psychology* 32 (1993), 125–46.

31. C. A. Bail et al., 'Exposure to Opposing Views on Social Media Can Increase Political Polarization', *Proceedings of the National Academy of Sciences* 115 (2018), 9216–21.

32. V. L. Banyard, 'Measurement and Correlates of Prosocial Bystander Behavior: The Case of Interpersonal Violence', *Violence and Victims* 23 (2008), 83–97; L. Hyers, 'Resisting Prejudice Every Day: Exploring Women's Assertive Responses to Anti-Black Racism, Anti-Semitism, Heterosexism, and Sexism', *Sex Roles* 56 (2007), 1–12; L. Hyers, 'Alternatives to Silence in Face-to-Face Encounters with Everyday Heterosexism: Activism on the Interpersonal Front', *Journal of Homosexuality* 57 (2010), 539–65.

33. J. H. Kuklinski and N. L. Hurley, 'It's a Matter of Interpretation', in

Political Persuasion and Attitude Change, ed. D. C. Mutz, R. Brody and P. Sniderman, Ann Arbor: Michigan University Press, 1996, 125–44.

34. M. Dobbs and W. D. Crano, 'Outgroup Accountability in the Minimal Group Paradigm: Implications for Aversive Discrimination and Social Identity Theory', Personality and Social Psychology Bulletin 27 (2001), 355–64; M. J. Monteith, 'Self-Regulation of Prejudiced Responses: Implications for Progress in Prejudice-Reduction Efforts', *Journal of Personality and Social Psychology* 65 (1993), 469–85.

35. C. D. Batson, *The Altruism Question: Toward a Social-Psychological Answer*, Hillsdale, NJ: Erlbaum, 1991.

36. Bettencourt et al., 'Cooperation and the Reduction of Intergroup Bias'; Gaertner and Dovidio, *Reducing Intergroup Bias*; Marcus-Newhall et al., 'Cross-Cutting Category Membership with Role Assignment'.

37. M. J. Monteith and G. L. Walters, 'Egalitarianism, Moral Obligation, and Prejudice-Related Personal Standards', *Personality and Social Psychology Bulletin* 24 (1998), 186–99; E. A. Plant and P. G. Devine, 'Responses to Other-Imposed Pro-Black Pressure: Acceptance or Backlash?', *Journal of Experimental Social Psychology* 37 (2001), 486–501.

Index